THE SUFIS

THE SUFIS

IDRIES SHAH

INTRODUCTION BY ROBERT GRAVES

ANCHOR BOOKS
A DIVISION OF RANDOM HOUSE, INC.
NEW YORK

FIRST ANCHOR BOOKS EDITION, 1971

Illustration: *The Islanders*. Sufic illustrative calligraphy, in the hand of
"Mohamed, son of Shafiq, 1291," of the Mevlevi ("Dancing") Dervishes.
The image of a ship with people standing in it is apparent.

Library of Congress Cataloging-in-Publication Data
Shah, Idries, 1924–
    The Sufis/by Idries Shah; introduction by Robert Graves.
        p.   cm.
    "Originally published in hardcover by Doubleday in 1964"
    —T.p. verso.
    1. Sufism.   I. Title.
BP189.S38   1990   90-40927
297'.4—dc20   CIP

ISBN 0-385-07966-4

www.anchorbooks.com

PRINTED IN THE UNITED STATES OF AMERICA
28   27   26   25   24   23   22   21   20   19

Contents

Introduction

The Sufis are an ancient spiritual freemasonry whose origins have never been traced or dated; nor do they themselves take much interest in such researches, being content to point out the occurrence of their own way of thought in different regions and periods. Though commonly mistaken for a Moslem sect, the Sufis are at home in all religions: just as the "Free and Accepted Masons" lay before them in their Lodge whatever sacred book—whether Bible, Koran, or Torah—is accepted by the temporal State. If they call Islam the "shell" of Sufism, this is because they believe Sufism to be the secret teaching within all religions. Yet according to Ali el-Hujwiri, an early authoritative Sufi writer, the Prophet Mohammed himself said: "He who hears the voice of the Sufi people and does not say *aamin* [Amen] is recorded in God's presence as one of the heedless." Numerous other traditions link him with the Sufis, and it was in Sufi style that he ordered his followers to respect all People of a Book, meaning those who respected their own sacred scriptures—a term later taken to include Zoroastrians.

Nor are the Sufis a sect, being bound by no religious dogma however tenuous and using no regular place of worship. They have no sacred city, no monastic organization, no religious instruments. They even dislike being given any inclusive name which might force them into doctrinal conformity. "Sufi" is no more than a nickname, like "Quaker," which they accept good-humoredly. "We friends" or "people like us" is how they refer to themselves, and they recognize one another by certain natural gifts, habits, qualities of thought. Sufi schools have indeed gathered around particular teachers, but there is no graduation and they exist only for the convenience of those who work to perfect their studies by close association with fellow Sufis. The characteristic Sufic signature is found in widely dispersed literature from at least the second millennium B.C., and although their most obvious impact on civilization was made between the eighth and eighteenth centuries A.D., Sufis are still active as ever. They number some fifty million. What makes them so difficult to discuss is that their mutual recognition cannot be explained in ordinary moral or psychological terms—whoever understands it is himself a Sufi. Though awareness of this secret quality or instinct can be sharpened by close contact with Sufis of experience, there are no hierarchical degrees among them, only a general undisputed recognition of greater or lesser capacity.

Sufism has gained an Oriental flavor from having been so long protected by Islam, but the natural Sufi may be as common in the West as in the East, and may come dressed as a general, a peasant, a merchant, a lawyer, a schoolmaster, a housewife, anything. To be "in the world, but not of it," free from ambition, greed, intellectual pride, blind obedience to custom, or awe of persons higher in rank—that is the Sufi's ideal.

Sufis respect the rituals of religion insofar as these further social harmony, but broaden religion's doctrinal basis wherever possible and define its myths in a higher sense— for instance, explaining angels as representations of man's higher faculties. The individual devotee is offered a "secret garden" for the growth of his understanding, but never required to become a monk, nun or hermit, like the more conventional mystics; and he thereafter claims to be enlightened by actual experience—"he who tastes, knows"—not by philosophic argument. The earliest known theory of conscious evolution is of Sufi origin but, though much quoted by

Darwinians in the great nineteenth-century controversy, it applies to the individual rather than to the race. The child's slow progress into manhood or womanhood figures as only a stage in his development of more spectacular powers for which the dynamic force is love, not either asceticism or the intellect.

Enlightenment comes with love—love in the poetic sense of perfect devotion to a Muse who, whatever apparent cruelties she may commit or however seemingly irrational her behavior, knows what she is doing. She seldom rewards her poet with any express sign of her favor, but confirms his devotion by its revivifying effect on him. Thus Ibn El-Arabi (1165–1240), a Spanish Arab from Murcia whom the Sufis call their Master Poet, wrote in his *Tarjuman el-Ashwaq* (Interpreter of Desires):

> If I bow to her as is my duty
> And if she never returns my salutation
> Have I just cause for complaint?
> Lovely woman feel no obligation.

This love theme was later used in an ecstatic cult of the Virgin Mary, who until the Crusades had occupied an unimportant position in the Christian religion. Her greatest veneration today is precisely in those parts of Europe that fell strongly under Sufic influence.

Ibn El-Arabi says of himself:

> I follow the religion of Love.
> Now I am sometimes called
> A Shepherd of gazelles [divine wisdom]
> And now a Christian monk,
> And now a Persian sage.
> My beloved is Three—
> Three yet only one;
> Many things appear as three,
> Which are no more than one.

Give her no name,
As if to limit one
At sight of whom
All limitation is confounded.

The poets were the chief disseminators of Sufi thought,
earned the same reverence as did the *ollamhs,* or master
poets, of early medieval Ireland, and used a similar secret
language of metaphorical reference and verbal cipher.
Nizami the Persian Sufi writes: "Under the poet's tongue
lies the key of the treasury." This language was a protection
both against the vulgarizing or institutionalizing of a habit
of thought only proper to those that understand it, and
against accusations of heresy or civil disobedience. Ibn El-
Arabi, summoned before an Islamic inquisition at Aleppo
to defend himself against charges of nonconformity, pleaded
that his poems were metaphorical, the basic message being
God's perfection of man through divine love. He had, for
precedent, the incorporation in the Jewish Scriptures of the
erotic Song of Solomon, which was officially interpreted by
the Pharisee sages as a metaphor of God's love for Israel;
and by the Catholic authorities as a metaphor of God's love
for his Church.

In its most advanced form the secret language uses Semitic
consonantal roots to conceal and reveal meanings; and
Western scholars seem unaware that even the popular
Thousand and One Nights is Sufic in content, and that its
Arabic title *Alf layla wa layla* is a code phrase indicating its
main content and intention: "Mother of Records." Yet what
seems at first sign Oriental occultism is an ancient and
familiar Western habit of thought. Most English and
French schoolchildren begin history lessons with a picture of
their Druidic ancestors lopping mistletoe from a sacred oak.
Although the Druids are credited by Caesar with ancestral
mysteries and a secret language, the lopping seems so simple
a ceremony, mistletoe being still used in Christmas decora-

tions, that few readers pause to consider what it means. The current view that the Druids were virtually emasculating the oak makes no sense.

Now, all other sacred trees, plants and herbs have peculiar properties. The alder's timber is waterproof and its leaves yield a royal red dye; birch is the host of the hallucigenetic fly-cap mushroom; oak and ash attract lightning for a holy fire; the mandrake root is antispasmodic. The foxglove yields digitalis which accelerates the beat of the heart; poppies are opiates; ivy has toxic leaves and its flowers provide bees with the last honey of the year. But the berries of the mistletoe, widely known in folklore as an "allheal," have no medicinal properties, though greedily eaten by wood pigeons and other nonmigratory birds in winter. The leaves are equally valueless; and the timber, though tough, can be put to few uses. Why then was the mistletoe singled out as the most sacred and curative of plants? The only answer can be that the Druids used it as an emblem of their own peculiar way of thought. Here is a tree that is no tree, but fastens itself alike on oak, apple, poplar, beech, thorn, even pine, grows green, nourishing itself on the topmost branches when the rest of the forest seems asleep, and the fruit of which is credited with curing all spiritual disorders. Lopped sprigs of it are tied to the lintel of a door and invite sudden and surprising kisses. The symbolism is exact, if we can equate Druidic with Sufic thought, which is not planted like a tree, as religions are planted, but self-engrafted on a tree already in existence; it keeps green though the tree itself is asleep, in the sense that religions go dead by formalism; and the main motive power of its growth is love, not ordinary animal passion or domestic affection but a sudden surprising recognition of love so rare and high that the heart seems to sprout wings. Strangely enough, the Burning Bush from which God appeared to Moses in the desert is now thought by Biblical scholars to have been an acacia glorified by the red leaves of a *locan-thus*, the Eastern equivalent of mistletoe.[1]

The Irish Muse-goddess Bridget was threefold like the Muse celebrated by Ibn El-Arabi; and not threefold merely in the sense of being at once maiden, nymph and crone, but in that of presiding over three spiritual realms— poetry, healing and handicraft. It need not greatly concern us whether this concept is native to Ireland, or whether it came from the East along with the complicated arabesques of medieval Irish illumination art and the curiously Persian or Arabian forms of ninth-century Irish poems. Certainly a well-known ninth-century Celtic cross is distinguished by bearing the Arabic formula *Bismillah er-Rahman, er-Rahim* (In the name of Allah, the Compassionate, the Merciful) as proof that Sufism is consistent with both religions.

It should perhaps matter more that all the noblest Islamic art and architecture is Sufic, and that healing, especially of psychosomatic disorders, is every day practiced by Sufis to-day as a natural love duty, though not until they have studied for at least twelve years. The *ollamhs* were also healers and studied twelve years in their woodland schools. The Sufi physician must not accept any payment more valu-able than a handful of barley, nor impose his own will on the patient, as most modern psychiatrists do; but having put him into deep hypnosis he must make him diagnose his own disorder and prescribe the cure. The physician then gives advice on how to prevent a recurrence of the symptoms, though the demand for a cure must come directly from the patient, not from his family or well-wishers.[2]

[1] The great Sufi poet Rumi wrote:
    In Winter the bare boughs that seem to sleep
    Work covertly, preparing for their Spring.
Though he did not mention the mistletoe, or any other *locanthus,* here is the visible emblem of the secret process of thought to which his lines refer.

[2] A clinical account of one aspect of this practice is contained in Dr. Jafar Hallaji's "Hypnotherapeutic Techniques in a Central Asian Community," International Journal of Clinical and Experimental Hypnosis, October, 1962, pp. 271 et seq.

After their conquest by the Saracens beginning in the eighth century A.D., Spain and Sicily became centers of Moslem civilization renowned for religious austerity. The northern scholars who flocked there to buy Arabic works for translation into Latin did not however demand orthodox Islamic doctrine but only Sufi literature and occasional scientific treatises. The songs of the troubadors—the word is unconnected with *trobar*, "to find," but represents the Arabic root TRB, meaning "lutanist"—are now authoritatively established as of Saracen origin. Yet Professor Guillaume points out in *The Legacy of Islam* that poetry, romances, music and dance, all Sufi specialties, were no more welcomed by the orthodox authorities of Islam than by Christian bishops. Arabic, in fact, although a carrier both for the Moslem religion and for Sufi thought, remained independent of either.

In 1229, the island of Majorca, where I have lived since 1929, was captured by King James of Aragon from the Saracens, who had held it for five centuries. He thereupon chose as his emblem a bat, which still appears above the arms of Palma, our capital. This bat emblem had long puzzled me, and the local tradition that it stood for "vigilance" did not seem a sufficient explanation, because the bat, in Christian usage, is an ill-omened creature associated with witchcraft. But I remembered that James I stormed Palma with the help of the Knights Templars and of two or three dissident Moorish noblemen living elsewhere in the island; that the Knights Templars had educated James in *le bon saber*, or wisdom; and that during the Crusades, the Knights Templars were accused of collaboration with Saracen Sufis. It therefore occurred to me that "bat" might have another meaning in Arabic, and be a signal to James's local Moorish allies, presumably Sufis, of his schooling in their own wisdom.

I wrote to Idries Shah Sayed, who replied:

The Arabic for bat is KHuFFaaSH, from the three-consonant root KH-F-SH. A second meaning of this

root is "to overthrow," ruin, trample down, probably
because bats haunt ruined buildings. James's emblem
was thus a simple rebus proclaiming himself "the
Conqueror;" as in Spanish he was known as *El Rey
Jaime, el Conquistador*. But this is not the whole story.
In Sufi literature, especially the love poetry of Ibn El-
Arabi of Murcia which was current throughout
Spain, "ruin" stands for the mind ruined by unregen-
erate thought and awaiting reedification.

The only other meaning of this root is "weak-eyes, seeing only by night." This can convey much more than to
be "blind as a bat." Sufis speak of the unregenerate as
blind to true reality; but also of themselves as blind to
things which are important to the unregenerate. Like
the bat, the Sufi is asleep to "things of the day"—
the familiar struggle for existence which the ordinary
man finds all-important—and vigilant while others are
asleep. In other words, he keeps awake the spiritual
attention dormant in others. That "mankind sleeps in
a nightmare of unfulfillment" is a commonplace of Sufi
literature. Your Palma tradition of "vigilance" as a
meaning of "bat" need not therefore be discounted.

Thus the palma emblem combines King James's overt
boast that he has broken the power of the fanatical Moslems who ruled Majorca, with a covert use of metaphor reassuring his allies that he is one of their fraternity. It may
be questioned whether King James spoke Arabic fluently,
but for most of his advisors it will have been their second
language, if not their first. Moreover, many thousands of
writers have made play with the associated meanings of
Arabic roots, even in countries where the language itself
is not spoken. Urdu and Persian poets, whose languages
are Indo-European and not Semitic, treat the roots somewhat as if they were algebraic formulae.

A coronation robe worn by Roger II, King of Sicily
(1093–1154) and later also used by Frederick II of Hohen-

staufen, Holy Roman Emperor (1194–1250) is on display at
the Weltliche-Schatzkammer, Vienna. Idries Shah Sayed
has explained its symbolism to me:

> In the center stands a palm tree, containing the nine
> elements of the "magic square of fifteen," a compli-
> cated diagram attributed to Geber (Jabir) the Sufi and
> reverenced alike by the Latin alchemists and the Chin-
> nese Taoists. The palm tree (NaKHL) is chosen be-
> cause the triconsonantal root NKHL also means "a fine
> essence descending almost impalpably," such as the di-
> vine element *baraka* or "blessedness." Words from the
> same root include sifted flour and a gentle drizzle of
> rain. Since the palm is a holy tree associated with birth
> among the Arabs, its appearance on a coronation robe
> means "Source of Blessedness." Moreover, the word for
> "palm tree" is *tariqat*, which is the Sufi technical term
> for "Being on the Path"—that is to say, Sufism. On
> either side of the palm a tiger is shown dragging down
> a camel. NMR is the Arabic root for "tiger," and JML
> for "camel." Thus the NMR overcomes the JML. But
> NMR also stands for "woolen garment" and for "unim-
> paired honor;" and since "Sufi" can mean "clad in
> wool," and since unimpaired honor is, with love, one
> of the two main pillars of Sufism, "Sufi" can be sub-
> stituted for "tiger." Thus "The Sufi overcomes JML."
> JML, too, means not only "camel," but also "elegance."
> As an indication that both the tiger and the camel are
> human, they wear similar stripes, but the camel has
> fewer, meaning that unimpaired honor is not altogether
> inelegant. Thus: "Under this divine source of Sufic
> blessedness, the unimpaired honor of the Wool-clad
> overcomes mere elegance."

That absorption with the theme of love leads to ecstasy,
all Sufis know. But whereas Christian mystics regard
ecstasy as a union with God, and therefore the height of
religious attainment, Sufis admit its value only if the de-

votee can afterward return to the world and live in a manner consonant with his experience. Western literature has been profoundly affected by the theme of man's spiritual tempering through love, spread mainly by such Spanish Arabs as the tenth-century Ibn Masarra of Córdoba, Ibn Barrajan of Seville, Abu Bakr of Granada (a Majorcan by birth), and Ibn Qasi of Agarabis in Portugal. The best known Sufi scholar was the twelfth-century Averroës (Ibn Rushd) who transformed Christian scholastic thought.

Sufis have always insisted on the practicality of their viewpoint. Metaphysics for them are useless without practical illustrations of prudent human behavior, supplied both by popular legends and fables. Since the Popes had excommunicated the Donatist heretics for denying that a blessing conferred by an evil-living priest was equal to that conferred by a saint, the attitude "Don't do as I do, but do as I tell you," had become a commonplace in Catholic churches. Gospel authority was found in Matthew xxiii, 2 et seq., where Jesus tells his disciples to obey the Pharisaic teaching in every detail but not to model themselves on the more formalistic Pharisees. Christians are content to use Jesus as the perfect and final exemplar of human behavior. The Sufis, however, while admitting him as a divinely inspired prophet, quote the text from the fourth Gospel: "Is it not written in your Law, I said, ye are gods?"—which means that judges and prophets are entitled to interpret God's law —and hold that this quasi divinity should suffice any man or woman, there being no god but God. They have similarly refused to accept the Lamaism of Tibet, and Indian theories of divine incarnation; and though charged by orthodox Moslems with being influenced by Christianity, they accept the Nativity only as a parable of the powers latent in man which can set him apart from his unilluminated brothers. Likewise they interpret the supernatural traditions of the Koran as metaphorical, and to be literally believed in by the unenlightened alone. Paradise, for example, has not, they say, been experienced by any living man; its *houris* ("creatures of light") offer no analogy to any human beings and should be given no physical attributes, as in vulgar fable.

Instances abound in all European literature of the debt to the Sufis. The legend of Wilhelm Tell is found in Attar's *Parliament of the Birds* (twelfth century) long before its appearance in Switzerland; and that the Germanic archer guilds (if we can trust the *Malleus Maleficarum*, a witch-hunting manual of 1460), shot "in the Devil's name" at apples similarly placed suggests Saracen influence. Although Don Quixote (pronounced "Kishotte" by the Aragonese and Provençals) seems the most Spanish of all Spaniards, Cervantes himself acknowledges his indebtedness to an Arabic source.

This attribution has been dismissed as a quixotic joke by scholars; but Cervantes' stories often closely follow those of Sidi Kishar, a legendary Sufi teacher sometimes equated with Nasrudin, including the famous incident of his mistaking mills (water mills, however, not windmills) for giants. The Spanish word *Quijada* (Quixote's real name, according to Cervantes) derives from the same Arabic root KSHR as Kishar, and retains its sense of "threatening grimaces." The Blessed Raymond Lully, a Majorcan mystic and martyr, admits to having written his famous poem *The Book of the Lover and His Beloved* (1283) on the Sufic model. And Brother Anselm of Turmeda, a Catalan Christian mystic, was well known also as the illuminated Sufi sage Abdulla el-Tarjuman, "the Interpreter."

Friar Roger Bacon, who lectured on philosophy at Oxford and is buried there, had studied in Saracen Spain; but carefully avoiding a direct reference to the "Illuminates," for fear of offending the university authorities, he calls this way of thought merely "Eastern," a word which in Arabic is formed from the same root as "illuminism." Professor Asín of Madrid and his associates have traced Bacon's indebtedness to the illuminates of the Córdoba school founded by Ibn Masarra (883–931). This school was developed by the Jewish Sufic sage Solomon ben Gabirol (1021–1058) known

to the Saracens as Suleiman ibn Yahya ibn Jabriol, and to
the Christians as Avicebron. Avicebron has now been established as the vital influence behind St. Francis of Assisi's founding of the Franciscan Order, which Bacon joined
in 1247. A passage from one of Bacon's Latin works refers
to the Sufic evolutionary theory:

> Nor do the natural philosophers know of this, neither
> the whole assembly of Latin writers. And because this
> science is not known to the generality of students it
> necessarily follows that they are ignorant of all that
> depends upon it, as regards the generation of animate
> things, of plants and beasts, and men; for, being igno-
> rant of what comes before, they are necessarily ignorant
> of what follows.

Though Friar Bacon has been looked on with awe and
suspicion because he studied the "Black Arts," the word
"black" does not signify "evil." It is a play on two Arabic
roots FHM and FHHM, pronounced *fecham* and *facham*,
one of which means "black" and the other "wise." The same
play occurs in the arms of Hugues de Payns ("of the
Pagans"), born in 1070,[8] who founded the Order of
Knights Templars: namely three Saracen heads sable, bla-
zoned as if cut off in battle, but really denoting heads of
wisdom.

The Moslem Sufis were fortunate enough to protect themselves against charges of heresy by the efforts of El-Ghazali
(1058–1111), known in Europe as Algazel, who became
the highest doctrinal authority in Islam and reconciled Koranic religious myth with rationalistic philosophy, thus earn-
ing the title "Proof of Islam." Nevertheless, they were frequently the victims of pogroms in less enlightened regions,
and were forced to adopt secret passwords, grips, and other

[8] *Les familles chevelresques du Lyonnais.* His father's surname was
"The Moor." Count de Pagan, the family's historian, refers to the
very early contact with the Spanish Arabs which produced this unusual surname.

ruses in self-protection. In the West, no Christian Sufi of sufficient ecclesiastical authority could be found to protect his fellows at the great Church councils, but Sufi thought continued to be a secret force running parallel to orthodox Christianity. Hence the admiration, mixed with suspicion, which greeted Friar Roger Bacon, the Blessed Raymond Lully (who has waited seven hundred years for canonization), and other Sufis credited with strange powers and stranger doctrines. Yet the Sufic works of Ghazali were cited by Averroës and Abu Bakr—"Abubacer"—writers of immense prestige at the Christian universities.

"The Sufis are an ancient spiritual freemasonry. . . ." Indeed, Freemasonry itself began as a Sufi society. It first reached England in the reign of King Aethelstan (924–939) and was introduced into Scotland disguised as a craft guild at the beginning of the fourteenth century, doubtless by the Knights Templars.[4] Its reformation in early eighteenth-century London, by a group of Protestant sages who mistook its Saracen terms for Hebrew, has obscured many of its early traditions. Richard Burton, translator of the *Thousand and One Nights*, being both a Freemason and a Sufi, first pointed out the close relation between the two societies, but he was not sufficiently advanced in either to realize that Freemasonry had begun as a Sufi group. Idries Shah Sayed now shows that it was a metaphor for the "reedification," or rebuilding, of spiritual man from his ruined state; and that the three working instruments displayed on modern Masonic lodges represent three postures of prayer. "Buizz" or "Boaz" and "Solomon, Son of David," who are honored by Freemasons as builders at King Solomon's temple at Jerusalem, were not Solomon's Israelite subjects or Phoenician

[4] There is a shadowy tradition among Masons of the Craft's Saracenic origins. Haydn's *Dictionary of Dates* (1867, p. 347) quotes Masonic historians in saying that "it is said that architects from the African coast, Mahometans, brought it into Spain, about the ninth century." That the successive degrees mark the actual passing through certain definite spiritual experiences, allegorized by their rituals, is less understood.

allies as is supposed, but Abdel-Malik's Sufi architects who
built the Dome of the Rock on the ruins of Solomon's temple, and their successors. Their real names included Thuban abdel Faiz ("Izz"), and his "great grandson," Maaruf,
the son (disciple) of David of Tay, whose Sufic code name
was Solomon, because he was the "son of David." The archi-
tectural measurements chosen for this Temple, as for the
Kaaba building at Mecca, were numerical equivalents of
certain Arabic roots conveying holy messages, every part of
the building being related to every other in definite proportion.

According to English academic principle, a fish is not the
best teacher of ichthyology, nor is an angel of angelology.
Hence most authoritative modern books and articles about
Sufism are written by historically minded European and
American university professors who have never swum in
Sufic depths nor soared to ecstatic Sufic heights, and do not
even understand Perso-Arabic poetic wordplay. I pleaded
with Idries Shah Sayed to remedy this lack of accurate public
information, if only to reassure natural Sufis in the West
that they are not alone in their peculiar habits of thought,
and that their intuitions can be sharpened by others' experience. He consented, though aware that this would be a
task of great difficulty. Idries Shah Sayed happens to be in
the senior male line of descent from the prophet Mohammed,
and to have inherited the secret mysteries from the Caliphs,
his ancestors. He is, in fact, a Grand Sheikh of the Sufi
Tariqa ("Rule"), but since all Sufis are by definition equal
and responsible only to themselves for their own spiritual
achievements, "Sheikh" is a misleading title. It does not
mean "leader" so much as "fugleman," the old army term for
the soldier who stood in front of a company on the parade
ground as an exemplar in arms-drill.

The difficulty that he foresaw (though many years resi-
dent in Europe and as conversant with English and the
main European languages as with Arabic, Pushtu, Urdu,
classical and modern Persian) is that readers of this book

must be assumed to have perceptions out of the ordinary, a poetic imagination, a strong sense of honor, and to have already stumbled on the main secret, which is a great deal to expect. Nor does he wish to be thought a missionary. Sufi teachers do their best to discourage disciples, and accept none that come "empty-handed," that is to say, who lack an inborn sense of the central mystery. A disciple learns less from his teacher in the way of literary or therapeutic tradition than from watching him deal with the problems of daily life; and must not plague him with questions but accept on trust a great deal of apparent illogic and foolishness which will make eventual sense. Many of the main Sufic paradoxes are current in the form of comic stories, especially those centered around the Khoja (schoolmaster) Nasrudin, and occur also in the fables of Aesop, whom the Sufis accept as one of their ancestors.

The court fool of the Spanish kings with his bladder stick, his motley clothes, cock crest, jingling bells, simple wisdom and utter disrespect of authority is a Sufi figure. His jokes were accepted by the sovereigns as having a deeper wisdom than the most solemn advice of eldest councillors. When Philip II of Spain was accentuating his persecution of Jews, he decided that every Spaniard with Jewish blood must wear a hat of a certain shape. Foreseeing trouble, the fool appeared the same evening with three such hats. "For whom are these, fool?" asked Philip. "One for me, nuncle, one for thee, and one for the Grand Inquisitor." And since it was true that numerous medieval Spanish aristocrats had married into rich Jewish families, Philip thereupon abandoned his plan. In much the same way, Charles I's court fool Charlie Armstrong (once a Scottish sheep stealer), whom he had inherited from his father, tried to oppose Archbishop Laud's Arminian Church policy, which seemed bound to end in an armed clash with the Puritans. Charles scornfully asked Archie's advice in religious policy, and was told: "Give great praise to God, nuncle, and little laud to the Devil." Laud, who was touchy about his smallness, had Charlie

Armstrong expelled from court; which brought his master no luck.

In effect, this book is not addressed to intellectuals or other orthodox thinkers, or to anyone who will fail to recognize it at once as addressed to himself. The economics of publication will of course distribute the book mostly among readers without much sense of what the author is saying; yet if he had written in a way that they clearly understood, he would have been saying something altogether different. An awkward position; and if anyone deserves the blame for publication, it is myself. Nevertheless Idries Shah Sayed supplies a great deal of unexpected information—besides what I have already quoted—such as the Saracen origin of the rosary and of Hans Andersen's Ugly Duckling, or Chaucer's debt to well-known Sufi poets, emphasizing these secondary phenomena without prejudice to the primary phenomenon of Sufi thought. The book will at least be available to a great number of people who share this peculiar way of thinking with one or two intimate friends, and whom it will doubtless surprise as much as it has surprised me.

DEYA   *Robert Graves*
MAJORCA

Author's Preface

The last thing that is intended in the writing of this book is that it should be considered inimical to scholasticism or to the academic method. Scholars of the East and the West have heroically consecrated their whole working lives to making available, by means of their own disciplines, Sufi literary and philosophical material to the world at large. In many cases they have faithfully recorded the Sufis' own reiteration that the Way of the Sufis cannot be understood by means of the intellect or by ordinary book learning. That this fundamental has not prevented them from trying to bring Sufism within the compass of their own understanding is a tribute to their intellectual honesty and their faith in their own system of examination.

It would, however, be false to Sufism not to affirm that it cannot be appreciated beyond a certain point except within the real teaching situation, which requires the physical presence of a Sufi teacher. For the Sufi, it is no accident that the "secret doctrine" whose existence has for uncounted time been suspected and sought proves so elusive to the seeker. If, say, communism is a religion without a god, academic study of Sufism without being to any extent a "working Sufi" is Sufism without its essential factor. If this assertion militates against the rational tradition that an individual can find truth merely through the exercise of the faculties with which he finds himself endowed, there is only one answer. Sufism, the "secret tradition," is not available on the basis of assumptions which belong to another world, the world of intellect. If it is felt that truth about extraphysical fact must be sought only through a certain way of thinking, the rational and "scientific" one, there can be no contact between the Sufi and the supposedly objective seeker.

Sufi literature and preparatory teaching is designed to help to bridge the gap between these two worlds of thought. Were it not possible to provide any bridge at all, this book would be worthless, and should not have been attempted.

Sufism, considered as a nutrient for society, is not intended to subsist within society in an unaltered form. That is to say, the Sufis do not erect systems as one would build an edifice, for succeeding generations to examine and learn from. Sufism is transmitted by means of the human exemplar, the teacher. Because he is an unfamiliar figure to the world at large, or because he has imitators, does not mean that he does not exist.

We find traces of Sufism in derelict organizations from which this element of human transmission of *baraka* has ceased; where the form alone remains. Since it is this outer shell which is most easily perceptible to the ordinary man, we have to use it to point to something deeper. Unlike him, we cannot say that such and such a ritual, such and such a book, incarnates Sufism. We start with human, social, literary material that is both incomplete (because now unaccompanied by the impact of the living exemplar, the teacher) and secondary, in that it is only partially absorbed. Historical facts, such as religious and social organization, when they persist, are secondary, external phenomena which depend upon organization, emotion and outward show for their survival. These factors, so essential for the continuation of familiar systems, are, Sufistically speaking, only the substitute for the vitality of organism, as distinct from appearance and sentiment.[1]

A Sufi school comes into being, like any other natural factor, in order to flourish and disappear, not to leave

1 See annotation "Outlook."

traces in mechanical ritual, or anthropologically interesting survivals. The function of a nutrient is to become transmuted, not to leave unaltered traces.

The great Sufi teacher Jami refers to this tendency when he says that if the beard is allowed to grow too bushy, it will vie with the hair of the head in its claims for attention or prominence.

It will easily be understood that both the "organic" and "human exemplar" claims of Sufism remove it immediately from the purview of conventional study.

There is, however, some value in paying attention to Sufi influences upon human culture. In the first place, we can observe attempts to bridge the gap between ordinary thinking and Sufi experience, contained in poetic, literary and other media, which have been designed to lead the ordinary, attenuated or embryonic human consciousness into a greater perception and realization. Secondly, it is maintained by Sufis that even in cultures where authoritarian and mechanical thinking have choked comprehensive understanding, human individuality will have to assert itself, somewhere, even if this be only through the primitive sense that life must have more meaning than the officially propagated one.

In this book, emphasis has been placed upon the diffusion of Sufic thought during a certain phase (from the seventh century of the current era) for illustrative purposes. If, in the process, material which is completely new has been presented, this is not done for any purpose of scholastic effort. Scholasticism is interested in accumulating information and making deductions from it. Sufism is engaged upon developing a line of communication with ultimate knowledge, not with combining individual facts, however historically exciting, or theorizing in any way at all.

Sufism, it should be remembered, is Eastern thought only insofar as it retains beliefs—such as the human exemplar—which have fallen into abeyance in the West. It is occult and mystical inasmuch as it follows a path other than that which has been represented as the true one by authoritarian and dogmatic organization. Sufism claims that the latter attitude constitutes only a part, only a phase, in the human story. Claiming a "real" source of knowledge, Sufism cannot accept the pretensions of the temporary phase which, viewed from within itself, is currently considered to be the "logical" one.

A great deal of the material presented here is incomplete because it is not possible to increase the amount of formal literature about Sufism without the balance of Sufic practice. Much of it, nevertheless, is unknown outside traditional Sufic circles. It is not intended to influence traditional scholasticism, with which it has only the most superficial connection; and one which cannot be carried far without distortion.

Sufism is known by means of itself.

It is interesting to note the difference between science as we know it today, and as it was seen by one of its pioneers. Roger Bacon, considered to be the wonder of the middle ages and one of humanity's greatest thinkers, was the pioneer of the method of knowledge gained through experience. This Franciscan monk learned from the Sufis of the illuminist school that there is a difference between the collection of information and the knowing of things through actual experiment. In his *Opus Maius,* in which he quotes Sufi authority, he says:

> There are two modes of knowledge, through argument and experience. Argument brings conclusions and compels us to concede them, but it does not cause certainty nor remove doubts in order that the mind may remain at rest in truth, unless this is provided by experience.

This Sufi doctrine is known in the West as the scientific method of inductive proceeding, and subsequent Western science is largely based upon it.

Modern science, however, instead of accepting the idea that experience was necessary in all branches of human thought, took the word in its sense of "experiment," in which the experimenter remained as far as possible outside the experience.

From the Sufi point of view, therefore, Bacon, when he wrote these words in 1268, both launched modern science and also transmitted only a portion of the wisdom upon which it could have been based.

"Scientific" thinking has worked continuously and heroically with this partial tradition ever since. In spite of its roots in the work of the Sufis, the impairment of the tradition has prevented the scientific researcher from approaching knowledge by means of itself—by "experience," not merely "experiment."

experience vs experiment

The Situation

Humanity is asleep, concerned only with what is useless, living in a wrong world. Believing that one can excel this is only habit and usage, not religion. This "religion" is inept. . . .

Do not prattle before the People of the Path, rather consume yourself. You have an inverted knowledge and religion if you are upside down in relation to Reality.

Man is wrapping his net around himself. A lion (the man of the Way) bursts his cage asunder.

(The Sufi master Sanai of Afghanistan, teacher of Rumi, in *The Walled Garden of Truth*, written in 1131 A.D.)

The Islanders

The ordinary man repents his sins:
the elect repent of their heedlessness.
(Dhu'l-Nun Misri)

Most fables contain at least some truth, and they often
enable people to absorb ideas which the ordinary patterns
of their thinking would prevent them from digesting. Fables
have therefore been used, not least by the Sufi teachers, to
present a picture of life more in harmony with their feelings
than is possible by means of intellectual exercises.

Here is a Sufic fable about the human situation, summarized and adapted, as must always be, suitably to the time
in which it is presented. Ordinary "entertainment" fables
are considered by Sufi authors to be a degenerated or infe-
rior form of art.

Once upon a time there lived an ideal community in a
far-off land. Its members had no fears as we now know
them. Instead of uncertainty and vacillation, they had pur-
posefulness and a fuller means of expressing themselves.
Although there were none of the stresses and tensions which
mankind now considers essential to its progress, their lives
were richer, because other, better elements replaced these
things. Theirs, therefore, was a slightly different mode of

existence. We could almost say that our present perceptions are a crude, makeshift version of the real ones which this community possessed.

They had real lives, not semilives.

We can call them the El Ar people.

They had a leader, who discovered that their country was to become uninhabitable for a period of, shall we say, twenty thousand years. He planned their escape, realizing that their descendants would be able to return home successfully, only after many trials.

He found for them a place of refuge, an island whose features were only roughly similar to those of the original homeland. Because of the difference in climate and situation, the immigrants had to undergo a transformation. This made them more physically and mentally adapted to the new circumstances; coarse perceptions, for instance, were substituted for finer ones, as when the hand of the manual laborer becomes toughened in response to the needs of his calling.

In order to reduce the pain which a comparison between the old and new states would bring, they were made to forget the past almost entirely. Only the most shadowy recollection of it remained, yet it was sufficient to be awakened when the time came.

The system was very complicated, but well arranged. The organs by means of which the people survived on the island were also made the organs of enjoyment, physical and mental. The organs which were really constructive in the old homeland were placed in a special form of abeyance, and linked with the shadowy memory, in preparation for its eventual activation.

Slowly and painfully the immigrants settled down, adjusting themselves to the local conditions. The resources of the island were such that, coupled with effort and a certain form of guidance, people would be able to escape to a further island, on the way back to their original home. This was the first of a succession of islands upon which gradual acclimatization took place.

The responsibility of this "evolution" was vested in those individuals who could sustain it. These were necessarily only a few, because for the mass of the people the effort of keeping both sets of knowledge in their consciousness was virtually impossible. One of them seemed to conflict with the other one. Certain specialists guarded the "special science."

This "secret," the method of effecting the transition, was nothing more or less than the knowledge of maritime skills and their application. The escape needed an instructor, raw materials, people, effort and understanding. Given these, people could learn to swim, and also to build ships.

The people who were originally in charge of the escape operations made it clear to everyone that a certain preparation was necessary before anyone could learn to swim or even take part in building a ship. For a time the process continued satisfactorily.

Then a man who had been found, for the time being, lacking in the necessary qualities rebelled against this order and managed to develop a masterly idea. He had observed that the effort to escape placed a heavy and often seemingly unwelcome burden upon the people. At the same time they were disposed to believe things which they were told about the escape operation. He realized that he could acquire power, and also revenge himself upon those who had undervalued him, as he thought, by a simple exploitation of these two sets of facts.

He would merely offer to take away the burden, by affirming that there was no burden.

He made this announcement:

"There is no need for man to integrate his mind and train it in the way which has been described to you. The human mind is already a stable and continuous, consistent thing. You have been told that you have to become a crafts-

man in order to build a ship. I say, not only do you not need
to be a craftsman—you do not need a ship at all! An islander
needs only to observe a few simple rules to survive and remain integrated into society. By the exercise of common
sense, born into everyone, he can attain anything upon
this island, our home, the common property and heritage of
all!"

The tonguester, having gained a great deal of interest
among the people, now "proved" his message by saying:

"If there is any reality in ships and swimming, show us
ships which have made the journey, and swimmers who
have come back!"

This was a challenge to the instructors which they could
not meet. It was based upon an assumption of which the
bemused herd could not now see the fallacy. You see,
ships never returned from the other land. Swimmers, when
they did come back, had undergone a fresh adaptation
which made them invisible to the crowd.

The mob pressed for demonstrative proof.

"Shipbuilding," said the escapers, in an attempt to reason
with the revolt, "is an art and a craft. The learning and the
exercise of this lore depends upon special techniques. These
together make up a total activity, which cannot be examined
piecemeal, as you demand. This activity has an impalpable
element, called *baraka*, from which the word 'barque'—a
ship—is derived. This word means 'the Subtlety,' and it cannot be shown to you."

"Art, craft, total, *baraka*, nonsense!" shouted the revolutionaries.

And so they hanged as many shipbuilding craftsmen as
they could find.

The new gospel was welcomed on all sides as one of liberation. Man had discovered that he was already mature! He
felt, for the time at least, as if he had been released from
responsibility.

Most other ways of thinking were soon swamped by

the simplicity and comfort of the revolutionary concept. Soon it was considered to be a basic fact which had never been challenged by any rational person. Rational, of course, meant anyone who harmonized with the general theory itself, upon which society was now based.

Ideas which opposed the new one were easily called irrational. Anything irrational was bad. Thereafter, even if he had doubts, the individual had to suppress them or divert them, because he must at all costs be thought rational.

It was not very difficult to be rational. One had only to adhere to the values of society. Further, evidence of the truth of rationality abounded—providing that one did not think beyond the life of the island.

Society had now temporarily equilibrated itself within the island, and seemed to provide a plausible completeness, if viewed by means of itself. It was based upon reason plus emotion, making both seem plausible. Cannibalism, for instance, was permitted on rational grounds. The human body was found to be edible. Edibility was a characteristic of food. Therefore the human body was food. In order to compensate for the shortcomings of this reasoning, a makeshift was arranged. Cannibalism was controlled, in the interests of society. Compromise was the trademark of temporary balance. Every now and again someone pointed out a new compromise, and the struggle between reason, ambition and community produced some fresh social norm.

Since the skills of boatbuilding had no obvious application within this society, the effort could easily be considered absurd. Boats were not needed—there was nowhere to go. The consequences of certain assumptions can be made to "prove" those assumptions. This is what is called pseudo-certainty, the substitute for real certainty. It is what we deal in every day, when we assume that we will live another day. But our islanders applied it to everything.

Two entries in the great *Island Universal Encyclopaedia* show us how the process worked. Distilling their wisdom from the only mental nutrition available to them, the island's savants produced, in all honesty, this kind of truth:

SHIP: *Displeasing.* An imaginary vehicle in which impostors and deceivers have claimed it possible to "cross the water," now scientifically established as an absurdity. No materials impermeable to water are known on the Island, from which such a "ship" might be constructed, quite apart from the question of there being a destination beyond the Island. Preaching "shipbuilding" is a major crime under Law XVII of the Penal Code, subsection J, *The Protection of the Credulous.* SHIPBUILDING MANIA is an extreme form of mental escapism, a symptom of maladjustment. All citizens are under a constitutional obligation to notify the health authorities if they suspect the existence of this tragic condition in any individual.

See: *Swimming; Mental aberrations; Crime (Major).*
Readings: Smith, J., *Why "Ships" Cannot be Built,* Island University Monograph No. 1151.

SWIMMING: *Unpleasant.* Supposedly a method of propelling the body through water without drowning, generally for the purpose of "reaching a place outside the Island." The "student" of this unpleasant art had to submit himself to a grotesque ritual. In the first lesson, he had to prostrate himself on the ground, and move his arms and legs in response to the commands of an "instructor." The entire concept is based upon the desire of the self-styled "instructors" to dominate the credulous in barbaric times. More recently the cult has taken the form of epidemic mania.

See: *Ship; Heresies; Pseudoarts.*
Readings: Brown, W., *The Great "Swimming" Madness,* 7 vols., Institute of Social Lucidity.

The words "displeasing" and "unpleasant" were used on the island to indicate anything which conflicted with the new gospel, which was itself known as "Please." The idea behind this was that people would now please themselves, within the general need to please the State. The State was taken to mean all the people.

It is hardly surprising that from quite early times the very thought of leaving the island filled most people with terror. Similarly, very real fear is to be seen in long-term prisoners who are about to be released. "Outside" the place of captivity is a vague, unknown, threatening world.

The island was not a prison. But it was a cage with invisible bars, more effective than obvious ones ever could be.

The insular society became more and more complex, and we can look at only a few of its outstanding features. Its literature was a rich one. In addition to cultural compositions there were numerous books which explained the values and achievements of the nation. There was also a system of allegorical fiction which portrayed how terrible life might have been, had society not arranged itself in the present reassuring pattern.

From time to time instructors tried to help the whole community to escape. Captains sacrificed themselves for the reestablishment of a climate in which the now concealed shipbuilders could continue their work. All these efforts were interpreted by historians and sociologists with reference to conditions on the island, without thought for any contact outside this closed society. Plausible explanations of almost anything were comparatively easy to produce. No principle of ethics was involved, because scholars continued to study with genuine dedication what seemed to be true. "What *more* can we do?" they asked, implying by the word "more" that the alternative might be an effort of quantity. Or they asked each other, "What *else* can we do?" assuming that the answer might be in "else"—something different. Their real problem was that they assumed themselves able to formulate the questions, and ignored the fact that the questions were every bit as important as the answers.

Of course the islanders had plenty of scope for thought and action within their own small domain. The variations of ideas and differences of opinion gave the impression of freedom of thought. Thought was encouraged, providing that it was not "absurd."

Freedom of speech was allowed. It was of little use without the development of understanding, which was not pursued.

The work and the emphasis of the navigators had to take on different aspects in accordance with the changes in the community. This made their reality even more baffling to the students who tried to follow them from the island point of view.

Amid all the confusion, even the capacity to remember the possibility of escape could at times become an obstacle. The stirring consciousness of escape potential was not very discriminating. More often than not the eager would-be escapers settled for any kind of substitute. A vague concept of navigation cannot become useful without orientation. Even the most eager potential shipbuilders had been trained to believe that they already had that orientation. They were already mature. They hated anyone who pointed out that they might need a preparation.

Bizarre versions of swimming or shipbuilding often crowded out possibilities of real progress. Very much to blame were the advocates of pseudoswimming or allegorical ships, mere hucksters, who offered lessons to those as yet too weak to swim, or passages on ships which they could not build.

The needs of the society had originally made necessary certain forms of efficiency and thinking which developed into what was known as science. This admirable approach, so essential in the fields where it had an application, finally outran its real meaning. The approach called "scientific," soon after the "Please" revolution, became stretched until it covered all manner of ideas. Eventually things which could not be brought within its bounds became known as "unscientific," another convenient synonym for "bad." Words were unknowingly taken prisoner and then automatically enslaved.

In the absence of a suitable attitude, like people who, thrown upon their own resources in a waiting room, feverishly read magazines, the islanders absorbed themselves in finding substitutes for the fulfillment which was the original (and indeed the final) purpose of this community's exile.

Some were able to divert their attention more or less successfully into mainly emotional commitments. There were different ranges of emotion, but no adequate scale for measuring them. All emotion was considered to be "deep" or "profound"—at any rate more profound than nonemotion. Emotion, which was seen to move people to the most extreme physical and mental acts known, was automatically termed "deep."

The majority of people set themselves targets, or allowed others to set them for them. They might pursue one cult after another, or money, or social prominence. Some worshiped some things and felt themselves superior to all the rest. Some, by repudiating what they thought worship was, thought that they had no idols, and could therefore safely sneer at all the rest.

As the centuries passed, the island was littered with the debris of these cults. Worse than ordinary debris, it was self-perpetuating. Well-meaning and other people combined the cults and recombined them, and they spread anew. For the amateur and intellectual, this constituted a mine of academic or "initiatory" material, giving a comforting sense of variety.

Magnificent facilities for the indulging of limited "satisfactions" proliferated. Palaces and monuments, museums and universities, institutes of learning, theaters and sports stadiums almost filled the island. The people naturally prided themselves on these endowments, many of which they considered to be linked in a general way with ultimate truth, though exactly how this was so escaped almost all of them.

Shipbuilding was connected with some dimensions of this activity, but in a way unknown to almost everyone.

Clandestinely the ships raised their sails, the swimmers continued to teach swimming. . . .

The conditions on the island did not entirely fill these dedicated people with dismay. After all, they too had originated in the very same community, and had indissoluble bonds with it, and with its destiny.

But they very often had to preserve themselves from the attentions of their fellow citizens. Some "normal" islanders tried to save them from themselves. Others tried to kill them, for an equally sublime reason. Some even sought their help eagerly, but could not find them.

All these reactions to the existence of the swimmers were the result of the same cause, filtered through different kinds of minds. This cause was that hardly anyone now knew what a swimmer really was, what he was doing, or where he could be found.

As the life of the island became more and more civilized, a strange but logical industry grew up. It was devoted to ascribing doubts to the validity of the system under which society lived. It succeeded in absorbing doubts about social values by laughing at them or satirizing them. The activity could wear a sad or happy face, but it really became a repetitious ritual. A potentially valuable industry, it was often prevented from exercising its really creative function.

People felt that, having allowed their doubts to have temporary expression, they would in some way assuage them, exorcise them, almost propitiate them. Satire passed for meaningful allegory; allegory was accepted but not digested. Plays, books, films, poems, lampoons were the usual media for this development, though there was a strong section of it in more academic fields. For many islanders it seemed more emancipated, more modern or progressive, to follow this cult rather than older ones.

Here and there a candidate still presented himself to a swimming instructor, to make his bargain. Usually what amounted to a stereotyped conversation took place.

"I want to learn to swim."

"Do you want to make a bargain about it?"

"No. I only have to take my ton of cabbage."

"What cabbage?"

"The food which I will need on the other island."

"There is better food there."

"I don't know what you mean. I cannot be sure. I must take my cabbage."

"You cannot swim, for one thing, with a ton of cabbage."

"Then I cannot go. You call it a load. I call it my essential nutrition."

"Suppose, as an allegory, we say not 'cabbage,' but 'assumptions,' or 'destructive ideas'?"

"I am going to take my cabbage to some instructor who understands my needs."

This book is about some of the swimmers and builders of ships, and also about some of the others who tried to follow them, with more or less success. The fable is not ended, because there are still people on the island.

The Sufis use various ciphers to convey their meaning. Rearrange the name of the original community—El Ar—to spell "Rcal." Perhaps you had already noticed that the name adopted by the revolutionaries—"Please"—rearranges to form the word "Asleep."

The Background
I. The Travelers and the Grapes

There are three forms of culture: worldly
culture, the mere acquisition of information;
religious culture, following rules; elite
culture, self-development.
(The master Hujwiri, *Revelation of the Veiled*)

There is a story in Aesop's fables about a young mole who
went to his mother and told her that he could see. Now, as
most people know, sight is something traditionally lacking
in moles. This one's mother decided to test him. She accordingly placed in front of him a piece of frankincense, and
asked him what it was.

"A stone," said the little mole.

"Not only are you blind," his mother answered, "but
you have lost your sense of smell as well."

Aesop, esteemed traditionally by Sufis as a practical
teacher in an immemorial tradition of wisdom gained
through the conscious exercise of the mind, body and perceptions, is not allowed much distinction by the overt meaning of this tale. The lameness of some of the morals (actually
superficial glosses) of the Aesopian stories has been noticed
by many students.

We can analyze the story to see what it really means, if
we know something of the Sufi tradition and its method of
concealing meanings in literature.

"Mole" in Arabic (*khuld,* from the radical KHLD) is written in the same way as *khalad,* which stands for "eternity, paradise, thought, mind, soul," according to the context. Because only the consonants are written, there is no way of telling, in isolation, which word is intended. If this word were used poetically in a Semitic language and then translated into Greek by someone who did not understand the double meaning, the play upon words would be lost.

Why the stone and scent? Because, in Sufi tradition, "Moses [*a guide to his people*] made a stone as fragrant as musk" (Hakim Sanai, *The Walled Garden of Truth*).

"Moses" symbolizes a guiding thought, which transforms something apparently inanimate and inert into something "as fragrant as musk"—something with what might almost be called a life of its own.

Our story now shows us that the "mother" of the thought (its origin, matrix, essential quality) presents "frankincense" (impalpable experience) to the thought, or mind. Because the individual (the mole) is concentrating upon "sight" (trying to develop faculties in the wrong order) it even loses the power to use the ones which it should have.

The human being, according to the Sufis, instead of reaching within himself in a certain manner in order to find and attain his development, searches outside, and follows illusions (metaphysical systems wrongly developed) which in fact cripple him.

What is the inner potentiality of the "mole?" We can now look at the whole group of words in Arabic which belong to the root KHLD which we are considering:

Khalad (KHaLaD)   =   ever abiding, long-lasting
Khallad (KHaLLaD)   =   to perpetuate a thing
Akhlad (AKHLaD)   =   to lean toward, to adhere
                                        faithfully to (a friend)
Khuld (KHuLD)   =   eternity, paradise, continuity
Khuld (KHuLD)   =   mole, field rat, lark (bird)
Khalad (KHaLaD)   =   thought, mind, soul

El-Khualid (EL-KHUALiD) = mountains, rocks,
                             supporters (of a
                             pot)

To the Sufi, this grouping of words around a basic root
conveys essentials for human forward development. It is
almost a map of Sufism. The mole, because of coincidence,
can be chosen as the symbol of the mind, or thought. In
the same mind there is eternity, continuity, support. Sufism
is concerned with the perpetuation of the human consciousness through its source in the mind. Faithfulness in association with others is an essential of this task.

The Aesopian story, therefore, does not mean, as its
commentators would believe, that "It is easy to unmask an
impostor." We need not deny that the tale could have fulfilled this function for centuries. But the use of the incense
and the mole, plus the Sufi tradition that certain secrets are
concealed in such words as those of Aesop, helps us to unlock the door. Looking at a great deal of literary and philosophical material in this light, we are irresistibly reminded
of the message of Rumi, himself, like Aesop, a great fabulist
of Asia Minor. He says that the canal may not itself drink,
but it performs the function of conveying water to the
thirsty. Those who are interested in this interpretation of
the mole symbolism might well feel that the light-hearted
potted wisdom of Aesop has been the carrier of the nutrition
which we now find in it.

Rumi lived nearly two thousand years after Aesop, and
he said: "A tale, fictitious or otherwise, illuminates truth."

There is no need to pursue the Arabic language itself as
the actual source of the Semitic version from which this
Aesopian tale comes. Arabic is useful to us as a tool because,
as philologists have demonstrated, it retains in close association words grouped according to a primitive pattern
whose meanings have become very corrupted in the other
Semitic languages.

There are, in the West as well as the East, quite nu-

merous examples of similar crystallization of teaching in
literature, ritual and folk belief. Many such phenomena are
considered unimportant: like the jokes attributed to
Nasrudin, Joe Miller and others, read for their face value.
Much of Omar Khayyam's poetry, intended to make the
reader think clearly through reducing life to absurdity, has
been taken in the superficial sense that Khayyam was a
"pessimist." Platonic material, intended according to the
Sufis to show the limitations of formal logic and the ease of
falling into false reasoning, has been considered defective,
and nothing more. In some cases, as with Aesop, the canal
still carries the water, though it is not recognized as a
canal. In other formulations, people carry on meaningless
rituals and beliefs which they have rationalized until they
have no real dynamic and are really only of antiquarian
interest. The great Sufi poet Jami says of them: "The dry
cloud, waterless, can have no rain-giving quality." And yet
such cults, often mere counterfeits of carefully organized
symbolism based on poetic analogy, are often seriously
studied. Some people think that they contain certain metaphysical or magical truths, others that they are themselves
of historical importance.

In the cases where a cult or grouping of people are following a theme mapped out originally on certain word
groupings, it is impossible to understand them or even to
trace their history unless we know that this is what originally happened. Because of its peculiarly mathematical
nature, and because it was chosen as the framework for
presenting certain knowledge to the East and West during
the middle ages, Arabic is most important in this study.

Again, because of the almost algebraic method of producing words from a basic three-letter form, Arabic has a great
simplicity which would hardly have been expected by anyone who does not know it. In many cases we are dealing
only with words, groups of consonants, not with grammar,
syntax, even with the Arabic letters, because they can all be
rendered sufficiently well for our purpose by means of Latin

letters. We substitute one letter for another. At the most we modify that letter in order to tell us which one the original was. This, in substance, is an art which has been used very widely in the countries of the East where Arabic letters and Sufi lore have penetrated, and used by people who have no deep knowledge of Arabic itself. Arabic, then, was discovered to be susceptible to use as a code by certain people in the East and also in the Latin West of the middle ages.[1]

The relationship of parent to child (mole and mother) is used by Sufis to denote the training toward full "sight" as well as the ultimate relationship between the Sufi and the ultimate "sight" of objective truth. To the Sufi, religious incarnation or effigy conveying this relationship is merely a rough and secondary method of portraying something which has happened to an individual or a group—a religious experience showing them the way to self-realization.

"The perfected Sufi is great, exalted; he is sublime. Through love, work and harmony he has attained the highest degree of mastership. All secrets are open to him; and his whole being is imbued with magical effulgence. He is the Guide and the Traveler on the Way of infinite beauty, love, attainment, power, fulfillment; the Guardian of the Most Ancient Wisdom, the Trailblazer to the highest secrets; the beloved friend whose very being elevates us, bringing new meaning to the spirit of humanity."

This is one portrayal of the Sufi, by a contemporary writer who is not himself a Sufi, though he has lived among the followers of the Way of Love.

The Sufi seems to the unregenerate man to change, but to those with inner perception he remains the same, because his essential personality is within, and not without. A scholar in Kashmir, which for centuries was a center of Sufi teaching, made in the seventeenth century what would today be called a survey of the general characteristics of Sufi mystics. This was Sirajudin, who traveled in all the adjacent coun-

[1] See annotation "Languages."

tries, and even to Java, China and the Sahara, talking to Sufis and collecting their unwritten lore.

"The Sufi," he says, "is the complete man. When he says, 'among roses, be a rose, among thorns, be a thorn,' he is not inevitably referring to social behavior. The Sufis are poets and lovers. According to the ground in which their teaching grows, they are soldiers, administrators or physicians. According to the eyes of the beholder they may seem magicians, mystics, practitioners of incomprehensible arts. If you revere them as saints, you will benefit by their sainthood; but if you work with them as associates, you will benefit from their company. To them, the world is a fashioning instrument, which polishes mankind. They, by identification with the processes of continuous creation, are themselves fashioners of other complete men. Some talk, others are silent, some walk it seems restlessly, others sit and teach. To understand them you must bring into action an intelligence which is an intuitive one, normally held down by its friendly enemy, the intelligence of the logical mind. Until you can understand illogicality, and the meaningfulness of it, shun the Sufis except for limited, precise, self-evident services."[2]

A Sufi, the Sufis, cannot be defined by any single set of words or ideas. By a picture, moving and made up of different dimensions, perhaps. Rumi, one of the greatest mystical masters, tells us in a famous passage that the Sufi is:

Drunk without wine; sated without food; distraught; foodless and sleepless; a king beneath a humble cloak; a treasure within a ruin; not of air and earth; not of fire and water; a sea without bounds. He has a hundred moons and skies and suns. He is wise through universal truth—not a scholar from a book.[3]

[2] *Safarnama* of Sirajudin Abbasi, 1649.
[3] The Rev. Canon Sell, a specialist of Sufism, seems to think that this booklessness is something to do with theology, of all things: "Mere learning from books will not make a theologian," he says, in a

Is he a man of religion? No, he is far, far more: "He is beyond atheism and faith alike—what are merit and sin to him? He is hidden—seek him!"

The Sufi, as we are told in these most famous words from the thirteenth-century *Diwan of Shams of Tabriz*, is hidden; hidden more deeply than the practitioner of any secret school. Yet individual Sufis are known in their thousands, throughout the East. Settlements of Sufis are found in the lands of the Arabs, the Turks, the Persians, Afghans, Indians, Malays.

The more the dogged searchers of the Western world have tried to dig out the secrets of the Sufi, the more hopelessly complex the task has seemed to be. Their work thus litters the fields of mysticism, Arabism, Orientalism, history, philosophy and even general literature. "The secret," in the Sufi phrase, "protects itself. It is found only in the spirit and the practice of the Work."

A distinguished professor of archaeology is perhaps the greatest living Western authority on the Sufis—because he is a Sufi, not because he is an academician.

The ordinary man or woman in the East often looks upon the Sufi as the Westerner might imagine an Oriental mystic should be. A man endowed with supernatural powers, inheritor of secrets handed down from uncounted ages, symbolic of wisdom and timelessness. The Sufi can read your thoughts, transport himself from one place to another in an instant, is in a special continuing relationship with things of another world.

Sufis are usually believed to have healing powers, and there is no scarcity of people who will tell you how they were made whole by Sufis through a glance or in some other inexplicable manner.[4] Sufis are thought to excel at their chosen vocations: and numerous individuals are

footnote to this. (Dr. Sell, *Sufism*, Christ. Lit. Soc., 1910, p. 63.) He finds Rumi difficult, saying (*Ibid.*, p. 69), "it is only very patient students who can find the esoteric meaning of the poet."

[4] See annotation "Consciousness."

pointed out as proof of this belief. They make mistakes, so the contention is, far less frequently than other people; and they approach things in a manner which nobody else would. Yet their actions are vindicated by events. This fact is attributed to a form of foreknowledge. They believe themselves to be taking part in the higher evolution of humanity.

If popular beliefs, which may include what amounts to saint worship throughout the Middle East, are far-reaching, they are eclipsed by legends and traditions of Sufi masters, personalities revered by members of all faiths. The Sufi ancients could walk on water, describe events taking place at vast distances, experience the true reality of life. And much more in the same vein. When one master spoke, his hearers went into a state of mystical rapture and developed magical powers. Wherever Sufis went, mystics of other persuasions, often of great prominence, became their disciples—sometimes without a word having been spoken.

In the material world, Sufi ascendancy is based upon work and creativity, and generally accepted because of the achievements of individual Sufis. Sufi philosophical and scientific discoveries are widely considered to have been achieved through their special powers. The conventional theosophist or intellectual finds himself in the uncomfortable position that, although he must often deny the likelihood of a special form of consciousness accessible to an elite of this kind, he has to accept that Sufis are national heroes in some countries, and are responsible for the development of classical literature in others. It is estimated that between twenty and forty million people are members of, or affiliated to, Sufi schools; and the Sufis are increasing in numbers.

The Sufi may be your neighbor, the man across the street, the woman who does your chores; a recluse at times, rich or poor.

No investigation into the reality of Sufism can be made entirely from the outside, because Sufism includes participation, training and experience. Although Sufis have written

innumerable books, these may apply to specific circumstances, seem to contradict one another, cannot be understood by the uninitiated, or are found to have meanings
other than the superficial one. They are usually studied by
outsiders only very superficially.

One difficulty of getting to grips with Sufism through its
Eastern literature has been noticed by many scholars who
have made the attempt, including Professor Nicholson, who
labored long to understand and make available Sufic thinking to the West. In presenting selections of some Sufi writings he admits that "a great deal is peculiar and unique,
so that the writings in which it occurs seldom impart their
real significance except to those who possess the key to
the cipher, while the uninitiated will either understand
them literally or not at all."[5]

A book such as the present one "designs itself" in a Sufistic manner; for by definition it must follow a Sufic, not a
conventional, pattern, and hence its material and treatment
are of a special nature, not subject to approach by means of
familiar criteria. This is the method known as "scatter," by
which an impact is considered effective by virtue of its multiple activity.

In ordinary life, certain forms of understanding become
possible because of experience. The human mind is what it
is partly because of the impacts to which it has been exposed, and its ability to use those impacts. The interaction
between impact and mind determines the quality of the
personality. In Sufism this normal physical and mental
process is engaged in consciously. The result is felt to be
more efficient; and "wisdom," instead of being a matter of
time, age and accident, is regarded as inevitable. Sufis liken
this process to the analogy between a savage who eats
everything and a discriminating man who eats what is good
for him as well as tasty.

It would be absurd to attempt to convey the meaning of

[5] R. A. Nicholson, *Tales of Mystic Meaning*, London, 1931,
p. 171.

Sufi thought and action in a conventional, simplified or conversational manner, for the above reasons. This absurdity is summarized by the Sufi tag as "sending a kiss by messenger." Sufism may be natural, but it is also a part of higher human development, and conscious development at that. An adequate vehicle for its presentation usually does not exist in societies where it has not been operating in this advanced form. On the other hand, a climate for its presentation (part literary, part expository, part example and so on) has been prepared in other areas.

Metaphysically minded people, and especially those who feel that they are comfortable in the domain of mysticism or "inner perception," have no greater start on the generality of humanity where the acceptance of Sufism is concerned. Their subjectivity, especially where it is linked with a strong sense of personal uniqueness "caught" from other people, can in fact be a serious disability.

There is no simplified Sufism; yet it disappears from the area of cognition of such ill-defined minds as may be confident that they can understand it, penetrate anything "spiritual" by virtue of what is truly a woolly, self-assumed perceptiveness. To the Sufi, such a personality, however vocal he may be (and he often is) hardly exists at all.

Anyone who says, "It is all so indescribable, but I just *feel* what you mean," is unlikely to be able to profit by Sufism. For Sufis are working, are carrying out an effort to awaken a certain field of consciousness by means of an approach which is specialized, not fortuitous. Sufism does not trade in airy-fairiness, mutual admiration, or lukewarm generalities. When the "bite" disappears, so, too, does the Sufic element from a situation. The converse is also true. Sufism is not directed to a section of the community—for no such section exists—but to a certain faculty within individuals. Where this faculty is not activated, there is no Sufism. It contains "hard" as well as "soft" realities, discord as well as harmony, the sharp brightness of awakening as well as the gentle dark of a lulling to sleep.

This central factor is well expressed in Sufi poetry, which is often perfect in a technical sense, and sometimes human, sometimes startlingly different. Generations of conventional prosodists have spent their lives analyzing this unique property by a different yardstick—in terms of a poet's "variations in quality." One Sufi poet replies like this:

O cat with a taste for sour cream; connoisseur of shades of bitterness! You belong to the litter that has agreed about yogurt. You hate with equal meaning the cheese, butter, and milk warm from the udder. You are no cheesemonger, you say? Verily, he is closer to you than your jugular vein.

And another, with an oddly modern echo of reference to slick writings:

Shall we paint a perfect picture, or design a perfect rug? Then shall we thump our tongues all night to find out wherein each has strayed from perfection? This is good; this is a task for a complete man; and for such a child as is intent upon the consistency of the materials which alone will give perfection to his mud pie.

Anyone who has tasted the firm, but not too hard, aseptic cheeses of the contemporary supermarket will be able to share the poet's feelings about food, if nothing else.

Hilaly, accused of "using a sword to sever a thread," said: "Shall I rather use honey to drown a camel?"

There are imitation Sufis, who try to benefit from the prestige which attaches to the name. Some of them have written books, which only add to a general perplexity among outsiders.

It is possible that much of the Sufic spirit may be transmitted in writing, if one accepts the fact that Sufism has to be experienced continually as well as tested vicariously. It does not depend upon the impact only of artistic forms, but of life upon life.

Sufism, in one definition, is human life. Occult and meta-

physical powers are largely incidental, though they may
play their part in the process, if not in personal prominence
or satisfaction. It is axiomatic that the attempt to become a
Sufi through a desire for personal power as normally understood will not succeed. Only the search for truth is valid,
the desire for wisdom the motive. The method is assimilation, not study.

In observing the Sufis by means of what are in fact derivations of Sufi techniques, we shall have to look at many
things which may be important at first, but which will cease
to have the same significance as we proceed. This technique
can easily be illustrated. A child learns to read by master-
ing the alphabet. When he can read words he retains the
knowledge of the letters, but reads whole words. If he were
to concentrate upon letters, he would be severely handicapped by what was useful only at an earlier stage. Both
words and letters should now have a more settled perspective. Thus the Sufic method.

The process is easier than it sounds, even if only because
doing a thing may often be easier than describing it.

I report a glimpse of Sufis in a circle (*halka*), the basic
unit and very heart of active Sufism. A group of seekers is
attracted to a teaching master, and attends his Thursday
evening assembly. The first part of the proceedings is the
less formal time, when questions are asked, and students
received.

On this occasion, a newcomer had just asked our teacher,
the Agha, whether there was a basic urge toward mystical
experience, shared by all humanity.

"We have a word," replied the Agha, "which sums all this
up. It describes what we are doing, and it summarizes our
way of thinking. Through it you will understand the very
reason for our existence, and the reason why mankind is
generally speaking at odds. The word is *Anguruzuminab-
stafil.*" And he explained it in a traditional Sufi story.

Four men—a Persian, a Turk, an Arab, and a Greek—
were standing in a village street. They were traveling com-

panions, making for some distant place; but at this moment they were arguing over the spending of a single piece of money which was all that they had among them.

"I want to buy *angur*," said the Persian.

"I want *uzum*," said the Turk.

"I want *inab*," said the Arab.

"No!" said the Greek, "we should buy *stafil*."

Another traveler passing, a linguist, said, "Give the coin to me. I undertake to satisfy the desires of all of you."

At first they would not trust him. Ultimately they let him have the coin. He went to the shop of a fruit seller and bought four small bunches of grapes.

"This is my *angur*," said the Persian.

"But this is what I call *uzum*," said the Turk.

"You have brought me *inab*," said the Arab.

"No!" said the Greek, "this in my language is *stafil*."

The grapes were shared out among them, and each realized that the disharmony had been due to his faulty understanding of the language of the others.

"The travelers," said the Agha, "are the ordinary people of the world. The linguist is the Sufi. People know that they want something, because there is an inner need existing in them. They may give it different names, but it is the same thing. Those who call it religion have different names for it, and even different ideas as to what it might be. Those who call it ambition try to find its scope in different ways. But it is only when a linguist appears, someone who knows what they really mean, that they can stop the struggling and get on with the eating of the grapes."

The group of travelers which he had been describing, he continued, were more advanced than most, in that they actually had a positive idea of what they wanted, even though they could not communicate it. It is far more common for the individual to be at an earlier stage of aspiration than he thinks. He wants something but does not know what it is—though he may think that he knows.

The Sufic way of thinking is particularly appropriate in

a world of mass communication, when every effort is directed toward making people believe that they want or need certain things; that they should believe certain things; that they should as a consequence do certain things that their manipulators want them to do.

The Sufi speaks of wine, the product of the grape, and its secret potential, as his means of attaining "inebriation." The grape is seen as the raw form of the wine. Grapes, then, mean ordinary religion; while wine is the real essence of the fruit. The travelers are therefore seen to be four ordinary people, differing in religion. The Sufi shows them that the basis of their religions is in fact the same. He does not, however, offer them wine, the essence, which is the inner doctrine waiting to be produced and used in mysticism, a field far more developed than mere organized religion. That is a further stage. But the Sufi's role as a servant of humanity is brought out by the fact that, although he is operating on a higher level, he helps the formal religionist as far as he can, by showing him the fundamental identity of religious faith. He might, of course, have gone on to a discussion of the merits of wine; but what the travelers wanted was grapes, and grapes they were given. When the wrangling over smaller issues subsides, according to the Sufi, the greater teaching may be imparted. Meanwhile, some sort of primary lesson has been given.

The basic urge toward mysticism is never, in the unaltered man, clear enough to be recognized for what it is.

Rumi, in his version of this story (*Mathnawi*, Bk. II) alludes to the Sufi training system when he says that the grapes, pressed together, produce one juice—the wine of Sufism.

The Sufis often start from a nonreligious viewpoint.[6] The answer, they say, is within the mind of mankind. It has to be liberated, so that by self-knowledge the intuition becomes the guide to human fulfillment. The other way, the way of

---

[6] "Words cannot be used in referring to religious truth, except as analogy." (Hakim Sanai, *The Walled Garden of Truth*.)

training, suppresses and stills the intuition. Humanity is turned into a conditioned animal by non-Sufi systems, while being told that it is free and creative, has a choice of thought and action.

The Sufi is an individual who believes that by practicing alternate detachment and identification with life, he becomes free. He is a mystic because he believes that he can become attuned to the purpose of all life. He is a practical man because he believes that this process must take place within normal society. And he must serve humanity because he is a part of it. The great El-Tughrai, contemporary of Omar Khayyam, wrote this warning in 1111 A.D.: "O Man, that art so full of information penetrating into secrets; listen, for in silence is safety from slips—'They have fostered thee for a purpose, did thou but understand it. Have a care to thyself, lest thou feed with lost sheep.'" This was translated by Edward Pococke in 1661.

In order to succeed in this endeavor, he must follow the methods which have been devised by earlier masters, methods for slipping through the complex of training which makes most people prisoners of their environment and of the effect of their experiences. The exercises of the Sufis have been developed through the interaction of two things—intuition and the changing aspects of human life. Different methods will suggest themselves intuitively in different societies and at various times. This is not inconsistent, because real intuition is itself always consistent.

The Sufi life can be lived at any time, in any place. It does not require withdrawal from the world, or organized movements, or dogma. It is coterminous with the existence of humanity. It cannot, therefore, accurately be termed an Eastern system. It has profoundly influenced both the East and the very bases of the Western civilization in which many of us live—the mixture of Christian, Jewish, Moslem and Near Eastern or Mediterranean heritage commonly called "Western."

Mankind, according to the Sufis, is infinitely perfectable.

The perfection comes about through attunement with the whole of existence. Physical and spiritual life meet, but only when there is a complete balance between them. Systems which teach withdrawal from the world are regarded as unbalanced.

Physical exercises are linked with theoretical patterns. In Sufi psychology there is an important relationship between, for instance, the doctrine of the "Seven Stages of Man"[7] and the integration of personality; and between movement, experience and the progressive attainment of a higher personality.

When, and where, did the Sufi way of thinking start? This is, to most Sufis, slightly irrelevant to the work at hand. The "place" of Sufism is within humanity. The "place" of your sitting-room carpet is on the floor of your house—not in Mongolia, where its design may have originated.

"The practice of the Sufis is too sublime to have a formal beginning," says the *Asrar el Qadim wa'l Qadim* (Secrets of the Past and Future). But as long as one remembers that history is less important than the present and the future, there is a great deal to be learned from a review of the spread of the modern Sufi trend since it branched out from the areas which were Arabized nearly fourteen hundred years ago. By a glance at this period of development, the Sufis show how and why the message of self-perfection may be carried into every conceivable kind of society, irrespective of its nominal religious or social commitment.

Sufism is believed by its followers to be the inner, "secret" teaching that is concealed within every religion; and because its bases are in every human mind already, Sufic development must inevitably find its expression everywhere. The historical period of the teaching starts with the explosion of Islam from the desert into the static societies of the Near East.

[7] The "stages" in Sufi literature correspond with the transmutation of seven "selves," the technical term for which is *Nafs*. See annotation "Seven Men."

Toward the middle of the seventh century, the expansion of Islam beyond the borders of Arabia was challenging, and was soon to overthrow, the empires of the Middle East. Each one had a venerable tradition in the political, military and religious spheres. The armies of Islam, originally composed mainly of Bedouins, but then swollen by recruits of other origins, struck northward, eastward and to the west. The Caliphs fell heir to the lands of the Hebrews, the Byzantines, the Persians and the Graeco-Buddhists; the conquerors reached the south of France in the West, and the valley of the Indus in the East. Those political, military and religious conquests form the nucleus of the Moslem countries and communities of today, which extend from Indonesia in the Pacific to Morocco on the Atlantic.

It is from this background that the Sufi mystics became known in the West, and they maintained a current of teaching which links people of intuition from the Far East to the farthest West.

The early Caliphs had possessed themselves of more than millions of square miles, uncounted riches and the political supremacy of the known world of the middle ages. The centers of learning of the ancients, and particularly the traditional schools of mystical teaching, had almost all fallen into their hands. In Africa, the ancient communities of Egypt, including Alexandria; and farther west, Carthage, where St. Augustine had studied and preached esoteric, pre-Christian doctrines.[8] Palestine and Syria, the homes of secret traditions; Central Asia, where the Buddhists were most firmly entrenched; and northwest India with its venerable background of mysticism and experiential religion—all were within the empire of Islam.

To these centers traveled the Arab mystics, anciently known as the Near Ones (*muqarribun*), who believed that essentially there was a unity among the inner teachings of all faiths. Like John the Baptist, they wore camels' wool,

[8] See annotation "St. Augustine."

and may have been known as Sufis (People of Wool),
though not for this reason alone. As a result of these contacts with the Hanifs[9] each one of the ancient centers of
secret teaching became a Sufi stronghold. The gap between
the secret lore and practice of Christians, Zoroastrians,
Hebrews, Hindus, Buddhists and the rest had been
bridged. This process, the confluence of essences, has never
been grasped by non-Sufis as a reality, because such observers find it impossible to realize that the Sufi sees and
contacts the Sufic stream in every culture, as a bee will suck
from many flowers without becoming a flower. Even the
Sufic usage of "confluence" terminology to denote this function has not penetrated far.[10]

Sufi mysticism differs tremendously from other cults claiming to be mystical. Formal religion is for the Sufi merely a
shell, though a genuine one, which fulfills a function. When
the human consciousness has penetrated beyond this social
framework, the Sufi understands the real meaning of religion. The mystics of other persuasions do not think in this
manner at all. They may transcend outer religious forms,
but they do not emphasize the fact that outer religion is
only a prelude to special experience. Most ecstatics remain
attached to a rapturous symbolization of some concept derived from their religion. The Sufi uses religion and psychology to pass beyond all this. Having done so, he "returns to
the world," to guide others on the way.

Professor Nicholson emphasizes this vision of religion from
an objective viewpoint, in translating Rumi thus:[11]

If there be any lover in the world, O Moslems, 'tis I.
If there be any believer, or Christian hermit, 'tis I.
The wine dregs, the cupbearer, the minstrel, the harp, and
    the music,

[9] See annotation "Hanifs."
[10] See annotation "Confluence."
[11] R. A. Nicholson, *The Mystics of Islam*, London, 1914, pp. 161
et seq.

The beloved, the candle, the drink and the joy of the
    drunken—'tis I.
The two-and-seventy creeds and sects in the world
Do not really exist: I swear by God that every creed and
    sect—'tis I.
Earth and air and water and fire, nay, body and soul too—
    'tis I.
Truth and falsehood, good and evil, ease and difficulty from
    first to last,
Knowledge and learning and asceticism and piety and faith
    —'tis I.
The fire of Hell, be assured, with its flaming limbos,
Yes, and Paradise and Eden and the Houris—'tis I.
This earth and heaven with all they hold,
Angels, Peris, Genies and Mankind—'tis I.

Rumi has broken through the limitations of the ordinary
consciousness. Now he is able to see things as they really
are, to understand the affinity and unity of seemingly different things, to perceive the role of man, and especially of
the Sufi. This is something far more advanced than what
is ordinarily called mysticism.

It was not always safe, in the face of vast numbers of
enthusiastic and victorious Moslem zealots, to claim, as the
Sufis did, that human realization came only from within
and not through just doing certain things and not doing
certain other things. At the same time, the Sufic attitude
was that mysticism must be taken out of its utterly secret
character if it were to become a force which would penetrate all humanity.

In their own tradition, the Sufis saw themselves as in-
heritors of one single teaching—elsewhere split into so many
facets—which could be made to serve as the instrument
of human development. "Before garden, vine or grape was
in the world," writes one, "our soul was drunken with immortal wine."

The groundwork for the wide diffusion of Sufic thought

and action was laid by the masters of the classical period—which may be taken as the first eight hundred years after the appearance of Islam—between about 700 A.D. and 1500 A.D. Sufism was based upon love, operated through a dynamic of love, had its manifestation through ordinary human life, poetry and work.

Because the Sufis recognized Islam as a manifestation of the essential upsurge of transcendental teaching, there could be no interior conflict between Islam and Sufism. Sufism was taken to correspond to the inner reality of Islam, as with the equivalent aspect of every other religion and genuine tradition.

The great Sufi Khayyam, in his *Rubaiyat*, stresses this interior experience, which has no real connection with the theological version of what people consider, by default, to be real religion:

In cell and cloister, monastery and synagogue, one lies
In dread of hell: one dreams of paradise.
But none that know the divine secrets
Has sown his heart with suchlike fantasies.

The phase into which what we call Sufism now entered was different in respect of climate and environment, but identical in respect of continuity of teaching. Rigid ecclesiastics—formalists—might not have recognized this, but they were relatively unimportant—"He who can see all the picture can both understand it and cater for it." Professor E. G. Browne comments: "But even the genuine Sufis differed considerably one from another for their system was essentially individualistic and little disposed towards propagandism. The fully developed *arif*, gnostic, or Adept, had passed through many grades and a long course of discipline under various *pirs*, *murshids*, or spiritual directors, ere he attained to the gnosis (*irfan*) which viewed all existing religions as more or less faint utterances of that great underlying Truth with which he had finally entered into communion; and he neither conceived it as possible nor desir-

able to impart his conceptions of this Truth to any save
those few who, by a similar training, were prepared to receive it."[12]

It is sometimes difficult for a conventionally minded person to grasp how far-reaching the rule of essential Sufic
action really is. Since Sufism was bound to exist in Islam as
elsewhere, it could easily be taught through Islam. It is
instructive to note that two legalistic and theological com-
pendia, obviously straining to present Sufism publicly as
religiously orthodox, were written by Sufi giants—the *Taaruf*
of Kalabadhi of Bokhara (died 995) and the first public
Persian treatise, the *Kashf* of Hujwiri (died 1063). Both
authors are of the highest Sufi rank, yet each often speaks as
if he were an observer, not an initiate, as Omar Khayyam
also frequently does, to the mystification of some of his trust-
ingly literalist commentators. These authors are full of hidden meanings, never reproduced in translation, and it was
precisely in this way that many of the Orders of medieval
Sufism proceeded. They continued their work, which was
entirely valid within the Islamic world. Yet, as some Sufis
note, "Sufism was even taught at one time exclusively by
signs." The end product, the Completed Man, is the same in
both cases. The symbolism and chain of experience whereby
Islam and other systems are reconciled through Sufi practice
is another matter, vouchsafed only to practitioners and concealed in the dictum: "He who tastes, knows."

Although many explanations are given—for various reasons—for the adoption of the word "Sufi," there is one
significant one which is taught to those who join these
mystics—the word contains, in enciphered form, the concept
of Love. Also encoded, this time by means of a conventional
numerical cipher, are the following words, which convey
an abbreviated message—above; transcending; correcting; a
bequest; sufficiency in or at a reasonable time. Sufism, then,
is a transcendental philosophy, which corrects, is handed

---

[12] E. G. Browne, *A Literary History of Persia,* 1909, p. 424.

down from the past, and is suitable to the contemporary community.

All religion is subject to development. To the Sufi, the evolution of the Sufi is within himself and also in his relationship with society. The development of the community, and the destiny of all creation—including even nominally inanimate creation—is interwoven with the destiny of the Sufi. He may have to detach himself for a period from society —for a moment, a month, or even more—but ultimately he is interlinked with the eternal whole. The Sufi's importance, therefore, is immense, and his actions and appearance to others will seem to vary in accordance with human and extrahuman needs. Jalaluddin Rumi emphasizes the evolutionary nature of human effort, which is true both in the individual and the group: "I died as inert matter and became a plant. And as a plant I died and became an animal. I died as an animal, and became a man. So why should I fear losing my 'human' character? I shall die as a man, to rise in 'angelic' form. . . ." (Mathnawi, III, Story XVII)

This attitude explains in a Sufic manner something of the seeming differences in conduct and attitude of the Sufis. Keeping pace with the realities of the community, the Sufis of the early Islamic period stressed the need for renunciation and discipline—factors which were very much lacking in the expanding and prosperous society which was forming on the basis of military success in the Near East. The ordinary historians fail to note this fact, and consequently look at the Sufis historically, believing that they can descry an independent development within the ranks of the devotees. Rabia, the woman Sufi saint, for instance (died 802), is said to have emphasized love; Nuri (died 907), shunning the world. Then, we are told, came a further departure, with a more involved view of life—speculative and philosophical. And much more, a following of supposed trends from without the cult.

This development is undoubtedly a fact, but its explanation is, according to the Sufi, very much unlike its superficial appearance. In the first place, the elements of Sufism were always there in their entirety, within the human mind. Various forms of the teaching were stressed at different times— "No man spends all his time enraged."

Individuals like Rabia were chosen as exemplars of certain aspects of the teaching. Uninitiated readers of the records, deprived of the necessary contextual framework, have quite naturally assumed that such and such a Sufi spent all his time in self-mortification; that before, say, Bayazid (died 875) there was no similarity to Vedantism and Buddhism, and so on. Perhaps these conclusions were inevitable, given the poverty of materials available to the ordinary student. On the other hand, there must always have been many Sufis who were willing to explain this point; to them, naturally, a generally known one. But it is inherent in scholastic thinking that something written down has a greater validity than something said or experienced; and it is thus more than likely that the living representatives of Sufism have been but rarely consulted on these points by academicians.

The recognition of the climate established by Islam as a suitable one for projecting Sufi wisdom is easy to trace. In spite of the development of an unauthorized clergy in Islam, those narrow-minded scripturists who stuck to a dogmatic interpretation of the religion, Islam provided better conditions for propagating an inner doctrine than any of its precursors in the same area. Religious minorities were guaranteed freedom from persecution—an immunity which was rigidly adhered to during the period when the Sufis were becoming visibly active. Islam itself was a matter of legal definition. What was a believer? At the minimum, a person who would repeat the phrase *La-illaha-illa-Allah, Mohammed ar-Rasul-Allah*—"Nothing worshiped but the divinity, the Praised one the messenger of the worshipful" —which is generally understood as, "There is no God but Allah, and Mohammed is His Prophet." The unbeliever was a person who actively denied the words of this creed.

Nobody could see into the heart; so belief could not be defined, only inferred.

Provided that a person could assert that he subscribed to this formula, he could not be proceeded against for heresy. No dogma as to the nature of this divinity and the relationship with the Prophet was fixed; and there was nothing in the phrase of affirmation which could not be subscribed to by a Sufi. His interpretation might be more mystical than that of the scholastics, but no power existed, no ordained priesthood, for instance, which could finally establish the ascendancy of the clerics. Ultimately, Islam as a community was regulated by the interpretations of the doctors of law. They could not define Allah, who was beyond human definition, nor could they precisely interpret Messengership, a unique relationship of deity and man. Before very long, Sufis were able freely to say such things as: "I am an idol worshiper; for I understand what idol worship means, and the idolator does not."

The breakup of the old order in the Near East, according to Sufi tradition, reunited the "beads of mercury" which were the esoteric schools operating in the Egyptian, Persian and Byzantine empires into the "stream of quicksilver" which was intrinsic, evolutionary Sufism.

The Sufis even established the principle, often to be accepted by Islamic courts of law, that seemingly irreverent statements made in a state of mystical ecstasy could not be taken at their face value for penal purposes. "If a bush can say, 'I am Truth,'" said a famous Sufi, "so can a man."

There was, too, a well-established belief among the general public that Mohammed had had a special relationship with other mystics, and that the devout and highly respected "Seekers of Truth"[13] who surrounded him during his lifetime might have been the recipients of an inner doctrine which he imparted in private. Mohammed, it will be remembered, did not claim to bring any new religion. He was

[13] *Tulab el Haqq.*

continuing the monotheistic tradition which he stated was working long before his time. He inculcated respect for members of other faiths, and spoke of the importance of spiritual teachers of many kinds. The Koran itself was revealed by mystical methods, and provided many indications of mystical thinking.

In the religious sphere, the Koran maintains the unity of religions and the identical origin of each—"Every nation had a Warner." Islam accepted Moses, Jesus and others as inspired prophets. Further, the recognition of Mohammed's mission by numerous former Jews, Christians and Magians (including priests), some of whom had traveled to Arabia during his lifetime seeking a teacher, provided a further basis for the belief in a continuity of ancient, not localized, teaching, of which previous highly organized religions might be merely elaborations or popularizations.

This is why, in Sufi tradition, the "Chain of Transmission" of Sufi schools may reach back to the Prophet by one line, and to Elias by another. One of the most respected seventh-century Sufi masters—Uways, who died in 657—never met Mohammed, though he was living in Arabia at the same time and outlived him. Again, it is authoritatively on record that the name "Sufi" was in use before the declaration of his prophetic mission by Mohammed.[14] It is essential to grasp this sense of continuity of inner teaching, and also the belief in the evolution of society, if the Sufis are to be understood to any real extent.

But perhaps the greatest contribution of Islam to the spread of Sufic thinking was its lack of exclusivism and its acceptance of the theory that civilization was evolutionary, even organic. Islam, unlike any of its predecessors, insisted that truth became available to all peoples at specific times in their development; and that Islam, far from being a new religion, was no more and no less than the last in the chain of great religions addressed to the peoples of the world. In

[14] *Kitab el-Luma.*

stating that there would be no prophet after Mohammed, Islam in its sociological sense reflected the human consciousness that the age of the rise of new theocratic systems was at an end. The events of the succeeding fifteen hundred years have shown this to be only too true. It is, for reasons of the development of society as we have it today, inconceivable that new religious teachers of the caliber of the founders of world religions should attain any prominence comparable to that achieved by Zoroaster, Buddha, Moses, Jesus, and Mohammed.

After the full development of the Islamic civilization in the middle ages, the contact between the indwelling otherworldliness streams of all peoples was to attain a far greater closeness than during the legendary days when practical mysticism was confined to relatively small, very secretive groups. Now Sufism began to spread in a number of different ways. The teachers who specialized in concentration and contemplation counteracted the greater trend toward materiality by balancing materialism with asceticism. Asceticism, warned the great Sufi Hasan of Basra (died 728), can be masochistic, in which case its use is due to a lack of fortitude. Every Sufi had to go through a period of training—long or short according to his capacity—before he could be considered sufficiently balanced to be "in the world but yet not of it." Adapting their teachings to the needs of society, Sufi poets and singers created masterpieces which were to become a part of the classical heritage of the East. In circles where entertainment and frivolity prevailed, the Sufi techniques adjusted themselves in music and dance, in teaching through romantic and wonderful tales, and especially in humor. The concentration on the theme of love, and the separation of the human being from his goal, was early introduced into military spheres, where chivalry and the theme of the quest of the beloved and of an ultimate fulfillment produced further literature and the formation of chivalric orders, subsequently significant in East and West.

The Background
II. The Elephant in the Dark

A man, never having seen water, is thrown
blindfolded into it, and feels it. When
the bandage is removed, he knows what it is.
Until then he only knew it by its effect.
(Rumi, *Fihi Ma Fihi*)

With the expansion of science and the arts in medieval
Saracendom, the Sufi genius asserted itself when Sufis became physicians and scientists, and left symbols in their
buildings and decorative art (some of them are nowadays
called arabesques) which were designed to maintain in
visible form certain eternal truths believed by the Sufis to
summarize the human soul in search of, and in progress
toward, final harmony and integration with all creation.[1]

The results of the intensely practical system of the Sufis,
though often obscure to outsiders through ignorance of the
system's real meaning, are to be found throughout the thinking, the art and the magico-occult phenomena of the East
and West alike. Approaching closer to the Sufic experience,
we must glimpse the methods of thinking and the basic ideas

[1] It baffles some twentieth-century scientists to know that, almost
one thousand years before Einstein, the dervish Hujwiri was in technical literature discussing the identity of time and space in applied
Sufi experience. (*Revelation of the Veiled*, "Recapitulation of Their
Miracles")

of these mystics. We could start with a poem, a joke, a symbol.

The pathways into Sufic thinking are, it is traditionally said, almost as varied as the number of Sufis in existence. Religion, for instance, cannot be accepted or rejected out of hand, until the student knows exactly what religion means. The essential unity of all religious faith is not agreed on throughout the world, say the Sufis, because most of the believers are not at all aware as to what *religion* itself essentially *is*. It does not have to be what it is generally assumed to be.

To the Sufi, the religionist and scoffer are like a believer in the flatness of the earth arguing with one who holds that it is cylindrical in shape—neither has any real experience of it.

This brings out a fundamental difference between the method of the Sufis and that of other metaphysical systems. It is too often taken for granted that a person must either be a believer or an unbeliever, or perhaps an agnostic. If a believer, he will expect to be offered a faith or a system which seems to him to fulfill what he thinks are his needs. Few people tell him that he may not understand what his needs are.

The Sufi's world has extra dimensions; to him things are meaningful in a sense which they are not to people who follow only the training which is imposed upon them by ordinary society.

Such people "squint." "A hungry man, asked to total two and two, will answer, 'Four (or even eight) *loaves of bread*.'"

The totality of life cannot be understood, so runs Sufi teaching, if it is studied only through the methods which we use in everyday living. This is partly because, although the question, "What is it all about?" can of course be posed in a nominally reasonable sequence of words, the answer is not to be expressed in a similar way. It comes through experience, and enlightenment. An instrument which can assess a small thing cannot necessarily assess a large thing. "Practice your knowledge, for knowledge without practice is a body without life."—Abu Hanifa.[2] A scientist may tell you that space and time are the same thing, or that matter is not solid at all. He may be able to prove it by his own methods. This, however, will make little difference to your understanding, and none at all to your experience, of what all this involves. All matter is infinitely divisible, shall we say. But for most practical purposes there is a limit to the number of divisions which you can make of a piece of chocolate if it is still to function as you expect a piece of chocolate to function. So on the one hand you may be looking at a piece of chocolate, on the other an object which you want to divide into as many pieces as possible. The human mind tends to generalize from partial evidence. The Sufis believe that they can experience something more complete.

A traditional Sufi story illuminates this question in one of its aspects, and shows the difficulties which beset even scholars when they approach the Sufis with a view to understanding them by applying limited methods of study:

An elephant belonging to a traveling exhibition had been stabled near a town where no elephant had been seen before. Four curious citizens, hearing of the hidden wonder, went to see if they could get a preview of it. When they arrived at the stable they found that there was no light. The investigation therefore had to be carried out in the dark.

One, touching its trunk, thought that the creature must resemble a hosepipe; the second felt an ear and concluded that it was a fan. The third, feeling a leg, could liken it only to a living pillar; and when the fourth put his hand on its back he was convinced that it was some kind of throne. None could form the complete picture; and of the part

2 Abu Hanifa is the founder of one of the four great Islamic schools of law, the Fourth School. He was the Sufi teacher of Daud of Tai (died 781). Daud passed on his teachings to his disciple Maaruf Karkhi ("Solomon the King") the founder of the Sufi fraternity called "The Builders."

which each felt, he could only refer to it in terms of things which he already knew. The result of the expedition was confusion. Each was sure that he was right; none of the other townspeople could understand what had happened, what the investigators had actually experienced.

The average person, wanting to inform himself as to what the Sufis' thinking is, will normally address himself to reference books. He may look up the word "Sufi" in an encyclopaedia, or have recourse to books by scholars of various kinds, experts in religion and mysticism.

If he does so, he will find a most admirable example of the "elephant in the dark" mentality.

According to one Persian scholar, Sufism is a Christian aberration. A professor at Oxford thinks that it is influenced by the Hindu Vedanta. An Arab-American professor speaks of it as a reaction against intellectualism in Islam. A professor of Semitic literature claims traces of Central Asian Shamanism. A German will have us find in it Christianity plus Buddhism. Two very great English Orientalists put their money on a strong Neoplatonic influence; yet, one of them will concede that it was perhaps independently generated. An Arab, publishing his opinions through an American university, assures his readers that Neoplatonism (which he invokes as a Sufic ingredient) is itself Greek plus Persian. One of the greatest Spanish Arabists, while claiming an initiation of Christian monasticism, plumps for Manichaeism as a Sufi source. Another academician of no less repute finds Gnosticism among the Sufis; while the English professor who is the translator of a Sufistic book prefers to think of it as "a little Persian sect." But another translator finds the mystical tradition of the Sufis "in the Koran itself." "Although the numerous definitions of Sufism which occur in Arabic and Persian books on the subject are historically interesting, their chief importance lies in showing that Sufism is undefinable."[3]

[3] Prof. R. A. Nicholson, *The Mystics of Islam*, London, 1914, p. 25.

A Pakistani view of Rumi (1207–1273) considers him the heir of virtually all the great currents of ancient thought as represented in the Near East. To those who have been in real contact with Sufis and who have attended their meetings, no mental adjustment or effort of will is needed to consider Sufism as containing within itself the myriad threads which appear in such non-Sufi systems as Gnosticism, Neoplatonism, Aristotelianism, and so on. "Numberless waves, lapping and momentarily reflecting the sun—all from the same sea," says the master Halki. The mind which has on the other hand been coached to believe in the distinctiveness or monopoly of ideas of certain schools will not easily be able to bring this synthesizing understanding into the contemplation of Sufism.

Dr. Khalifa Abdu-Hakim shows that he is able to refer to all the philosophical schools whose ideas are shared with Rumi, without being compelled to consider one as derived from the other. He says: "His *Mathnawi* is a crystal of many facets. In it we see reflected the broken lights of Semitic monotheism, Greek intellectualism, Plato's theory of ideas and Aristotle's theory of causation and development, the One of Plotinus and the ecstasy that unites with the One, the controversial questions of the *mutakallimun* (Schoolmen), the *Erkenntnistheoretisch* problems of Ibn Sina and al-Farabi, Ghazali's theory of Prophetic Consciousness and Ibn El-Arabi's monism."

Which does not mean to imply, if my position is not yet clear, that Rumi has concocted a system of mysticism out of the above ingredients. "Pears are not found only in Samarkand."

The world literature on Sufism is large—a great number of Sufi texts have been translated by Western scholars. Few, if any, have had the advantage of experiencing Sufism, or knowing its oral lore or even the order in which its formal material is studied. This is not to say that their labors have not been very much worthwhile. They have been most useful to the Orientalist, but may tend to be incoherent. Like the legendary scribe who had to accompany his letter and read it himself because of its illegibility, many of these works need a Sufi's commentary.

The effect of the translations and discursive books on Sufism upon the uninitiated student must be remarkable, and certainly will not be easily forgotten. The method of approaching the question of translations has its quaintnesses. Setting aside the matter of differences between translators in matters of accuracy and meaning (which have caused much feline though really irrelevant activity among them), we find that the literary material offered the captive reader in translated form may undergo strange adventures.

Sometimes attempts are made to reproduce in English the cadence or the original rhymes of Eastern poetry, because the translator feels that this device helps to convey the sense of the original. But other translators hold the opposite view, and eschew any attempt to reproduce meter, because they claim that it is impossible of attainment or otherwise undesirable. Some texts, again, are translated with the aid of non-Sufi (generally Moslem, even formal Christian theological) commentaries. Then there are the partial translations, selectively presented, having suffered excisions which the translator somehow considers himself entitled to make. The less he knows about the practices of the Sufi, the braver these mutilations seem to be. Yet Sufi writings are never solely literary, philosophical or technical material.

There is a translation of a Persian book into English, not from Persian, but from a French translation of an Urdu rendering of a classical Persian abridgment of an Arabic original. There are modern versions of Persian classics, sometimes edited to remove references offensive to current Iranian religious beliefs. Add to these the works of Christian (missionary), Hindu and Western neo-Hindu—and Western neo-Sufi—nonacademic writers and popularizers. The presentation of Sufism to the average literate man in a

Western language reveals a condition of literature which is perhaps unmatched in any other field.

This kaleidoscopic process has its own special incidental delights. The warping tendency, to find a term for which seems impossible, unless it be "polychotomy" (on the pattern of dichotomy) had in fact reached an amusing point nearly a thousand years ago. This was when the Jewish thinker Avicebron of Málaga (c. 1020–c. 1050 or 70) wrote the *Fount of Life,* a book based upon Sufi illuministic philosophy. Because he wrote in Arabic, many authoritative Christians of the northern European school, then imbibing "Arab" learning, thought that he was an Arab. Some at least considered that he was a Christian, "sound in doctrine," and they said so. The Franciscans accepted his teachings, which they eagerly transmitted into the Christian stream of thought, having culled them from a Latin translation made about a century after Avicebron's death.

A lady of academic distinction who has written authoritatively on Middle Eastern mysticism has felt more than one part of the elephant; for in one and the same book she says Sufism "might have been directly effected (sic) by Buddhistic ideas;" and that the earliest Sufis "can have had little contacts with Hellenistic literature of any kind"—yet their ideas were derived from Hellenistic sources. Then she ends her study of the Sufic way with the decision that "Its real origin and source are to be found in the agelong desire of the human soul for God."

Sufi activity has had a considerable influence upon the Christian West, so much so that a better than average case could be made out for the Sufi assertion that objective truth contains within it a dynamic which can hardly be gainsaid. This vitalistic force, however, depends for its correct expression upon correct alignment of the human receptor. If this preparation is absent, the Sufic current is liable to take a peculiar turn. Especially susceptible to this warping is the elective or fragmentary handling of the Sufi stream. An excellent illustration might be made from the fate of Ghazali's work in Europe.

Ghazali of Central Asia (1058–1111) wrote a book called *Destruction of the Philosophers,* which was soon translated in part and used by Catholic apologists against Moslem and Christian schools alike. The portion which came into the hands of the West, however, was only that part which was devoted to a preparatory exposition of philosophy. Ghazali's Sufi works have to be read as a whole, and his opinions about the value of Sufic exercises must also be followed if he is to be understood aright. This book, however, was answered by another Arab, Ibn Rushd of Córdoba (1126–1198). Under the name Averroës, he, too, was translated. He did not succeed in refuting Ghazali at all by his scholastic methods, but thought that he had done so. Yet Averroism dominated Western and Christian scholastic thought for no less than four hundred years—from the twelfth to the end of the sixteenth century. Taken together, Ghazali's fragments and Averroës' Aristotelianism constituted a double Sufic current (action and reaction) which nurtured a Christendom wholly ignorant (as far as scholastics were concerned) of the initiating cause of both Ghazalism and Averroism.

"It is necessary to note," says Rumi, "that opposite things work together, even though nominally opposed." (*Fihi Ma Fihi*)

The fundamental Sufi awareness that Sufism is both a teaching and a part of an organic evolution is seldom shared by those who make it their concern to attempt a study of the system. There is consequently almost no possibility that the outsider will be able to form accurate conclusions. Relying upon his discursive faculty alone, he is incapacitated before he begins. It is the externalist of today, as much as of yesterday, whom Rumi addresses in his *Mathnawi:*

> *Danad o ki nekbakht wa muharam ast:*
> *Ziraki az Iblis wa ishq Adam ast.*

Which is to the effect that:

He who is fortunately enlightened [the Sufi]
Knows that sophistry is from the devil and love from Adam.

If the Sufis confuse the scholar by their seeming inconsistencies and sometimes cause him to hedge his conclusions with too many qualifications to be of great value, they can rouse the theologian to holy wrath. Love, an active principle of Sufic development and experience, the mechanism and the goal alike, cannot be admitted as genuine. The Reverend Professor W. R. Inge, in *Christian Mysticism*, hastens to hurl himself at what he takes to be the target: "The Sufis, or Mohammedan mystics, use erotic language very freely, and appear, like true Asiatics, to have attempted to give a sacramental or symbolic character to the indulgence of their passions."

This classic sample conjures up visions of certain Western scholars who have embraced Sufism, revealing them to be imitation Asiatics addicted to erotic language (in secret, for they do not publish it) which itself covers up the indulgence of their passions. They, in turn, might be able to comfort themselves with the opinion of a Cambridge professor who sees Sufism, more respectably, as "the development of the primordial religion of the Aryan race." And if Sufi symbolism is not in fact such, but rather represents experiences actually lived, then we might well find that the Sufis are even more versatile than their staunchest supporters know. The Sufi literalist would be able to swallow a hundred oceans, worship idols while not worshiping them, travel to China in a state of drunkenness—being in the world and yet not of it the while—not to mention his hundred moons and suns.

Advocates of a literal interpretation of mystical expressions are, of course, already adequately answered by such specialists as Evelyn Underhill:

"Symbol—the clothing which the spiritual borrows from the material plane—is a form of artistic expression. That is to say, it is not literal but suggestive; though the artist who used it may sometimes lose sight of this distinction. Hence the persons who imagine that the 'spiritual marriage' of St. Catherine or St. Teresa veils a perverted sexuality, that the vision of the Sacred Heart involved an incredible anatomical experience or that the divine inebriation of the Sufis is the apotheosis of drunkenness, do but advertise their ignorance of the mechanism of the arts: like the lady who thought that Blake *must* be mad because he said that he had touched the sky with his finger."[4]

It must be admitted that it is easier for the scholar to approach and describe one aspect of the Elephant in the Dark than it is for him to form a coherent outside view of Sufism. Many scholars suffer from a psychological incapacity to handle this theme. "Apart from incapacity itself," says Ghazali, "other shortcomings prevent the reaching of inner truth. One such is knowledge acquired by external means." (*Alchemy of Happiness*)

In addition to the unscalable wall of Sufi experience, there is the problem of the Sufi personality. Any ordinary survey of Sufic writings and careers would be enough to bewilder the least doctrinaire investigator. Among the Sufis have been former Zoroastrian, Christian, Hindu, Buddhist and other priests; Persians, Greeks and Arabs, Egyptians, Spaniards and Englishmen. There are in the ranks of the Sufi masters theologians, a reformed captain of *banditti*, slaves, soldiers, merchants, viziers, kings and artists. Only two are well known to many contemporary Western readers. They are the poet and mathematician Omar Khayyam of Persia, and the prince Abu ben-Adam of Afghanistan— the subject of a poem by Leigh Hunt: "Abu ben-Adam, may his tribe increase. . . ."

Among those directly influenced by Sufism we can name at random Raymond Lully, Goethe, President de Gaulle, and Dag Hammerskjold of the United Nations.

[4] *Mysticism*, London, 1911; New York, 1960.

Writing often under threat of inquisitorial persecution, Sufis have prepared books reconciling their practices with orthodoxy and defending the use of fanciful imagery. In order to obscure the meanings of ritualistic factors, or for the necessary purpose of appearing mere compilers of Sufi compendiums, they have handed down manuscripts from which the Sufic essence is to be distilled only by those who have the necessary equipment. Adapting their workings to different places, epochs and temperaments, they have in turn stressed the roles of asceticism, piety, music and movement, solitude and gregariousness. Only the respectably religious of the Sufi manuals are available outside Sufi circles.

That a person may be completely ignorant of the coherence behind Sufi teaching and yet appreciate the work of its great poets has been demonstrated again and again by translators. Gertrude Bell, an indefatigable student and translator into English of the great Hafiz, was hailed by the Orientalist Sir Denison Ross for her scholarship and judgment. Yet she is the first to admit that "Exactly on what grounds he [Hafiz] is appreciated in the East it is difficult to determine, and what his compatriots make of his teaching it is perhaps impossible to understand."[5]

This makes all the more interesting her shot in the dark, when she tries to form some opinion as to what Hafiz really is getting at: "From our point of view, then, the sun of his philosophy seems to be that there is little of which we can be certain, that little must always be the object of all men's desire; each of us will set out upon the search for it along a different road, and none will find his road easy to follow, each may, if he be wise, discover compensations for his toil by the wayside."[6] She does not see the Sufi activity as a process—as the Sufis see it—but could not fail to glimpse the strange and wholly Sufic character of Hafiz in speaking of, and seeing, a panorama of human thought in what

[5] See annotation "Hafiz."
[6] G. L. Bell, *Poems from the Divan of Hafiz*, London, new ed. 1928, p. 81.

is to us the present, and was of course to him the distant future:

It is as if his mental eye, endowed with wonderful acuteness of vision, had penetrated into those provinces of thought which we of a later age were destined to inhabit.[7]

Hafiz' prescience was too evident to be missed; but it was also startling. She can come to no conclusion about it.

To return to our elephant, the scholars are happily much less doctrinaire than the ecclesiastics. For the Sufis, both resemble the visitors to the elephant's house. Is it possible that they have, indeed, all seen a part of the parts? The Sufis say, "This is not a religion; it *is* religion;" and, "Sufism is the essence of all religions." Is there, then, among the Sufis and elsewhere, a tradition that there is a secret doctrine passed down by initiation and preserved by a chain of succession; which might account for the outside observer according to his prejudice seeing almost every form of religion among the writings of the Sufis?

In order to determine this, we shall have to refer to the opinions of the Sufis on this point, which has generally been disregarded by non-Sufi students; and also follow the traditions of other schools, as well as the transmission in the middle ages and other times of a belief in an inner teaching beyond formalized religion. The search is by no means an uninteresting one.

"Formerly," according to the Sheikh Abu el-Hasan Fushanji, "being a Sufi was a reality without a name. Today it is a name without a reality." This statement, taken at face value, is generally considered to mean that people calling themselves Sufis abounded, while the real pursuit of the Sufis was not understood. And, although this, too, might be an interpretation of the saying, it is here intended to clarify a completely different point.

[7] *Ibid.*

The urge to trace a historical phenomenon to definite beginnings, so well marked in the present phase of learning, is undoubtedly bound up with the need of the ordinary mind to have a beginning and, if possible, an end for everything. Almost everything known to man through his ordinary senses has for him a beginning and an end. To know what something is gives a sensation of stability, a feeling of security. The label has been stuck on the book, now it can be placed on the shelf—the A to Z of something or other. There are various more or less accepted methods of establishing beginnings and endings, or creating substitutes for them. They may be created by concocted myths and legends, which often deal with how things started and how they will finish. Another way is that of the Chinese emperor who decreed that history would start with him, and that all earlier books should be destroyed. A third technique is to assume that a certain event, located in time and perhaps in space, represents a beginning. This was generally the religious way, and it is very strongly marked in familiar Christianity, whose official dogma depends upon it, St. Augustine notwithstanding.

The belief that a certain unique religious event brought about a complete change in human destiny released within Christendom a great force of energy, but at least two factors seriously limited its effect. The first was time, which in the event showed that there was a limit to the natural and even artificial expansion of Church Christianity, and a limit to its dynamic within its own domain. The other was a scholastic problem. Because the teaching of Jesus was held to be unique (although perhaps "foreshadowed and foretold in prophecy"), it was difficult to attain a spiritual perspective which was not conditioned by this belief. Religion, mysticism, spirituality could not now easily be looked upon as a natural development or a common possession of mankind. According to the Sufis, the main counterbalance to the power of formalized Christianity was the continued experience of the real tradition of which it is a distortion.

Before even the tenth century, when Islam possessed the most powerful culture and expanding civilization of the known world, the theory of a secret doctrine, a teaching which had been cherished from the earliest times, had made its way from this center of gravity to the West. The first, and most powerful, classical Sufi school in Europe was founded in Spain well over a thousand years ago.[8] The tradition was not, as might be thought, invented in the West to account for the ascendancy of the Arabized countries. It fitted in well enough with, and was even incidentally encouraged by, Islam, which view of religion we have noted as also that of a continuous process represented in every community. It existed in the Far East, and it would awaken a response in the hearts of those who still retained memories of earlier spiritual teachings. It was, in part, the theory of theosophy which accounted for different religious manifestations among communities which, according to doctrinaire religion of another brand, should not exist at all.

This sense of the unity of inner, experiential or symbolic religion was undoubtedly at work in the days when the peoples of the ancient world equated each others' gods one with the other—Mercury with Hermes, Hermes with Thoth are examples. And it is this theosophical theory which the Sufis considered to be their own tradition, though not limited to the religious domain. Hence, as the Sufi has it:

I am in the pagan; I worship at the altar of the Jew; I am the idol of the Yemenite, the actual temple of the fire worshiper; the priest of the Magian; the inner reality of the cross-legged Brahmin meditating; the brush and the color of the artist; the suppressed, powerful personality of the scoffer. One does not supersede the other—when a flame is thrown into another flame they join at the point of "flameness." You throw

[8] Sufis accompanied the Arab armies which conquered Spain in 711 A.D.

a torch at a candle, and then you say, "See! I have an-
nihilated the candle's flame!" (Ishan Kaiser in *Speech
of the Sages*)

The Sufis use a new point of view in order to overcome
the conditioning which materialistic, one-sided society has
imposed. All philosophy has been cheapened because the
teaching of "wisdom" has become capsulated. People endlessly repeat truisms to one another, without really *experiencing* what they mean. If a Sufi says, "What is needed
is a new approach," it is by no means unlikely that everyone
who hears him will at once agree (because the statement
sounds significant) and will immediately forget all about it.
The meaning of the words has not sunk in. "Take the
wheat, not the measure in which it is contained." (Rumi,
Mathnawi, Bk. II)

So important is it to free the thinking from the adhesions
of rigid thinking that the great Rumi has started both of
his major works with exercises in this process. In this sense
he keeps pace with the procedure which is normally followed in Sufi teaching schools; and, though the externalist
translators probably do not know it, two of his books are in
fact commentaries upon the stages and states of the Sufic
development as manifested in the flesh in a Sufi school.

In *Fihi Ma Fihi*, at the very beginning, Rumi takes a
saying of Mohammed which had passed into common
speech and become a proverb, sagely passed from lip to lip.
Mohammed is reported as having said, "The worst of sages
is a visitor of princes; the best of princes is a visitor of sages."

Rumi points out that the inner meaning of this teaching
is that the meaning of "visiting" depends upon the quality
of the visitor and the visited. If a great sage visits a prince,
it is the prince who benefits; and hence he is to be considered as having himself "visited" the sage. This is very far
from being a mere juggling with words, as some less re-
flective people have supposed.

With what amounts to shock tactics, the *Mathnawi* opens

its teaching, after the celebrated "Song of the Reed," with
what looks like a fairy tale about a prince out hunting and
a beautiful girl. As the audience settles down to enjoy the
conventional story, Rumi starts to manipulate it to create
thought in the mind and to combat the tendency to "sleep,"
which is Sufistically taken to be the usual reaction to folk-
tales.

A prince, out hunting, saw on the road a beautiful hand-
maiden. He fell in love with her, and bought her. Soon
afterward she became ill. In desperation, the potentate offered his doctors anything they might desire of worldly
goods to cure her. They were unable to do so, and the girl's
condition became worse. The prince, utterly distraught with
love and fear, ran to a mosque and implored divine aid.

He saw a vision in which an ancient assured him that a
physician would soon appear. The following day, as predicted, this personage arrived. The doctor looked at the girl
and realized that every remedy tried by the leeches had
been useless and worse. He understood that her illness was
concerned with her inward condition. Adopting a psychological method, he asked her questions and made her talk,
until he discovered that she was in love with a certain goldsmith of Samarkand.

He told the prince that a cure would be effected by bringing the goldsmith to the girl's bedside, and he agreed. The
goldsmith, for his own part, saw in the prince's summons
only a recognition of his own importance in goldsmithing.
He did not realize what his fate was to be.

When he arrived, they were married, and the girl recovered completely. Thus far the anodyne of the story may
well have taken effect upon the audience, who surrender
themselves to the delights of all being well that ends well.

But the physician now prepared medicine for the goldsmith; a medicine which made his inner faults so evident
that the maiden saw him as he was and started to hate him.
He died, and the girl was able to love the prince, who was
always intended for her.

Apart from the complicated imagery of the tale in the original, the teaching contains an impact at many levels. It is not just a matter of telling a tale with one crude moral; it is a commentary upon some of the processes of life.

Hadrat-i-Paghman says of this story: "Ponder it, for unless you feel it through, you will be like the little child who wants everything right and cries when things do not seem to be right. You will make a prison for yourself, a prison of emotion. When you are in this prison, you will hurt yourself on the sharpness of the bars which you have yourself arranged."

Formerly, Sufi ideas and teachings were actually lived— and there could be a Sufi without a name for his cult. Then came the modern period, in which the name exists, but the living of it is difficult, and has had to be adapted to the "veiling"—conditioning—which starts in the cradle and ends almost in the grave.

Exactly how old is the word "Sufism?" There were Sufis at all times and in all countries, says the tradition. Sufis existed as such and under this name before Islam. But, if there was a name for the practitioner, there was no name for the practice. The English word "Sufism" is anglicized from the Latin, *Sufismus*; it was a Teutonic scholar who, as recently as 1821, coined the Latinization which is now almost naturalized into English. Before him there was the word *tasawwuf*—the state, practice or condition of being a Sufi. This may not seem an important point, but to the Sufis it is. It is one reason why there is no static term in use among Sufis for their cult. They call it a science, an art, a knowledge, a Way, a tribe—even by a tenth-century portmanteau term, perhaps translatable as psychoanthropology (*nafsaniyyatalinsaniyyat*)—but they do not call it Sufism.

Tarika-sufiyya stands for the Sufi Way; and makes a very good English parallel because *tarika* stands for Path, as well as a way of doing something, and also conveys the notion of following a path, a line or streak—the Path of the Sufi. Sufism is referred to by different names in accordance with the sense in which it is being discussed. Thus, *ilm-al-maarifat* (the science of Knowing) may be found; or *el-irfan* (the gnosis); and the organized Orders or groups tend to be called the *tarika*. Similarly, the Sufi is known as the Seeker, the Drunken man, the enlightened one, the good, the Friend, the Near One, the dervish, a Fakir (humble, poor in spirit), or *Kalandar*, knower (gnostic), wise, lover, esoterist. Because there would be no Sufism without the Sufis, the word always applies to people, and cannot be considered as an abstract form, as, say, "philology" or "communism" could mean respectively the study of words or a theory of communalist action. Sufism, then, involves the body of the Sufis as well as the actual practice of their cult. It cannot really mean any theoretical presentation of the Way of the Sufis. There is no theoretical or intellectual Sufism; any more than there can be a Sufi movement, which latter is a redundancy, because all Sufic being is movement and a movement embracing all phenomena of a similar kind. There are, for instance, "Christian Sufis," a phrase which could be used, and has been used, by Sufis in general. The Sufi is even called *masihi-i-batini* (esoteric Christian) in some connections.

If a Sufi were to present to a conventionally cataloging mind certain facts about the Sufis, a mental or electrical computer might well wreck itself in the attempt to work them into some kind of system. Fortunately, however, there are still numbers of people who can accept information on various levels, and who will be able to form a pattern out of them. Here is a series of facts about the Sufis:

The Sufis appear in historical times mainly within the pale of Islam. They have produced great theologians, poets, scientists. They accepted atomic theory and formulated a science of evolution over six hundred years before Darwin. They have been hailed as saints, executed and persecuted as heretics. They teach that there is only one underlying truth within everything that is called religion.

Some have said, "I believe in nothing;" others, "I believe

in everything." Some say, "Let there be no levity among
Sufis;" others, "There is no Sufi without humor." Scholasticism and mysticism are opposed to one another. But the
Sufis gave rise to, among others, a school of each. Were these
Moslem schools? No, they were Christian, associated with
the Augustinians and St. John of the Cross, as Professor
Palacios and others have established. From being an Oriental mystic, the Sufi now appears as the antecessor of
Catholic mystics and philosophers. Let us add a few more
facts. The coffee which we drink was traditionally first used
by Sufis, to heighten awareness. We wear their clothes
(shirt, belt, trousers); we listen to their music (Andalusian,
measured music, love songs); dance their dances (waltz,
Morris dancing); read their stories (Dante, Robinson
Crusoe, Chaucer, William Tell); employ their esoteric
phrases ("moment of truth," "human spirit," "ideal man");
and play their games (cards).[9] We even belong to derivations of their societies, such as Freemasonry, and certain
chivalric orders. Such Sufic elements are examined at a later
stage in this book.

The monk in his cell, the Fakir on the mountaintop, the
merchant in his shop, the king on his throne—these can be
Sufis, but this is not Sufism. The Sufi tradition has it that
Sufism is a leaven ("Sufism is yeast") within all human
society. If it has never been removed from the field of academic study this is because it was never made available to
scholasticism as a subject of investigation. Its very diversity
prevents it from being systematized in the semipermanent
manner which would make it static enough to investigate.
"Sufism," according to the Sufi, "is an adventure in living,
necessary adventure."

If Sufism is an adventure, a goal of human perfection attained by reviewing and awakening within humanity a
higher organ of fulfillment, completion, destiny, why is it so
difficult to assess, to locate in time, to pin down? It is precisely because Sufism is carried out in every community

[9] See annotation "Tarot."

and at every time that it has such diversity—and this is one
of its secrets. The Sufi does not need the mosque, the Arabic
language, litanies, books of philosophy, even social stability.
The relationship with humanity is evolutionary and adaptive. The Sufi does not depend upon his repute of being
able to perform magic or miracles—this is less than incidental, though he may have that reputation. The magico-
religious practitioner of other systems starts from the other
end of the scale; his reputation is built upon his miracles,
and probably sustained by them. The Sufi has a reputation,
but this is secondary to his work, his being as a part of the
Sufi organism.

The moral ascendancy, or the magnetic personality,
which the Sufi attains is not his goal but the by-product of
his inner attainment, the reflection of his development.

A Sufi says: "The moth, if it could think, might well believe that the candle flame is desirable because it seems to
represent perfection. The flame is the product of the wax,
the wick and the spark which kindles. Is the human moth
seeking the flame or the spark itself? Observe the moth. His
destiny, to be destroyed by the flame, is visible to you and
hidden to him." (*Tongue of the Dumb*, quoting Paisecm)

He is, of course, judged by the world at large only in the
light of what he says and does. Supposing that he has become a millionaire. The outside observer, realizing that this
man has become a millionaire since he embarked upon a
way of life called Sufism, may look upon the phenomenon
as a millionaire-producing process. To the Sufi in question,
however, it is the inner realization and evolution which has
given him his inner attainment. The money may be an outward reflection of it, but this is of far less account than the
Sufic experiences. This does not mean, as many people
would assume, that he has become a millionaire obsessed
by mysticism, and that money has no meaning for him. Such
a development would not be possible for a Sufi, because the
material and the metaphysical are linked in a form best
regarded as a continuum. He would be the kind of mil-

lionaire who is not only rich, but also completely psychologically integrated. It is difficult for many people to absorb this fundamental fact sufficiently well for it to be of any use to them.

In the popular practice, current from Calcutta to California, the ordinary person will rise to the philosophical heights of repeating sagely to himself or anyone who will listen that "money is not everything," or that "money does not bring happiness." The very fact that such an idea can be voiced shows that it is rooted in a previous assumption that money can be considered to be in some way of transcendental importance. Practice shows that it is not. But the homespun philosopher cannot grasp why this might be. The penniless man's most pressing problems seem soluble by money. The priest tells him that money is not a good thing. When he gets money he may not as a result feel fulfilled. And these three factors he is incapable of integrating.

Modern psychology has done some good, where, for instance, it has pointed out that the urge to make money may be a symptom of insecurity. But it has not yet integrated itself; historically it is still struggling sometimes against the tide. The Sufi attitude starts to operate on a different basis. All life is struggle, says the Sufi, but the struggle must be a coherent one. The average man is struggling against too many things all at once. If a confused and incomplete person makes money, or becomes a professional success, he still remains a confused and incomplete person.

Psychology learns as it goes along, Sufism has already learned; it transforms the mind from its natural and acquired incoherence into an instrument whereby human dignity and destiny may be carried a stage further.

Freudian and Jungian psychology have not the freshness to the Sufi mind which they have conveyed to the West. Freud's sexual arguments are noted by the Sufi Sheikh Ghazali in his *Alchemy of Happiness* (written over nine hundred years ago) as being standard among Moslem theologians. The Jungian archetypal theory did not originate with Professor Jung, but was stated by the Sufi master, Ibn El-Arabi—as Professor Rom Landau notes in *The Philosophy of Ibn Arabi*. (New York, Macmillan, 1959, p. 40 et seq.)

Sufis of all orders are steeped in Ghazali's *Alchemy of Happiness* and Ibn El-Arabi's works, and hence they are familiar with these supposedly modern modes of thinking and their limitations.

Sufism is not susceptible to study through psychology for several reasons. The most interesting of these to the Westerner will probably be that Sufism is itself a far more advanced psychological system than any which has yet developed in the West. Neither is this psychology Eastern in essence, but human. It is unnecessary to affirm this fact without support. We may mention Jung's admission that Western psychoanalysis is only that of a beginner compared to that of the East:

"Psychoanalysis itself and the lines of thought to which it gives rise—surely a distinctly Western development—are only a beginner's attempt compared to what is an immemorial art in the East."[10]

And yet Jung has referred only to certain parts of Eastern thought. The whole cannot be studied by means of the parts, and the beginner cannot judge the work of the adept, in any field, Sufism included.

The so-called scientific approach to the human phenomenon and man's relationship with the rest of being is every bit as limited as ordinary philosophy. Like discursive reason, science operates only within the convenient circle of what fits in with its preconceptions, as Professor Graves reminds us:

". . . scientists are careful to express their suppositions in mathematical formulas which, applied artistically to such problems as the structure of the atom or the inner temperature of stars, give 'beautiful' results. They are applied only

[10] C. G. Jung, *Modern Man in Search of a Soul*, London, 1959, pp. 250–51; and see annotation "Consciousness."

to safe, prepared cases—though remaining unworkable in unstereotyped ones: there must be a sympathetic equivalence between formula and case. . . . A beautiful result is as good as a demonstrable proof and can be superseded only by a still more beautiful result."[11]

Again the doctrine that the whole cannot be studied by means of the parts, plus the fact that a thing cannot study all of itself simultaneously. The Sufi master Pir-i-Do-Sara says:

"Can you imagine a mind observing the whole of itself— if it were all engaged in observation, what would it be observing? If it were all engaged in being mind, what would do the observing? Observation of self is necessary while there is a self as distinct from the nonself part. . . ."[12]

The Sufis affirm that the organism known generally as Sufism has been the one stream of direct, evolutionary experience which has been the determining factor in all the great schools of mysticism. In order to verify this as far as possible, there is some interest in following the movement of Sufic ideas. If they prove to have a penetrative power, an ability to influence thought and action in divers communities, the inner dynamism of the system can very well be inferred. Is there, in other words, reason to suppose that the Sufic stream has the power to influence human thinking in, say, western Europe? During the fairly well documented classical period of Sufism, has it penetrated through the screen of the dark ages, providing power and development for communities which have a different background? Is Sufism organic in this respect?

This suggestion implies that, from remote times, Sufi masters have transmitted their lore into almost every society. Sufi tradition claims that this has been the fact. In more modern times this claim can only be tested by the visible appearance of Sufi practices in communities far removed

[11] Robert Graves, *The Crowning Privilege*, London, 1959, pp. 306–7.
[12] *Mountain of Illumination*, XVI, verses 9951–57, MS.

from the Sufi centers of Asia. The essence of Sufi activity would not be so visible. All that one could hope to find would be traces here and there, like the radioactive tracers sometimes injected into the human bloodstream, of characteristic Sufi lore and practice which still maintained its local color.

Take an example. If Alfonso the Sage wrote in Arabic, this might be evidence of Arabian influence. If, however, the symbol of a Sufi initiatory society were found among the Irish of the ninth century (it was), this might, with other evidence, point to a drift of Sufic lore to the West.

We have looked at certain outstanding characteristics of Sufism, but have not noted in starker relief the need for the superficially plausible facts of Sufi expression. Here, then, as near as they may be transmitted by ordinary words, are the rest of Sufi convictions:

Sufis believe that, expressed in one way, humanity is evolving to a certain destiny. We are all taking part in that evolution. Organs come into being as a result of the need for specific organs (Rumi). The human being's organism is producing a new complex of organs in response to such a need. In this age of the transcending of time and space, the complex of organs is concerned with the transcending of time and space. What ordinary people regard as sporadic and occasional bursts of telepathic or prophetic power are seen by the Sufi as nothing less than the first stirrings of these same organs. The difference between all evolution up to date and the present need for evolution is that for the past ten thousand years or so we have been given the possibility of a conscious evolution. So essential is this more rarefied evolution that our future depends upon it. It can be called "learning how to swim," in the words of our fable.

How are these organs developed? By the Sufi method. How do we know that we are developing them? Only through experience. In the Sufi system there are a number of "stages." The attainment of these stages is marked by an unmistakable if ineffable experience. This experience, when it comes, activates the organ in question, gives us a relief from our climb upward, and grants us sufficient strength to continue the climb. The attainment of stages is permanent. Until one of these stages has been reached, the photographic plate, as it were, may have been exposed and developed, but has not been fixed; and actual experiences are the fixative substance.

This is the meaning of mystical experience, which, however, when indulged in without proper harmony with evolution seems merely to be something sublime—a sensation of omnipotence or of grace, but no assurance of where the happy or unhappy mortal is going next.

Sufis believe that Sufic activity produces and concentrates what might be termed a centrifugal or magnetic force. This force calls to similar force elsewhere. With the coming together of such forces, work continues. This is an explanation of the mysterious "messages" which Sufi teachers get, telling them to repair to such and such a place, in order to respond to the call of the force there which has become derelict (in the sense of abandoned) or needs their reinforcing.

This is as far as anything in Sufism can be explained in formal terms. As for the rest, the only valid thing is the Sufic watchword: "He who tastes not, knows not." (Rumi)

The Subtleties of Mulla Nasrudin

When you arrive at the sea, you
do not talk of the tributary.
(Hakim Sanai, *The Walled Garden of Truth*)

Mulla (Master) Nasrudin is the classical figure devised by
the dervishes partly for the purpose of halting for a moment situations in which certain states of mind are made
clear. The Nasrudin stories, known throughout the Middle
East, constitute (in the manuscript *The Subtleties of the
Incomparable Nasrudin*) one of the strangest achievements
in the history of metaphysics. Superficially, most of the Nasrudin stories may be used as jokes. They are told and retold
endlessly in the teahouses and the caravanserais, in the
homes and on the radio waves, of Asia. But it is inherent
in the Nasrudin story that it may be understood at any one
of many depths. There is the joke, the moral—and the little
extra which brings the consciousness of the potential mystic
a little further on the way to realization.

Since Sufism is something which is lived as well as something which is perceived, a Nasrudin tale cannot in itself
produce complete enlightenment. On the other hand, it
bridges the gap between mundane life and a transmutation

of consciousness in a manner which no other literary form yet produced has been able to attain.

The Subtleties has never been presented in full to a Western audience, probably because the stories cannot properly be translated by a non-Sufi, or even be studied out of context, and retain the essential impact. Even in the East the collection is used for study purposes only by initiate Sufis. Individual "jokes" from the collection have found their way into almost every literature in the world, and a certain amount of scholastic attention has been given them on this account—as an example of culture drift, or to support arguments in favor of the basic identity of humor everywhere. But if because of their perennial humorous appeal the stories have proved their survival power, this is entirely secondary to the intention of the corpus, which is to provide a basis for making available the Sufi attitude toward life, and for making possible the attainment of Sufic realization and mystical experience.

The Legend of Nasrudin, appended to the *Subtleties* and dating from at least the thirteenth century, touches on some of the reasons for introducing Nasrudin. Humor cannot be prevented from spreading; it has a way of slipping through the patterns of thought which are imposed upon mankind by habit and design. As a complete system of thought, Nasrudin exists at so many depths that he cannot be killed. Some measure of the truth of this might be seen in the fact that such diverse and alien organizations as the British Society for the Promotion of Christian Knowledge and the Soviet Government have both pressed Nasrudin into service. The S. P. C. K. published a few of the stories as *Tales of the Khoja;* while (perhaps on the principle of "If you cannot beat them, join them") the Russians made a film of Nasrudin under the name of *The Adventures of Nasrudin.* Even the Greeks, who accepted few other things from the Turks, consider him a part of their cultural heritage. Secular Turkey, through its information department, has published a selection of the metaphysical jokes attributed to this supposed Moslem preacher who is the archetype of the Sufi mystic. And yet the dervish Orders were suppressed by law in republican Turkey.

Nobody really knows who Nasrudin was, where he lived, or when. This is truly in character, for the whole intention is to provide a figure who cannot really be characterized, and who is timeless. It is the message, not the man, which is important to the Sufis. This has not prevented people from providing him with a spurious history, and even a tomb. Scholars, against whose pedantry in his stories Nasrudin frequently emerges triumphant, have even tried to take his *Subtleties* to pieces in the hope of finding appropriate biographical material. One of their "discoveries" would have warmed the heart of Nasrudin himself. Nasrudin said that he considered himself upside down in this world, argues one scholar; and from this he infers that the supposed date of Nasrudin's death, or his "tombstone," should be read not as 386, but 683. Another professor feels that the Arabic numerals used would, if truly reversed, look more like the figures 274. He gravely records that a dervish to whom he appealed for aid in this ". . . merely said, 'Why not drop a spider in some ink and see what marks he makes in crawling out of it. This should give the correct date or show something.'"

In fact, 386 means 300 + 80 + 6. Transposed into Arabic letters, this decodes as SH, W, F, which spells the word ShaWaF: "to cause someone to see; to show a thing." The dervish's spider would "show" something, as he himself said.

If we look at some of the classical Nasrudin stories in as detached a way as possible, we soon find that the wholly scholastic approach is the last one that the Sufi will allow:

Nasrudin, ferrying a pedant across a piece of rough water, said something ungrammatical to him. "Have you never studied grammar?" asked the scholar.

"No."

"Then half of your life has been wasted."

A few minutes later Nasrudin turned to the passenger. "Have you ever learned how to swim?"

"No. Why?"

"Then *all* your life is wasted—we are sinking!"

This is the emphasis upon Sufism as a practical activity, denying that the formal intellect can arrive at truth, and that pattern-thinking derived from the familiar world can be applied to true reality, which moves in another dimension.

This is brought out even more forcefully in a wry tale set in a teahouse; a Sufi term for a meeting place of dervishes. A monk enters and states:

"My master taught me to spread the word that mankind will never be fulfilled until the man who has *not* been wronged is as indignant about a wrong as the man who actually *has* been wronged."

The assembly is momentarily impressed. Then Nasrudin speaks:

"My master taught *me* that nobody at all should become indignant about anything until he is sure that what he thinks is a wrong is in fact a wrong—and not a blessing in disguise!"

Nasrudin, in his capacity as a Sufi teacher, makes frequent use of the dervish technique of himself playing the part of the unenlightened man in the story, in order to highlight a truth. A famous tale denying the superficial belief in cause and effect makes him the victim:

Mulla Nasrudin was walking along an alleyway one day when a man fell from a roof and landed on top of him. The other man was unhurt—but the Mulla was taken to the hospital.

"What teaching do you infer from this event, Master?" one of his disciples asked him.

"Avoid belief in inevitability, even if cause and effect seem inevitable! Shun theoretical questions like: 'If a man falls off a roof, will his neck be broken?' *He* fell—but *my* neck is broken!"

Because the average person thinks in patterns and cannot accommodate himself to a really different point of view, he loses a great deal of the meaning of life. He may live, even progress, but he cannot understand all that is going on. The story of the smuggler makes this very clear:

Nasrudin used to take his donkey across a frontier every day, with the panniers loaded with straw. Since he admitted to being a smuggler when he trudged home every night, the frontier guards searched him again and again. They searched his person, sifted the straw, steeped it in water, even burned it from time to time. Meanwhile he was becoming visibly more and more prosperous.

Then he retired and went to live in another country. Here one of the customs officers met him, years later.

"You can tell me now, Nasrudin," he said. "Whatever *was* it that you were smuggling, when we could never catch you out?"

"Donkeys," said Nasrudin.

This story also emphasizes one of the major contentions of Sufism—that preternatural experience and the mystical goal is something nearer to mankind than is realized. The assumption that something esoteric or transcendental must be far off or complicated has been assumed by the ignorance of individuals. And that kind of individual is the least qualified to judge the matter. It is "far off" only in a direction which he does not realize.

Nasrudin, like the Sufi himself, does not violate the canons of his time. But he adds a new dimension to his consciousness, refusing to accept for specific, limited purposes that truth, say, is something that can be measured as can anything else. What people call truth is relative to their situation. And he cannot find it until he realizes this. One of the Nasrudin tales, a most ingenious one, shows that until one can see through relative truth, no progress can be made:

One day Nasrudin was sitting at court. The King was complaining that his subjects were untruthful. "Majesty," said Nasrudin, "there is truth and truth. People must practice real truth before they can use relative truth. They always try the other way around. The result is that they take liberties with their man-made truth, because they know instinctively that it is only an invention."

The King thought that this was too complicated. "A thing must be true or false. I will *make* people tell the truth, and by this practice they will establish the habit of being truthful."

When the city gates were opened the next morning, a gallows had been erected in front of them, presided over by the captain of the royal guard. A herald announced: "Whoever would enter the city must first answer the truth to a question which will be put to him by the captain of the guard."

Nasrudin, who had been waiting outside, stepped forward first.

The captain spoke: "Where are you going? Tell the truth—the alternative is death by hanging."

"I am going," said Nasrudin, "to be hanged on those gallows."

"I don't believe you!"

"Very well, then. If I have told a lie, hang me!"

"But that would *make it* the truth!"

"Exactly," said Nasrudin, "*your* truth."

The would-be Sufi must also understand that standards of good and bad depend upon individual or group criteria, not upon objective fact. Until he experiences this internally as well as accepting it intellectually, he will not be able to qualify for inner understanding. This shifting scale is exemplified by a story of the chase:

A king who enjoyed Nasrudin's company, and also liked to hunt, commanded him to accompany him on a bear hunt. Nasrudin was terrified.

When Nasrudin returned to his village, someone asked him: "How did the hunt go?"

"Marvelously."

"How many bears did you see?"

"None."

"How could it have gone marvelously, then?"

"When you are hunting bears, and when you are me, seeing no bears at all *is* a marvelous experience."

Internal experience cannot be transmitted through repetitiousness, but has to be constantly refreshed from the source. Many schools continue to operate long after their actual dynamic is exhausted, becoming mere centers repeating a progressively weakened doctrine. The name of the teaching may remain the same. The teaching may have no value, may even oppose the original meaning, is almost always a travesty of it. Nasrudin emphasizes this as one of the points in his "Duck Soup" story:

A kinsman came to see the Mulla from somewhere deep in the country, bringing a duck as a gift. Delighted, Nasrudin had the bird cooked and shared it with his guest. Presently, however, one countryman after another started to call, each one the friend of the friend of the "man who brought you the duck." No further presents were forthcoming.

At length the Mulla was exasperated. One day yet another stranger appeared. "I am the friend of the friend of the friend of the relative who brought you the duck."

He sat down, like all the rest, expecting a meal. Nasrudin handed him a bowl of hot water.

"What is this?"

"That is the soup of the soup of the soup of the duck which was brought by my relative."

The sharpened perception which the Sufi attains sometimes enables him to experience things which are imperceptible to others. Ignorant of this, members of other schools generally give away their lack of perception by saying or doing something which is so obviously the result of spiritual immaturity that the Sufi can read him like a book. In these circumstances Sufis seldom trouble to say anything. The perception, however, is illustrated by another Nasrudin tale:

Nasrudin called at a large house to collect for charity. The servant said, "My master is out."

"Very well," said the Mulla; "even though he has not been able to contribute, please give your master a piece of advice from me. Say: 'Next time you go out, don't leave your face at the window—someone might steal it.'"

People do not know where to look when they are seeking enlightenment. As a result, it is hardly surprising that they may attach themselves to any cult, immerse themselves in all manner of theories, believing that they have the capacity to distinguish the true from the false.

Nasrudin taught this in several ways. On one occasion a neighbor found him down on his knees looking for something.

"What have you lost, Mulla?"

"My key," said Nasrudin.

After a few minutes of searching, the other man said, "Where did you drop it?"

"At home."

"Then why, for heaven's sake, are you looking here?"

"There is more light here."

This is one of the most famous of all Nasrudin tales, used by many Sufis, commenting upon people who seek exotic sources for enlightenment. Acting it on the stage was a part of the repertoire of Karl Vallentin, the late "metaphysical clown" of Munich.

The mechanism of rationalization is one which effectively bars the deepening of perception. The Sufic impact may often be wasted because the individual will not properly absorb it.

A neighbor came to borrow Nasrudin's clothesline.

"I am sorry, but I am drying flour on it."

"But how can you dry flour on a line?"

"It is less difficult than you think, when you don't want to lend it."

Nasrudin here presents himself as the evasive part of

the mind, which will not accept that there are other ways of approaching truth than the conventional patterns.

In the development of the human mind, there is a constant change and limit to the usefulness of any particular technique. This characteristic of Sufi practice is ignored in repetitious systems, which condition the mind and create an atmosphere of attainment or nearness to attainment, without actually producing it. Nasrudin figures as the character in a story which seeks to make this clear:

The Mulla nearly fell into a pool of water. A passer-by saved him in the nick of time. Every time they met in future, the man reminded Nasrudin about how he had prevented him from getting wet.

Ultimately, unable to stand it any longer, the Mulla took his friend to the pool, jumped in as far as the neck, and shouted: *"Now* I am as wet as I would have been if I had never met you! Will you leave me alone?"

The ordinary joke or fable, containing only one point or emphasis, cannot be compared to the Nasrudin system—ideally a participation-recital which exercises an inward as well as an outward or superficial effect. The parable, fable and ordinary joke are considered mystically sterile because they lack penetration or true regenerative force.

While the complex ingenuity and intention of the Nasrudin story is far ahead of, say, the Baldakiev figure of the Russians, the Arab Joha, or Bertoldo of the Italians—all well-known comical figures—something of the difference of depth in stories can be assessed by means of the Mulla's jokes and their equivalent in their sporadic occurrence elsewhere.

A Zen story provides an interesting example. In this a monk asks a master to give him a version of the reality beyond reality. The master snatches up a rotten apple; and the monk perceives the truth by means of this sign. We are left in the dark as to what lies behind, or leads up to, the illumination.

The Nasrudin story about an apple fills in a great deal of

missing detail: Nasrudin is sitting among a circle of disciples, when one of them asks him the relationship between things of this world and things of a different dimension. Nasrudin says, "You must understand allegory." The disciple says, "Show me something practical—for instance an apple from Paradise."

Nasrudin picks up an apple and hands it to the man. "But this apple is bad on one side—surely a heavenly apple would be perfect."

"A celestial apple would be perfect," says Nasrudin; "but as far as you are able to judge it, situated as we are in this abode of corruption, and with your present faculties, this is as near to a heavenly apple as you will ever get."

The disciple understood that the terms which we use for metaphysical things are based upon physical terms. In order to penetrate into another dimension of cognition, we have to adjust to the way of understanding of that dimension.

The Nasrudin story, which may well be the original of the apple allegory, is designed to add to the mind of the hearer something of the flavor which is needed to build up the consciousness for experiences which cannot be reached until a bridge has been created.

This gradual building up of inner consciousness is characteristic of the Nasrudin Sufic method. The flash of intuitive illumination which comes as a result of the stories is partly a minor enlightenment in itself, not an intellectual experience. It is also a steppingstone toward the reestablishing of mystical perception in a captive mind, relentlessly conditioned by the training systems of material life.

A Nasrudin joke, detached (perhaps by translation) from its technical terminology, can still pass current on its humorous value. In such cases much of its impact may be lost. An example is the salt and wool joke:

Nasrudin is taking a load of salt to market. His donkey wades through a stream, and the salt is dissolved. When it reaches the opposite bank, the ass is frisky because his load is lightened. But Nasrudin is angry. On the next market day he packs the panniers with wool. The animal is almost drowned with the increase of weight when it takes up water at the ford.

"There!" says Nasrudin triumphantly, "that'll teach you to think that you gain something every time you go through water!"

In the original story, two technical terms are used, salt and wool. "Salt" (*milh*) is the homonym for "being good, wisdom." The donkey is the symbol for man. By shedding his burden of general goodness, the individual feels better, loses the weight. The result is that he loses his food, because Nasrudin could not sell the salt to buy fodder. The word "wool" is of course another word for "Sufi." On the second trip the donkey had an increase of his burden through the wool, because of the intention of his teacher, Nasrudin. The weight is increased for the duration of the journey to market. But the end result is better, because Nasrudin sells the damp wool, now heavier than before, for a higher price than dry wool.

Another joke, found also in Cervantes (*Don Quixote*, Ch. 5) remains a joke although the technical term "fear" is merely translated and not explained:

"I shall have you hanged," said a cruel and ignorant king to Nasrudin, "if you do not prove that you have deep perceptions such as have been attributed to you." Nasrudin at once said that he could see a golden bird in the sky and demons within the earth. "But how can you do this?" the King asked. "Fear," said the Mulla, "is all you need."

"Fear," in the Sufi vocabulary, is the activation of conscience whose exercises can produce extrasensory perception. This is an area in which the formal intellect is not used, and other faculties of the mind are called into play.

Yet Nasrudin, in a manner wholly unique, manages to use the very fabric of intellectuality for his own purposes. An echo of this deliberate intent is found in the *Legend of Nasrudin*, where it is recounted that Hussein, the founder of the system, snatched his messenger-designate Nasrudin from the very clutches of the "Old Villain"—the crude system of thought in which almost all of us live.

"Hussein" is associated in Arabic with the concept of virtue. "Hassein" means "strong, difficult of access."

When Hussein had searched the whole world for the teacher who was to carry his message through the generations, he was almost at the point of despair when he heard a commotion. The Old Villain was upbraiding one of his students for telling jokes. "Nasrudin!" thundered the Villain, "for your irreverent attitude I condemn you to universal ridicule. Henceforth, when one of your absurd stories is told, six more will have to be heard in succession, until you are clearly seen to be a figure of fun."

It is believed that the mystical effect of seven Nasrudin tales, studied in succession, is enough to prepare an individual for enlightenment.

Hussein, eavesdropping, realized that from every situation comes forth its own remedy; and that this was the manner in which the evils of the Old Villain could be brought into their true perspective. He would preserve truth through Nasrudin.

He called Nasrudin to him in a dream and imparted to him a portion of his *baraka*, the Sufi power which interpenetrates the nominal significance of meaning. Henceforth all the stories about Nasrudin became works of "independent" art. They could be understood as jokes, they had a metaphysical meaning; they were infinitely complex and partook of the nature of completion and perfection which had been stolen from human consciousness by the vitiating activities of the Old Villain.

Baraka, looked at from the ordinary viewpoint, has many "magical" qualities—although it is essentially a unity and the fuel as well as the substance of objective reality. One of these qualities is that anyone who is endowed with it, or any object with which it is associated, retains a quota of it, no matter how much it may be altered by the impact of unregenerate people. Hence the mere repetition of a Nasrudin jest takes with it some *baraka;* pondering brings more. "So that by this method the teachings of Nasrudin in the line of Hussein were impressed forever within a vehicle which could not be utterly distorted beyond repair. Just as all water is essentially water, so within the Nasrudin experiences there is an irreducible minimum which answers a call, and which grows when it is invoked." This minimum is truth, and through truth, real consciousness.

Nasrudin is the mirror in which one sees oneself. Unlike an ordinary mirror, the more it is gazed into, the more of the original Nasrudin is projected into it. This mirror is likened to the celebrated Cup of Jamshid, the Persian hero; which mirrors the whole world, and into which the Sufis "gaze."

Since Sufism is not built upon artificial conduct or behavior in the sense of external detail, but upon comprehensive detail, the Nasrudin stories must be experienced as well as thought about. Further, the experiencing of each story will contribute toward the "homecoming" of the mystic. One of the first developments of homecoming is when the Sufi shows signs of superior perception. He will be able to understand a situation, for example, by inspiration, not formal cerebration. His actions, as a result, may sometimes baffle observers working on the ordinary plane of consciousness; but his results will nevertheless be correct.

One Nasrudin story, showing how the right result comes for the Sufi through a special mechanism ("the wrong method," to the uninitiated) explains much of the seeming eccentricities of Sufis:

Two men came before Nasrudin when he was acting in his capacity of magistrate. One said, "This man has bitten my ear—I demand compensation." The other said, "He bit it himself." Nasrudin adjourned the case and withdrew to his chambers. There he spent half an hour trying to bite his own ear. All that he succeeded in doing was falling over in the attempt, and bruising his forehead. Then he returned to the courtroom.

"Examine the man whose ear was bitten," he ordered. "If his forehead is bruised, he did it himself, and the case is dismissed. If not, the other one did it, and the bitten man is compensated with three silver pieces." The right verdict had been arrived at by seemingly illogical methods.

Here Nasrudin arrived at the correct answer, irrespective of the apparent logic of the situation. In another story, himself adopting the role of fool ("the Path of Blame," to the Sufi), Nasrudin illustrates, in extreme form, ordinary human thinking:

Someone asked Nasrudin to guess what he had in his hand.

"Give me a clue," said the Mulla.

"I'll give you several," said the wag. "It is shaped like an egg, egg-sized, looks, tastes and smells like an egg. Inside it is yellow and white. It is liquid within before you cook it, coalesces with heat. It was, moreover, laid by a hen. . . ."

"I know!" interrupted the Mulla. "It is some sort of cake."

I tried a similar experiment in London. At three tobacconists I successively asked for "cylinders of paper filled with particles of tobacco, about three inches long, packed in cartons, probably with printing on them."

None of the people who sold cigarettes all day long could identify what I wanted. Two directed me elsewhere—one to their wholesalers, another to a shop which specialized in exotic imports for smokers.

The word "cigarette" may be a necessary trigger to describe paper cylinders filled with tobacco. But the trigger habit, depending upon associations, cannot be used in the same way in perceptive activities. The mistake is in carrying over one form of thinking—however admirable in its proper place—into another context, and trying to use it there.

Rumi tells a story which resembles Nasrudin's tale of the egg, but emphasizes another significant factor. A king's son had been placed in the hands of mystical teachers who reported that they now could not teach him any more. In order to test him, the King asked him what he had in his hand. "It is round, metallic and yellow—it must be a sieve," the boy replied. Sufism insists upon a balanced development of inner perceptions and ordinary human conduct and usage.

The assumption that just because one is alive, one is perceptive, is denied by Sufism, as we have already seen. A man may be clinically alive, but perceptively dead. Logic and philosophy will not help him in attaining perception. One aspect of the following story illustrates this:

The Mulla was thinking aloud.

"How do I know whether I am dead or alive?"

"Don't be such a fool," his wife said; "if you were dead your limbs would be cold."

Shortly afterward Nasrudin was in the forest cutting wood. It was midwinter. Suddenly he realized that his hands and feet were cold.

"I am undoubtedly dead," he thought; "so I must stop working, because corpses do not work."

And, because corpses do not walk about, he lay down on the grass.

Soon a pack of wolves appeared and started to attack Nasrudin's donkey, which was tethered to a tree.

"Yes, carry on, take advantage of a dead man," said Nasrudin from his prone position; "but if I had been alive I would not have allowed you to take liberties with my donkey."

The preparation of the Sufi mind cannot be adequate until the man knows that he has to make something for himself—and stops thinking that others can make it for him. Nasrudin brings the ordinary man under his magnifying lens:

One day Nasrudin went into the shop of a man who sold all kinds of miscellaneous things.

"Have you leather?"

"Yes."

"And nails?"

"Yes."

"And dye?"

"Yes."

"Then why don't you make yourself a pair of boots?"

The story emphasizes the role of the mystical master, essential in Sufism, who provides the starting point for the would-be seeker to do something about himself—that something being the "self-work" under guidance which is the outstanding characteristic of the Sufi system.

The Sufi quest cannot be carried out in unacceptable company. Nasrudin emphasizes this point in his tale of the ill-timed invitation:

The hour was late, and the Mulla had been talking to his friends in a teahouse. As they left, they realized that they were hungry. "Come and eat at my home, all of you," said Nasrudin, without thinking of the consequences.

When the party had nearly arrived at his house, he thought he should go on ahead and tell his wife. "You stay here while I warn her," he told them.

When he told her, she said, "There is nothing in the house! How dare you invite all those people!"

Nasrudin went upstairs and hid himself.

Presently hunger drove his guests to approach the house and knock on the door.

Nasrudin's wife answered. "The Mulla is not at home!"

"But we saw him going in through the front door," they shouted.

She could not think, for the moment, of anything to say.

Overcome by anxiety, Nasrudin, who had been watching the interchange from an upstairs window, leaned out and said, "I could have gone out again by the back door, couldn't I?"

Several of the Nasrudin tales emphasize the falsity of the general human belief that man has a stable consciousness. At the mercy of inner and outer impacts, the behavior of almost anyone will vary in accordance with his mood and his state of health. While this fact is of course recognized in social life, it is not fully admitted in formal philosophy or metaphysics. At best, the individual is expected to create in himself a framework of devoutness or concentration through which it is hoped that he will attain illumination or fulfillment. In Sufism, it is the entire consciousness which has ultimately to be transmuted, starting from the recognition that the unregenerate man is very little more than raw material. He has no fixed nature, no unity of consciousness. Inside him there is an "essence." This is not yoked to his whole being, or even his personality. Ultimately, nobody automatically knows *who* he really is. This in spite of the fiction to the contrary. Thus Nasrudin:

The Mulla walked into a shop one day.

The owner came forward to serve him.

"First things first," said Nasrudin; "did you see me walk into your shop?"

"Of course."

"Have you ever seen me before?"

"Never in my life."

"Then how do you know it is *me?*"

Excellent as this may be as a mere joke, those who regard it as the idea of a stupid man, and containing no deeper significance, will not be people who are in a position to benefit from its regenerative power. You extract from a Nasrudin story only a very little more than you put into it; if it appears to be no more than a joke to a person, that person is in the need of further self-work. He is caricatured in the Nasrudin interchange about the moon:

"What do they do with the moon when it is old?" a stupid man asked the Mulla.

The answer fitted the question: "They cut each old moon up into forty stars."

Many of the Nasrudin tales highlight the fact that people seeking mystical attainment expect it on their own terms, and hence generally exclude themselves from it before they start. Nobody can hope to arrive at illumination if he thinks that he knows what it is, and believes that he can achieve it through a well-defined path which he can conceive at the moment of starting. Hence the story of the woman and the sugar:

When Nasrudin was a magistrate, a woman came to him with her son. "This youth," she said, "eats too much sugar. I cannot afford to keep him in it. Therefore I ask you formally to forbid him to eat it, as he will not obey me."

Nasrudin told her to come back in seven days.

When she returned, he postponed his decision for yet another week.

"Now," he said to the youth, "I forbid you to eat more than such and such a quantity of sugar every day."

The woman subsequently asked him why so much time had been necessary before a simple order could be given.

"Because, madam, I had to see whether I myself could cut down on the use of sugar, before ordering anyone else to do it."

The woman's request had been made, in accordance with most automatic human thinking, simply on the basis of certain assumptions. The first was that justice can be done merely by giving injunctions; secondly, that a person could in fact eat as little sugar as she wanted her son to eat; thirdly, that a thing can be communicated to another person by someone who is not himself involved in it.

This tale is not simply a way of paraphrasing the statement: "Do as I say, not as I do." Far from being an ethical teaching, it is one of grim necessity.

Sufi teaching can only be done by a Sufi, not by a theoretician or intellectual exponent.

Sufism, since it is the attunement with true reality, cannot be made closely to resemble what we take to be reality, but which is really more primitive short-term rule of thumb. For example, we tend to look at events one-sidedly. We also assume, without any justification, that an event happens as it were in a vacuum. In actual fact, all events are associated with all other events. It is only when we are ready to ex-

perience our interrelation with the organism of life that we
can appreciate mystical experience. If you look at any action which you do, or which anyone else does, you will
find that it was prompted by one of many possible stimuli;
and also that it is never an isolated action—it has consequences, many of them ones which you would never expect, certainly which you could not have planned.

Another Nasrudin "joke" underlines this essential circu-
larity of reality, and the generally invisible interactions
which occur:

One day Nasrudin was walking along a deserted road.
Night was falling as he spied a troop of horsemen coming
toward him. His imagination began to work, and he feared
that they might rob him, or impress him into the army. So
strong did this fear become that he leaped over a wall and
found himself in a graveyard. The other travelers, innocent
of any such motive as had been assumed by Nasrudin, became curious and pursued him.

When they came upon him lying motionless, one said,
"Can we help you—why are you here in this position?"

Nasrudin, realizing his mistake, said, "It is more complicated than you assume. You see, I am here because of *you;*
and you, *you* are here because of *me.*"

It is only the mystic who "returns" to the formal world
after literal experience of the interdependence of seemingly
different or unconnected things, who can truly perceive life
in this way. To the Sufi, any metaphysical method which
does not embrace this factor is a concocted (external) one,
and cannot be the product of what he calls mystical experience. Its very existence is a barrier to the attainment of its
purported aim.

This is not to say that the Sufi, as a result of his experiences, becomes divorced from the reality of superficial life.
He has an extra dimension of being, which operates parallel to the lesser cognition of the ordinary man. The Mulla
sums this up neatly in another saying:

"I can see in the dark."

"That may be so, Mulla. But if it is true, why do you sometimes carry a candle at night?"

"To prevent other people from bumping into me."

The light carried by the Sufi may be his conforming with the ways of the people among whom he is cast, after his "return" from being transmuted into a wider perception.

The Sufi is, by virtue of his transmutation, a conscious part of the living reality of all being. This means that he cannot look upon what happens—either to himself or to others—in the limited way in which the philosopher or theologian does. Someone once asked Nasrudin what Fate was. He said, "What you call 'Fate' is really assumption. You assume that something good or bad is going to happen. The actual result you call 'Fate.'" The question, "Are you a fatalist?" cannot be asked of a Sufi, because he does not accept the unsubstantiated concept of Fate which is implied in the question.

Similarly, since he can perceive the ramifications in depth of an event, the Sufi's attitude toward individual happenings is comprehensive, not isolated. He cannot generalize from artificially separated data. " 'Nobody can ride that horse,' the King said to me," said the Mulla; "but I climbed into the saddle." "What happened?" "I couldn't move it either." This is intended to show that when an apparently consistent fact is extended along its dimensions, it changes.

The so-called problem of communication, which engages so much attention, hinges on assumptions that are unacceptable to the Sufi. The ordinary man says, "How can I communicate with another man beyond very ordinary things?" The Sufi attitude is that "communication of things which have to be communicated cannot be prevented. It is not that a means has to be found."

Nasrudin and a Yogi, in one of the tales, both play the part of ordinary people who have, in fact, nothing to communicate to one another:

One day Nasrudin saw a strange-looking building at whose door a contemplative Yogi sat. The Mulla decided that he would learn something from this impressive figure, and started a conversation by asking him who and what he was.

"I am a Yogi," said the other, "and I spend my time in trying to attain harmony with all living things."

"That is interesting," said Nasrudin, "because a fish once saved my life."

The Yogi begged him to join him, saying that in a lifetime devoted to trying to harmonize himself with the animal creation, he had never been so close to such communion as the Mulla had been.

When they had been contemplating for some days, the Yogi begged the Mulla to tell him more of his wonderful experience with the fish, "now that we know one another better."

"Now that I know you better," said Nasrudin, "I doubt whether you would profit by what I have to tell."

But the Yogi insisted. "Very well," said Nasrudin. "The fish saved my life all right. I was starving at the time, and it sufficed me for three days."

The meddling with certain capacities of the mind which characterizes so-called experimental mysticism is something which no Sufi would dare to do. The product of consistent experimentation countless centuries ago, Sufism actually deals in phenomena which are still elusive to the empiric:

Nasrudin was throwing handfuls of bread all round his house. "What are you doing?" someone asked.

"Keeping the tigers away."

"But there are no tigers around here."

"Exactly. Effective, isn't it?"

One of several Nasrudin tales which are found in Cervantes' *Don Quixote* (Ch. 14) warns of the dangers of rigid intellectualism:

"There is nothing which cannot be answered by means of my doctrine," said a monk who had just entered a teahouse where Nasrudin was sitting with his friends.

"And yet just a short time ago," replied the Mulla, "I was

challenged by a scholar with an unanswerable question."

"If only I had been there! Tell it to me, and I shall answer it."

"Very well. He said, 'Why are you trying to get into my house by night?'"

The Sufi perception of beauty is associated with a power of penetration which extends beyond the ken of the usual forms of art. One day a disciple had taken Nasrudin to view, for the first time, a beautiful lakeland scene.

"What a delight!" he exclaimed. "But if only, if only . . ."

"If only what, Mulla?"

"If only they had not put water into it!"

In order to reach the mystic goal, the Sufi must understand that the mind does not work in the manner in which we assume that it does. Furthermore, two people may merely confuse one another:

One day the Mulla asked his wife to make a large quantity of *halwa*, a heavy sweetmeat, and gave her all the ingredients. He ate nearly all of it.

In the middle of the night, Nasrudin woke her up.

"I have just had an important thought."

"Tell it to me."

"Bring me the rest of the *halwa*, and I will tell you."

When she had brought it, she asked him again.

The Mulla first finished up the *halwa*.

"The thought," said Nasrudin, "was: 'Never go to sleep without finishing up all the *halwa* that has been made during that day.'"

Nasrudin enables the Sufi Seeker to understand that the formal ideas current about time and space are not necessarily those which obtain the wider field of true reality. People who believe, for instance, that they are being rewarded for past actions and may be rewarded in future for future doings, cannot be Sufis. The Sufi time conception is an interrelation—a continuum.

The classic story of the Turkish bath caricatures it in a manner which enables something of the idea to be grasped:

Nasrudin visited a Turkish bath. Because he was dressed in rags, he was cavalierly treated by the attendants, who gave him an old towel and a scrap of soap. When he left, he handed the amazed bath men a gold coin. The next day he appeared again, magnificently attired, and was naturally given the best possible attention and deference.

When the bath was over, he presented the bath keepers with the smallest copper coin available.

"This," he said, "was for the attendance *last* time. The gold coin was for your treatment of me *this* time."

The residue of pattern-thinking, plus a distinct immaturity of mind, cause people to attempt to enroll themselves in mysticism on their own terms. One of the first things taught to the disciple is that he may have an inkling of what he needs, and he may realize that he can get it from study and work under a master. But beyond that he can make no conditions. This is the Nasrudin tale which is used to inculcate this truth:

A woman brought her small son to the Mulla's school. "Please frighten him a little," she said, "because he is rather beyond my control."

Nasrudin turned up his eyeballs, started to puff and pant, danced up and down and beat his fists on the table until the horrified woman fainted. Then he rushed out of the room.

When he returned and the woman had recovered consciousness, she said to him, "I asked you to frighten the boy, not me!"

"Madam," said the Mulla, "danger has no favorites. I even frightened myself, as you saw. When danger threatens, it threatens all equally."

Similarly, the Sufi teacher cannot supply his disciple with only a small quantity of Sufism. Sufism is the whole, and carries with it the implications of completeness, not of the fragmentation of consciousness which the unenlightened may use in his own processes, and may call "concentration."

Nasrudin pokes a great deal of fun at the dabblers, who

hope to learn, to steal, some deep secret of life, without actually paying for it:

A ship seemed about to sink, and the passengers were on their knees praying and repenting, promising to make all kinds of amends if only they could be saved. Only Nasrudin was unmoved.

Suddenly, in the midst of the panic he leaped up and shouted, "Steady, now, friends! Don't change your ways—don't be too prodigal. I think I see land."

Nasrudin hammers away at the essential idea—that mystical experience and enlightenment cannot come through a rearrangement of familiar ideas, but through a recognition of the limitations of ordinary thinking, which serves only for mundane purposes. In doing this, he excels beyond any other available form of teaching.

One day he entered a teahouse and declaimed, "The moon is more useful than the sun."

Someone asked him why.

"Because at night we need the light more."

The conquest of the "Commanding Self" which is an object of the Sufi struggle is not achieved merely by acquiring control over one's passions. It is looked upon as a taming of the wild consciousness which believes that it can take what it needs from everything (including mysticism) and bend it to its own use. The tendency to employ materials from whatever source for personal benefit is understandable in the partially complete world of ordinary life, but cannot be carried over into the greater world of real fulfillment.

In the story of the thieving bird, Nasrudin is carrying home a piece of liver and the recipe for liver pie. Suddenly a bird of prey swoops down and snatches the meat from his hand. As it wings away, Nasrudin calls after it, "Foolish bird! You may have the liver, but what will you do without the recipe?"

From the kite's point of view, of course, the liver is sufficient for its needs. The result may be a satiated kite, but it gets only what it thinks it wants, not what could have been.

Since the Sufi is not always understood by other people, they will seek to make him conform to their idea of what is right. In another Nasrudin bird story (which also appears in Rumi's poetic masterpiece, the *Mathnawi*), the Mulla finds a king's hawk perched on his window sill. He has never seen such a strange "pigeon." After cutting its aristocratic beak straight and clipping its talons, he sets it free, saying, "*Now* you look more like a bird. Someone had neglected you."

The artificial division of life, thought and action, so necessary in ordinary human undertakings, has no place in Sufism. Nasrudin inculcates this idea as a prerequisite to understanding life as a whole. "Sugar dissolved in milk permeates all the milk."

Nasrudin was walking along a dusty road with a friend, when they realized that they were very thirsty. They stopped at a teahouse and found that they had between them only enough money to buy a glass of milk. The friend said: "Drink your half first; I have a twist of sugar here which I will add to my share."

"Add it now, brother, and we shall both partake," said the Mulla.

"No, there is not enough to sweeten a whole glass."

Nasrudin went to the kitchen, and came back with a saltcellar. "Good news, friend—I am having *my* half with salt—and there is enough for the whole glass."

Although, in the practical but nonetheless artificial world which we have created for ourselves, we are accustomed to assuming that "first things come first," and that there must be an A to Z of every thing, this assumption cannot hold good in the differently orientated metaphysical world. The Sufi Seeker will learn, at one and the same time, several different things, at their own levels of perception and potentiality. This is another difference between Sufism and the systems which rest on the assumption that only one thing is being learned at any one moment.

A dervish teacher comments upon this multiform relationship of Nasrudin with the Seeker. The tale, he says, is in a way like a peach. It has beauty, nutrition, and hidden depths—the kernel.

A person may be emotionally stirred by the exterior; laugh at the joke, or look at the beauty. But this is only as if the peach were lent to you. All that is really absorbed is the form and color, perhaps the aroma, the shape and texture.

"You can eat the peach, and taste a further delight—understand its depth. The peach contributes to your nutrition, becomes a part of yourself. You can throw away the stone—or crack it and find a delicious kernel within. This is the hidden depth. It has its own color, size, form, depth, taste, function. You can collect the shells of this nut, and with them fuel a fire. Even if the charcoal is of no further use, the edible portion has become a part of you."

As soon as the Seeker gains some degree of insight into the real workings of existence, he ceases to ask the questions which once seemed such urgently relevant ones to the whole picture. Further, he sees that a situation can be changed by events which seemingly have no relevance to it. The tale of the blanket spotlights this:

Nasrudin and his wife woke one night to hear two men fighting below their window. She sent the Mulla out to find out what the trouble was. He wrapped his blanket over his shoulders and went downstairs. As soon as he approached the men, one of them snatched his one and only blanket. Then they both ran off.

"What was the fight about, dear?" his wife asked as he entered the bedroom.

"About my blanket, apparently. As soon as they got that, they went away."

A neighbor went to Nasrudin, asking to borrow his donkey. "It is out on loan," said the Mulla.

At that moment the donkey was heard to bray, somewhere inside the stable.

"But I can hear it bray, over there."

"Whom do you believe," said Nasrudin; "me or a don**key**?"

Experience of this dimension of reality enables the Sufi to avoid selfishness and the exercise of the mechanism of rationalization—the way of thought which imprisons a part of the mind. Nasrudin, in playing the part of a typical human being for a moment, brings this point home to us:

A yokel came to the Mulla and said, "Your bull gored my cow. Am I entitled to any compensation?"

"No," said the Mulla at once; "the bull is not responsible for its actions."

"Sorry," said the crafty villager, "I put it the wrong way around. I meant that it was *your* cow which was gored by *my* bull. But the situation is the same."

"Oh, no," said Nasrudin; "I think I had better look up my lawbooks to see whether there is a precedent for this."

Because the whole body of intellectual human thought is expressed in terms of external reasoning, Nasrudin as the Sufi teacher returns again and again to an exposure of the falsity of ordinary assessment. Attempts at putting into speech or writing the mystical experience itself have never succeeded, because "those who know do not need it; those who do not know cannot gain it without a bridge." Two stories of some importance are often used in conjunction with Sufi teaching to prepare the mind for experiences outside the usual habit-patterns.

In the first tale, Nasrudin is visited by a would-be disciple. The man, after many vicissitudes, arrives at the hut on the mountain side where the Mulla is sitting. Knowing that every single action of the illuminated Sufi is meaningful, the newcomer asks Nasrudin why he is blowing on his hands. "To warm myself in the cold, of course."

Shortly afterward, Nasrudin pours out two bowls of soup, and blows on his own. "Why are you doing that, Master?" asks the disciple. "To cool it, of course," says the teacher.

At this point the disciple leaves Nasrudin, unable to trust any longer a man who uses the same process to arrive at different results—heat and cold.

Examining a thing by means of itself—the mind by means of the mind, creation as it appears to a created but undeveloped being—cannot be done. Theorizing based on such subjective methods may hold good in the short run, or for specific purposes. To the Sufi, however, such theories do not represent truth. While he obviously cannot provide an alternative in mere words, he can—and does—magnify or caricature the process in order to expose it. Once this is done, the door is open for seeking an alternative system of assessment of the correlation of phenomena.

"Every day," says Nasrudin to his wife, "I am more and more amazed at the efficient way in which this world is organized—generally for the benefit of mankind."

"What exactly do you mean?"

"Well, take camels for instance. Why do you suppose they have no wings?"

"I have no idea."

"Well, then; just imagine, if camels had wings, they might nest on the roofs of houses and destroy our peace by romping about above and spitting their cud down at us."

The role of the Sufi teacher is stressed in his famous story of the sermon. It shows (among other things, as in all Nasrudin tales) that no start can be made on completely ignorant people. Further, that those who know need not be taught. Finally, that if there are some enlightened people in a community, there is no need for a new teacher.

Nasrudin was invited to give a discourse to the inhabitants of a nearby village. He mounted the rostrum and began.

"O people, do you know what I am about to tell you?"

Some rowdies, seeking to amuse themselves, shouted, "No!"

"In that case," said the Mulla with dignity, "I shall ab-

stain from trying to instruct such an ignorant community."

The following week, having obtained an assurance from
the hooligans that they would not repeat their remarks, the
elders of the village again prevailed upon Nasrudin to address them.

"O people!" he began again; "do you know what I am
about to say to you?"

Some of the people, uncertain as to how to react, for he
was gazing at them fiercely, muttered, "Yes."

"In that case," retorted Nasrudin, "there is no need
for me to say more." He left the hall.

On the third occasion, when a deputation had again
visited him and implored him to make one further effort, he
presented himself before the assembly.

"O people! Do you know what I am about to say?"

Since he seemed to demand a reply, the villagers shouted,
"Some of us do, and some of us do not."

"In that case," said Nasrudin as he withdrew, "let those
who know tell those who do not."

In Sufism one cannot start the "work" at a predetermined point. The teacher must be allowed to guide each
would-be illuminate in his own way. Nasrudin was once
approached by a young man who asked him how long it
would take before he became a Sufi.

He took the young man to the village. "Before I answer
your question, I want you to come with me, as I am going
to see a music-master about learning to play the lute."

At the musician's house Nasrudin inquired about the
fees.

"Three pieces of silver for the first month. After that, one
silver piece a month."

"Splendid!" shouted the Mulla; "I shall be back in a
month's time!"

The sixth sense which the Sufi acquires, which is assumed by theoreticians to be a sense of complete prescience,
of almost divine all-knowledge, is nothing of the kind. Like

all the other senses it has its limitations. Its function is not
to make the Perfected Man all-wise, but to enable him to
fulfill a mission of greater perception and fuller life. He
no longer suffers from the sense of uncertainty and incom-
pleteness which is familiar to other people. The story of the
boys and the tree is taken to convey this meaning:

Some boys wanted to run away with Nasrudin's slippers.
As he came along the road they crowded around him and
said, "Mulla, nobody can climb this tree!"

"Of course they can," said Nasrudin. "I shall show you
how, then you will be able to do it."

He was about to leave his slippers on the ground, but
something warned him, and he tucked them into his belt
before starting his climb.

The boys were discomfited. "What are you taking your
slippers for?" one shouted up to him.

"Since this tree has not been climbed, how do I know
that there is not a road up there?" the Mulla answered.

When the Sufi is using his intuition, he cannot explain
his actions plausibly.

The sixth sense also gives the possessor of *baraka* the
means apparently to create certain happenings. This capacity comes to the Sufi by a means other than using formal
reasoning:

"Allah will provide recompense," said Nasrudin to a man
who had been robbed.

"I don't see how it could work," said the man.

Nasrudin immediately took him into a nearby mosque,
and told him to stand in a corner. Then the Mulla started
to weep and wail, calling upon Allah to restore to the
man his twenty silver coins. He made such a disturbance
that the congregation made a collection and handed that
sum to the man.

"You may not understand the means which operate in
this world," said Nasrudin; "but perhaps you will understand what has happened in Allah's house."

Participating in the working of reality is very different

from intellectual extensions of observed fact. In order to demonstrate this, Nasrudin once took the slowest of lumbering oxen to a horse race which accepted all entrants.

Everyone laughed, for it is well known that an ox cannot run at any speed.

"Nonsense," said the Mulla; "it certainly will run very fast indeed, given a chance. Why, when it was a calf, you should have seen how it ran. Now, though it has had no practice, no occasion to run, it is fully grown. Why should it not run even faster?"

The story also combats the belief that just because a thing—or person—is old, it is necessarily better than something which is young. Sufism as a conscious and living activity is not tied to the past or hidebound tradition. Every Sufi who is living today represents every Sufi who has lived in the past, or who will ever live. The same amount of *baraka* is there, and immemorial tradition does not increase its romance, which remains constant.

A further depth of this tale points out that the disciple (the calf) may develop into someone with an apparently different function (the ox) from what one might have assumed. The clock cannot be turned back. Those who rely upon speculative theory cannot rely upon Sufism.

The absence of an intuitive faculty in mankind in general produces an almost hopeless situation; and many Nasrudin tales emphasize this fact.

Nasrudin plays the part of the insensitive, ordinary dervish in the story of the bag of rice. One day he disagreed with the prior of a monastery at which he was staying. Shortly afterward, a bag of rice was missing. The chief ordered everyone to line up in the courtyard. Then he told them that the man who had stolen the rice had some grains of it in his beard.

"This is an old trick, to make the guilty party touch his beard involuntarily," thought the real thief, and stood firm.

Nasrudin, on the other hand, thought, "The prior is out to revenge himself upon me. He must have planted rice in my beard!" He tried to brush it off as inconspicuously as he could.

As his fingers combed his beard, he realized that everyone was looking at him.

"I *knew*, somehow, that he would trap me sooner or later," said Nasrudin.

What some people take to be "hunches" are often really the products of neurosis and imagination.

The spirit of scepticism about metaphysical matters is by no means confined to the West. In the East it is not uncommon for people to say that they feel that discipleship in a mystical school will deprive them of their autonomy, or otherwise rob them of something. Such people are generally ignored by Sufis, because they have not yet reached the stage where they realize that they are already prisoners of a far worse tyranny (that of the Old Villain) than anything which could be devised for them in a mystical school. There is one succinct Nasrudin joke, however, which points this out:

"I hear a burglar downstairs," the Mulla's wife whispered to him one night.

"Not a sound," replied Nasrudin. "We have nothing for him to steal. With any luck, *he* might leave something behind."

Nasrudin, burglar of many empty houses, always leaves something behind—if the inhabitants recognize it.

In Sufism, practical methods of instruction are essential. This is partly because Sufism is an active undertaking; partly because, although people pay lip service to truths when they are told them, the reality of the truth does not usually penetrate beyond their discursive faculty.

Nasrudin was mending the roof one day when a man called him down into the street. When he went down he asked the man what he wanted.

"Money."

"Why did you not say so when you called to me?"

"I was ashamed to beg."

"Come up to the roof."

When they reached the roof, Nasrudin started to lay the tiles again. The man coughed, and Nasrudin, without looking up, said, "I have no money for you."

"What! You could have told me that without bringing me up here."

"Then how would you have been able to recompense me for bringing me down?"

A great many things are instantly obvious to the Sufi, which cannot be arrived at by the average man. An allegory is used to explain some of the amazing acts of Sufi initiates, based upon supersensory powers. To the Sufi, these are no more miraculous than any of the ordinary senses are to the layman. Just how they work cannot be described; but a rough analogy can be drawn.

"Mankind is asleep," said Nasrudin, when he had been accused of falling asleep at court one day. "The sleep of the sage is powerful, and the 'wakefulness' of the average man is almost useless to anyone."

The King was annoyed.

The next day, after a heavy meal, Nasrudin fell asleep, and the King had him carried into an adjoining room. When the court was about to rise, Nasrudin, still slumbering, was brought back to the audience chamber.

"You have been asleep again," said the King.

"I have been as awake as I needed to be."

"Very well, then, tell me what happened while you were out of the room."

To everyone's astonishment, the Mulla repeated a long and involved story that the King had been reciting.

"How did you do it, Nasrudin?"

"Simple," said the Mulla; "I could tell by the expression on the face of the King that he was about to tell that old story again. That is why I went to sleep for its duration."

Nasrudin and his wife are presented in the next story as two ordinary people, who are man and wife, yet separated

in understanding of each other by the fact that ordinary
human communication is faulty and insincere. The communication between Sufis is of a different order. Further,
it is hopeless to try to use the crudity and dishonesty of ordinary communication for mystical purposes. At least, the
various methods of communication are combined by Sufis to
produce an altogether different signaling system.

The Mulla's wife was angry with him. She accordingly
brought him his soup boiling hot, and did not warn him
that it might scald him.

But she was hungry herself, and as soon as the soup was
served, she took a gulp of it. Tears of pain came to her eyes.
But she still hoped that the Mulla would burn himself.

"My dear, what is the matter?" asked Nasrudin.

"I was only thinking about my poor old mother. She used
to like this soup, when she was alive."

Nasrudin took a scalding mouthful from his own bowl.

Tears coursed down his cheek.

"Are you crying, Nasrudin?"

"Yes, I am crying at the thought that your old mother is
dead, poor thing; and left someone like you in the land of
the living."

Seen from the standpoint of reality, which is the Sufi one,
other metaphysical systems contain several severe drawbacks,
some of which are worth considering. What a mystic has to
say of his experiences, when reported in words, always constitutes a nearly useless distortion of fact. Furthermore, this
distortion can be repeated by others impressively enough to
appear profound; but it has in itself no illuminative value.
For the Sufi, mysticism is not a matter of going somewhere
and gaining enlightenment, and then trying to express
something of it. It is an undertaking which correlates with
his very being and produces a link between all humanity
and the extra dimension of understanding.

All these points—and several more—are made concurrently
in one of the Nasrudin tales:

The Mulla had returned to his village from the imperial

capital, and the villagers gathered around to hear what he had to say of his adventures.

"At this time," said Nasrudin, "I only want to say that the King spoke to me."

There was a gasp of excitement. A citizen of their village had actually been spoken to by the King! The titbit was more than enough for the yokels. They dispersed to pass on the wonderful news.

But the least sophisticated of all hung back, and asked the Mulla exactly what the King had said.

"What he said—quite distinctly, mind you, for anyone to hear—was 'Get out of my way!'"

The simpleton was more than satisfied. His heart expanded with joy. Had he not, after all, heard words actually used by the King; and seen the man to whom they had been addressed?

The story is popularly current among the folk tales of Nasrudin, and its obvious moral is aimed against name droppers. But the Sufic meaning is important in preparing the dervish mind for the experiences which replace superficial ones like this.

It is more than interesting to observe the effect of Nasrudin tales upon people in general. Those who prefer the more ordinary emotions of life will cling to their obvious meaning, and insist upon treating them as jokes. These include the people who compile or read small booklets of the more obvious jests, and who show visible uneasiness when the metaphysical or "upsetting" stories are told them.

Nasrudin himself answers these people in one of his shortest jokes:

"They say your jokes are full of hidden meanings, Nasrudin. Are they?"

"No."

"Why not?"

"Because I have never told the truth in my life, even once; neither will I ever be able to do so."

The ordinary individual may say, with a sense of profundity, that all humor is really serious; that every joke carries a message on a philosophical level. But this message system is not that of Nasrudin. The cynical humorist, it may be supposed, like the Greek philosopher, may point out absurdities in our thoughts and actions. This is not the role of Nasrudin either—because the over-all effect of Nasrudin is something more profound. Since the Mulla stories all have a coherent relationship with one another and with a form of reality which the Sufi is teaching, the cycle is a part of a context of conscious development which cannot be correctly related to the snipping of the ordinary humorist or the sporadic satiricism of the formal thinker.

When a Nasrudin tale is read and disgested, something is happening. It is this consciousness of happening and continuity which is central to Sufism.

In reply to the question, "What method lacks Sufism?" Khoja Anis said, "Without continuity, there is no Sufism; without being and becoming, there is no Sufism; without interrelation, there is no Sufism."

This truth is to an extent transmitted by words. Better still, it is partially conveyed by the mutual action of the words and the reaction of the hearer. But the Sufi experience comes by means of a mechanism which takes over at the point where words leave off—the point of action, of "working with" a master.

Nasrudin once illustrated this in his famous "Chinese" story. He had gone to China, where he gathered a circle of disciples, whom he was preparing for enlightenment. Those who became illuminated immediately ceased attending his lectures.

A party of his undeveloped followers, desiring more illumination, traveled from Persia to China to continue their studies with him.

After their first lecture, he received them.

"Why, Mulla," one of them asked, "do you lecture on secret words which we (unlike the Chinese) can understand? They are *namidanam* and *hichmalumnist!* They mean, in Persian, merely 'I don't know' and 'Nobody knows.'"

"What would you have me do instead—lie my head off?" asked Nasrudin.

Sufis use technical terms to render an approximate equivalent of mysteries which are experiences not to be verbalized. Until the Seeker is ready to "catch" the experience, he is protected from making the mistake of trying to investigate it intellectually by the very use of these technicalities. Itself the result of conscious specialization, Sufism has discovered that there is no short cut to enlightenment. This does not mean that the enlightenment may take a long time. It does mean that the Sufi must stick to the Path.

Nasrudin, playing the part of the man who seeks a short cut, figures in a joke which conveys this idea:

It was a wonderful morning, and the Mulla was walking home. Why, he thought to himself, should he not take a short cut through the beautiful woodland beside the dusty road?

"A day of days, a day for fortunate pursuits!" he exclaimed to himself, plunging into the greenery.

Almost at once, he found himself lying at the bottom of a concealed pit.

"It is just as well I took this short cut," he reflected, as he lay there; "because if things like this can happen in the midst of such beauty—what catastrophe might not have developed on that uncompromisingly tiresome highway?"

Under somewhat similar circumstances, the Mulla was once seen investigating an empty nest:

"What are you doing, Mulla?"

"Looking for eggs."

"There are no eggs in last year's nest!"

"Don't be too sure," said Nasrudin; "if you were a bird and wanted to protect your eggs, would you build a *new* nest, with everyone watching?"

This is another of the Mulla's tales which appear in *Don Quixote*. The fact that this joke can be read in at least two ways might deter the formalist thinker, but provides the dervish with the opportunity of understanding the duality of real being, which is obscured by conventional human thinking. Hence what is its absurdity to the intellectual becomes its strength to the intuitively perceptive.

Contact between Sufis sometimes takes place by means of signs, and communication can be carried on through methods which are not only unknown, but could appear incomprehensible, to the mind conditioned in the ordinary way. This, of course, does not prevent the pattern-thinker from trying to make sense out of what seems nonsense. In the end he gets the wrong interpretation, though it may satisfy him.

Another mystic stopped Nasrudin in the street, and pointed at the sky. He meant, "There is only one truth, which covers all."

Nasrudin was accompanied at the time by a scholar, who was seeking the rationale of Sufism. He said to himself, "This weird apparition is mad. Perhaps Nasrudin will take some precautions against him."

Sure enough, the Mulla rummaged in his knapsack and brought out a coil of rope. The scholar thought, "Excellent, we will be able to seize and bind up the madman if he becomes violent."

Nasrudin's action had, in fact, meant, "Ordinary humanity tries to reach that 'sky' by methods as unsuitable as this rope."

The "madman" laughed and walked away. "Well done," said the scholar; "you saved us from him."

This story has given rise to a Persian proverb, "A question about the sky—the answer about a rope." The proverb, often invoked by non-Sufi clerics or intellectuals, is often used in a contrary sense to its initiatory one.

Knowledge cannot be attained without effort—a fact which is fairly generally accepted. But the ludicrous methods which are used to project effort, and the absurdity of the efforts themselves, effectively close the gateway to knowledge for people who try to transfer the learning systems of one field into that of another.

Yogurt is made by adding a small quantity of old yogurt to a larger measure of milk. The action of the *bacillus bulgaricus* in the seeding portion of yogurt will in time convert the whole into a mass of new yogurt.

One day some friends saw Nasrudin down on his knees beside a pond. He was adding a little old yogurt to the water. One of the men said, "What are you trying to do, Nasrudin?"

"I am trying to make yogurt."

"But you can't make yogurt in that way!"

"Yes, I know; but just *supposing* it takes!"

Almost anyone will smile at the idiocy of the ignorant Mulla. Some people believe that many forms of humor depend for their enjoyment value on the knowledge that one would not be as much of a fool as the person laughed at. Millions of people who would not try to make yogurt with water would attempt to penetrate esoteric thinking by equally futile methods.

One tale attributed to Mulla Nasrudin goes a long way toward distinguishing between the mystical quest in itself and the form which is based upon lesser, ethical or formally religious criteria:

A Chinese sage is represented as having said to Nasrudin, "Each person must regard his behavior as he would regard that of the other. You must have in your heart for the other what you have in your heart for yourself."

This is not a paraphrase of the Christian Golden Rule, though it contains the same sentiment. It is, in fact, a quotation from Confucious (born 551 B.C.).

"This would be an astonishing remark," replied the Mulla, "for anyone who paused to realize that what a man desired for himself is likely to be as undesirable in the end as what he would desire for his enemy, let alone his friend.

"What he must have in his heart for others is not what he wants for himself. It is what *should* be for him, and what *should* be for all. This is known only when inner truth is known."

Another version of this reply says tersely, "A bird ate poisonous berries, which did it no harm. One day it collected some for its meal, and sacrificed its lunch by feeding the fruit to its friend, a horse."

Another Sufi master, Amini of Samarkand, comments tersely on this theme, as did Rumi before him: "A man wished another man to kill him. Naturally he wished this for everyone else, since he was a 'good' man. The 'good' man is, of course, the man who wants for others what he wants for himself. The single problem of this is that what he wants is often the last thing which he needs."

Again there is the insistence in Sufism upon the reality which must precede the ethic—not the ethic merely set up in isolation and assumed to have some sort of universal validity which even general consideration can show to be absent.

The Nasrudin stories cannot, incidentally, be read as a system of philosophy which is intended to persuade people to drop their beliefs and embrace its precepts. By its very construction, Sufism cannot be preached. It does not rely upon undermining other systems and offering a substitute, or a more plausible one. Because Sufi teaching is only partially expressed in words, it can never attempt to combat philosophical systems on their own terms. To attempt to do so would be to try to make Sufism accord with artificialities—an impossibility. By its own contention, metaphysics cannot be approached in this way; so Sufism relies upon the composite impact—the "scatter" dissemination. The would-be Sufi may be prepared or partially enlightened by Nasrudin. But in order to "mature" he will have to engage in the practical work, and benefit from the actual presence of a master and of other Sufis. Anything else is referred to by the pithy term, "Trying to transmit a kiss by personal messenger." It is a kiss, sure enough; but it is not what was intended.

If Sufism is accepted to be the methodology whereby the

injunctions of religious teachers may be given their real expression, how is the would-be Sufi to find a source of instruction for an instructor he must have?

The true master cannot prevent the growth and development of supposedly mystical schools which accept pupils and perpetuate the counterfeit version of illuminative teaching. Still less, if we are to see the facts objectively, is the tyro able to distinguish between a true and a false school. "The false coin exists only because there is such a thing as true gold," runs the Sufi dictum—but how can the true be distinguished from the false by someone who has no training in so doing?

The beginner is saved from complete insensitivity because within him there is a vestigial capacity to react to "true gold." And the teacher, recognizing the innate capacity, will be able to use it as a receiving apparatus for his signals. True, in the earlier stages, the signals transmitted by the teacher will have to be arranged in such a way as to be perceptible to the inefficient and probably distorting mechanism of the receiver. But the combination of the two elements provides a basis for a working arrangement.

At this stage the teacher marks time to a great extent. Several Nasrudin tales, in addition to their entertainment value, emphasize the initial seemingly incomplete harmony between the teacher and the taught which occupies a preparatory period:

A number of would-be disciples came to the Mulla one day and asked him to give them a lecture. "Very well," he said, "follow me to the lecture hall."

Obediently they lined up behind Nasrudin, who mounted his donkey back to front, and moved off. At first the youths were confused, later they remembered that they should not question even the slightest action of a teacher. Finally they could not bear the jeers of the ordinary passers-by.

Sensing their unease, the Mulla stopped and stared at them. The boldest of them all approached him.

"Mulla, we do not quite understand why you are riding that donkey face to tail."

"Quite simple," said the Mulla. "You see, if you were to walk in front of me, this would be disrespect to me. On the other hand, if I had my back to you, it would mean disrespect toward you. This is the sole possible compromise."

To someone whose perception is sharpened, more than one dimension of this and other stories becomes apparent. The net effect of experiencing a tale at several different levels at once is to awaken the innate capacity for understanding on a comprehensive, more objective manner than is possible to the ordinary, painstaking and inefficient way of thinking. The Sufi, for instance, sees in this story, at one and the same time, messages and linkages with the other sphere of being which not only help him on his way but also give him positive information. To a small extent the ordinary thinker may be able to experience (*mutatis mutandis*) the different perspectives by considering them separately. For instance, Nasrudin is able to observe the pupils by sitting back to front. He is unconcerned as to what other people will think of him, while the undeveloped students are still sensitive to public (and uninformed) opinion. He may be sitting back to front, but he is still mounted, while they are not. Nasrudin, in violating the ordinary conventions, even making himself appear ridiculous, is stating that he is different from the average person. Since, too, he has been along that path before, he does not need to face forward, to look where he is going. Again, in that position, uncomfortable by average standards, he is able to keep his equilibrium. He is, again, teaching by doing and being, not by words.

Such considerations, transposed into the field of metaphysics and then experienced concurrently, provide the total yet composite impact of the Nasrudin story upon the progressing mystic.

Nasrudin's guile, made necessary by the need to slip through the mesh which has been arranged by the Old

Villain, appears in one story after another. His seeming madness is characteristic of the Sufi, whose actions may be inexplicable and appear mad to the onlooker. In story after story he stresses the Sufi assertion that nothing can be had without paying for it. This paying may take one of many forms of sacrifice—of cherished ideas, of money, of ways of doing things. This latter point is essential because the Sufi quest is impossible if the areas employed in the journey are already occupied by elements which prevent the journey being pursued.

And yet, in the end, Nasrudin gets away scot-free. This indicates the fact that although deprivation in the early stages of Sufism may appear to be "paying," in the true sense the Seeker does not pay at all. He does not pay, that is to say, anything of ultimate worth.

The Sufi attitude toward money is a special one, far removed from the shallower, philosophical or theological assumption that money is the root of evil, or that faith is in some way opposed to money.

One day Nasrudin asked a wealthy man for some money.

"What do you want it for?"

"To buy an elephant."

"If you have no money you will not be able to maintain an elephant."

"I asked for *money,* not advice!"

The link here is with the elephant in the dark. Nasrudin needs money for the "work." The rich man, Nasrudin realizes, cannot readjust his ideas to see how the money would be spent; he would need a plausible scheme of finance to be put before him. Nasrudin uses the Sufi word "elephant" to stress this. Naturally the rich man does not understand.

Nasrudin is poor; the word being the same one which is used by Sufis to denote one of their number—Fakir. When he does in fact obtain money, he does so by a method, and uses it in a way which is incomprehensible to the formalist thinker:

One day the Mulla's wife was upbraiding him for being poor.

"If you are a man of religion," she said, "you should pray for money. If that is your employment, you should be paid for it, just as anyone else is paid."

"Very well, I shall do just that."

Going into the garden, Nasrudin shouted at the top of his voice, "O God! I have served you all these years without financial gain. My wife now says that I should be paid. May I therefore, and at once, have a hundred gold pieces of my outstanding salary?"

A miser who lived in the next house was at that moment on his roof counting his riches. Thinking that he would make a fool of Nasrudin, he threw down in front of him a bag containing exactly a hundred golden dinars.

"Thank you," said Nasrudin, and hurried into the house. He showed the coins to his wife, who was very impressed.

"Forgive me," she said, "I never really believed that you were a saint, but I now see that you are."

During the next day or two, the neighbor saw all manner of luxuries being delivered at the Mulla's house. He began to grow restive. He presented himself at Nasrudin's door.

"Know, fellow," said the Mulla, "I am a saint. What do you want?"

"I want my money back. I threw down that bag of gold, not God."

"You may have been the *instrument,* but the gold did not come as a result of my asking *you* for it."

The miser was beside himself. "I shall take you at once to the magistrate, and we will have justice."

Nasrudin agreed. As soon as they were outside, Nasrudin said to the miser, "I am dressed in rags. If I appear beside you before the magistrate, the disparity of our appearances may well prejudice the court in your favor."

"Very well," snarled the miser, "take my robe and I will wear yours."

They had gone a few yards farther when Nasrudin said, "You are riding and I am on foot. If we appear like this before the magistrate he may well think that he should give the verdict to you."

"I know who is going to win this case, no matter what he looks like! *You* ride on my horse."

Nasrudin mounted the horse, while his neighbor walked behind.

When their turn came, the miser explained what had happened to the judge.

"And what have you got to say to this charge?" the judge asked of the Mulla.

"Your honor. This man is a miser, and he is also suffering from delusions. He has the illusion that *he* gave me the money. In true reality, it came from a higher source. It merely *appeared* to this man to have been given by him."

"But how can you prove that?"

"There is nothing simpler. His obsessions take the form of thinking that things belong to him when they do not. Just ask him to whom this robe belongs. . . ." Nasrudin paused and fingered the robe which he was wearing.

"That is mine!" shouted the miser.

"Now," said Nasrudin; "ask him whose horse I was riding when I came to this court. . . ."

"You were riding *my* horse!" screamed the plaintiff.

"Case dismissed," said the judge.

Money is looked upon by the Sufis as an active factor in the relationship between people, and between people and their environment. Since the ordinary perception of reality is shortsighted, it is not surprising that the normal human use of money is equally limited in perspective. The joke about the frogs in the Nasrudin collection explains something of this flavor:

A passer-by saw Nasrudin throwing money into a pool, and asked him why he was doing it.

"I was on my donkey. He had slipped and was slithering down the side of this pool, about to overbalance and fall.

There seemed no hope that either of us would survive a serious fall. Suddenly the frogs in the water began to croak. This frightened the donkey. He reared up and by this means he was able to save himself.

"Should the frogs not benefit from having saved our lives?"

Whereas on the ordinary plane this joke is taken to show Nasrudin as a fool, the deeper meanings are direct reflections of Sufi financial attitudes. The frogs represent people, who cannot use money. Nasrudin rewards them because of the general rule that a reward follows a good action. That the croaking of the frogs was accidental, seemingly, is another factor to ponder. In one respect, at least, the frogs were less blameworthy than ordinary people would be. They probably did not think that they were capable of using money, correctly or otherwise. This story is also used in the sense of "casting pearls before swine," in answer to a questioner who asked a Sufi why he did not make his knowledge and wisdom available to all and sundry, and especially to people who (like the frogs) had showed him kindness and what they thought to be understanding.

In order to understand the wider aspects of Sufi thought, and before progress can be made along lines outside the web cast over humanity by the Old Villain, the dimensions provided by Nasrudin must be visited. If Nasrudin is like a Chinese box, with compartment within compartment, at least he offers numerous simple points of entry into a new way of thinking. To be familiar with the experience of Nasrudin is to be able to unlock many doors in the more baffling texts and practices of the Sufis.

As one's perceptions increase, so does the power of extracting nutrition from the Nasrudin tales. They provide for the beginner what the Sufis call a "blow"—calculated impact which operates in a special way, preparing the mind for the Sufi undertaking.

Looked upon as nutrition, the Nasrudin blow is called a

coconut. This term is derived from a Sufi statement: "A monkey threw a coconut from a treetop at a hungry Sufi, and it hit him on the leg. He picked it up; drank the milk; ate the flesh; made a bowl from the shell."

In one sense, they fulfill the function of the literal blow which occurs in one of the most terse of the Mulla tales:

Nasrudin handed a boy a pitcher, told him to fetch water from a well, and gave him a clout on the ear. "And mind you don't drop it!" he shouted.

An onlooker said, "How can you strike someone who has done nothing wrong?"

"I suppose," said Nasrudin, "that you would prefer me to strike him *after* he has broken the pitcher, when the pitcher and water are both lost? In my way the boy remembers, and the pot and contents are also saved."

Since Sufism is a comprehensive work, it is not only the Seeker who must learn, like the boy. The work, like the pitcher and the water, has its own rules, outside the mundane methods of arts and sciences.

Nobody can set off on the Sufi path unless he has the potentiality for it. If he tries to do so, the possibilities of error are too great for him to have a chance of bringing back the water without breaking the pot.

Sometimes Nasrudin stories are arranged in the form of aphorisms, of which the following are examples:

It is not in fact so.

Truth is something which I never speak.

I do not answer *all* the questions; only those which the know-alls secretly ask themselves.

If your donkey allows someone to steal your coat—steal his saddle.

A sample is a sample. Yet nobody would buy my house when I showed them a brick from it.

People clamor to taste my vintage vinegar. But it would not be forty years old if I let them, would it?

To save money, I made my donkey go without food. Unfortunately the experiment was interrupted by its death. It died before it got used to having no food at all.

People sell talking parrots for huge sums. They never pause to compare the possible value of a *thinking* parrot.

Sheikh Saadi of Shiraz

He who sleeps on the Road will lose either
his hat or his head.

(Nizami, *Treasury of Mysteries*)

The *Gulistan* (Rose Garden) and *Bustan* (Orchard) of
Saadi of Shiraz (1184–1291) are two classics of Sufism
which provide the moral and ethical basis of the reading
of millions, in India, Persia, Pakistan, Afghanistan and
Central Asia. Saadi was at times a wandering dervish, was
captured by the Crusaders and made to dig ditches until
ransomed; visited the centers of learning of the East and
wrote poetry and literature which has not been surpassed.
He was educated in Baghdad at the great college founded
by Nizam, the friend of Khayyam and Minister of Court of
the Shah. His affiliation was with the Naqshbandi Order
of Sufis, and he was closely associated with Sheikh Shahabudin Suhrawardi, the founder of the Suhrawardi School,
and also Najmuddin Kubra, the "Pillar of the Age," one
of the greatest Sufis of all time.

Saadi's influence upon European literature is acknowledgedly very considerable. He is one of the group whose
writings gave substance to the *Gesta Romanorum*, source
book for many Western legends and allegories. Scholars

have traced many of Saadi's influences in literature such as that of Germany. Translations of his works are first found in the West in the seventeenth century. Like most other Sufi work, however, the interior meaning of Saadi is hardly known at all through his literary interpreters. A typical comment by a recent commentator shows this clearly. It is not so much an opinion of Saadi as an indication of the mind of the author: "It is exceedingly doubtful whether he was a Sufi by temperament. In him the didactic subordinates the mystic."

In actual fact, the cautionary tales, rhymes, soulful analogies used by Saadi are multifunctional. On the ordinary level they do indeed contribute toward the ordinary stabilization of ethic. But Professor Codrington almost alone among Western commentators sees deeper:

"The allegory in the *Gulistan* is particular to Sufis. They cannot give their secrets to those who are unprepared to receive or interpret them correctly, so they have developed a special terminology to convey these secrets to initiates. Where no words exist to convey such thoughts, special phrases or allegories are used."

It is not in the West alone that people expect esoteric knowledge to be handed to them upon a plate. Saadi himself points this out in one of his stories.

He was traveling with some devout companions toward the Hejaz in Arabia. A boy near Beni Hilal Oasis started to sing in such a way that the camel of a scoffer of mysticism began to dance, then ran off into the desert. "I commented," says the Sheikh, " 'good Sir, you remain unmoved, but that song has affected even an animal.' "[1]

His teaching about self-examination refers not only to the ordinary need to practice what one preaches. On the Sufi Way there must be a certain kind of self-examination. This comes at a stage earlier than that at which one can understand the admonitions of a teacher. "If you will not

[1] This and other extracts are from Aga Omar Ali Shah's translation (MS).

reprove yourself," Saadi says, "you will not welcome reproof from another."

Such is the persistence of mechanical adulation of the retired life that a candidate for Sufi studies must first be informed as to the place of retirement. "Fettered feet in the presence of friends is better than living in a garden with strangers," he remarks. Only under certain circumstances is withdrawal from the world needed. Anchorites, who are nothing more than professional obsessives, have given the impression that the desert or mountains are the places where the mystic must spend his whole life. They have mistaken a thread for the whole carpet.

The importance of time and place in Sufi exercises is another matter which Saadi stresses. Ordinary intellectuals will be unable to believe that thought varies in quality and effectiveness in accordance with circumstances. They will plan a meeting for a certain time and place, will start an academic conversation and keep it going under any circumstances, insensitive to the Sufi cognition that only on "occasion," according to the Sufi, can the human mind escape from the machine within which it revolves.

This principle, familiar in ordinary life under the guise of "There is a time and a place for everything," is stressed by the *Gulistan* in a typical manner. Tale thirty-six of the chapter on the manners of dervishes seems to be a mere exercise in moral instruction or etiquette. When expounded in the Sufi atmosphere, it reveals fresh dimensions.

A dervish entered a house of a generous man, and found an assembly of literati there. There was a constant interchange of pleasantries and the air was thick with the results of intellectual exercise. Someone invited him to contribute. "You must accept from a smaller intellect only one couplet," said the dervish. The company implored him to speak.

> Like a bachelor before the women's bathhouse
> door, I face the table, hungry for food.

The couplet means not only that this was a time for food,

not talk; it also conveys that the intellectual prattling was merely a setting for real understanding.

The story continues that the host at once said that very soon meatballs would be provided. "For the starving man," replied the dervish, "plain bread is meatball enough."

Those who are impatient to learn without knowing that they are not fitted for learning Sufism in their crude state are often reprimanded by the *Gulistan,* in stories and poetry. "How can the sleeper arouse the sleeper?" Saadi asks in a familiar Sufi phrase. While it may be true that a man's actions should accord with his words, it is also most true that the observer himself must be in a position to assess these actions. Most people are not. "A conference of the wise is like the bazaar of the clothsellers. In the latter place you cannot take away anything unless you pay money. In the former, you can only carry away that for which you have the capacity."[2]

The selfishness of the would-be disciple in seeking his own development and interests is another subject that is stressed among the Sufis. A balance has to be struck between wanting something for oneself and wanting it for the community as well. The link between the Sufis and the Brethren of Sincerity, hardly noticed by outside observers, is stressed in Saadi's section on this problem. The Brethren were a society of savants who prepared recensions of available knowledge and published them anonymously, in the cause of education, none desirous of increasing his own repute through this dedication. Because they were a secret society, little was known about them; because "sincerity" is associated with the Sufis, Sufi teachers were often asked about them. Saadi gives this lesson about the mysterious Brethren in tale forty-three:

A wise man was asked about the Brethren of Sincerity. He said, "Even the least among them honors the wishes of his

2 "Many a 'learned' man is destroyed by ignorance and by the learning which is of no use to him." (Hadrat Ahmed ibn Mahsud, the Sufi)

companions above his own. As the wise say: 'A man engrossed in himself is neither brother nor kinsman.' "

The place won by the *Gulistan* as a book of moral uplift invariably given to the literate young has had the effect of establishing a basic Sufic potential in the minds of its readers. Saadi is read, and enjoyed, because of his thoughts, his poems, the entertainment value of his books. In later years, when he comes to be affiliated to a Sufi teaching school, the inner dimensions of the tales can be revealed to the student. He has something upon which to build. This preparatory material is almost nonexistent in other cultures.

Secrets revealed prematurely—and there are some in Sufism which can actually be communicated without the whole of the teaching—can cause more harm than good. Unless the recipient is prepared, he can misuse the power of which the Sufis are guardians. Saadi explains this in a story which, overtly, is little more than the amplification of a well-worn proverb:

A man had an ugly daughter. He married her to a blind man because nobody else would have her. A doctor offered to restore the blind man's sight. But the father would not allow him, for fear that he would divorce his daughter. "The husband of an ugly woman," concludes Saadi, "is best blind."

Generosity and liberality are two of the important factors which, when applied energetically and correctly, go to prepare the candidate for Sufihood. When it is said, "You get nothing free," there is very much more to it than that. The manner of giving, the thing which is given, the effect of the giving upon the individual—these are the factors which determine the progress of the Sufi. There is a strong link between the concept of persistence and bravery with that of liberality. In ordinary discipleship as known in other systems, where the inner understanding of the mechanism of progress is in disarray, the disciple will think in terms of struggle. He gets nothing without struggle, he thinks; and he is encouraged to think in this way.

But Saadi pinpoints the problem in one of his smaller aphorisms. A person, he says, went to a sage and asked whether it was better to be valorous or liberal. He answered, "He who is liberal does not have to be valorous." This is a most important aspect of Sufi training. It will also be noticed that the form in which the teaching is couched gives Saadi the extra possibility of pointing out (through the mouth of the sage) that questions put in a certain way—either/or—are not necessarily to be answered in that way.

In his chapter on the advantages of contentment, Saadi conceals Sufi teachings in several stories which are seemingly aimed at those who do not exercise correct etiquette. A number of dervishes, reduced to an extremity of hunger, wanted to accept some food from an evil man, known for his liberality. Saadi himself advises them, in a famous poem:

> The lion does not eat the dog's leavings
> Though he die of hunger in his lair.
> Resign your bodies to starvation:
> Do not beg the base for favors.

The way and position in which this story is given shows to the Sufi that Saadi is warning against the dervish following any attractive creed outside of his own, while he is in a period of trial consequent upon his Sufi dedication.

The real Sufi has something within him which cannot be reduced in value by association with lesser men. Saadi has made this theme most attractive in one of his elegant moral tales, showing where real dignity resides:

A king was hunting in a wilderness with some courtiers when it became very cold. He announced that they would sleep in a peasant's hovel until morning. The courtiers insisted that the monarch's dignity would suffer if he were to enter such a place. The peasant, however, said, "It is not your Majesty who will lose; but I who will gain in dignity from being so honored." The peasant received a robe of honor.

Fariduddin Attar, the Chemist

A monkey saw a cherry through the clear glass of a bottle, and thought he would take it. Passing his hand into the neck of the bottle, he closed his fist over the cherry. Now he found that he could not withdraw his hand. The hunter, who had set this trap, now came along. The monkey, impossibly hampered by the bottle, could not run away, and he was caught. "At least I have the cherry in my hand," he thought. At that moment the hunter gave him a sharp tap on the elbow. The monkey's hand opened, and came out of the bottle. The hunter now had the fruit, the bottle and the monkey.

(*Book of Amu-Daria*)

"To abandon something because others have misused it may be the height of folly; the Sufic truth cannot be encompassed in rules and regulations, in formulas and in rituals—but yet it is partially present in all these things."

These words are attributed to Fariduddin the Chemist, a great illuminate and author, and an organizer of the Sufis. He died over a century before the birth of Chaucer, in whose works references to Attar's Sufism are to be found. More than a hundred years after his death the foundation of the Order of the Garter showed such striking parallels with his initiatory Order that this can hardly be a coincidence.

Fariduddin was born near Omar Khayyam's beloved Nishapur, and his father bequeathed him a pharmacy, which is one reason given for his surname and Sufi style Attar—the Chemist. Of his life, a great many stories are told —some of them involving miracles, others containing his teachings. He wrote a hundred and fourteen works for the Sufis, the most important of which is undoubtedly the *Parliament of the Birds*, a forerunner of *Pilgrim's Progress*. Still a classic of Sufism and Persian literature alike, the *Parliament* describes the Sufi experiences, and is itself based in plan on earlier Sufic quest themes. It unfolds meanings which become perceptible with the Sufic awakening of the mind.

The story of Attar's conversion, which the Sufis use to illustrate the need for balance between material and metaphysical things, is given by Daulat-Shah, in the classic *Memoirs of the Poets*. It is not accepted as literal reporting, but allegorical. Attar was in his shop one day, among his numerous and varied merchandise, when a wandering Sufi appeared at the door, gazing in with his eyes filled with tears. Fariduddin at once told the man to be gone. "It is not difficult for me," replied the traveler. "I have nothing to carry; nothing but this cloak. But you, you with your costly drugs? You would do well to consider your own arrangements for going on your way."

This impact so profoundly impressed Attar that he renounced his shop and his work, and withdrew into a Sufi settlement for a period of religious retreat under the aegis of the master Sheikh Ruknuddin. While a great deal is made of his aesthetic practices, he himself maintained the importance of the body, even saying, "The body is not different from the soul, for it is a part of it; and both are a part of the Whole." His teachings are not only embodied in his poetical works, but also in the traditional rituals which are believed by Sufis to be a part of them. Reference to this will be made later; it is the sphere where Sufic poetry, teaching and "work" (*amal*) coincide.

Attar was one of the Sufis most deeply versed in the biographies of the earlier historical Sufis, and his only prose work, *Memoirs of the Friends* (or *Recital of the Saints*), is devoted to a collection of these lives. It was on his wanderings to Mecca and elsewhere after he quit the Sufi circle of Ruknuddin that he decided to make the collection.

In his old age Attar was visited by the young Jalaluddin Rumi, and he presented him with one of his books. Rumi made more public the initiatory aspects of the Sufic lore which Attar pursued. Later he was to refer to him as his own soul: "Attar traversed the seven cities of love, and we have reached only a single street."

Attar died, as he had lived, teaching. His last action was deliberately calculated to make a man think for himself. When the barbarians under Jenghiz Khan invaded Persia in 1220, Attar was seized, by now a man of one hundred and ten years of age. One Mongol said, "Do not kill this old man; I will give a thousand pieces of silver as a ransom for him." Attar told his captor to hold out, for he would get a better price from someone else. A little later another man offered only a quantity of straw for him. "Sell me for the straw," said Attar, "for that is all that I am worth." And he was slain by the infuriated Mongol.

Attar's romantic and quest writings have been shown by Garcin de Tassy to resemble the *Roman de la Rose,* and belong, of course, to the direct Sufic stream of romance teaching which antedates its appearance in Europe. A romance piece which gave rise to later material on a similar Sufic theme was written by Majriti the Córdoban. It is probable that the romance material reached Western Europe through Spain and southern France, rather than through Syria, where the Sufic compositions of this genre were well established. Western scholars who believe that the Grail legend entered Europe through the Crusaders base this assumption only on the Syrian sources. Syria and Andalusia, however, were strongly linked. The transformation of "Q" into "G" (*Qarael Muqaddas* [Holy Recital] for *Garael Mugaddas*) is Hispano-Moorish, not Syrian. De Tassy notes that the *Roman de la Rose* has analogies with two Sufic streams of literature—that of the *Birds and the Flowers,* and above all with the *Parliament of the Birds* of Attar. The exact version which stimulated the versions of the *Roman* known in Europe is not, of course, available; and it is more than possible that the origin was a verbal one, passed on through Sufi teaching in the widespread Sufic circles of Spain.

The *Rose of Bakawali* romance in India contains much that throws light upon the Sufic usage of this most dynamic imagery. And the *Parliament* itself, apart from the fragmentary indications in Chaucer and elsewhere, was translated into French and published in Liége in 1653. It was also translated into Latin in 1678.

In the Order of Khidhr (who is St. George and also Khidr, the patron saint of the Sufis, the hidden guide, sometimes thought to be Elias), which exists to this day, passages from the *Mantiq ut-Tair* (Parliament of the Birds) of Attar are quoted. This is a part of the ceremonial of initiation:

The sea was asked why it was dressed in blue, the color of mourning, and why it became agitated as if fire made it boil. It answered that the blue robe spoke of the sadness of separation from the Beloved, "that it was the fire of Love which made it boil." Yellow, continues the recital, is the color of gold—the alchemy of the Perfected Man, who is refined until he is in a sense gold. The robe of initiation consists of the Sufi blue mantle, with a hood, and a yellow band. Together these two colors when mixed make green, the color of initiation and nature, truth and immortality. The *Mantiq* was written about one hundred and seventy years before the foundation of the mysterious Order of the Garter, which was originally known as the Order of St. George.

The Sufi Order which Attar is credited with having created, and probably developed, and which certainly carries the tradition of his concentrating, carries out exercises designed to produce and maintain the harmony of the participant with the whole of creation, and it closely resembles the other Orders of Sufism, the *tarikas*. The stages of development of a Sufi, while they may take a different sequence in different individuals, are portrayed in the *Parliament of the Birds*.

The birds, who represent humanity, are called together by the hoopoe, the Sufi, who proposes that they should start on a quest to find their mysterious King. He is called Simurgh, and he lives in the Mountains of Kaf. Each bird, after at first being excited by the prospect of having a King, begins to make excuses as to why he should not himself take part in the journey toward the hidden King. The hoopoe, after hearing the plea of each, replies with a tale which illustrates the uselessness of preferring what one has or might have to what one should have. The poem is full of the Sufi imagery, and has to be studied in detail in order to be properly understood. The Ring of Solomon, the nature of Khidr the hidden guide, anecdotes of the ancient sages, fill its pages.

Eventually the hoopoe tells the birds that in the quest they have to traverse seven valleys. First of all is the Valley of the Quest, where all kinds of perils threaten, and where the pilgrim must renounce desires. Then comes the Valley of Love, the limitless area in which the Seeker is completely consumed by a thirst for the Beloved. Love is followed by the Valley of Intuitive Knowledge, in which the heart receives directly the illumination of Truth and an experience of God. In the Valley of Detachment the traveler becomes liberated from desires and dependence.

In the interchange in which the hoopoe deals with the nightingale, Attar exposes the uselessness of ecstatics, mystics who follow romance for its own sake, who intoxicate themselves with yearnings, who indulge ecstatic experience, and are out of touch with human life.

The passionate nightingale came forward, beside himself with fervor. In each one of his thousand varying chirrupings he gave vent to a different mystery of meaning. He spoke so eloquently of mysteries that all the other birds fell silent.

"I know the secrets of love," he said. "Throughout the night I give my love call. I myself teach the secrets; and it is my song which is the lament of the mystic flute, and

which the lute wails. It is I who set the Rose in motion,
and move the hearts of lovers. Continuously I teach new
mysteries, each moment new notes of sadness, like the
waves of the sea. Whoever hears me loses his wits in rapture,
contrary to his normal way. When I am long bereft of my
love the Rose, I lament unceasingly. . . . And when the
Rose returns to the world in Summer, I open my heart to
joy. My secrets are not known to all—but the Rose
knows them. I think of nothing but the Rose; I wish nothing but the ruby Rose.

"To reach the Simurgh, that is beyond me—the love of
the Rose is enough for the nightingale. It is for me that
she flowers. . . . Can the nightingale live but one night
without the Beloved?"

The hoopoe cried, "O laggard, busy with the mere shape
of things! Leave off the pleasures of seductive form! The
love of the face of the Rose has merely driven thorns into
your heart. It is your master. However beautiful the Rose,
the beauty vanishes in a few days. Love for something so
perishable can only cause revulsion in the Perfected Man.
If the Rose's smile awakens your desire, it is only to hold you
ceaselessly in sorrow. It is she who laughs at you each Spring,
and she does not cry—leave the Rose and the redness."

Commenting upon this passage, one teacher remarks that
Attar refers not only to the ecstatic who does not take his
mysticism further than rapture. He also means the ecstatic's
parallel, the person who feels frequent and incomplete love,
and who, although deeply affected by it, is not regenerated
and altered by it to such an extent that his very being undergoes a change: "This is the fire of love which purifies, which
is different whenever it occurs, which sears the marrow and
makes incandescent the kernel. The ore separates from
the matrix, and the Perfected Man emerges, altered in such
a way that every aspect of his life is ennobled. He is not
changed in the sense of being different; but he is completed,
and this makes him considered powerful of men. Every
fiber has been purified, raised to a higher state, vibrates to

a higher tune, gives out a more direct, more penetrating note, attracts the affinity in man and woman, is loved more and hated more; partakes of a destiny, a portion, infinitely assured and recognized, indifferent to the things which affected him while he pursued the mere shadow of which this is the substance, however sublime that former experience may have been."

This teacher (Adil Alimi) warns that these sentiments will not appeal to all. They will be "disbelieved by the materialist; attacked by the theologian; ignored by the romantic; avoided by the shallow; rejected by the ecstatic; be welcomed but misunderstood by the theoretician and imitation Sufi." But, he continues, we must remember *qadam ba qadam* (step by step): "Before you can drink the fifth cup, you must have drunk the first four, each of them delicious."

He realizes that things, whether they be old or new, have no importance. Things that have been learned are of no value. The traveler is experiencing everything afresh. He understands the difference between traditionalism, for instance, and the reality of which it is a reflection.

The fifth valley is the Valley of Unification. Now the Seeker understands that what seemed to him to be different things and ideas are, in actuality, only one.

In the Valley of Astonishment, the traveler finds bewilderment and also love. He no longer understands knowledge in the same way as formerly. Something, which is called love, replaces it.

The seventh and last valley is that of Death. This is where the Seeker understands the mystery, the paradox, of how an individual "drop can be merged with an ocean, and still remain meaningful. He has found his 'place.'"

Fariduddin Attar's pen-name is Attar, the Chemist or Perfumer. While most historians assume that he adopted this descriptive word because his father had a pharmacy, the Sufi tradition is that "Attar" conceals an initiatory meaning. If we take the standard method of decoding by the Abjad system, known to almost every person literate in Arabic and

Persian, the letters can be substituted for the following figures:

A (yn)	=	70
Ta	=	9
Ta	=	9
Alif	=	1
Ra	=	200

The letters must be arranged in accordance with conventional Semitic orthography, as above. The *Hisab el-Jamal* (standard rearrangement of letters and numbers) is the simplest form of the use of the Abjad, used in very many poetic names. This rearrangement requires the totaling of the values of the letters (70 + 9 + 9 + 1 + 200), giving a total of 289. In order to provide a fresh "hidden" three-letter root, we have (again by standard procedure) to resplit the total, in order of hundreds, tens and units, thus:

$$289 = 200, 80, 9.$$

These three figures are recoded:

$$200 = R; 80 = F; 9 = T.$$

Now we look up in a dictionary the words which correspond with any arrangement of these three letters. In Arabic dictionaries, words are always listed in accordance with their basic (usually three-letter) roots, so this makes the task easy.

The three letters may be grouped only in the following ways: RFT, RTF, FRT, FTR, and TFR.

The only triliteral root which is concerned with religion, interior or initiatory meanings is the FTR root.

"Attar" is an encipherment of the concept of FTR, which is the message about his teaching that Fariduddin Attar is transmitting.

Attar was one of the greatest Sufi teachers. Before we look at the implications of the FTR root in Arabic, we can recapitulate his ideas. Sufism is a form of thinking clothed by Attar and his followers (including Rumi, his disciple) in a religious format. It is concerned with growth and the theme of the organic evolution of mankind. Its accomplishment is associated with the dawn after the dark, the breaking of bread after a fast, and intensive physical and mental action, unpremeditated because a response to intuitive impulses.

Does the root FTR contain (1) religious associations; (2) connections between Christianity and Islam—because the Sufis claim to be Moslems but also esoteric Christians; (3) the idea of speed or unpremeditated action; (4) humility; dervishism; (5) a strong impact (of ideas or movement, as applied in dervish schools for training Sufis); (6) "the grape"—Sufi poetic analogy for interior experience; (7) something which forces its way out of the bosom of nature?

Every one of these ideas is contained in the Arabic words derived from the FTR root, forming a mosaic of the Sufi existence. We may now examine the root and its use:

FaTaR   =   to cleave, to split a thing; to find out; to begin; to create a thing (God)

FuTR   =   a mushroom (that which forces its way upward by cleaving)

FaTaRa   =   to breakfast, to break a fast

TaFaTTaR   =   to split or crack

'IYD elFiTR   =   the Feast of the Breaking of the Fast

FiTRAT   =   natural disposition; religious feeling; the religion of Islam (submission to the divine will)

FaTIR   =   unleavened bread; unpremeditated or precipitate action; haste

FaTIRA   =   a small, flat cake, such as is used as a sacrament

FATiR   =   the Creator

FuTaiyRi   =   a worthless man, empty, blunt

FuTAR   =   a blunt thing, like a blunt sword

Attar is traditionally associated with having passed down the special Sufi exercise called "Halt!"—the Exercise of the Pause of Time. This takes place when the teacher, at a special time, calls for a complete freezing of movement by the students. During this "pause of time" he projects his *baraka* upon the people. Suddenly suspending all physical action is considered to leave the consciousness open to the receipt of special mental developments whose power is drained by muscular movement.

FTR, strangely enough, is in the Sufi word list, developed into QMM. This, again encoded by the same Abjad notation, produces the word QiFF—the Divine Pause. This "Pause" is the name given to the "Halt!" exercise, which is only carried out by a teaching master.

That the FTR root means, in a secondary sense, the mushroom, gives rise to an interesting speculation. Largely due to the initiative of Mr. R. Gordon Wasson, it has been determined that in ancient times there was (and still is in surprisingly many places) a widespread ecstatic cult based upon the eating of hallucinogenic mushrooms.

Is the FTR root connected with a mushroom cult? It is, in one sense, but not the sense which one would immediately assume. FTR is a mushroom, but not a hallucinogenic one. We have two sources for asserting this. In the first place, the Arabic word for a hallucinogenic fungus is from the root GHRB. Words derived from the GHRB root indicate a knowledge of the strange influence of hallucinogenic fungi, while the FTR words do not:

GHaRaBa = to go away, depart, have an eye tumor
GHaRaB = to forsake one's country, to live abroad
GHuRB[an] = the setting of a star; to be absent or remote
GHaRub = to be obscure, something not well understood, to become a stranger
GHaRaB = to go West

A-GHRaB   =   to do or say strange or immoderate
                     things; to laugh immoderately; to run
                     swiftly; to go far into the country
ISTa-GHRaB   =   to find a thing strange, extraordi-
                     nary; also, to laugh to excess
GHaRB   =   edge of a sword; tears; etc.
ESH el GHuRAB   =   toadstool (literally, "Bread of
                     the crow, of the intricate, of
                     the darkness, of the strange-
                     ness")

The second interesting evidence which indicates that the
Sufis used the FTR root to mean the interior experience
and not one which was induced by chemical means is contained in a passage from the works of the aptly named Mast
Qalandar (literally, "intoxicated dervish"), who undoubtedly comments upon a belief that hallucinogenic mushrooms
might provide a mystical experience, but claims that this is
incorrect.

First we can look at a literal rendering of the text:

"The Creator from the spreading of fervor and the
essence of religious feeling thus ordered the 'juice of
the grape' for the breakfasting of the Lovers (the Sufis),
and in the sacramental bread of the half understanders
he left a symbol. And this too learn and know, that the
Sufi illuminate is far from the crack and fissure of
deception which is distortion, and went near to that
other (initiatory) ecstatic feeling; and was far from
mushrooming and mushrooms of madness was far. And
the breakfasting was of the breakfast of truths on the
Way of uncrackedness. Finally after the spreading
(vine) and grape came and after that its juice made
wine, and supping (after abstinence), the Complete
Man was made fashioned strangely by the blunt scimi-
tar. But this bread is not from what they say, neither
from beneath the tree. Truly the Truth of Creation is
discovered and ecstasy may be solely known in this hid-

denness of the bread of the hungry and thirsty. His
drink is after his food. The Creator displays as the
Opener."

This remarkable passage has been considered to be the
ravings of a madman. Sheikh Mauji of the Azamia Sufis
interprets it in a page from his *Durud* (Recitals):

"There is a certain sensation which is true fervor and
which is associated with love. This stems from ancient
origins, and is necessary to mankind. Signs of it remain
in circles other than those of the Sufis, but now only
in symbolic form—as they have the Cross but we have
Jesus. The Seeker must remember that there are simili-
tudes of feeling which are illusory and which are like
madness, but not the madness which the Sufi means
when he talks of madness, as the author has used to
describe himself (Mast Qalandar). It is from this
source, the origin of what we call a wine, from a grape,
from a vine, the product of splitting and spreading, that
comes the true illumination. After a period of abstinence from wine or bread, the detachment from attachment, this force which is a form of Opening comes
about. This is the nutrient which is not a food in any
sense of being a known physical thing. . . ."

The original passage, which is in more or less literary
Persian, gives us the explanation of what it is that the "mad
dervish" is trying to do. It harps upon a single word-root:
and that root is FTR. No translation could possibly re-
create this poetic fact, because in translation the root cannot be maintained. In English, since the derivation of "split,"
"cake," "religious experience" and so on are from different
stems, we cannot maintain the almost eerie sense of carrying on one single sound.

This is an example: "Ya baradar, *Fatir* ast *tafattari fitrat*
wa dhati *fitrat*. . . ."

In the whole passage of one hundred and eleven words,

the word derived from the three-letter root FTR occurs no less than twenty-three times! And many of these usages of the words, though not incorrect, are so unusual (because there is so often a conventional word more apt in such a context) that there is absolutely no doubt that a message is being conveyed to the effect that chemical hallucinogens derived from fungi provide an undeniable but counterfeit experience.

Our Master Jalaluddin Rumi

He is enlightened whose speech and behavior accord, who
repudiates the ordinary connections of the world.

(Dhu'l-Nun, the Egyptian)

Maulana (literally, Our Master) Jalaluddin Rumi, who
founded the Order of the Whirling Dervishes, bears out in
his career the Eastern saying, "Giants come forth from Afghanistan and influence the world." He was born in Bac-
tria, of a noble family, at the beginning of the thirteenth
century. He lived and taught in Iconium (Rum) in Asia
Minor, before the beginning of the Ottoman Empire, whose
throne he is said to have refused. His works are written in
Persian, and so esteemed by the Persians for their poetic,
literary and mystical content that they are called "The
Koran in the Pehlevi tongue"—and this in spite of their
being opposed to the national cult of the Persians, the Shia
faith, criticizing its exclusivism.

Among the Arabs and the Indian and Pakistani Moslems, Rumi is considered to be one of the first rank of mystical masters—yet he states that the teachings of the Koran
are allegorical, and that it has seven different meanings. The
extent of Rumi's influence can hardly be calculated; though
it can be glimpsed occasionally in the literature and thought

of many schools. Even Doctor Johnson, best known for his unfavorable pronouncements, says of Rumi, "He makes plain to the Pilgrim the secrets of the Way of Unity, and unveils the Mysteries of the Path of Eternal Truth."

His work was well enough known within less than a hundred years of his death in 1273 for Chaucer to use references to it in some of his works, together with material from the teachings of Rumi's spiritual precursor, Attar the Chemist (1150–1229/30). From the numerous references to Arabian material which can be found in Chaucer, even a cursory examination shows a Sufi impact of the Rumi school of literature. Chaucer's use of the phrase, "As lions may take warning when a pup is punished . . ." is merely a close adaptation of *Udhrib el-kalba wa yata' addaba el-fahdu* ("Beat the dog and the lion will behave"), which is a secret phrase used by the Whirling Dervishes. Its interpretation depends on a play upon the words "dog" and "lion." Although written as such, in speaking the password, homophones are used. Instead of saying dog (*kalb*), the Sufi says heart (*qalb*), and in place of lion (*fahd*), *fuhid* (the neglectful). The phrase now becomes: "Beat the heart (Sufi exercises) and the neglectful (faculties) behave (correctly)."

This is the slogan which introduces the "beating the heart" movements encouraged by the motions and concentrations of the Mevlevi—Whirling—Dervishes.

The relationship between the *Canterbury Tales* as an allegory of inner development and the *Parliament of the Birds* of Attar is another interesting item. Professor Skeat reminds us that, like Attar, Chaucer has thirty participants in his pilgrimage. Thirty pilgrims seeking the mystical bird, the Simurgh makes sense in Persian, because *si-murgh* actually means "thirty birds."[1] In English, however, such a transposition is not possible. The number of pilgrims, made necessary in the Persian because of the requirements of

[1] See annotation "Simurgh."

rhyme, is preserved in Chaucer, deprived of double meaning. "The Pardoner's Tale" occurs in Attar; the pear-tree
story is found in Book IV of the Sufi work, the *Mathnawi*
of Rumi.

Rumi's influence, both in ideas and textually, is considerable in the West. Since most of his work has been translated into Western languages in more recent years, his impact has become greater. But if he is, as Professor Arberry
calls him, "surely the greatest mystical poet in the history
of mankind," the poetry itself in which so much of his teachings is couched can really only be appreciated in the original Persian. The teachings, however, and the methods
used by the Whirling Dervishes and other Rumi-influenced
schools, are not so elusive, providing that the way of putting esoteric truths is understood.

There are three documents by means of which Rumi's
work can be studied by the outside world. The *Mathnawi-i-
Manawi* (Spiritual Couplets) is Jalaluddin's masterwork—
six books of poetry and imagery of such power in the original that its recitation produces a strangely complex exaltation of the hearer's consciousness.

It was forty-three years in the writing. It cannot exactly
be criticized as poetry, because of the special intricacy of
ideas, form and presentation. Those who seek conventional
verse alone in it, as Professor Nicholson remarks, have to
skip. And then they lose the effect of what is in fact a special
art form, created by Rumi for the express purpose of conveying meanings which he himself concedes have no actual parallel in ordinary human experience. To ignore this
remarkable achievement is like selecting the taste without
the strawberry jam.

Nicholson, overstressing the role of the exquisite poetry in
the ocean of the *Mathnawi*, sometimes shows a preference
for formal verse.

"The *Mathnawi*," he says (Introduction, *Selections from
the Diwan of Shams of Tabriz*, p. xxxix), "contains a wealth
of delightful poetry. But its readers must pick their way

through apologues, dialogues, interpretations of Koranic texts, metaphysical subtleties and moral exhortations, ere all at once they chance upon a passage of pure and exquisite song."

To the Sufi, if not to anyone else, this book speaks from a different dimension, yet a dimension which is in a way within his deepest self.

Like all Sufi works, the *Mathnawi* will vary in its effect upon the listener in accordance with the conditions under which it is studied. It contains jokes, fables, conversations, references to former teachers and to ecstatogenic methods— a phenomenal example of the method of scatter, whereby a picture is built up by multiple impact to infuse into the mind the Sufi message.

This message, with Rumi as with all Sufi masters, is arranged partially in response to the environment in which he is working. He instituted dances and whirling movements among his disciples, it is related, because of the phlegmatic temperament of the people among whom he was cast. The so-called variation of doctrine or action prescribed by the various Sufi teachers is in reality nothing more than the application of this rule.

In his teaching system, Rumi used explanation and mental drill, thought and meditation, work and play, action and inaction. The body-mind movements of the Whirling Dervishes, coupled with the reed-pipe music to which they were performed, is the product of a special method designed to bring the Seeker into affinity with the mystical current, in order to be transformed by it. Everything which the unregenerate man understands has a use and a meaning within the special context of Sufism which may be invisible until it is experienced. "Prayer," says Rumi, "has a form, a sound and a physical reality. Everything which has a word, has a physical equivalent. And every thought has an action."

One of the really Sufic characteristics of Rumi is that, although he will uncompromisingly say the most unpopular thing—that the ordinary man, whatever his formal attainments, is immature in mysticism—he also gives the chance to almost anyone to attain progress toward the completion of human destiny.

Like many Sufis cast in a theological atmosphere, Rumi first addresses his hearers on the subject of religion. He stresses that the form in which ordinary, emotional religion is understood by organized bodies is incorrect. The Veil of Light, which is the barrier brought about by self-righteousness, is more dangerous than the Veil of Darkness, produced in the mind by vice. Understanding can come only through love, not by training by means of organizational methods.

For him, the earliest teachers of religions were right. Their successors, apart from a few, organized matters in such a way as virtually to exclude enlightenment. This attitude requires a new approach to the problems of religion. Rumi takes the whole question out of the normal channel. He is not prepared to submit dogma to study and argument. The real religion, he says, is other than people think it is. Therefore there is no virtue in examining dogma. In this world, he says, there is no equivalent to the things which are called the Throne (of God), the Book, Angels, the Day of Reckoning. Similes are used, and they are of necessity merely a rough idea of something else.

In the collection of his sayings and teachings called *In It What Is In It* (*Fihi Ma Fihi*), used as a textbook for Sufis, he goes even further. Mankind, he says, passes through three stages. In the first one, he worships anything—man, woman, money, children, earth and stones. Then, when he has progressed a little further, he worships God. Finally, he does not say, "I worship God," nor "I do not worship God." He has passed into the last stage.

In order to approach the Sufi Way, the Seeker must realize that he is, largely, a bundle of what are nowadays called conditionings—fixed ideas and prejudices, automatic responses sometimes which have occurred through the training of others. Man is not as free as he thinks he is. The first step is for the individual to get away from thinking that he understands, and really understand. But man has been taught that he can understand everything by the same process, the process of logic. This teaching has undermined him.

"If you follow the ways in which you have been trained, which you may have inherited, for no other reason than this, you are illogical."

The understanding of religion, and what the great religious figures taught, is a part of Sufism. Sufism uses the terminology of ordinary religion, but in a special manner which has always excited the anger of the nominally devout. To the Sufi, generally speaking, each religious teacher symbolizes, in his creed and especially in his life, an aspect of the way whose totality is Sufism. Jesus is within you, says Rumi; seek his aid. And then, do not seek from within yourself, from your Moses, the needs of a Pharaoh.

The way in which the different religious paths are symbolized for the Sufi is stated by Rumi when he says that the path of Jesus was struggling with solitude and overcoming lustfulness. The path of Mohammed was to live within the community of ordinary humanity. "Go by the way of Mohammed," he says, "but if you cannot, then go by the Christian way." Rumi here is not by any means inviting his hearers to embrace one or other of these religions. He is pointing to the ways in which the Seeker can find fulfillment; but fulfillment through the Sufic understanding of what the paths of Jesus and Mohammed were.

Similarly, when the Sufi speaks of God, he does not mean the deity in the sense in which it is understood by the man who has been trained by the theologian. This deity is accepted by some, the pious; rejected by others, the atheists. But it is a rejection or acceptance of something which has been presented by the scholastics and priesthood. The God of the Sufis is not involved in this controversy; because divinity is a matter of personal experience to the Sufi.

All this does not mean that the Sufi is trying to take away the exercise of the reasoning faculty. Rumi explains that reason is essential; but it has a place. If you want to have

clothes made you visit a tailor. Reason tells you which tailor
to choose. After that, however, reason is in suspense. You
have to repose complete trust—faith—in your tailor that he
will complete the work correctly. Logic, says the master,
takes the patient to the doctor. After that, he is completely
in the hands of the physician.

But the well-trained materialist, although he claims that
he wants to hear what the mystic has to tell him, cannot be
told the whole truth. He would not believe it. The truth is
not based upon materialism any more than upon logic. Hence
the mystic is working on a series of different planes, the
materialist on only one. The result of their contact would
be that the Sufi will even appear inconsistent to the materialist. If he says today something which he said differently
yesterday, he will appear to be a liar. At the very least, the
situation of being at cross-purposes will destroy any chance
of progress in mutual understanding.

"Those who do not understand a thing," Rumi observes,
"claim that it is useless. The hand and the instrument are
as flint and steel. Strike flint with earth. Will a spark be
made?" One of the reasons why the mystic does not preach
publicly is that the conditioned religious man, or the materialist, will not understand him:

A king's hawk settled upon a ruin inhabited by owls.
They decided that he had come to drive them out of their
home and take possession of it himself. "This ruin may seem
a prosperous place to you. To me, the better place is upon
the arm of the King," said the hawk. Some of the owls cried,
"Do not believe him. He is using guile to steal our home."

The use of fables and illustrations like this one is very
widespread among the Sufis; and Rumi is the master fabulist
of their number.

The same thought is often given by the master in many
different forms, in order to make it penetrate the mind.
Sufis says that an idea will enter the conditioned (veiled)
mind only if it is so phrased as to be able to bypass the
screen of conditionings. The fact that the non-Sufi has so

little in common with the Sufi means that the Sufis have to
use the basic elements which exist in every human being,
and which are not entirely killed by any form of conditioning. And these elements are precisely those which under-
lie the Sufi development. Of these the first and permanent
one is love. Love is the factor which is to carry a man, and
all humanity, to fulfillment:

"Mankind has an unfulfillment, a desire, and he struggles to fulfill it through all kinds of enterprises and ambi-
tions. But it is only in love that he can find fulfillment."

But love is itself a serious matter; it is something which
keeps pace with enlightenment. Both increase together. The
full potential fire of illumination is too powerful to be endured all at once:

"The heat of a furnace may be too great for you to take
advantage of its warming effect; while the weaker flame of a
lamp may give you the heat which you need."

Everyone, when he gets to a certain stage of mere personal
sophistication, thinks that he can find the way to enlightenment by himself. This is denied by Sufis, for they ask how a
person can find something when he does not know what it
is. "Everyone has become a gold seeker," says Rumi, "but the
ordinary do not know it when they see it. If you cannot
recognize it, join a wise man."

The ordinary man, thinking that he is on the path of enlightenment, often sees only a reflection of it. Light may be
reflected upon a wall; the wall is the host to the light. "Do
not attach yourself to the brick of the wall, but seek the eternal original."

"Water needs an intermediary, a vessel, between it and
the fire, if it is to be heated correctly."

How is the Seeker to set about his task of getting on the
right path? In the first place, he should not abandon work
and living in the world. Do not give up working, instructs
Rumi; indeed, "the treasure which you seek derives from it."
This is one reason why all Sufis must have a constructive
vocation. Work, though, is not only ordinary labor or even

socially acceptable creativity. It includes self-work, the
alchemy whereby man becomes perfected: "Wool, through
the presence of a man of knowledge, becomes a carpet. Earth
becomes a palace. The presence of a spiritual man creates a
similar transformation."

The man of wisdom is initially the guide of the Seeker.
As soon as possible this teacher dismisses the disciple, who
becomes his own man of wisdom, and then he continues
his self-work. False masters in Sufism, as everywhere else,
have not been few. So the Sufis are left with the strange
situation that whereas the false teacher may appear to be
genuine (because he takes pains to appear what the disciple
wants him to be), the true Sufi is often not like what the un-
discriminating and untrained Seeker thinks a Sufi should be
like.

Rumi warns: "Judge not the Sufi to be that which you
can see of him, my friend. How long, like a child, will you
prefer only nuts and raisins?"

The false teacher will pay great attention to appearance,
and will know how to make the Seeker think that he is a
great man, that he understands him, that he has great secrets
to reveal. The Sufi has secrets, but he must make them
develop within the disciple. Sufism is something which happens to a person, not something which is given to him. The
false teacher will keep his followers around him all the time,
will not tell them that they are being given a training which
must end as soon as possible, so that they may taste their
development themselves and carry on as fulfilled people.

Rumi calls upon the scholastic, the theologian, and the
follower of the false teacher: "When will you cease to worship and to love the pitcher? When will you begin to look
for the water?" Externals are the things which people usually
judge by. "Know the difference between the color of the
wine and the color of the glass."

The Sufi must follow all the routines of self-development;
otherwise mere concentration upon one will cause an im-
balance, leading to loss. The speed of development of dif-

ferent people varies. Some, says Rumi, understand all from
reading a line. Others, who have actually been present at
an event, know all about it. The capacity for understanding
develops with the spiritual progress of the individual.

The meditations of Rumi include some remarkable ideas,
designed to bring the Seeker into an understanding of the
fact that he is temporarily out of contact with complete
reality, even though ordinary life seems to be the totality of
reality itself. What we see, feel and experience in ordinary,
unfulfilled life, according to Sufic thinking, is only a part
of the great whole. There are dimensions which we can
reach only through effort. Like the submerged portion of
the iceberg, they are there, though unperceived under ordinary conditions. Also like the iceberg, they are far greater
than could be suspected by superficial study.

Rumi uses several analogies to explain this. One of the
most striking is his theory of action. There is, he says, such
a thing as comprehensive action, and there is also individual
action. We are accustomed to seeing, in the ordinary world
of sense, only individual action. Supposing a number of
people are making a tent. Some sew, others prepare the
ropes, some again weave. They are all taking part in a
comprehensive action, although each is absorbed in his individual action. If we are thinking about the making of
the tent, it is the comprehensive action of the whole group
which is important.

In certain directions, the Sufi says, life must be looked
upon as a whole, as well as individually. This getting into
tune with the whole plan, the comprehensive action of life,
is essential to enlightenment.

Little by little, as his experiences increase, the Sufi begins
to reshape his thinking along these lines. Before he had
actual experience of mysticism, he was either a scoffer, un-
committed, or had a completely illusory idea of the nature
of the experience, and especially of the teacher and the
path. Rumi gives him meditations designed to overcome the
overdevelopment of certain ideas which are current among

the uninstructed. Man expects to be given a golden key. But some are faster than others in developing. A man traveling through the darkness is yet traveling. The disciple is learning when he does not know that he is learning, and as a result he may well chafe. In winter, Rumi reminds him, a tree is collecting nutriment. People may think that it is idle, because they do not see anything happening. But in spring they see the buds. Now, they think, it is working. There is a time for collecting, and a time for releasing. This brings the subject back to the teaching: "Enlightenment must come little by little—otherwise it would overwhelm."

The tools of scholasticism, used sparingly by Sufis, are being replaced by esoteric training, and this has to be done in accordance with the capacities of the student. The tools of the goldsmith, our teacher remarks, in the hands of the cobbler are like seeds sown in sand. And the cobbler's tools in the farmer's hand are like straw offered to a dog, or bones to a donkey.

The attitude toward ordinary conventions of life undergoes an examination. The question of humanity's inner yearnings is seen, not as a Freudian need, but as a natural instrument inherent in the mind in order to enable it to attain to truth. People, Rumi teaches, do not really know what they want. Their inner yearning is expressed in a hundred desires which they think are their needs. These are not their real desires, as experience shows. For when these objectives are attained, the yearning is not stilled. Rumi would have seen Freud as someone who was obsessed by one of the secondary manifestations of the great yearning; not as someone who had discovered the basis of the yearning.

Again, people may appear evil in one's eyes—and yet to another individual they may seem fair. This is because in the one mind there is the idea of unpleasantness, in the other, the concept of goodness. "The fish and the hook are both present together."

The Sufi is learning the power of detachment, to be followed by the power of experiencing what he is considering, not just looking at it. In order to do this, he is instructed by the teacher to meditate upon Rumi's theme: "The satiated man and the hungry one do not see the same thing when they look upon a loaf of bread."

If a person is so untrained that he is influenced by his own bias, he cannot hope to make much progress. Rumi concentrates upon developing control; control through experience, not through mere theory as to what is good or bad, right or wrong. This belongs to the category of words: "Words, in themselves, are of no importance. You treat a visitor well, and speak a few kind words to him. He is happy. But if you treat another man to a few words of abuse, he will be hurt. Can a few words really *mean* happiness or sadness? These are secondary factors, and not real ones. They affect people who are weak."

The Sufi learner is developing through his exercises a new way of seeing things. He is also acting, reacting, differently in a given situation than he otherwise would. He understands the deeper meaning of such recommendations as this: "Take the pearl, not the shell. You will not find a pearl in every shell. A mountain is many times larger than a ruby." What seems almost trite to the ordinary man, perhaps passed on as a wise saw, becomes intensely meaningful to the Sufi, who finds in its depths contact with something that he calls "other"—the underlying factor which he is seeking. What may appear a stone to the ordinary man, continues Jalaluddin, further developing his theme, is a pearl to the Knower.

Now the elusiveness of spiritual experience is glimpsed by the Seeker. If he is a creative worker, he enters the stage when inspiration enters him sometimes, but not at other times. If he is subject to ecstatic experience, he will find that the joyous meaningful sense of completeness comes transitorily, and that he cannot control it. The secret protects itself: "Concentrate upon spirituality as you will—it

will shun you if you are unworthy. Write about it, boast of it, comment upon it—it will decline to benefit you; it will flee. But, if it sees your concentration, it may come to your hand, like a trained bird. Like the peacock, it will not sit in an unworthy place."

It is only when he is beyond this stage of development that the Sufi can communicate anything of the path to others. If he tries to do so before, "it will flee."

Here, too, the need for a delicate balance between extremes is essential, or the whole effort may be in vain. The net which is your mind, observes Rumi, is delicate. It has to be so adjusted as to catch its catch. If there is unhappiness, the net is torn. If it is torn, it will not be of use. By too great love and too great opposition alike, the net becomes torn. "Practice neither."

The five inner senses begin to function as the inner life of the individual is awakened. The food which is not a palpable food, spoken of by Rumi, starts to exercise a nutritious effect. The inner senses resemble in a way the physical ones, but "they are to them as copper to gold."

As individuals all vary in their capacities, the Sufis at this stage are developed in some ways and not in others. It is usual for a number of inner faculties and special abilities to develop concurrently and harmoniously. Changes in mood may occur, but they are not at all like the changes in mood which undeveloped people feel. Mood becomes a part of real personality, and the crudeness of ordinary moods is replaced by the alternation and interaction of higher moods, of which the lower ones are considered to be reflections.

The Sufi's conception of wisdom and ignorance undergoes a change. Rumi puts it like this: "If a man were entirely wise, and had no ignorance, he would be destroyed by it. Therefore ignorance is laudable, because it means continued existence. Ignorance is the collaborator of wisdom, in this sense of alternation, as night and day complement one another."

The working together of opposite things is another significant theme of Sufism. When apparent opposites are reconciled, the individuality is not only complete, it also transcends the bounds of ordinary humanity as we understand them. The individual becomes, as near as we can state it, immensely powerful. What this means, and how it takes place, are matters of personal experience outside the realm of mere writing. Rumi reminds us in another place, talking of the written words: "The book of the Sufis is not the darkness of letters. It is the whiteness of a pure heart."

Now the Sufi attains some of the insights which are associated with the developing of an infallible intuition. His feeling for knowledge is such that he can, by reading a book, often sift the fact from the fiction, the real intention of the author from other elements. Especially threatened by this faculty are the imitators, who claim to be Sufis, and whom he is able to see through. Yet his sense of balance shows him how far the imitator may be of value in the cause of Sufism. Rumi comments upon this function in the *Mathnawi*, and this teaching is faithfully passed on by Sufi teachers when they find that the student has reached this stage: "The imitator is like a canal. It does not itself drink, but may transit water to the thirsty."

As he progresses on the path, the Sufi realizes how immensely complex and even perilous it is, unless carried out in accordance with the method which has been developed through the ages. Using a fable, the *Mathnawi* records this stage of the experiences. A lion entered a stable, ate an ox which he found there, and sat in its place. The stable was dark, and the ox's owner entered and felt around for his animal. His hands passed over the lion's body. The lion said, "If there were any light, he would die of fright. He strokes me thus only because he takes me for an ox." Read as an ordinary story, this vivid sketch might be passed over as just a version of fools rushing in where angels fear to tread.

The understanding of true meanings behind inexplicable worldly happenings is another consequence of Sufi development. Why, for instance, does a certain phase in mystical study take one person longer than another, even if he is carrying out roughly the same routines? Rumi illustrates the experiencing of a special dimension in life which veils the complete workings of actuality, giving us an unsatisfactory view of the whole. Two beggars, he says, came to the door of a house. One was immediately satisfied, and given a piece of bread. He went away. The second was kept waiting for his morsel. Why? The first beggar was not greatly liked; he was given stale bread. The second was made to wait until a fresh loaf was baked for him. This story illustrates a theme which recurs frequently in Sufic teaching—that there is often one element in a happening which we do not know. Yet we base our opinions upon material which is incomplete. Small wonder that the uninitiated develops and passes on a "squint" which is self-perpetuating.

"You belong," sings Rumi in one verse, "to the world of dimension. But you come from nondimension. Close the first 'shop,' open the second."

All life and all creation is seen in a new and comprehensive form. The worker, to use the imagery of the *Mathnawi*, is "hidden in the workshop," hidden by the work, which has, as it were, spun a web over him. The workshop is the place of vision. Outside it is the place of darkness.

The Sufi's position as one with greater insight into matters of the world and of the whole, as opposed to the part, gives him a tremendous potentiality for power. But he can exercise this only in association with the rest of creation —first with the other Sufis, then with mankind, finally with all creation. His powers and his very being are linked with a new set of relationships. People come to him, and he realizes that even those who scoff have quite possibly come to learn rather than to score a point over him. He regards a great number of happenings as a sort of question and answer. A visit to a sage he considers to be the approach, "Teach me." Hunger may be a questing, a question: Send food." Abstinence from food is an answer, a negative one.

And, as Rumi concludes this passage, the answer to the existence of a fool is silence.

He is able to pass on a part of his mystical experience to certain others, some of the disciples who come to him, and who are adapted by their past experiences for such a development. This is sometimes done by mutual concentration exercises (*tajalli*), and its practice may develop into the true mystical experience. "At first," Rumi told his disciples, "enlightenment comes to you from the Adepts. This is imitation. But when it comes frequently, it is the experience of truth." A Sufi may often, during many of the stages of the search, seem to be unheeding of the feelings of others, or otherwise out of step with society. When this is so, it is because he has glimpsed the true character of a situation behind the apparent situation visible only partially to others. He acts in the best possible way, though he does not always know why he has said or done a thing.

Jalaluddin, in *Fihi Ma Fihi*, gives an illustration of just such a situation. A drunken man saw a King pass by with a highly prized horse. He called out some uncomplimentary remark about the horse. The King was angry, and summoned him to his presence later. "At that time," explained the man, "a drunkard was standing on that roof. I am not him, for he is gone." The King was pleased with the reply, and rewarded him. The drunk is the Sufi, just as is the sobered man. The Sufi, in his state of association with true reality, acted in a certain way. As a result he was rewarded. He had also performed a function in explaining to the King that people are not always responsible for their actions. He had, too, given the King a chance to perform a good action.

No ripe grape becomes unripe again, and human evolution cannot be stopped. It can be directed, however; and it can also be interfered with by those who do not know what true intuition is. Thus the teachings of the Sufis can become distorted; thus, too, can the Adept be treated if he allows himself to be seen too openly by the profane. As for actually preaching Sufic things to those without, Rumi, like other

Sufi teachers, is prepared always to make a general invitation:

> While the inner lamp of jewels is still alight,
> hasten to trim its wick and provide it with oil.

But he is in accord with the teachers who refuse to discuss the cult with all and sundry: "Summon horses to a place other than where grass is to be found; and they will question it"—no matter what it is.

The Sufis oppose the pure intellectuals and scholastic philosophers partly because they believe that such training of the mind in obsessive and one-track thinking is bad for that mind and for all other minds as well. Equally, those who think that all that matters is intuition or asceticism are strongly combated by Sufic teaching. Rumi insists upon the balance of all the faculties.

The union of mind and intuition which brings about illumination and the development which the Sufis seek is based upon love, always love—this insistent theme of Rumi is nowhere better expressed than in his writings, unless it be within the actual walls of a Sufi school. Just as intellectualism works with palpable materials, Sufism works with both perceptible and inner ones. Where science and scholasticism ever narrow their scope to take in smaller and smaller areas of study, Sufism continues to embrace every evidence of the great underlying truth, wherever it may be found.

This power of assimilation and ability to invoke symbolism, story and thought from the underground Sufic current has caused the outward commentators (even in the East) great excitement and new pastimes. They track down the origins of a story in India, an idea in Greece, an exercise among shamans. These elements they bear back delightedly to their desks, eventually to provide ammunition in the struggle in which their opponents are only each other. The unique atmosphere of Sufi schools is found in the *Math-*

nawi and *Fihi Ma Fihi.* But many externalists consider
that they are confusing, chaotic and loosely written.

True, both books are partially guides which have to be
used in conjunction with actual Sufic teaching and practice—work, thought, life and art. But even one commentator
who accepted the reality of this atmosphere as deliberately
created, and who repeated the Sufi account of this in print,
showed himself in personal contact to be rather bewildered
by the whole thing. Still, it must be said that he considered
himself to be a Sufi, although not admitted by any Sufic
method. Under the influence of such men, the Western
study of Sufism, now in a period of tremendous upsurge,
has become a little more Sufic, although it still has a very
long way to go. The "intellectual Sufi" is the latest fad in
the West.

Sufism, of course, has a technical terminology all its own,
and Rumi's verses teem with familiar and special varieties
of initiatory terms. He describes, for instance, in his third
great book, *The Diwan of Shams of Tabriz,* some of the
concepts of mind and activities which are projected within
a secret meeting of dervishes. Couched in rhapsodic verse,
the teachings of Sufi being "in thought and action" are
conveyed by a method especially devised for their projection:

Join the community, be like them, so see the joy of real
life. Go along the ruined street, and see the distraught (owners of the "ruined houses"). Drink the
cup of feeling, so that you do not feel shame (self-
consciousness). Shut both the eyes of the head, so
that you may see with the inner eye. Open the two
arms of your self, if you seek an embrace. Shatter the
earthen idol in order to see the face of idols. Why accept so great a dowry for a feeble hag—and for three
loaves why do you accept military servitude?
The Friend returns at night; tonight do not take a
draught—shut your mouth against food, that you gain

the food of the mouth. In the assembly of the kindly
Cupbearer, circle yourself—come into the Circle. How
long will you circle (around it)? Here is an offer—
leave one life, gain the Shepherd's kindliness. . . .
Cease thought except for the creator of thought—
thought for "life" is better than thought of bread. In
the amplitude of God's earth, why have you fallen
asleep in a prison? Abandon complicated thoughts—in
order to see the concealed answer. Be silent of speech,
to attain enduring speech. Pass "life" and "world," in
order to see the Life of the World.

Although the actuality of Sufi being cannot be assayed
by the more limited criteria of discursive thought, this poem
can be seen as an assembling of the salient factors in the
Rumi method. He stipulates a community, dedicated to perceiving reality, of which apparent reality is only a substitute. This cognition comes through contact with others, by
being engaged in group activity, as well as in personal
activity and thought. What actually is fundamental comes
only when certain patterns of thinking have been reduced
to their correct perspective. The Seeker must "open his
arms" to an embrace, not expect to be given anything while
he stands passively awaiting it. The "feeble hag" is the whole
array of mundane experiences, which are reflections of an
ultimate reality that bears hardly any comparison with what
seems to be truth. For the "three loaves" of ordinary life,
people sell their potentiality.

The Friend comes at night—comes, that is, when things
are still, and when the individual is not drugged by automatic thinking. The food which is a special nutrition of
the Sufi is not the same as the ordinary food; but it is an essential part of the human intake. Humanity is circling
around reality, in a system which is not the real system. It
must enter the circle instead of following its perimeter. The
relationship of the real awareness to what we consider to be
awareness is as of a hundred lives to one life. Certain

characteristics of life as we know it—the predatory and self-
ish ones, the many others which are barriers to progress—
must be outbalanced by benign factors.

Thought, not pattern-thinking, is the method. Thought
must be for all life, not for small aspects of it. Man is like
someone who has the choice of traversing the earth, but
has fallen asleep in a prison. The complications of mis-
placed intellectualism hide the truth. Silence is a prelude
to speech, real speech. The inner life of the world is gained
by ignoring the fragmentation implied by "life" and "world."

When Rumi died in 1273 he left his son Bahaudin to
carry on the generalship of the Mevlevi Order. Surrounded
in life by people of every creed, his funeral was attended by
people of every description.

A Christian was asked why he wept so bitterly at the
death of a Moslem teacher. His reply shows the Sufi idea of
recurrence of teaching and of the transmission of spiritual
activity:

"We esteem him as the Moses, the David, the Jesus of
the age. We are all his followers and his disciples."

The life of Rumi shows the mixture of transmitted lore
and personal illumination which is central to Sufism. His
family was descended from Abu Bakr, the Companion of
Mohammed, and his father was related to King Khwarizm
Shah. Jalaluddin was born in Balkh, a center of ancient
teaching, in the year 1207, and it is claimed in Sufi legend
that it was foretold by Sufi mystics that a great future would
be his. The King of Balkh, under the influence of powerful
scholastics, turned against the Sufis, and especially against
his kinsman, our Rumi's father. One Sufi master was
drowned in the Oxus by order of the Shah. This persecution foreshadowed the invasion of the Mongols, in which
Najmuddin (the Greatest), the Sufi leader, was killed on
the battlefield. It is this master who founded the Kubravi
Order, which is closely connected with the development of
Rumi.

The virtual destruction of Central Asia by Jenghiz Khan's

forces caused the dispersal of the Turkestan Sufis. Rumi's
father fled with his young son to Nishapur, where they met
another great teacher of the same Sufi stream, the poet Attar, who blessed the child and "spiritualized" him with the
Sufi *baraka*. He presented to the boy a copy of his *Asrar-
nama* (Book of Secrets), written in verse.

Sufi tradition has it that since the spiritual potential of
the young Jalaluddin had been recognized by the contemporary masters, their concern for his protection and development became the motive for the travels of the refugee party.
They left Nishapur with the saintly Attar's words in their
ears: "This boy will spark the fire of divine exaltation for
the world." The city was not safe. Attar, like Najmuddin,
awaited his turn for a martyr's grave, which he gained at
the hands of the Mongols not long afterward.

The Sufi group with their fledgling leader reached Baghdad, where they heard of the utter destruction of Balkh and
the slaughter of its inhabitants. For some years they wandered, performing the pilgrimage to Mecca, returning
northward to Syria and Asia Minor, visiting Sufi centers.

Central Asia was falling apart under the relentless blows
of the Mongols, and Islamic civilization, after less than six
hundred years of life, seemed about to be snuffed out.

Rumi's father ultimately made his headquarters not far
from Konia, which is associated with the name of St. Paul.
The city was at this time in the hands of the Seljuk mon-
archs, and the King invited Jalaluddin to settle there. He
accepted a professorial post, and continued instructing his
son in the Sufi mysteries.

Jalaluddin also came into contact with the Greatest
Master, the poet and teacher Ibn El-Arabi of Spain, who
was in Baghdad about this time. The contact was established
through Burhanudin, one of Rumi's teachers, who had made
his way to the Seljuk regions to find Rumi's father recently
dead. Replacing him as Rumi's mentor, he took him to
Aleppo and Damascus.

It was when he was nearly forty that Rumi started his

semipublic mystical teachings.[2] The mysterious dervish "Sun of the Faith of Tabriz" inspired him to produce a great deal of his finest poetry, and to couch his teachings in a manner and form they were to retain throughout the life of the Mevlevi Order. His work done, the dervish vanished after about three years, and no further trace of him was ever reported.

This "emissary from the unknown world" has been equated by Rumi's son with the mysterious Khidr, the guide and patron of the Sufis, who appears and then passes out of normal cognition after transmitting his message.

It was during this time that Rumi became a poet. For him, although acknowledgedly one of the greatest poets of Persia, poetry was only a secondary product. He did not regard it as any more than a reflection of the enormous inner reality which was truth, and which he calls love. The greatest love, as he says, is silent and cannot be expressed in words. Although his poetry was to affect men's minds in a way that can only be called magical, he was never carried away by it to the extent of identifying it with the far greater being of which it was a lesser expression. At the same time, he recognized it as something which could form a bridge between what he "really felt" and what he could do for others.

Adopting the Sufic methods of getting a thing into perspective, even at the risk of demolishing the fondest ideas, he himself assumes the role of critic of poetry. People come to him, he says, and he loves them. In order to give them something to understand, he gives them poetry. But poetry is for them, not for him, however great a poet he may be— "What, after all, is my concern with poetry?" In order to hammer home the message, as only a poet with the greatest contemporary reputation could dare to do, he states categorically that in comparison with the true reality, he has no

[2] His pen-name, Rumi, was chosen because the letters total by substitution 256, which is again transcribed by substitution into the three letters NUR. *Nur* is the Persian and Arabic word for "light."

time for poetry. This is the only nutrition, he says, that his visitors can accept, "so like a good host he provides it."

The Sufi must never allow anything to stand as a barrier between what he is teaching and those who are learning it. Hence Rumi's insistence upon the subsidiary role of poetry in the perspective of the real quest. What he had to communicate was beyond poetry. To a mind conditioned to the belief that there is nothing more sublime than poetic expression, such a feeling might produce a sense of shock. It is just this application of impact which is necessary to the Sufi cause, in the freeing of the mind from attachment to secondary phenomena, "idols."

Rumi, the inheritor of his father's chair, now projected his mystical teachings through artistic channels. Music, dancing and poetry were cultivated and used in the dervish meetings. Alternating with these were certain mental and physical exercises designed to open the mind to the recognition of its greater potential, through the theme of harmony. Harmonious development, through the medium of harmony, might be a description of what Rumi was practicing.

Studying such of his teachings as they can from the outside, many foreign observers have been bewildered by Rumi. One refers to his "very unoriental view that woman is not a mere plaything, but a ray of deity "

One poem of Rumi's, published in *The Diwan of Shams of Tabriz*, has caused a certain amount of confusion to the literalists. It appears to refer to Rumi's examination of all forms of current religion, old and new, and his conclusion that the essential truth lay in the inner consciousness of man himself, not in external organizations. This is true if we realize that, according to Sufi belief, the "examining" of these creeds is done in a special way. The Sufi does not necessarily literally travel from one country to another, seeking religions to study and taking what he can from them. Neither does he read books of theology and exegesis, in order to compare one with the other. His "journey" and his "examination" of other ideas takes place within himself. This is because the Sufi believes that, like anyone experienced in anything else, he has an inner sense against which he can measure the reality of religious systems. To be more specific, it would appear nonsensically cumbersome to approach a metaphysical subject by ordinary research methods. Anyone who said to him, "Have you read the book on such and such by so-and-so?" would be using the wrong approach. It is not the book, nor the author, but the reality of what that book and that man signify, which are important to the Sufi. In order to make his assessment of a person or his teachings, the Sufi needs only a sample. But this sample has to be accurate. He must, in other words, be placed into rapport with the essential factor in the teaching in question. A disciple, for instance, who does not thoroughly understand the system which he is following cannot convey enough of that system to the Sufi to enable an assessment to be made.

This is the poem in which Rumi speaks of the attaining of the rapport with the various faiths, and his reaction to them:

Cross and Christians, end to end, I examined. He was not on the Cross. I went to the Hindu temple, to the ancient pagoda. In neither was there any sign. To the heights of Herat I went, and Kandahar. I looked. He was not on height or lowland. Resolutely, I went to the top of the Mountain of Kaf. There only was the place of the 'Anqa bird. I went to the Kaaba. He was not there. I asked of his state from Ibn Sina: he was beyond the limits of the philosopher Avicenna. . . . I looked into my own heart. In that his place I saw him. He was in no other place. . . .

This "he" (which, in the original, could be either he, she or it) is the true reality. The Sufi is eternal, and his use of words like "drunkenness" or "grape" or "heart" is necessary but ultimately so approximate as to appear a travesty. As Rumi puts it:

Before garden, vine or grape were in the world
Our soul was drunken with immortal wine.

The Sufi may be compelled to use similes drawn from the familiar world at an early stage of transmission, but Rumi follows the standard Sufi formula very strictly. The crutches must be removed if the patient is to be able to walk by himself. The value of Rumi's mode of expression for the student is the fact that he makes this much more plain than most material available outside of Sufi schools. If certain external Orders have fallen into the habit of literally conditioning their followers to repetitious stimuli, marking time at a certain stage of development, retaining the attachment of the disciples to the "crutches," it is no fault of Jalaluddin Rumi.

Ibn El-Arabi: The Greatest Sheikh

> To the sinful and vicious, I
> may appear to be evil. But to
> the good—beneficent am I.
> (Mirza Khan, Ansari)

One of the most profound metaphysical influences upon
both the Moslem and Christian worlds is Ibn El-Arabi the
Sufi, called in Arabic "the Greatest Master." He was a
descendant of Hatim El-Tai, still famous among the Arabs
as the most generous man who ever lived and mentioned
in FitzGerald's *Rubaiyat*—"Let Hatim Tai cry 'Supper!':
Heed him not!"

Spain had been an Arab country for more than four hundred years when Ibn El-Arabi the Murcian was born in
1164. Among his names is "the Andalusian," and he was
undoubtedly one of the greatest Spaniards who ever lived.
It is commonly believed that there is no greater love poetry
than his; nor was there ever a Sufi who so profoundly impressed the orthodox theologians with the interior meaning
of his life and work.

His Sufi background, according to biographers, was that
his father was in contact with the great Abdul-Qadir
Jilani,[1] Sultan of the Friends (1077–1166). Ibn El-Arabi

[1] See annotation "Jilani."

himself is said to have been born as a result of the spiritual influence of Abdul-Qadir, who predicted that he would be a person of outstanding gifts.

His father was determined to give him the best possible education, something which was offered in Moorish Spain at the time to a degree almost unparalleled elsewhere. He went to Lisbon, where he studied law and Islamic theology. Next, while still a boy, he went on to Seville, where he learned the Koran and the traditions under the greatest scholars of the time. At Córdoba he attended the classes of the great Sheikh El-Sharrat, and distinguished himself in jurisprudence.

During this period, Ibn El-Arabi showed qualities of intellect far beyond those which distinguished his contemporaries, even though they were drawn from the scholastic elite in whose families such intellectual capacity was proverbial in the middle ages. During his adolescence, in spite of the severe discipline of the academic schools, he spent his free time almost entirely with the Sufis, and began to write poetry.

He lived in Seville for three decades, his poetry and eloquence winning for him a place second to none in the highly cultivated atmosphere of Spain, as well as in Morocco, which was itself a center of cultural life.

In some ways Ibn El-Arabi resembled El-Ghazali (1058–1111). Like him, he came from a Sufi family, and was to influence Western thought. Again like him, he was pre-eminent in Islamic lore. But whereas Ghazali first mastered Islamic scholasticism, found it insufficient, and then turned to Sufism at the height of his greatness, Ibn El-Arabi maintained, through associations and poetry, a continuous contact with the Sufic stream. Ghazali reconciled Sufism with Islam, making the scholastics understand that it was not a heresy, but an inner meaning of religion. Ibn El-Arabi's mission was to create Sufi literature and cause it to be studied in order that people might thus enter into the spirit of Sufism—discover the Sufis through their being and expression, whatever their cultural background might be.

How this process worked is exemplified in a comment by the distinguished Professor R. A. Nicholson, who translated El-Arabi's *Interpreter of Desires*:

> Some of the poems, it is true, are not distinguishable from ordinary love songs, and as regards a great portion of the text, the attitude of the author's contemporaries, who refused to believe that it had any esoteric sense at all, was natural and intelligible; on the other hand there are many passages which are obviously mystical and give a clue to the rest. If the sceptics lacked discernment, they deserve our gratitude for having provoked Ibn El-Arabi to instruct them. Assuredly, without his guidance the most sympathetic readers would seldom have hit upon the hidden meanings which his fantastic ingenuity elicits from an Arabic *qasida*.[2]

A very great deal of Ibn El-Arabi's writings remain in a like case up to this day, as far as others than Sufis are concerned. Some of his material is addressed to those who have a grasp of ancient mythology, and is couched in those terms. Some, which connects with Christianity, serves as a lead-in to people with a Christian commitment. Other poetry serves to introduce the Sufi Way by means of love poetry. No single individual can unravel all his work only by means of scholastic, religious, romantic or intellectual equipment. This brings us to another hint of his mission, which is contained in his name.

According to Sufi tradition, Ibn El-Arabi's mission was to "scatter" (Arabic *nashr*, NSHR) Sufi lore throughout

[2] *The Tarjuman Al-Ashwaq* (Interpreter of Desires), tr. R. A. Nicholson, London, 1911, p. 7. Professor Nicholson's opinions about Sufism must be treated with great reserve. An example is this astonishing remark, almost incomprehensible to a Sufi: "Professing to adore a universal abstraction, they make individual men the objects of their real worship." (*Selections from the Diwan-i-Shams-i-Tabriz*, tr. Nicholson, Cambridge, 1898, p. xxi.)

the contemporary scene, connecting it with the existing
traditions of the people. This sense of scatter is perfectly
legitimate and in accordance with Sufi thinking. As the
Sufic term for scatter (NSHR) was not at the time used
publicly, Ibn El-Arabi employed an alternative word for it.
He was known in Spain as Ibn Saraqa, "Son of a small
saw." Saraqa, however, from the root SRQ, stands for another word for saw, derived from the NSHR root. The
NSHR root when normally inflected means "publication,
spreading," as well as "sawing." It also means revivification.
Muhiyuddin, Ibn El-Arabi's personal name, translates as
"reviver of faith."[3]

Taking the NSHR root literally, as most scholars were
bound to do, has caused even such a respectable historian
as Ibn el-Abbar to conclude that his father was a carpenter.
He could only have been a "carpenter" in the secondary
sense known to Sufis who adopted guild terms for their
meetings, to account for the collection together in any one
place of a number of people who did not want to appear to
be a subversive group.

Taken on their own, some of the statements of Ibn El-
Arabi are startling. In *Bezels of Wisdom,* he says that God
is never to be seen in an immaterial form. "The sight of
God in woman is the most perfect of all." Love poetry, as
with everything else to the Sufi, is capable of reflecting a
complete and coherent experience of divinity, while concurrently fulfilling various other functions. Every Sufi experience is an experience in depth and in qualitative in-
finity. It is only to the ordinary man or woman that a word
has only one meaning, or an experience less than a large
number of equally valid, whole significances. This multiplicity of being is something which, although accepted as a
contention by non-Sufis, is frequently forgotten by them
when they deal with Sufi material. At best they can generally appreciate that there is an allegory—which means to
them just one alternative meaning.

[3] See annotation "NSHR."

To the theologians, committed to a literal acceptance of divine formalism, Ibn El-Arabi bluntly says that "Angels are the powers hidden in the faculties and organs of man." It is the Sufi's objective to activate these organs.

Unmindful of the difference between formulation and experience, Dante[4] took over Ibn El-Arabi's literary work and crystallized it within a currently possible framework. In so doing, he robbed Ibn El-Arabi's message of its Sufic validity, and merely left Professor Asín with an embalmed example of what to the modern mind almost amounts to piracy. Raymond Lully, on the contrary, took over literary material from Ibn El-Arabi, but in addition emphasized the importance of the Sufi exercises which are necessary to complete the Sufic experiences.

Ibn El-Arabi, who studied under the Spanish woman Sufi Fatima b. Waliyya, was undoubtedly subject to special psychic states, such as are cultivated by the Sufis. He refers to these on various occasions. Some of his work was written in trance, and its meaning did not become clear to him until some time after its writing down. When he was thirty-seven, he visited Ceuta, where the renowned Ibn Sabain (who advised the Holy Roman Emperor Frederick) had his school. There he had a strange vision or dream, which was interpreted by a famous scholar. The sage said: "Immeasurable. . . . If this individual is in Ceuta, it can be none other than the recently arrived young Spaniard."

The source of his inspiration was reverie in which the consciousness was still active. By the exercise of this Sufi faculty, he was able to produce from the innermost mind a contact with supreme reality—the reality which he explained underlay the appearances of the familiar world.

His teaching stressed the importance of this exercise of faculties which are unknown to most people, and consigned to credulous occultism by the many. "A person," he said, "must control his thoughts in a dream. The training of this

---

[4] Miguel Asín Palacios, *Islam and the Divine Comedy*, tr. H. Sunderland, New York, E. P. Dutton, 1926.

alertness will produce awareness of the intermediate dimension. It will produce great benefits for the individual. Everyone should apply himself to the attainment of this ability of such great value."[5]

It is quite hopeless to attempt an interpretation of Ibn El-Arabi from a fixed position. His teachings are derived from the inner experiences, then presented within a form which itself has a function. Where his poetry has a double meaning, and it often has, he intends not only to convey both meanings but to affirm that both are valid. Where it is expressed in terms used by others before him, it is not intended by him that this should be taken as evidence of outside influence. What he is doing here is to address himself to people in terminology which forms a part of their own cultural background. There are poems of Ibn El-Arabi's which can be read in a shifting sense—the meaning starting in one theme and drifting into another. He has done this deliberately, in order to prevent the automatic associative processes from carrying the reader away into ordinary enjoyment; because El-Arabi is a teacher, not an entertainer.

For Ibn El-Arabi, as for all Sufis, Mohammed represents the Perfected Man. At the same time, it is necessary to know what is meant by "Mohammed" in this context. Ibn El-Arabi is more explicit than most on this point. There are two versions of Mohammed—the man who lived in Mecca and Medina, and the eternal Mohammed. It is this latter one of whom he speaks. This Mohammed is identified with all the prophets, including Jesus. This idea has caused people with a Christian background to claim that Ibn El-Arabi or the Sufis or both were secret Christians. The Sufi claim is that all the individuals who have performed certain functions are in a sense one. This oneness they call in its origin *haqiqat-el-Mohammedia,* the Reality of Mohammed.

Jili, in his standard Sufi text, *The Perfect Man,* explains the incarnation of this Reality among all peoples. He seeks

[5] Quoted by Ibn Shadakin.

to describe the essential factor, by showing the multiplicity of what we call an individual. Mohammed, for instance, means The Praised One. Another name, which is only a description of a function, is Father of El-Qasim. In his name of Abdullah, he stands for its literal meaning—Servant of God. Names are qualities or functions. Incarnation is a secondary factor: "He is given names and in every age has a name which is appropriate to the guise in which he appears in that age. . . . When he is seen as Mohammed, he is Mohammed, but when he is seen in another form, he is called by the name of that form."

This is not a reincarnation theory, however much it may resemble one. The essential reality which activates the man called Mohammed or anything else has to be given a name in conformity with the environment. Those who have identified this attitude with the Logos doctrine of Plotinus are, according to the Sufis, ascribing a historical connection to a situation which has objective reality. The Sufis did not copy the Logos doctrine, though the idea of the Logos and of the Reality of Mohammed have a common source. Ultimately the source of Sufi information on this, as on other points, is the personal experience of the Sufi, not the literary formulation which has been one of its historical manifestations. The trap of historical thinking, which assumes no basic interior source for knowledge and has to seek literary and superficial inspiration, is constantly avoided by the Sufi. Several Western students of Sufism have, it must be admitted, emphasized that similarity of appearances, of terminology or of date do not prove transmission of the essential idea.

Ibn El-Arabi confused the scholars because he was what is called in Islam a conformist in religion while remaining an esotericist in inner life. Like all Sufis he claimed that there was a coherent, continuous and perfectly acceptable progression between formal religion of any kind and the inner understanding of that religion, leading to a personal enlightenment. This doctrine, naturally, could not be accepted by theologians, whose importance depended upon more or less static facts, historical material and the use of reasoning powers.

Although Ibn El-Arabi is loved by all Sufis, had an immense personal following among people of all kinds, and lived an exemplary life, he was undoubtedly a threat to formal society. Like Ghazali, his intellectual powers were superior to those of almost all his more conventional contemporaries. Instead of making use of these abilities to carve a place in scholasticism, he claimed, like many another Sufi, that when one has a powerful intellect, its ultimate function is to show that intellectuality is merely a prelude to something else. Such an attitude seems impossible arrogance—unless one has actually met such a person and known his humility.

Many people sympathized with him, but did not dare to support him, because they were working on a formal plane, and he on an initiatory one. One respected divine is on record as saying: "I have no doubt at all that Muhiyuddin (Ibn El-Arabi) is a deliberate liar. He is a chief among heretics and a hardened Sufi." The great theologian, Kamaludin Zamlaqani, however, exclaimed: "How ignorant are those who oppose the Sheikh Muhiyuddin Ibn El-Arabi! His sublime sayings and the precious words in his writings are too advanced for their understanding."

On a famous occasion, the renowned teacher Sheikh Izedin ibn Abdesalam was presiding over a group of students of the religious law. During a discussion the question of defining hypocritical heretics arose. Someone cited Ibn El-Arabi as a prime example. The teacher did not challenge the assertion. Later, when dining with the teacher, Salahuddin, who later became the Shiekh of Islam, asked him who was the most eminent sage of the age:

"He said, 'What is that to you? Eat on.' I realized that he knew, stopped eating and pressed him in God's name to tell me who it was. He smiled, then said, 'The Sheikh Muhiyuddin Ibn El-Arabi.' For a moment I was so amazed that I could say nothing. The Sheikh asked me what was the matter. I said, 'I am in wonderment because this very morning a man has stated that he is a heretic. On that occasion you did not contest it. Now you call Muhiyuddin the Magnetic Pole of the Age, the greatest man alive, the teacher of the world.'

"He said, 'But it was in a meeting of scholars, legists.'"

The main opposition to Ibn El-Arabi was due to his truly amazing collection of odes—love poetry known as the *Interpreter of Desires*. The poetry is so sublime, has so many possible meanings, is so full of fantastic imagery that it can exercise a magical effect upon the reader. For the Sufis it is regarded as the product of the most advanced development of human consciousness possible to man. It is only fair to add here that D. B. MacDonald considers Ibn El-Arabi's outpourings as "a strange jumble of theosophy and metaphysical paradoxes, all much like the theosophy of our day."

For scholars one of the important things about the *Interpreter* is that there is extant a commentary on the poems, made by the author himself, in which he explains how the imagery fits in with orthodox Islamic religion. How this came about can only be studied against the background of the book's history.

In the year 1202 El-Arabi decided to go on the pilgrimage. After spending some time in traveling through North Africa, he arrived in Mecca and there met a group of Persian immigrants, mystics who welcomed him into their fold, in spite of the fact that he had been accused of heresy and worse in Egypt. He narrowly escaped an attempt by a fanatic to murder him.

The chief of this Persian community was named Mukinuddin. He had a beautiful daughter, Nizam, devout and well versed in the religious law. His spiritual experiences in Mecca, and his symbolical rendering of the path of the mystic, are expressed in love poems dedicated to her. El-Arabi realized that human beauty was connected with divine reality; and for this reason he was able to produce poems which both celebrated the perfection of the maiden and also, in correct perspective, stood for a deeper reality. But the capacity to see the connection was denied to the formal religionists, who professed themselves scandalized. The poet's supporters have pointed out, often in vain, that real truth may be expressed in several different ways simultaneously. They refer to Ibn El-Arabi's use of myths and legends, as well as traditional history, to express the esoteric truths which are concealed within them, as well as the entertainment value which they have. Such a concept of the multiplicity of the meaning of one and the same factor was as little understood during his time as it is today. The nearest that the ordinary individual can get to this is to allow that "a beautiful woman is a divine work of art." He is not able to perceive the beautiful woman and the divinity at the same time. This is the entire problem of Sufi statement in a nutshell.

Ibn El-Arabi's *Interpreter* therefore reads, on the surface, as a collection of erotic poems. When he traveled to Aleppo in Syria, a stronghold of religious orthodoxy, he found that the divines of Islam were saying that he was a mere pretender, trying to justify his erotic poesy by claiming a deeper meaning. He immediately set to work on a commentary to bring the work into orthodox focus. The result was that the scholars were entirely satisfied, because the author had helped to support their own interpretations of the religious law by his explanations of the meaning of his work. For the Sufi, however, there was a third meaning to the *Interpreter*. Ibn El-Arabi, by using familiar terminology, was showing them that superficialities might be true, that human love might be completely valid; but that both of these things in actuality veiled an inner truth, or were an extension of it.

It is this inner reality which he refers to when he accepts all formalism, yet claims a truth behind and beyond it. Professor Nicholson has thus translated one of the poems which most shocked the devout, who believed that theirs was the road to human salvation:

> My heart is capable of every form:
> A cloister for the monk, a fane for idols,
> A pasture for gazelles, the votary's Ka'ba [temple],
> The tables of the Torah, the Quran.
> Love is the creed I hold: wherever turn
> His camels, Love is still my creed and faith.

The romantically minded person may take this as meaning that the familiar, quantitative kind of love with which his mind automatically associates these words is what the Greatest Sheikh means. For the Sufi, it is Sufism, of which the familiar "love," is only a part, a limited part beyond which, under ordinary circumstances, the average person never goes.

El-Ghazali of Persia

The words used to denote "states"
in Sufism are mere approximations.
(Kalabadhi)

While the Normans were consolidating their domains in
Britain and Sicily, and the flow of Saracenic knowledge to
the West was increasing through Arabized Spain and Italy,
the empire of Islam was less than five hundred years old.
The topheavy priesthood, whose functions were prohibited
by the religious law but immensely powerful in fact, was
desperately trying to reconcile Greek philosophical method
with the Koran and the traditions of the Prophet. Having
accepted scholasticism as the method whereby religion could
be interpreted, these dialecticians yet found themselves unable to demonstrate the truth of their beliefs by intellectual
means. Society had, through the circulation of knowledge,
outgrown formal dialectic. Excellent economic conditions
had produced a large intelligentsia which needed more than
dogmatic assurances or the assertion that the "State must be
right." Islam was the State. Islam seemed likely to fall apart.
A young Persian of Meshed, known as Mohammed El-
Ghazali (the Spinner), orphaned at an early age and
brought up by Sufis, was at this time at college in Central

Asia. He was destined to achieve two remarkable things, as a result of which both Islam and Christianity bear some of the characteristics which they still have today.

Orthodox Islam was opposed to Sufism, which was regarded as attempting to ignore the Law and substitute personal experience of what religion really meant—a very heretical idea. But Mohammed El-Ghazali it was who proved the only man able to reconcile Islam with intellectualism and "fixed the ultimate creed of the Ashariyya and established its dicta as the universal creed of Islam," as Professor Hitti says. So successful was this heretic in becoming the virtual father of the Moslem church, that even the most orthodox still call him by the highest academic title known, the Authority of Islam.

In under fifty years after their composition, his books were exerting a tremendous influence upon Jewish and Christian scholasticism. He not only anticipated in a remarkable fashion John Bunyan's *Holy War* and *Pilgrim's Progress*, but influenced Ramón Marti, Thomas Aquinas and Pascal, as well as numerous more modern thinkers.

Such books as the *Destruction of the Philosophers*, the *Alchemy of Happiness* and the *Niche for Lights* continue to be eagerly studied and contain a great deal of his teachings.

Known in the middle ages in Europe as Algazel, Abu-Hamid Mohammed El-Ghazali took up the questions which, as more than one writer notes, the Christian theologians gratefully handed over to the Moslem thinkers; and he returned the answers, arrived at by what Professor Hitti calls the "mystico-psychological" answer of the Sufi. The accepted position of Sufism, whereby it is acknowledged by many Moslem divines as the inner meaning of Islam, is a direct result of Ghazali's work.

The ideas which Ghazali passed on and which influenced both St. Thomas Aquinas the Dominican and St. Francis of Assisi, each in his own way, caused a confusion in the minds of writers on Western mysticism which endures to this day. To the Sufi, the Ghazalian stream in two different emphases is seen plainly in the work of both intellectual Dominicans and intuitive Franciscans. The two influences, separated because of the phenomenon of adaption and specialization in one Sufic method without the others, are so clearly definable that even if one did not know of any source for the inspiration of these Christian teachers, it would be possible to identify the Sufic stream.

Evelyn Underhill (*Mysticism*) has managed to convey the underlying unity of the seemingly separate streams of the two Christian schools. Apparently without having heard of the Sufi influences on Christian mysticism, she is able to note that both the Dominican and Franciscans were basically rooted in contemplation, and "because of this were able to interpret to the medieval world the great spiritual traditions of the past."

Ghazali, by using the Sufi concept that all religious and psychological activity is essentially of the same nature, representing a continuing tradition which can be furthered by certain individuals, arrived at the position where he could represent both the mystical and the theological worlds perfectly within their own contexts. In so doing, he was able to demonstrate the inner reality of religion and philosophy in such a way as to appeal to followers of any creed. The consequence was that, although his work was revered by followers of different traditions, there was a mistaken tendency to assume that he had been attempting a synthesis of religion. A Christian theologian, Dr. August Tholuck, puts his work in these terms, while agreeing that Ghazali's writings should be acceptable to Christianity. Tholuck's remarks on this subject are well worth noting, for they give an excellent example of the "elephant in the dark" form of thinker, who cannot believe in a single source for all genuine metaphysical teaching, and must try to account for the ingredients in any new appearance of a teacher:

"All that is good, worthy and sublime, which his great

soul had compassed, he bestowed upon Mohammedanism, and he adorned the doctrines of the Koran with so much piety and learning that in the form given them by him, they seem, in my opinion, worthy of the assent of Christians. Whatever was most excellent in the philosophy of Aristotle or in the Sufi mysticism, he discreetly adapted to the Mohammedan theology. From every school he sought the means of shedding light and honor upon religion, while his sincere piety and lofty conscientiousness imparted to all his writings a sacred majesty."

Hardly anything will shake the intellectualizing observer in his confidence that everything which he is studying is made up of a patchwork of other things.

At a time when few divines were considered capable of reciting a tradition of the Prophet correctly unless they were graybeards, Ghazali appointed a professor at the famous Nizamiyya Academy at Baghdad at the age of thirty-three. His intellect was of such an order as to be unsurpassed in Islam. For him, the real object of education was not merely to provide information, but the stimulation of an inner consciousness—a concept too revolutionary for the scholastics of the time. He propounded this theory in his *Ihya-el-ulum.* As in the case of Rumi (who spoke of the limitations of poetry only when he had become a great poet) Ghazali could afford to show up scholasticism by the time he had no less than three hundred thousand traditions of the Prophet by heart, and was the Authority of Islam.

His intellectual powers were yoked to a restlessness of mind which, as he says in his own autobiographical writings, made him tirelessly investigate every dogma and every doctrine which he came across; and this from his early youth.

While he was still teaching, Ghazali came to the conclusion that canon law (on which he wrote authoritative books) was an insufficient basis for reality, and he lapsed into scepticism.

Resigning his post, Ghazali spent twelve years—the traditional dervish period—in wanderings and meditation, returning to his Sufi background for the answers which he did not find in the ordinary world.

He confesses that he was an egoist, and craved applause and recognition. When he realized that this was a barrier to real understanding, he did not abruptly demean himself by choosing the "path of blame," the panacea offered to many mystics. He decided that he would use conscious development in order to arrive at objective truth.

During his period of detachment from the world, after he had abandoned his career as a scholastic, which had saved Moslem theology from decay, Ghazali relates how he battled with his Commanding Self. He had been wandering throughout the East, on pilgrimages and seeking enlightenment in the manner of the dervishes, when he entered a mosque. In the sermon, the Imam was ending his discourse with the words: "So speaks our leader Ghazali."

The wandering dervish said to himself, "O Commanding Self, how pleasant it is to you to hear this said! Yet I shall not tolerate this indulgence any more. I leave this place forthwith, to go where nobody talks of Ghazali."

The theologian, accepted master in matters of outer religion, knew that the realization of what might be meant by the term "God" was something which could only be appreciated by inner means, not accessible through the framework of any formal religion.

"I traveled to Syria," he says, "and remained there for two years. I had no other objective than that of seeking solitariness, overcoming selfishness, fighting passions, trying to make clear my soul, to complete my character." He did this because the Sufi cannot enter into understanding until his heart is prepared to "meditate upon God," as he calls it.

This period of time was sufficient only to give him sporadic flashes of spiritual fulfillment (foretaste)—the stage which is considered by most non-Sufi mystics to be the ultimate, but which is in fact only the first step.

It had become clear to him that "the Sufis are not men of

words, but of inner perception. I had learned all that could be learned by reading. The remainder could not be acquired by study or by talk."

Instead of being bemused by his ecstatic experiences, considering them the be-all and end-all of the mystical quest, Ghazali realized that "the so-called absorption in God, considered to be the *goal* of the Sufi, is in fact only the beginning."

He had exhausted scholasticism and intellectualism because he realized that they had an end, and so he was able to exhaust the preliminary stages which passed as mystical experience in a final sense. He was able to do this because he attained what he sought—a form of cognition which, like a directing beam, gave him a sense of certitude and a means of reaching the ultimate realization. "It is something," he reports, describing this perception, "as specific as if one had actually touched an object."

Relating happiness and fulfillment to a process of alchemical transmutation of the human mind, Ghazali gives a story of Bayazid, one of the early classical Sufi masters, in his *Alchemy of Happiness,* to stress how the *amour propre* (Commanding Self) must first be seen in its real light before any refining can actually be done:

A man came to Bayazid and said that he had fasted and prayed for thirty years, and yet had not come near to an understanding of God. Bayazid told him that even a hundred years would not be enough. The man asked why.

"Because your selfishness is working as a barrier between yourself and truth."

"Give me the remedy."

"There is a remedy, but it is impossible to you."

The man insisted, and Bayazid agreed to describe it to him.

"Go and shave your beard. Strip yourself naked, except for a loincloth. Fill a nose bag full of walnuts and go to the marketplace. There cry out, 'A walnut for every boy who

slaps me!' Then make your way to the court where the doctors of law are in session."

"But I really could not do that. Give me some other
method."

"This is the only method," said Bayazid, "but I have already told you, there is no answer for you."

Ghazali, like other dervish teachers, maintained that
Sufism was the inner teaching of all religions, and he used
many quotations from the Bible and Apocrypha to make his
points. He wrote an early critical work on distortions in
Christian ideals—*El Qawl el Jamil fil Raddi a la man
Ghayar el Injil.* As a consequence, of course, he has been
said to have been under Christian influence. He was, in
fact, less so than even the British Broadcasting Corporation
when it occasionally uses Sufi stories in its morning religious program, probably deriving them from secondary
sources, and using them in their esoteric sense when they
accord with nominal Christianity.

Ghazali was widely accused of preaching one thing and
secretly teaching another. This is undoubtedly true, if it is
accepted that he regarded active Sufism as a specialized undertaking suitable only for a limited number of people with
the capacity for Adepthood. The external and doctrinal
aspects of Islam which he enunciated with such impec-
cable orthodoxy were intended for those who could not follow the inner Sufi Way.

The Perfected Man (*insani kamil*), because of his living
in different dimensions at the same time, must appear to
follow more than one set of doctrines. A man who is swimming across a lake is carrying out actions and responding
to perceptions other than a man walking down a hill, for
instance. He is the same man; and he carries with him when
he is walking all the potentiality of swimming.

With extraordinary bravery he actually states this in his
Mizan el Amal (Balances of Work).

The Perfected Man has three frameworks of belief:

1. That of his surroundings.

2. That which he conveys to students in accordance with their capacity for understanding.

3. That which he understands from inner experience, only to be known among a special circle.

His *Mishkat el Anwar* (Niche for Lights) is both a commentary on the famous Light Verse of the Koran and a rendering of its initiatory significance.[1]

He explains that everything has an Outward and an Inward significance. They do not operate together, though they both work consistently within their own dimensions. The version which is available in general circulation, it is true, does not contain the interpretation which is handed down by the present representatives of the dervish fraternities; but this is only because the key to this extraordinary book cannot be expressed in words, but is an extension of personal experience. In other words, it cannot be understood unless it is experienced.

This fact, a basic one in Sufism and stressed by numerous Sufi writers, may easily be misunderstood by formal thinkers. In a translation of the *Niche* made in English by the Director of the School of Oriental Studies, Cairo, Mr. W. H. T. Gairdner speaks of the difficulty of understanding Ghazali on the subject of the point at which belief and disbelief meet, and much else:

"All these things are incommunicable mysteries, secrets, from the revealing of which our author (Ghazali) turns away at the exact moment when we expect the denouement. The art is supreme—but something more than tantalizing. Who were the Adepts to whom he *did* communicate these thrilling secrets? Were these communications ever written down for or by his brother initiates?"

Ghazali is referring to secrets which are experienced, and cannot be written down. He is not trying to tantalize at all.

There are really four parts of Ghazali's work. The first

[1] See annotation "Light Verse."

is the philosophical material which he placed at the disposal of Moslem theologians and intellectuals for the purpose of keeping the theoretical framework of the religion together. Then comes his metaphysical teachings as contained in such works as the *Niche* and the *Alchemy*. Afterward there are the meanings which are concealed in an enciphered form in his writings. Finally there is the teaching which extends from an understanding of the last two, which is partly transmitted orally and partly accessible to those who have followed correctly his mystical works and experiences.

Like all the classical dervishes, Ghazali made use of poetic symbolism and encipherment. His surname, chosen by himself, is generally rendered "El-Ghazali." Primarily this means "the Spinner." This appellation denotes "one who spins, works with material such as wool"—the code word for *Sufi*—and carried the connotation of the need to spin, or work upon, one's materials—and one's self. Also by vocation association it is linked with Fatima (which means "the Dyer"), Mohammed's daughter. From her all descendants of the Prophet trace their pedigree. They are believed to inherit the inner teaching of Islam, showing where it connects with all genuine metaphysical traditions.

The care with which these poetic names are chosen is shown by the numerous other associations of the work. Ghazali also stands for "gazelle" (the generic term for various types of antelope, such as the Oryx, which is a literal homonym for "a lover"). The three-letter root GH-Z-L from which the whole series of words is derived also produces the word GHaZaL, which itself is the standard Arabic and Persian technical term for a love poem, an amorous verse. Other derivations from this root include a spider's web (something spun), which is in this case intended to be a reference to action coming through faith. The action was the spinning of a web across a cave mouth where Mohammed and his companion Abu Bakr were hiding from their enemies, on a famous occasion.

A Sufi aware of these traditions therefore interprets El-

Ghazali's name in accordance with the principles on which it was chosen. To him, then, it means that Ghazali follows the path of Love, of Sufism ("wool"), which means work (spinning in this case). Ghazali has left these keynotes to be picked up by his successors, including the hint of the continuity of an inner doctrine (Fatima, the Dyer) within the religious context in which he lives.

The methodology of Ghazali is followed in the traditional Sufi orders, with various variations. He defended the special use of music to elevate the perceptions in his *Ihya*—and music is used in this way in the Mevlevi and Chishti Orders of dervishes. The tune known in the West as Ravel's *Bolero* is actually an adaptation of one of these specially composed pieces. He points out that in order to develop higher faculties, self-pride must be recognized and overcome. This forms another part of Sufi training and study. He points out that the consciousness must be transmuted, rather than suppressed or distorted.

It is this very use of the phraseology of alchemy by the Sufis of the middle ages which is responsible for a very great deal of confusion in the minds of later researchers as to what "alchemy" really does mean. Some say that it is a disguised form of a spiritual quest. Others reply that the laboratories of the alchemists have been examined and show every indication of having been used for real experiments. Works attributed to spiritual alchemists have been described as chemical treatises.

Thus Ghazali: "Alchemical gold is better than gold, but real alchemists are rare, and so are true Sufis. Who has but a smattering of Sufism is not superior to a learned man." (*Alchemy of Happiness*)

First of all it should be remembered that a great part of the alchemical tradition of the West came through Arabic sources, and that the so-called Emerald Tablet of Hermes the Thrice-Greatest is found in its earliest form in Arabic. Further, the first classical Sufi was Jabir Ibn al-Hayyan, surnamed the Sufi, the alchemist and occultist—the Latin Geber, who lived three centuries before Ghazali.

The "Great Work" is a translated Sufi phrase, and the doctrine of the microcosm and macrocosm (what is above is equal to what is below) is also found in Sufi tradition, and expounded by Ghazali. As Sufism is not a mere invention which took place at a certain point in time, it is inevitable that similar ideas should occur in other genuine inner traditions. Unless all these points are firmly grasped, there can be no advantage in observing the theory of transmutation from coarse to fine from an adequate standpoint.

Ghazali's *Revival of Religious Sciences* was publicly burned in Moslem Spain (before he had become the greatest religious authority in Islam) because it contained such statements as:

> The question of divine knowledge is so deep that it is really known only to those who have it. A child has no real knowledge of the attainments of an adult. An ordinary adult cannot understand the attainments of a learned man. In the same way, a learned man cannot understand the experiences of enlightened saints or Sufis.

The *Revival* contains most important expositions of the Sufi love ideal. Affinity of humanity for each other and of humanity for creation is stressed. Quoting the Sufi master Malik ibn Dinar, Ghazali says, in Book IV: "Just as birds of the same feather fly together, two persons having a quality common to both will join."[2]

Ghazali points out that a "mixture of a pig, a dog, a devil and a saint" is not a suitable basis for a mind which is attempting to attain deep understanding of things which this mixture by definition cannot attain. "You must stop looking at a cushion if you are trying to look at a lamp."

The way in which the unholy mixture is corrected, the

2 Sayed Nawab Ali's version, *Some Moral and Religious Teachings of Al-Ghazzali*, Lahore, 1960, p. 109.

method whereby the mirror is aligned in order to reflect properly, must be known and must be practiced. This is the knowledge and the practice which is the result of the Sufi specialization.

The specialized techniques of Sufism for arriving at the ability to learn and the learning itself, as well as the wisdom which is ultimately attained, are the result of the correct approach. "There are many degrees of knowledge," Ghazali stresses. "The mere physical man is like the ant crawling on paper, who observes black lettering and attributes its production to the pen and to nothing more." (*Alchemy of Happiness*)

What is the product of this specialization, as far as the ordinary world is concerned? Ghazali answers this in specific terms in the *Alchemy*. Some people rule their own bodies. "Those individuals who reach a certain height of power rule their own bodies, and those of others as well. Should they desire an invalid to recover, he does so. . . . They can make someone come to them, by an effort of will."

There are three qualities which are the consequence of Sufi specialization that can be expressed in terms perceptible to the ordinary reader:

1. The power of extra perception, consciously exerted.

2. The power to move bodies outside their own mass.

3. Immediate consciousness of knowledge. Even that which is normally acquired only by labor becomes theirs by illumination or insight.

These faculties may appear to be separate or strange, but they are in fact only a part of a higher stage of being or existence, and can be recognized by ordinary people only in this crude way. "This interrelation cannot be explained in the usual way; just as in more mundane things we cannot explain the effect of poetry to one whose ear cannot accept it, or color to one who lacks the function of sight."

Man, Ghazali points out, is capable of existing on several different planes. He does not normally know enough about them to be able to differentiate. He is on one of four planes.

"The first plane is when he is like a moth. It has sight, but no memory. It will be singed again and again on the same flame. The second is where he is like a dog. Once beaten, it will flee at the sight of a stick. The third is like that of a horse or a sheep. Both will run immediately, if they see a lion or a wolf, which are their natural foes. They will, however, not flee from a camel or a buffalo, even though both are much larger than their hereditary enemies." The fourth plane is that in which man entirely transcends these animal limitations. He is now able to exercise some foresight. The relationship between these stages in respect of locomotion can be likened to:

1. Walking on the land.
2. Being on a ship.
3. Riding in a chariot.
4. Walking on the sea.

Beyond all these there is the phase in which one might say that the man can fly by his own power through the air.

The commonalty remain in one of the first two stages. In these they do not endure as much as they should. Being static, they are invariably inimical to those who are in movement.

In his metaphysical work, Ghazali seldom troubles himself to exhort people to follow the Sufi path. In one passage, however, he does emphasize one argument. If, he says, what the Sufis are saying is true—that there is an urgent undertaking in life which bears a relationship with one's future state—it will matter very much in the future state. If, on the other hand, there is no such relationship, nothing will matter. Therefore, he asks, is it not better to give this point of view the benefit of the doubt? Later it will be too late.

Ghazali next turns in his *Alchemy* to the question of music in its psychological aspects. He notes the mechanism whereby music and dancing can be used for excitatory purposes. Music can be a method of producing emotional effect. He maintains, however, that there is an innocent function of music, in which it does not produce the pseudo-religious sentiments used by undiscriminating cults.

The Sufi use of music is different from the emotional use. Before a Sufi can participate in musical activities, including listening to music, it must be established by his director as to whether he will benefit correctly from the experience.

A story is related here to show how a Sufi teacher (Sheikh Gurjani) explained that a certain disciple was not yet fitted for the audition of music in the Sufi, objective, sense. In response to his request, the Sheikh said, "Fast for a week. Have delicious food cooked for you. If you then still prefer musical movement, take part in it."

Participation in music and "dancing" under any other circumstances is, says Ghazali, not only forbidden; it is actually harmful to the aspirant. Modern psychology has not yet realized that there is a special function of sound for elevating consciousness.

The reality of the true "state" of Sufi experience is very difficult to grasp for the outsider, because he is accustomed to thinking in terms which are different from this state. "Allowances must be made for him," Ghazali says, "because he is unaware of what these states are. It is like a blind man trying to understand the experience of seeing green herbage or running water."

At best the outsider can only relate the experience which is reported to him in terms of his own experiences—sensual, orgiastic, emotional. "Yet a wise man will not deny such states simply because he has not experienced them; because this form of opinion forming is disastrously foolish."

The deist view of the so-called mystical experience, which carries no superior knowledge but is merely a form of auto-intoxication, is not the one which Ghazali is trying to portray. Still less is he inclined to accept the contention that there is any sort of a descent of deity into man. The whole reportage is vitiated, and may even be voided, by the attempt to transpose it into a vehicle—words—which will not adequately convey it. A Sufi commentator on Ghazali notes that things which are comprehensive experiences "cannot be penned by a mumbling wordsmith, any more than he himself would accept a paper copy of a fruit as edible or nutritious."

The intellectual or externalist attempt to understand something vicariously, to force into a word pattern something which is beyond it, is "like someone who, seeing his face in a mirror, imagines that his face has in some way become imprisoned in a mirror."

In dervish meetings, there are examples of ecstatic convulsions and other signs of false experience or states. Once, Ghazali recalls, the great Sheikh Junayd reprimanded a youth who fell into frenzy at a Sufi meeting. "Never do that again, or leave my company," Junayd told him. Sufi belief is that outward evidences like this of supposedly inner changes are counterfeit or merely emotional. True experience carries no physical concomitant of this kind— whether it be "speaking in tongues" or rolling on the floor. The illustrious Mahmud Shabistari, in his *Secret Garden*, comments: "If thou know not these states, pass on, nor join the infidel in ignorant counterfeit. . . . But all learn not the secrets of the Way."

These demonstrations are, in a way, associated with the emotional use of words which is the shortcoming and ultimately the downfall of the formal religions. Making phrases connected with God, faith, or any religion is an external, at best an emotional, matter. This is one reason why Sufis will not discuss Sufism in the same context as religion. Different planes are involved.

Once there has been an inner experience of what is meant by the familiar phraseology of religion, the phrases cease to have any meaning at all, because the transition from the coarse to the finer has taken place. Ghazali illustrates this fact by a report. The Sufi master Fudayl (died 801) said: "If asked whether you love God, say nothing. This is because if you say, 'I do not love God,' you are an unbeliever. If, on the other hand, you say, 'I do love God,' your actions contradict you."

If a person knows what religious love is, he will express it in its own way, not in a way which is familiar to those who do not know. Everyone will be uplifted or the reverse in accordance with his own capacities and that with which he is familiar. Ghazali reports that a man collapsed in a perfume bazaar. People tried to revive him with sweet odors. Presently someone who knew him said, "I have been a dustman. This man is also one. He will be revived by the smell of that which is familiar to him." Accordingly some nauseating substance was held under his nose, and he immediately revived.

This kind of contention is generally anathema to those who seek to attribute familiar sensations to a higher order of being, and assume that they are experiencing at least some measure of the divine or mystical in forms which are nothing more than grosser ones. The grosser form is suitable to its context, and cannot be transposed. A petrol engine cannot be run on butter, even though butter is in its own place a very excellent thing. Nobody would think of referring to it seriously as petrol, however. The Sufi doctrine of a continuum of refinement of matter will here be seen to be quite different from that of other systems. The other two schools hold that materiality must either be shunned altogether, or that it must be made use of. In actual fact, every degree of materiality has its own function; and materiality extends in successive refinement until it becomes what has been generally considered to be separate—spirit.

Ghazali enunciated the doctrine that it is necessary to realize the multiple functions, at different levels, of what appears to be the same thing; e.g.: "The eye may see the large as small: the sun as the size of a bowl. . . . Intelligence understands that the sun is in fact many times larger than the earth. . . . The faculties of imagination and fantasy often produce beliefs and pass judgments which they consider to be products of the intelligence. The error is consequently in the lower mental processes to the unwary or insensitive." (*Niche of Lights*, first part.) By insensitive he means those who do not allow themselves to feel multiple impact and meaning. Among numerous illustrations of the working of this tendency, he says in his *Revival* some important things about the self.

The self means in one sense the personality of man, which is used to handle outside impacts and employ them for gratification. But it also means the inner or essential quality of the individual. In this capacity its formal name changes in accordance with its functions. If the essence operates correctly in reorganizing the emotional life and preventing confusion, it is known as the Peaceful Self. Operating in the field of conscience, when it is activated to remind the man or woman of certain matters, it is called the Accusatory Self. There has been tremendous confusion in this matter, because for purposes of examination and teaching, the essential self has to be given a name. Yet its differing modes of operation according to what work it is performing can give the impression that it is a number of different things; or even that it is at different stages of development. It is legitimate to represent the process as being composed of stages, but this is at best only an illustrative distinction. The Sufi whose consciousness is operating correctly will regard the different phases of the essence's transmutation in a special and distinctive way, not adequately duplicated in familiar terminology. When the essence is operating in a way normal to undeveloped man, it gives its potential to the mechanism which indulges primitive satisfactions, and is then known as the Commanding Self.

"Certain conditions," he stresses, "are easily understood and give the impression that everything can similarly easily be understood. But there are situations which can only be understood by those who see them in a certain [special] way. The ignorance of this [mechanism] gives rise to the common fault of assuming an uniformity in events."

In common with other Sufi teachers, Ghazali finds that

he has to repeat his argument in different forms as his text demands it. This is partly because the Sufi method may require the same standpoint to be taken up in different sets of ideas. It is also because, as is so often seen in study groups, people may give lip service to an important contention, yet not be permeated with it. The contention must actually operate as a dynamic force within the mind of the student. In many cases, because he is accustomed to being conditioned or trained, the student will accept a contention as a conditioning. The result of this will be that he merely thinks that he has absorbed it, because he responds in a predictable way whenever a certain stimulus of contention is applied to him. Such conditioning, if it has taken place, must be broken before the Sufi effect can manifest itself.

The misunderstanding involved in the use of the terms "Son of God" (attributed to Jesus) and "I am the Truth" (said by the Sufi Hallaj)[3] is due entirely to this question. The attempt to express a certain relationship in language not prepared for it causes the expression to be misunderstood.

The individual, Ghazali says in the *Revival*, may pass through stages of interior development analogous to those of human growing up. This gradual development causes his experiences to take different forms. Hence, a Sufi may not need a certain physical experience because his development has substituted a capacity for a more coherent, better experience. "Every stage of life, for example, is marked by a fresh kind of enjoyment. Children like playing and have no conception of the pleasures of marriage which they will develop the capacity for later. The adult, in his turn, will in his younger days have no capacity for the enjoyment of riches and greatness which is experienced by the middle-aged. The latter, in their turn, may consider earlier delights as much less significant than their current ones. More developed individuals, of course, will consider incomplete, impalpable or sporadic the conventionally familiar indul-

[3] See annotation "Hallaj."

gences when compared with their new capacities for appreciation."

The alternation of allegories, which prevents their becoming crystallized into mere conditioning mechanisms, is a common procedure in the living teaching of Sufi schools. Ghazali in his works often changes his teaching in an outward sense, while the inner meaning remains the same. In his *Minhaj el-Abidin*, he treats of the progress of the alchemizing of the consciousness in seven "valleys" of experience—the Valleys of Knowledge, Turning Back, Obstacles, Tribulations, Lightning, Abysses and Praise. This is the more theological frame of projection of the Sufi message, and forms the medium through which the Moslem and Christian devout of the middle ages was able to gain a glimpse of Sufi teaching. It is interesting to note that Bunyan and Chaucer used this Sufi material, drawing heavily upon its imagery to provide a stiffening for Catholic thinking. Eastern teachers such as Attar and Rumi maintained contact with the more direct stream of meaning of the "quest" theme; probably because they were practical, as well as theoretical, teachers with their own schools.

Man's happiness undergoes successive refinements in accordance with his "state of being," according to Ghazali. This teaching, which will not accept the usual human view that there is one standard form of happiness, an abstraction, is a marked feature of Sufi lore.

"Man contains diverse possibilities, each responding to its own type of enjoyment. Initially there is the physical one. In a similar way there is the moral faculty, which I call real reason, which enjoys the attainment of as much knowledge as possible. There are thus the outward and inward indulgences. In accordance with their refinement, so will they be preferred.

"A man, then, who has a capacity for acceptance of a perfection of Being will prefer the contemplation of this. Even in the present life the happiness of the right-seekers is incomparably greater than can be imagined."

Omar Khayyam

True devotion is for itself: not to
desire heaven nor to fear hell.
(Rabia el-Adawia)

The quatrains of Omar, son of Abraham the Tentmaker,
have been translated into almost every language in the
world. Nothing in his reputed life as schoolfellow of the
great Assassin, friend of Nizam the Great Vizier, courtier
and epicure, is as unlikely as the adventures which have
befallen him in translation. It has become a commonplace
that the *Rubaiyat* translated by FitzGerald more faithfully
represents the Irish poet than the Persian. Yet this is itself
a superficial assessment, because Omar represents not himself but a school of Sufi philosophy. It is necessary not only
to know what Omar really said, but what he meant by it.

There is a further interest in the fact that in amalgamat-
ing ideas from several Sufi poets and putting them out in the
name of Omar, FitzGerald unconsciously maintained a
Sufic impact in English literature.

Let us start with FitzGerald's translating. In Quatrain 55,
he makes Omar speak specifically against the Sufis:

> The Vine had struck a Fibre; which about
> If clings my Being—let the Sufi flout;

Of my Base Metal may be filed a Key,
That shall unlock the Door he howls without.

This seems to mean, if it means anything at all, that Omar is opposed to the Sufi. And that what the Sufi seeks may actually be found by Omar's method, not his own.

To any ordinary inquirer this poem would immediately dispose of the likelihood that Omar was a Sufi.

The Sufis believe that within mankind there is an element, activated by love, which provides the means of attaining to true reality, called mystical meaning.

If we turn to the original poem from which Quatrain 55 was translated, looking for flouting Sufis or not, this is the meaning which we find in Persian:

When the Original Cause determined my being
I was given the first lesson of love.
It was then that the fragment of my heart was made
The Key to the Treasury of Pearls of mystical meaning.

There is no Sufi, door, howl, flout, vine or fiber. But the words used are Sufi technical terms.

While it has been generally accepted that Khayyam was a poet without much honor in his own country until reintroduced by the esteem which FitzGerald's translation caused in the West, this again is not strictly accurate. Khayyam, it is true, was not as universally prized as Saadi, Hafiz, Rumi and other Sufi poets. The function of the collection of poems which passes under his name was slightly different. It is doubtful whether any Sufis were asked as to what they thought of Khayyam. And it must be admitted that even if they were asked, few of them would care to discuss the matter with an outsider.

Immense and painstaking labor has been devoted to the task of assessing which quatrains from the many collections of Omarian verse are original or genuine. From the Sufi point of view, since Omar was not the teacher of a school of mystics but a single teacher and the exemplar of a school, the question is void of importance. Much interest has been shown by literary researchers in the possible influence upon Omar of the blind poet Abu el-Ali el-Maari. In the *Luzum,* written a generation before Khayyam, Maari published very similar poetry which is said to be reminiscent of Khayyam.

Maari wrote like Khayyam, and Khayyam like Maari, a Sufi would say, because they were both writing from the point of view of the same school. Khayyam probably copied Maari just as much as two swimmers copy each other if they swim together, having learned, separately or together, from the same source.

This is the impasse which develops when one party (the literary) is looking at one facet of a work, and another party (the mystic) at the intention or influence within a certain context.

Khayyam is the Sufi voice, and the Sufi voice, to the Sufi, is timeless. In poetry it will not submit readily to time-centered theories. That Khayyam has been rediscovered in Persian through the fame of translations is correct—if we amend this to read, "Khayyam was not well known to non-Sufis until comparatively recently in Persia. However, through the efforts of Western scholars, his work has become known very widely to non-Sufis there."

Professor Cowell, who introduced Omar to FitzGerald, and taught him Persian, found the Sufi content in Khayyam through talks with Indian scholars of Persian. Some later scholars have concluded that these people misled the professor. Some Western experts will have no Sufic content in Khayyam. The Reverend Dr. T. H. Weir, a lecturer in Arabic (Khayyam wrote in Persian), wrote a book about Omar in which he is quite clear about this. "The truth is," he says (in his *Omar Khayyam the Poet*), "that one cannot read half a dozen lines of Omar without seeing that there is no mysticism here, any more than in Burns." He does not tell us what kind of mysticism he is referring to, or how he would identify it.

FitzGerald himself was confused about Omar. Sometimes he thought that he was a Sufi, sometimes not. But he had himself absorbed a great deal of Sufi thought. Heron-Allen, who made a most careful analysis, shows that material which people had thought was concocted by FitzGerald often came from other Persian poets. These authors were the ones which have since Chaucer most influenced English writers—the Sufis Attar, Hafiz, Saadi and Jami.

Perhaps intentionally but probably accidentally, Fitz-Gerald had become soaked in Sufic teachings from what are Persian basic texts. These matured in his mind until they emerged, mixed with Omar, to form the *Rubaiyat* in English. Had FitzGerald known about the special teaching technique used by Khayyam—following up a line of thought in order to imply its shallowness—he might have provided something even more effective in its impact.

The translator also missed the stress placed by Khayyam on the Sufic state of understanding which comes after "inebriation," contained in such passages at this:

I cannot live without wine,
Without the cup's draught I cannot carry my body.
I am the slave of that breath in which the Saki says
"Take one more cup"—and I cannot do so.

This is a clear reference to the condition attained under Sufi teachers when what was an ecstatic experience develops into a real perception of the hidden dimension beyond the metaphorical drunkenness.

FitzGerald's version of Khayyam has never been improved upon in English because, in order for Sufi ideas to be transmitted to any extent in any generation, there must be a certain measure of harmony between the ideas and the formulation of the time.

This is not to say that everyone could see this content in Omar. He captured Swinburne, Meredith and millions of people seeking a way of thinking outside the conventions within which they felt themselves imprisoned. But others sensed that this was in some way a threat to convention. A

celebrated doctor of divinity, Dr. Hastie, did not attempt
to understand the depth in Khayyam.

He found the FitzGerald version "of the rudest wit and
shallowest reflection, lean and flashy songs." FitzGerald himself had produced a "new-patched Omar;" exciting "miserable, self-deluded, unhealthy fanatics of his Cult." This
"cult" was "a literary craze and delusion, infatuation and
spurious idolatry."

Did the reverend gentleman feel his values threatened by
one who was, after all, only a "tipsy toper, cowardly scamp,
bankrupt, blustering purblind braggart?"

Omar was perhaps as often understood in the East as in
the West. Perturbed because so many English-speaking
Moslem students in India were enthused over Khayyam in
FitzGerald's translation, at least one orthodox Moslem
divine circulated a warning. In *The Explanation of Khayyam* (Molvi Khanzada, Lahore, 1929), a widely circulated
pamphlet, he did what he could to fit the problem into
his own perspective. First he argues, not without reason,
that FitzGerald did not know Persian really well. Secondly,
he insists that Cowell did not know it well either ("both
scrawled badly, like small children"). People who wanted
to read Khayyam should study Persian first, not English.
Even before Khayyam they would then be able to get a
proper basis of Islam before passing on to complicated matters like Sufism. Finally, Khayyam is a generic term applied
to a way of teaching which the Sufis have and which would
in any case be misleading if taken on its own, out of books
and without a master.

Khayyam was a great cult in England. His devotees
formed clubs, planted roses from Nishapur on FitzGerald's
grave, sought to emulate him in their poetry. The literary
cult multiplied, in spite of the fact that it was known that
the oldest available manuscript was written three hundred
and fifty years after its author's death—almost as if all we
knew about St. John of the Cross was in a document

written yesterday, and we had to base our assessment of him on that and very little else.

From the Sufi point of view, Khayyam's poetry has multiple functions. It may be read for its apparent content alone; it may be recited under certain conditions in order to provide special improvements in the range of consciousness; it may be "decoded" to obtain material of use in Sufic studies.

It is a part of the Sufi heritage, and as such performs a comprehensive role whose understanding is itself a part of Sufi specialization.

It is reported of Khan Jan-Fishan Khan, chief of the Hindu-Kush Sufis and a great nineteenth-century master, that he used the quatrains of Omar in his teaching. A disciple reports:

Three new members came to the Khan. He received them, told them to go away and study Khayyam, then to report on him. In a week they reported, on his reception day. The first said that the effect of the poems had been to make him think and to think as he had not thought before. The second said that he thought Khayyam a heretic. The third felt that there was some deep mystery in Khayyam, which he hoped he would eventually be able to understand.

The first was kept on as a disciple. The second was sent to another teacher. The third was sent back to study Khayyam for another week. A disciple asked the Khan whether this was a method of assessing the potentialities of the would-be Sufis. "We already knew something about them, through intuitive means," said the master, "but what you consider a test is partly a test and partly a fragment of their training. Further, it has the function of helping to train the watchers as well. This is Sufism—it is a composite, if you like, of study, feeling and the interaction of people and thought."

I was present one day when an enthusiastic German follower of Omar read a complicated and wordy analysis of Khayyam and his sources to a Sufi master. Beginning with the contention that Omar was discovered by von Hammer

almost forty years before Cowell and FitzGerald, he ended
by showing to his own satisfaction that almost every type of
philosophical theory was embodied in the *Rubaiyat*. The
sage listened to him in complete silence. Then he told a
story, and here it is.

A scholar went to a Sufi master and asked him about the
seven Greek philosophers who fled to Persia from the
tyranny of Justinian, who had closed their philosophical
schools. "They were of our number," replied the Sufi.

Delighted, the scholar went away and wrote a treatise on
the Greek origins of Sufic thought.

One day he met a traveling Sufi, who said, "The master
Halimi and the great Rumi quote Jesus as a Sufi teacher."

"Perhaps he means that the Greek knowledge passed to
the Christians and also to the Sufis," thought the scholar.
He wrote this into his treatise.

The original master, on a pilgrimage, passed through the
scholar's hometown one day. Meeting him, he said, "And
the heretics, and thousands who do not know it, are of our
number."[1]

My friend, the Sufi, looked closely at the German scholastic. "Wine contains water, sugar, fruit, color. Mix these together and you will not produce wine.

"We are sitting in a room. Suppose a man said, 'The
Chinese have rooms. Therefore all rooms are copied from
them. There is a carpet here. This means Mongol influence.
A servant just entered—this, surely is a Roman habit. Or is
it a Pharaonic one? Now, through the window I see a bird.
Research has shown that birds were almost certainly seen
through windows by ancient Egyptians. What a wonderful
amalgam of inherited customs this place is!' What would you
think of such a man?"

Omar's so-called theory of transmigration was assessed by
Professor Browne, one of the greatest British authorities on
Persian literature and author of the standard *Literary His-*

[1] See annotation "Hidden Sufis."

tory of Persia, who quotes a traditional tale about the poet,
supposed to prove that he believed in reincarnation.

The poet was one day about to pass an old college in
Nishapur, accompanied by a group of his students. A
string of donkeys, carrying bricks for the repair of the building, entered. One, however, refused to pass through the
gates. Omar looked at the scene, smiled and went up to the
donkey, reciting an extempore poem:

> O one who has gone and returned,
> Your name has been lost from among names.
> Your nails are combined into hooves:
> Your beard, a tail, now on the other end.

The ass now readily entered the college grounds. The
disciples, puzzled, asked their teacher, "Wise one, what does
this mean?"

"The spirit which is now within that ass was once inside
the body of a teacher in this college. It was reluctant to go in
as a donkey. Then, finding that it had been recognized by
a fellow teacher, it had to enter the precincts."

But Omar was not (as has been thought by externalists)
indicating a possibiilty that some element of human entity
might attach itself to another living form. Neither was he
just taking an opportunity of tilting at the sterile scholasticism of his time. Nor was he showing that he could influence donkeys by means of verse.

If he was not showing off in front of his disciples, not
playing a joke, not carrying out some private activity
mysterious to the unenlightened onlooker, not preaching
a form of reincarnation, not essentially versifying—what
was he doing?

He was doing what all Sufi teachers do—applying a complex impact for the benefit of the students, allowing them to
participate in the fact of accompanying a teacher through
a comprehensive experience. This is a form of demonstrative
communication which is known only to those who have
been through the rough-and-tumble of a Sufi school. The

moment the process is split up by the inquiring mind, in an attempt to relate it to a single, even a double, rational meaning, the meaning itself drops away.

The disciple learns through this method things which cannot be conveyed by any other. Reproduce them in print, and unless you add a caution, trying to indicate their special character, the situation will appear to the most earnest inquirer as obscure at best.

The name which Omar chose for his own—Omar Khayyam—decodes by numerical cipher to *Ghaqi*—Squanderer of Goods; a name used for a man who does not care for the ordinary things of this world, when dissipation of attention upon them prevents his developing of meaningful perception of another dimension.

One of Omar's most telling poems against mechanical thinkers—academic or emotional—might still be used with every justification to reproach his later self-appointed critics and expounders:

O ignorant ones—the Road is neither this nor that!

The Secret Language
I. The Coalmen

How can the Essence which itself has not
found the giver of Being—how can it
become a giver of Being?

(Jami)

Neither Sufism in translation of its literary forms nor the writings of many Eastern poets can be well understood without a knowledge of the secret language (the "hidden tongue") which is used to communicate ideas and concepts. Literal translation of Sufi words or encoded terms has caused an almost unbelievable confusion in the West, especially in the transmission of "secret lore." The problem started in its literary form in the twelfth century, when the allegorical alchemies were translated. It continues in almost unbroken succession to the present day, when Sufi books are still appearing with a literal interpretation given to what are in fact poetic complications, so written as to be clear only to the Sufi.

It is impossible to give a full account of all the systems used in secret-language form by the Sufis. But we can point out some cases, examples which make the idea clear and also shed light on puzzles still lingering in the West.

First we must go into the matter a little further.

The illustrious poet Nizami, in his *Treasury of Mysteries,* is one of the many who have referred to the cryptography of the Sufis. It is a form of communication among the enlightened ones. It has the advantage of connecting mundane thinking with the greater dimensions, the "other world" from which ordinary humanity is cut off. The language will vary in its formulation according to the time and culture in which it is used, but its essence and working remain the same.

In classical Sufi times this language is based upon Arabic, though examples of pre-Islamic use of the system are to be found.

Nizami, in one poem, gives this clue about the language:

A time will come when our die is stamped on a new coin. [The Sufi speech] does not belong to any known tongue. Under the poet's tongue lies the key to the *Treasury*. The prophet and the poet are the kernel: others the shell.

The secret language, because it is not only a cipher to prevent the profane from understanding things with which they cannot correctly attune themselves, and because it is thought to connect with a greater reality, is immensely complicated in effect. It is the subject of Sufi study in the circles of the teachers, and once its method of procedure is understood, at least one layer of its working is revealed. If we look at the extract from Nizami, we see how double meaning is used to throw the ordinary literary reader off the scent. "Our die . . . stamped on a new coin" may be taken to mean a life to come, or even the possibility of reincarnation. But this automatic association is not intended thus. Following, in the original Persian, the basic knowledge that the passage is a clue, we find that the "key to the *Treasury*" is the title of the book itself. (*The Treasury of Mysteries*) In a secondary sense it may be taken to mean a treasury of knowledge, but our poet is being more specific.

The secret language, although it has expression in the familiar world, is considered to be in a special relationship with the extrafamiliar one. Hence it is in its literary expression both an art form and also a lead-in to the reaches where there is no "known tongue."

If we return to an earlier stage in encipherment, the basic system is the Abjad scheme, a fairly simple substitution cipher, often coupled with allegorization of the recipherment. This is widely used in literature. Many people read it, or at least look for it, almost as a matter of course, especially poets and writers. Hebrew and Arabic both use similar numerical equivalents for the Semitic letters, also now applied to many other languages. These are the letters and their equivalents:

Letter	Number	Letter	Number	Letter	Number
ALIF	1	YA	10	QAF	100
BA	2	KAF	20	R	200
JIM	3	LAM	30	SH	300
DAL	4	MIM	40	T	400
HA	5	NUN	50	TH	500
WAU	6	SIN	60	KH	600
Z	7	AYN	70	DZ	700
HH	8	FA	80	DH	800
TT	9	SD	90	TZ	900
				GH	1000

While the Arabic letters have equivalents up to one thousand, the Hebrew alphabet has equivalents only up to four hundred, inclusive. For mnemonic purposes this arrangement of letters is always memorized as follows, as a string of meaningless words, adding diacritical points to make pronunciation possible:

ABJAD HAWAZ HUTY KALMAN SAFAS QURSHAT THAKHDZ DHATZAGH.

In Persian, Urdu and other non-Semitic languages, the letters are given slightly different sounds in some cases, but this does not affect the use of the letters, whose numerical values remain constant.

Date names, dates of birth or death, words expressing the character or aspirations of a person, all are often evolved from the scheme. Ignorant repetition of the meaningless words has in some places endowed the barbarous Abjad "words" with spurious *baraka*, the belief in special inherent functions, but this belongs to the realm of repetitious magical procedures and is not important.

Here is an example of how one might use the scheme. Supposing that we want to name a book, showing that it has a certain sort of disguised content, perhaps records of secret processes. We could name it *Source of Records*, in Arabic *Umm el Qissa*. We examine the words which we have chosen, with their meanings:

UMM = mother, matrix, source, principle, prototype
EL = of
QISSA = record, story, tale

Umm el Qissa, we now see, may mean something equivalent to: Mother of Records, Source of Story, Prototype of Tales. We now, if all these alternatives are agreeable to us, encipher the letters by substituting their numerical equivalents from the standard Abjad list. Now we add them together. The sum is 267.

Now we have to find a sufficiently descriptive or poetic title for our book, made up of letters which, when added, give us the same number 267.

Our rearrangement can give us the phrase: *Alf layla wa layla*. This means *Thousand and One Nights*. The title of a book, or the author's name, will often give a most important indication of the emphasis which is to be placed upon the book, and what can be discovered from it. In the case of the *Arabian Nights*, the person who named the work intended to convey that herein would be found certain essential stories. A study of the stories themselves, and their decoding according to the rules of the secret language, gives us the intention or concealed meaning and use of the stories. Many of them are encoded Sufi teaching stories, descriptions of psychological processes, or enciphered lore of one **kind** or another.

However complicated all this may appear, in fact the investigation is inevitable and not difficult for anyone who is working with this kind of material. Most people who do so have been coached in the methodology by their own teachers. It can be said to be a part of Sufi literary training —the point at which literature is shown to be the vehicle for much more complex experiences than those on the literary level as usually understood.

We can now look at the mysterious word "Sufi," itself the subject of puzzlement and questioning. Decoded by the scheme, we find it to be made up as follows:

S = 90; W = 6; F = 80; Y = 10. These are the consonants used in the spelling of the word. They total 186. In order to decode, we have to arrange the numbers in hundreds, tens and units: 100, 80, 6. These are now retransformed into their equivalent letters: 100 = Q; 80 = F; 6 = U. These can be rearranged in any of several ways, to form three-letter roots in Arabic, all indicative of some aspect of Sufism. The main interpretation is FUQ, which means "Above, transcending." Sufism is, as a consequence, spoken of as the Transcendent philosophy.

The names of Sufi authors and teachers have been chosen with the greatest care. They represent a quality, formulation or emphasis which it is intended should be read into their works, or at least the work in which they appear.

Sufis therefore do not approach their teachers' names externally, as the product of their environment (Bokhara, Arabia, and so on); nor as indications of professions (the Chemist, Painter, Spinner). Their names have first to be decoded.

Attar, for instance, means the Chemist, or the Seller of Perfumes. On the poetical level, such a name is sufficiently descriptive. Decoded, to gain the essence of the name, we have the number 280. Restoring the numbers to their order of greatness (hundreds, then tens), we have 200 and 80.

Reconverting into letters: 200 = R; 80 = F. The word which represents the essence (*dhat*) is RF. The dictionary shows us that in Arabic this word stands for the concept of "the fluttering of a bird." Attar's masterpiece *The Parliament of the Birds* is a reference to this. More than this, he has chosen the RF root to convey its alternative meanings: "to flash (light); to twinkle; shining (color); to be shaken by the wind."

The flash refers to intuition, the shining to the projection of teaching and the use of colors by the Sufis. The shaking, used in this root as of a plant in the wind, means the movement of the exercises of the dervish. Attar further chooses the plant allegory because Sufism is of a growing, adaptive, organic and necessary nature, according to its followers. The wind which is taken as shaking the plant is the divine wind, the impalpable force which is known by its effect (on the plant) as much as by anything else.

Shams of Tabriz, the inspirer of some of Rumi's poetry and at one time his associate, is a mysterious figure to the externalist. He is referred to in literature under the sobriquet of *zardoz*, Persian for "worker in golden thread," people having in consequence inferred that this was his mundane occupation. His whole name was Shamsuddin-i-Tabriz. When it is decoded, we find that this was a poetic name, carefully chosen by the Abjad method. His real name, converted and reconverted into letters, spells *khit*, "thread, string," and is connected with gossamer and also the particles which seem to dance in the sun's rays. Since his name "Shams" also means "sun" when literally translated, the play upon words becomes obvious. His other names, such as *parinda* (the Flyer) can be similarly decoded to produce meaningful descriptions.

In initiatory words, the Abjad provides even more profound meanings, familiar to every practicing Sufi. No person may be a teacher of Sufism unless he has himself been through the succession of experiences which are essential. When he has been through these, he is changed, so that he remains an ordinary human being only in the obvious sense. His functions have changed, and he is now a "herdsman." What is it that gives him that character? It is a cognition which is called "certitude," which the Sufi illuminate, the "arrived man," or "whole one," now possesses. In this he differs from the ordinary man, who is a prey to the fluctuations of his own lack of stabilization. This is expressed in the derivations of the word for certitude.

Certitude stands for infallible guidance, and the word for it is *yaqina,* formed of the elements YQN. These are transposed into 160, split again into 100 and 60, reconverted into QSS. The dictionary shows that this word stands for "taking the marrow out of a bone." It can also mean "herdsman," or "to become a priest." Sufis therefore consider that the essence of certitude and its expression is the "retrieving of the very marrow, the shepherding of others, the exercising the commanding authority and endowment usually invested in what is called a priest in mechanical religion." It may be noted that the Sufi cannot benefit another person beyond the extent to which his function is acknowledged by that person. As a shepherd he can look after the external needs of a flock; as a priest he has the inner qualities to cater for their essential progress. This, to the Sufi, is the meaning of priest—that he should have arrived at some sort of certitude which places him into contact with the greater dimension, not that he should be mechanically created by order or study. A priest is the result of a development. No such priests exist in familiar religion.

We can carry the Abjad method, where used by organization, much further than isolated cases. In Sufi circles, instead of numerical substitution, rhyme or homonym is used to confuse the noninitiate as to the symbolism of ritual. Several mysterious societies in the West are offshoots of Sufi circles, and can easily be traced back through a knowledge of the Sufi organization, historical possibility, or the secret language. The Builders is one. Another is the Coalmen.

In Arabic (and thence to Persian), the word FeHM, from the Semitic root FHM, means "to understand, perceive." From it are derived the words "to make a person understand," and so on.

A Sufi circle called the *fehmia* (Perceivers) traces its philosophical pedigree to Bayazid of Bistam. There are two letters "h" in Arabic. A word using the second "h" is also pronounced like FeHM, but means Coalman, or charcoal dealer.

Its members, to commemorate this in ritual, actually put charcoal on their faces. Freemasons are in some Arabic dictionaries called charcoal burners or Coalmen.

An Italian secret society, originally devoted to doing good and to the ends of mutual protection, was called the *Carbonari*, the charcoal burners. There can be no reasonable doubt, on historical, geographical and linguistic evidence, that this is a deteriorated form of the Perceivers. According to Sufi lore, when the dynamic element of a living teacher deserts a circle, it becomes repetitive and loses its interior quality. Whatever may be the truth of this, the *Carbonari* are an excellent example to study.

The myth of the foundation of the *Carbonari* claims that King Francis I of France (died 1515) when out hunting strayed into Scotland, which bordered his territories. He was found and befriended by charcoal burners. These, however, were not ordinary people, but a band of mystics, who had been instructed by an ancient sage. Francis joined them and became their protector. If we realize that the country which bordered France was Spain, and not Scotland, and Sufiized Spain at that,[1] we begin to see another line of connection with the Sufi charcoal men. "Scotland" seems to be not a mistake, as has been thought, but a code name for Spain. This is borne out by the fact that the Freemasons

[1] The last great expulsion of Moslems from Spain was in 1609, when a million unrepentant Moors were deported. In Francis I's time, nothing is more likely than fugitive associations of Sufis in the forests, instructed by "ancients."

also state that early lodges were founded in "Scotland," and they speak of "Scottish rites."

From being a mystical society, the *Carbonari* became ethical, then political. They were joined by many Freemasons.[2] There are many more points of resemblance between the Sufi circle and the Italian. Engravings of *Carbonari* meetings show the members ranged in the same way as in Sufi meetings. The smallest unit of the *Carbonari* was called the *baracca*, the "hut."

But among the Sufi Coalmen, *baraka* is a word for a meeting, originally a signal to call meetings. No less interesting is the fact that it was the reputation of the Sufi Coalmen that they could give a *baraka* (blessing) to brides in country districts. In England even today brides often call in the chimney sweep—with sooty face—to give them a kiss just after the wedding ceremony. El-Aswad, the Black Man, is one of the important and mysterious figures in both North European and Spanish-Arab accounts of witchcraft rites (non-Catholic ceremonies) in many parts of Europe.[3]

Millions of words could be written on concealed Sufic meanings. Sometimes they are contained in phrases, some of them not very meaningful in their apparent sense, but repeated with a fervor which has baffled the uninitiated. Here is one such slogan.

"Seek knowledge, even as far as China," the phrase which is on all Sufi lips, has more than a literal or even a figurative

[2] Secret meanings in rituals and ideas diffused from Spain may thus be considered to remain "in suspension" or fossilized in many contemporary systems, where the original meaning has been lost. It is interesting to note that even in Spain today, some of these meanings may be clearer to simple peasants than they are to the non-Arabist erudite of North Europe. Professor E. G. Browne, the celebrated Orientalist, reports a debased Arabic script as still in use for love letters by Spanish peasants in the early part of this century. (E. G. Browne, *Literary History of Persia*, Cambridge University Press, 1956, Vol. I, p. 9)

[3] It is said that, under Louis XVIII and Charles X, over twelve thousand Freemasons in Paris were also *Carbonari* initiates.

sense. This meaning is unlocked by analyzing the use of the word "China," interpreted through the secret language.

"China" is the code word for mind concentration, one of the Sufi practices, an essential prerequisite to Sufic development. The phrase is important partly because it provides an example of the coincidence in interpretation possible in either the Arabic or Persian languages. Neither has any real connection with the other. The fact that the word for "China" in both, though spelled and pronounced differently, decodes to substantially the same concept, invests this phrase with a special significance for the Sufi.

This is the method of decoding:

CHINA. In Arabic SYN (letters Saad, Ya, Nun). Equivalent numbers: 90, 10, 50. Totaled, these letters yield the number 150. Splitting by hundreds, tens and units: 100 + 50 (no units remain). Retranslated into numbers: 100 = Q, plus 50 = N. Q and N recombined to form a word: QN. The word QN (in the form QaNN) represents, in Arabic, the concept of "scrutinizing, observing," and is therefore taken as a symbol of concentration, focus. The injunction now reads: "Seek knowledge, even as far as concentration (of the mind)."

CHINA. In Persian CHYN (letters Che, Ya, Nun). Equivalent numbers: 3, 10, 50. Before translating into numbers, the Persian letter Che (CH) is first exchanged for its nearest equivalent in the Abjad scheme, which is J. The three sums totaled: 3 + 10 + 50 = 63. Separated into tens and units: 60 + 3. These numbers retranslated into letters: 60 = SIN; 3 = JIM. The word we now have to determine is a combination of S and J. SJ (pronounced SaJJ) means "to plaster or coat, as with clay." Reverse the order of the letters (a permissible change, one of very few allowed by the rules) and we have the word JS. The word is pronounced JaSS. This means "to inquire after a thing; to scrutinize (hidden things); to ascertain (news)." This is the root of the word for "espionage," and hence the Sufi is called the Spy of the Heart. To the Sufi the scrutinization for the purpose of ascertaining hidden things is an equivalent, poetically speaking, with the motive for concentrating the mind.

In their official documents, and in referring to one another, the *Carbonari* always used the term "good cousins." This is an interesting example of translation from Arabic, and also of the transposing of Semitic roots, through alliteration, into another language—in this case Italian. "Good cousin" in Arabic is the same word which is used of the ancient Sufis mentioned in the Koran, the *muqaribin*, the Near Ones, "close kindred." The Semitic radical QRB from which the word is derived is cleverly perpetuated in the first syllable of the Italian word *Carbonari*, the K-R-B sound. There are many other resemblances of this kind in this and other usages of initiatory societies, most of which must remain concealed from outsiders, since they are still in use.

The Secret Language
II. The Builders

Detach from fixed ideas and
preconceptions. And face what is
to be your lot.
(Sheikh Abu-Said Ibn Abi-Khair)

"Sufi-ism," said Sir Richard Burton, was "the Eastern parent
of Freemasonry."[1] Whether Burton was a Freemason or not,
there is no doubt that he was a Sufi.

Freemasonry has been upheld by distinguished people in
many countries, reviled and persecuted, linked with politics,
reduced to the relative informality of staid businessmen's
frolics, penetrated by Rosicrucianism, attacked as a Jewish
imposture by the Nazis. It would not be seemly for a Freemason to engage upon a public portrayal of any part of the
craft's symbolism or beliefs—indeed it is more than probable
that a member would be under an oath of secrecy whereby
he must preserve every part of the brotherhood's workings
from all who are not initiated. The source of material purporting to be Masonic for the nonmember, therefore, is
bound to be fairly one-sided—the inner workings of
Masonry provided by renegades and probably by opponents
of the craft.

When a study is made of all available literature purporting

[1] F. Hitchman, *Burton*, Vol. I, p. 286.

to contain Masonic secrets, certain definite outlines appear, which might justifiably be considered to form a reasonable amount of true information, on the no-smoke-without-fire principle. Be that as it may, what interests the Sufi is the fact that, out of the material which claims to be partially or wholly Masonic, a very great deal is at once seen to concur with matters of everyday Sufi initiatory practice. Either Freemasonry is, as Burton claimed, derived from the Sufis; or else the substance of the frequent and plentiful exposes, which may not be of Freemasonry at all, are in fact exposures of a Sufic cult other than Freemasonry. For the purposes of this study we shall approach this exciting part of the inquiry from the only perspective open to us. Parallels will be sought between what the exposers claim to be Freemasonry, and what we know of Sufic schools.

One of the best methods of tracing Arab-Sufi transmission to the West is through terminology. When a certain word is used with an esoteric significance, it is generally worthwhile studying it and seeking a parallel between the two systems. The fundamental word which we find most used in Masonic exposures is composed of the three Hebrew letters A, B, L. Transliterated into Arabic letters, this word proves to be the password of the Sufi society called the Builders (al-Banna); and the Arabic word for Mason is also al-Banna. Far from ending here, the parallels are only just beginning.

As in the case of the troubadors (TRB, Arabic root), the Builders (first said to have flourished under this name in the ninth century) chose this triliteral word with care, searching the dictionary for a term which would embrace as many aspects of their oganization as possible. The result, analyzed by inflecting the Arabic root in the normal manner, provides this list of characteristics of the school:

ABL = monk, sexton, etc.; hierophancy
ALB = to gather people together; grouping
LaBA = to stop, to halt at a place

BaLA = to give a thing, to be beneficent

BAL = heart, mind; attention; state; boldness; welfare

Even without other information which exists about this Sufi school, we can already glean something of their organization and objectives through this breakdown of their secret word. The first word intimates initiation, the second the congregation, the third the stages of the Path of the Sufis, the fourth the giving (of love and charity) which was their means of expression, the fifth various aspects of their activities and training. Why was the word written in Hebrew, and not in Arabic? Some late hand has reshaped the Arabic origins of the craft into a form more acceptable to people with a Judeo-Christian tradition; and we can safely assume from the published materials that it was to just such a community that the modern form of Masonry as we know it in the West was addressed.

To the Sufi Builders, these three letters symbolized three meditation postures. The Kufic letter *alif* was the kneeling position. Dhu'l-Nun Misri, one of the greatest Sufi teachers, is believed to have formulated it in this shape. It became powerful in Turkey during the sixteenth century. Western writers say "it is strangely like the Masons." It was illustrated by a set square, a primal symbol of the Masons. In Arabic, again, the word *square* is RBA—which summarizes meditation very well in its alternative meaning of "waiting, restraint." The second letter, *ba*, is written in Arabic letters like a boat with a dot under it. This forms a fairly passable diagram of its symbol—the level—also used in Masonry. This conveys the emblematic meaning of "prostration and concentration." The final letter, *lam*, is likened to a rope. In shape it is very much like a hook or curving piece of rope. It means to the Builder "the rope which binds all in union."

There are, according to the Sufis, ninety-nine divine names or attributes. The development of the effect of all these names produces the complete individual. The hundredth name is a secret, and becomes known to the Seeker only when he has become imbued with the spirit of the others. The number thirty-three is used by the Builders to denote one third of the total training system which produces the first grade of enlightenment. In the numerical system of the Arabic alphabet (where every letter has a number) thirty-three provides: 30 = letter L; 3 = letter J. This is the only way in which the number can be split up by this system. If the letters L and J are then considered to spell a word, they constitute the password or initiatory meaning of the first third of Sufi enlightenment. Is there a word LJ or JL in Arabic? Indeed there is. There are both. LJ spells "flame," and Sufistically stands for the illumination, the burning desire of love. JL spells "illustrious." The flaming sword which is reputedly a Masonic emblem is used by the Builders to correspond with this meaning—the thirty-three names.

What of the hundredth name? This, strange though it may seem, seems to be the (now corrupted) original of the strange G-like symbol found within the Masonic star in items of regalia. In the cult of the Builders, this G is the Arabic letter Q, which it closely resembles.[2] And Q stands for the secret, the final element. In the same Arabic letter-number notation, Q is equivalent to the number one hundred.

This method of codes within codes, and using letters and numbers to convey matters which only the initiated understand is characteristic of dervish poets; and since it occurs in too many particulars for it to be mere coincidence, the Masonic usage and the Sufi one are identical. Take the matter a stage further. If we add the letter Q, the hidden power, to the three-letter word ALB, eliding the letter A, in Arabic we have a further panorama of hidden meanings:

Q-ABL = beforehand, first, prior (primacy of the cult)

[2] In Colloquial Arabic, the Q sound may be rendered, especially by non-Arabs, as G. The tendency is more marked still in some countries which use Arabic words, but themselves lack the guttural Q sound.

Q-ALB = heart (Sufi symbol for contemplation and in-
         ner metaphysical contact)[8]
L-aQB = title, honorific (the distinction of the cult)

And, whether by accident or design, the three letters
Q,L,B, when added together according to the Arabic notation, produce 132. This can be read as $32 + 1 = 33$. But,
according to the Builders, it is an intimation of the secret
teaching passed on with great secrecy by one whose name,
when calculated by the same method in Arabic, provides
the number thirty-three. And this is how they spell it:

$$
\left.
\begin{array}{rcl}
M & = & 40 \\
H & = & 8 \\
M & = & 40 \\
M & = & 40 \\
D & = & 4
\end{array}
\right\} 132
$$

The word, spelled according to Arab orthography, is
Mohammed. We are now at the stage when the Builders
reveal that the Sufic lore which they practice was a part
of the secret teaching of Mohammed himself.

This figure of thirty-three, or the letter Q, the Sufi Builders inscribe within a pentagram, and sometimes in a star
composed of two triangles. In other esoteric traditions, these
superimposed triangles are explained as standing for male
and female principles, as air and fire, and so on. But to the
Sufi Builder, the lower triangle is the shaped Arabic nu-
meral seven. The upper one is the outline of the number
eight. And, taken together, the six sides of the two triangles
comprise the number six. This, to them, means the series
786. And 786 is the religious formula *Bismillah ar-Rahman,
ar-Rahim,* reduced to figures by direct substitution. The
meaning of the phrase is the same as that found on a Sufic
crucifix from ninth-century Ireland—In the name of Allah,
the Beneficent, the Merciful.

The Kaaba (cubical temple) of Mecca was rebuilt in

[8] See annotation "QALB."

608 A.D., when Mohammed was thirty-five years old, and five years before he started his teaching. This temple was built with thirty-one courses of stone and wood.[4] The Sufis add: "with Earth and Sky, thirty-three."

It would be improper to go any further in presenting material which both Freemasons and organized dervish fraternities possess and consider to be of high initiatory significance.[5] But there are incidental facts which can be mentioned, and are of some general interest. Freemasonry, according to some of its historians, came to England in the time of Aethelstan (about 894–939), the Saxon king who brought England into close contact with the rest of Europe. His life covered almost the same period as that of the illustrious Spanish Sufi Ibn Masarra (883–931) from whose illuminist school a tremendous and continuing influence upon Western thought has been traced. It was during the same century that Dhu'l-Nun the Egyptian, the Sufi and reputed founder of the dervish Order of Builders, lived and taught. Dhu'l-Nun, revered by all Sufis, is referred to as having been of Nubian ("black") origin, giving a connection with the adoption of "black" (fehm) and "knowledge, understanding" (fehm) by the dervish school of the Coalmen, which we associate with the *Carbonari*.

"Black" is also another word for Egypt, said to be derived from the color of the soil. The Black Art is thought by many to mean nothing more than "the Egyptian Art," or the "Art of Understanding." By a similar process of thought, the Black Virgins of the middle ages could be translated as the "Wise Virgins." The confusion between the Black Art, the Hermetic Art and the Egyptian Secrets has appeared and reappeared throughout medieval literature. The misunderstanding exists only because of ignorance of the similarity of "black" and "wise" in Arabic by foreigners.

---

[4] Azraqi, quoted by Wistenfeld in Creswell: *Early Muslim Architecture*, London, 1958, p.I. The two other courses are, of course, the earth and sky, according to Sufi symbolism.

[5] For one cryptic interchange, see annotation "Dots."

The connection between Black Art, alchemy and Rosi-crucianism has baffled many students, who have assumed for the most part that all these things were dabbled in by Europeans of the middle ages just because of a general credulity and desire to penetrate secrets and find a hidden teaching.

The connection beween the Shriners and the Masons has seemed to many observers to be absurd, or some sort of a false association. A Shriner must be a Mason. His ritual is avowedly based upon a myth and ritual connected with the Holy Temple in Mecca. What possible connection, it is sometimes asked, could there be between the Mecca temple of the Moslems and the Temple of Solomon and its build-ing? There could be a very close connection indeed. First let it be noted that charges against ancient Sufis included the terrible allegation that a mime of the Mecca pilgrimage ceremonies could be carried out anywhere with equal validity to an actual pilgrimage. Secondly, let us remember that the great Sufi teacher Maaruf Karkhi (died 815) is known as Son of David, and also as "king," a common Sufi appellation. The Son of David, by association, was Solomon. Solomon it was who rebuilt the Temple. Why Son of David? Because Karkhi was the disciple of the illus-trious teacher Daud el Tai. Daud is Arabic for David.

This David died in 781. Less than a century before, about 691, the Saracens rebuilt the Temple of Solomon on the site which is now known as the Dome of the Rock. This, and no earlier one, is the Temple whose servants were the Knights Templars, accused of Saracenic leanings. It is no accident that after the dissolution of the Order of the Templars the Freemasons took on Templar traditions.

It should not be forgotten that the Kaaba (literally, the Cube) is the foursquare temple of Mecca. The "black stone" of Mecca is set in an outer corner of the Kaaba. It is thus correctly described as the Kaaba (Cube) stone, easily ren-dered as the Cubic Stone. It is also called *hajarel aswad* (black stone). "Black," as we have noted, is rendered as "coal," and the "stone of black" can be rendered as *hajarel fehm*, "stone of wisdom," or even, in translation, "stone of the wise." Second only to this place for all Moslems is the sanctified spot known as the Temple of Solomon in Palestine.

Sufi tradition has it that a band of early classical Sufis were a number of men who assembled in the Mecca temple and devoted themselves to its service. On the fall of Jerusalem to the Arabs, the first act of the Moslems was to repair to the site of the Solomonic Temple to acquire it for Islam. That the Sufi tradition was continued in respect of the Dome of the Rock is evidenced by the fact that its later interior decorations contain Sufi symbolic designs. Templar churches and other indications show the influence of the Saracen version of the Solomonic Temple.

There are two lines of diffusion of this lore to the West —initially through Saracen Spain, with or without Jewish amalgamation of ideas (because Jews were active in co-operation with the Arab Cabalists), and again through the Crusades, when members of the cult known as the Builders may very well have found similar rituals among the dervishes of the Near East.

Finally, the darkness-and-light motif attributed to Freemasonry has dervish parallels so close that these alone would give one cause to wonder. The dervishes speak of light as truth, illumination. Black, as we have already noted, is associated with wisdom (being homonymous with it in Arabic); and white, too, stands for understanding. Knowing the true meaning of wisdom and light, of good and bad, of the real "darkness" of the ignorant is the central point in dervish activity. Sufis ultimately in this connection depend upon the Light Verse in the Koran (Sura 24, 35), which says: "Rejectors' deeds are like darkness: darkness upon darkness. No light at all has he who has not Allah's light." This theme is taken up in careful detail by Ghazali, whom we know influenced all the scholastic West. He wrote a book on the subject of light and darkness—the *Niche for Lights.*

The dervish usage of the light and darkness theme carries on through the literature. A fair sample is in the *Secret Garden* of Shabistari, composed in 1319: "The dervish path is dark in both worlds; yet it is but the gloom that on the horizon of the desert gladdens the wayfarer and tells the tents are near at hand. . . . Within a day of darkness shineth light."

Johnson Pasha's translation (*The Dialogue of the Gulshan-i-Raz,* Cairo, 1903), whether from Masonic or Builder sources, is not unknown in English literature. Pope, for instance (*Dunciad,* Bk. IV), could have been using a Sufi allegory when he wrote:

> Of darkness visible, so much be lent.
> As half to show, half veil, the deep intent.

From our knowledge of dervish usage, we can interpret the mysterious message in a curious and repeated Mason's mark which appears in medieval buildings. This is a mark which looks like the figure four. If the professional Masons of the middle ages were connected with dervish orders in the West, as the Eastern building workers certainly were, we have a concealed message here.

The Sufi diagram known as the Magic Square of fifteen is drawn thus:

4	9	2
3	5	7
8	1	6

This square adds up to the number fifteen, whichever way the lines of figures (one to nine) are added up. It is used in Cabalism as a code frame by means of which to convey a message. This is done by drawing lines to link up the numbers which it is intended to emphasize. The Mason's mark which we are considering looks something like this:

If this figure is superimposed upon the frame, we can read off which numbers have been involved in the message. The outline crosses all the squares of the figure, except the one occupied by the number eight!

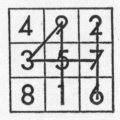

Eight symbolizes the number of perfect expression, the octagon, representing, among other things, the cube. The figure also covers eight of a total of nine squares. The meaning here is "The eight (balance) is the way to the nine." Nine stands in Arabic for the letter *Ta*, whose hidden meaning is "secret knowledge."

The outline is given additional significance when it is realized that the figure which looks like a four with a bar (sometimes a curve) attached is also a rough representation of the Arabic word *hoo*—the dervish liturgical word, chanted in order to produce ecstatic states.

That the Masons are connected with alchemy through this sign alone is made more likely by the fact that this magic square has been found in use in China and commented upon by recent alchemical researchers, who there link it with both alchemy of the symbolic kind and the Taoist tradition. If further indications were needed, one could refer to the fact that this same magic square is used by Geber, the patron of both Eastern and Western alchemy, and (as Professor Holmyard remarks) used also by the Sufi society of which Geber was a member.

Far from an irregular and haphazard collecting of mysterious and unconnected lore, the alchemists, Freemasons, Rosicrucians, *Carbonari* and others were almost certainly intermingled, because of Sufic symbolic constituents in their original or early objective—the development of human consciousness.

The Secret Language
III. The Philosopher's Stone

Deep in the sea are riches beyond compare.
But if you seek safety, it is on the shore.
(Saadi, Rose Garden)

Robert of Chester, an Englishman who studied in Saracen Spain, introduced alchemy to Christendom of the middle ages in a book which he finished in 1144. This was a translation of an Arabic book, and in it, as Professor Holmyard notes (*Alchemy,* London, 1957, p. 103), he states categorically that this science was not at that time known in the "Latin world."

Ever since this time there has been a struggle between the two interpretations of the "Art." Was it intended literally, or was alchemy a spiritual or mental developmental system? Almost inevitably, the fact that it was tackled both in the chemical and initiatory manner has been missed by many researchers. The consequence has been that some claim that alchemy was the forerunner of chemistry, exclusively concerned with producing the Philosopher's Stone; others that it stems from early attempts to gild or plate metals and pass them off as gold or silver; others that it is a sublime art which deals only with the potentialities of the human consciousness.

The facts are far less complicated than they have appeared to those who have not linked Sufi allegory with what is often only derivative literature. The first thing to remember is that the people who are indiscriminately lumped together as alchemists, and whose work has so often been treated as a whole, in actual fact constitute several different kinds of people, working along different or analogous lines.

Goldsmiths' recipes, originating at an early date, are no proof that alchemical terminology was not used by mystics. Two people, each supposed to have attained the elixir, may very well be in the one instance a charlatan, in the other a mystical teacher. Abundant evidence in the literature of the middle ages points to a constant struggle toward a form of mental development, couched in alchemical terminology.

The mistake was not rectified when the French chemist M. P. E. Berthelot, in 1888 and 1893, examined a wide variety of alchemical documents. A thorough worker, he found that the earliest available were under two thousand years old. Further, he found books containing metallurgical recipes for working and tinting metals—manuals of craftsmen in which the texts were mixed with a certain amount of spirituality. It was concluded, before most of the readers of this book were born, that alchemy was a sort of aberration, a degeneration of metallurgy and very early chemistry carried out by Greeks in Egypt.

The material was not examined in the light of the idea that alchemy was the terminology adopted by a teaching school for the projection of its allegorized message, which originated completely outside the metallic context.

The literature of alchemy, lumped together as one phenomenon, is so immense that lifetimes have been spent in an attempt to understand it. It includes forgeries of greater or lesser plausibility in Greek, Latin, Arabic and later Western languages. These writings are sometimes incoherent, veiled in symbolism and shot through with allegory and such bizarre imagery as dragons, changing colors, blazing swords, metals and planets.

The assumption that the quest of transmutation is an enterprise arising out of a misunderstanding of artisans' documents is quite insufficient to explain the consistent use of terminology by the alchemists. If we read the Arabic words for which Latin equivalents were chosen by translators, we can judge whether the Latins were trying real metallic transmutation or something else, from their use of these terms. In other words, we can tell the chemists from the spiritualists. This is one of the tools which unlocks the story of medieval alchemy.

We have to start at an early stage, with the father of alchemy as we know it, Jabir Ibn el-Hayyan. Jabir has been acknowledged by both the Arab and the European alchemists as the patron of the art since the eighth century. All alchemy as such known to us since that time contains the doctrine of three elements—salt, sulphur and mercury. These must be correctly combined to produce the Philosophical Gold. It is stressed by many alchemists, one might almost say all of them, that these substances are not the same as those which we know as salt, sulphur and mercury. Further, Geber, as Jabir was known in the West, is recorded by Professor Holmyard as having introduced the sulphur and mercury doctrine which "appears to have been unknown to the ancients."

Alchemy as it has been practiced since the eighth century bears the stamp of Jabir Ibn el-Hayyan. Who was he, and what did he mean by his sulphur and mercury? According to the Latin as well as Arabic books, Jabir was surnamed El-Sufi, the Sufi.[1]

He acknowledges in his works the Imam Jafar Sadiq (700–765) as his master, and speaks of him in the most respectful terms. And Jafar Sadiq is the great Sufi teacher whose name appears on almost all the "chains of transmission" of the lore of Sufism, which is itself called alchemy by such authorities as Rumi and Ghazali. Ghazali even

[1] Alchemy was called the Sophic Art in the middle ages.

names one of his most important books *The Alchemy of Happiness*. Ibn El-Arabi says that the "Great Names" are called gold and silver.

What is the Sophistical Stone, the Stone of the Philosophers, as it is called, which would transmute base metals into precious ones? All we have to do here is to retranslate certain words into Arabic, and see what their technical usage is among the Sufis, and we find what Jabir was talking about.

The regeneration of an essential part of humanity, according to the Sufis, is the goal of mankind. The separation of man from his essence is the cause of his disharmony and unfulfillment. His quest is the purification of the dross and the activation of the gold. The means of achieving this is found within man—it is the Philosopher's Stone. The Arabic word for stone is associated with the word for "hidden, forbidden." Hence the stone symbol was adopted in accordance with the normal rule of assonance in use among Sufis.

The stone, the hidden thing, so powerful, is also called the Azoth in the West. Azoth is traced by Orientalists to one of two words—*el-dhat* (or *ez-zat*), meaning essence or inner reality; or else to *zibaq*, mercury. The stone, according to the Sufis, is the *dhat*, the essence, which is so powerful that it can transform whatever comes into contact with it. It is the essence of man, which partakes of what people call the divine. It is "sunshine," capable of uplifting humanity to a next stage.

We can go much further than this. Three elements went toward the production of the *dhat*, after being submitted to the "work," which is a translation of the word *amal*. These elements are sulphur (*kibrit*, homonym of *kibirat*, "greatness, nobility"); salt (*milh*, homonym of *milh*, "goodness, learning"); and mercury (*zibaq*, sharing the radix for "to open a lock, to break").[2]

[2] Paracelsus (1493–1541) notes: "Mercury is the spirit, sulphur is the soul, salt is the body."

Unless we know how the words were used and also what they are equivalents for, we cannot unlock alchemy. Ibn El-Arabi himself reveals two of the meanings when he says that sulphur stands for the divine; mercury for nature. The interaction in correct proportion produced the Azoth, the ennobled essence. Translation into Latin lost the assonance which the Sufi works had, but their interpretation continued (for the benefit of non-Arabs) in the books in Persian, like Ghazali's *Alchemy of Happiness*.

The transmission of the lore of alchemy is also stated to have been in the hands of ancient masters, some of whom are named. These include Hermes, according to the Eastern and Western writers, known to the Arabs as Idris. Western authors and practitioners accept the transmission from Hermes to such an extent that alchemy is often called by them the Hermetic Art, and has been so styled ever since they accepted this origin from the Arabs.

The Spanish-Arab historian Said of Toledo (died 1069) gives this tradition of Thoth, or Hermes: "Sages affirm that all antediluvian sciences originate with the first Hermes, who lived in Sa'id, in Upper Egypt. The Jews call him Enoch and the Moslems Idris. He was the first who spoke of the material of the superior world and of planetary movements. He built temples to worship God . . . medicine and poetry were his functions. . . . [He] warned of a catastrophe of fire and water before the Flood. . . . After the Flood the sciences, including alchemy and magic, were carried out at Memphis, under the more renowned Hermes the Second."[3]

The Thrice-Great Hermes, who quite possibly did represent three different teachers, is not only the reputed originator of alchemy. His name appears among the ancient masters of what is now called the Way of the Sufis. In other words, both the Sufis and the alchemists claim Hermes as an initiate of their craft. So Jafar Sadiq the Sufi, Jabir the

---

[3] Cf. Asín Palacios, *Ibn Masarra*, p. 13.

Sufi and Hermes the reputed Sufi are all credited by alchemists of both East and West as being masters of their
craft.

The methods of concentration, distillation, maturing and
mixing, endowed with chemical names, is nothing other
than an organization of the mind and body to produce a
human, not a chemical effect. That there were imitators
who practiced physical chemistry is in no doubt whatever.
But it is equally true to say that there were until fairly
recently (and they still linger in some places) people who
believed that spiritual things had a physical parallel.

Who was Jafar Sadiq, master of Jabir, and his teacher?
None other than the Sixth Imam, or Leader, descendant
of Mohammed through Fatima, believed by many to be of the
direct line which transmitted the inner teaching of Islam,
confided to them by Mohammed himself, called Sufism.

Jabir Ibn el-Hayyan was for a long time a close companion of the Barmecides, the viziers of Haroun el-Rashid.
These *barmakis* were descended from the priests of the
Afghan Buddhist shrines, and were held to have at their
disposal the ancient teaching which had been transmitted
to them from that area. Haroun el-Rashid himself was a
constant associate of Sufis, and there are instances on record
of his making reverential pilgrimages to meet Sufi masters.

The assumption that alchemical lore came from Egypt
direct from the writings of Thoth, or something of that
kind, is unnecessary to this thesis. According to Sufi tradition the lore was transmitted through Dhu'l-Nun the
Egyptian, the King or Lord of the Fish, one of the most
famous of classical Sufi teachers.

Who was Hermes, or how was he generally conceived of?

He was the god who carried the souls of the dead to the
underworld, and carried messages from the gods. He was
the link between the extrahuman and the terrestrial. He
moved, like Mercury, his equivalent, at immense speed,
negating time and space, just in the way that inner experience does. He is an athlete, a developed man, and is con-

sidered therefore to resemble the "perfected man" of the Sufi in his outward aspect. In his earlier statues, he is shown as a matured man, a man of age and wisdom, thought of as correct results of right development. He invented the lyre and caused, as Sufis and others do, an altered state in the hearers by means of music. He cast a giant into a sleep with his flute, which action was taken as an indication of the hypnotic character of the personification of Hermes as a Sufic type. The connection with this hypnotic activity and both mysticism and medicine is obvious.

The ancient lore and its preservation and transmission is well anchored to this Hermes figure. He has a female double—Sesheta—associated with the building of temples, and the keeper of books in which ancient wisdom was preserved. Like the aspiring human being of the Sufis and also the Sufi Truth (*simurgh*), he is represented as a bird. Sometimes he is a man with the head of an ibis, where the head would indicate aspiration or attainment in the mind, localized in the head.

The world was created through a word from Thoth—eight characteristics (four symbolized as gods, four as goddesses) were made from a sound which he uttered. The eightfold character of Sufi teaching is symbolized by the octagonal diagram for the word *hoo,* the Sufi sound.

Whatever other deities or legends may have become confused with the personalities of Hermes, Mercury and Thoth, the main elements of intermediation between human and divine, wisdom, music, letters and medicine, remain.

In the threefold figure—Egyptian, Greek and Roman—like has been equated with like. His association with a form of wisdom which was transmitted to man from divine sources remains. It is undoubtedly far more comprehensive than the alchemical format which was later given to it.

For centuries people were baffled by the reputed teaching of Thrice-Great Hermes, inscribed on an Emerald Tablet, which the Arabs communicated as the great inner principle of the Great Work. This was the ultimate authority of the alchemists, and may be rendered thus:

The truth, certainty, truest, without untruth. What is above is like what is below. What is below is like what is above. The miracle of unity is to be attained. Everything is formed from the contemplation of unity, and all things come about from unity, by means of adaptation. Its parents are the Sun and the Moon. It was borne by the wind and nurtured by the Earth. Every wonder is from it, and its power is complete. Throw it upon earth, and earth will separate from fire. The impalpable separated from the palpable. Through wisdom it rises slowly from the world to heaven. Then it descends to the world, combining the power of the upper and the lower. Thus you shall have the illumination of all the world, and darkness will disappear. This is the power of all strength—it overcomes that which is delicate and penetrates through solids. This was the means of the creation of the world. And in the future wonderful developments will be made, and this is the way.

I am Hermes the Threefold Sage, so named because I hold the three elements of all the wisdom. And thus ends the revelation of the work of Sun.

This is the same as the Sufi dictum (Introduction to the *Perception of Jafar Sadiq*): "Man is the microcosm, creation the macrocosm—the unity. All comes from One. By the joining of the power of contemplation all can be attained. This essence must be separated from the body first, then combined with the body. This is the Work. Start with yourself, end with all. Before man, beyond man, transformation."

If it can be established that there was such a thing as metallurgical lore which resembled alchemy, and also that there was spiritual alchemy without chemical experimentation, there is still another point missed by commentators.

Jabir (or his followers, at least some of them Sufis) actually did carry out chemical research. They made discoveries which are acknowledgedly the basis of modern chemistry. To the modern mind, this means that they were trying for the Philosopher's Stone—were attempting actual metallic transmutation. Could they have gone through the years of experiment and endured with patience the reverses which all alchemists encountered, unless they were convinced that there was a theoretical possibility of success? Would they have carried out such serious experiments merely as a blind, in societies which frowned upon individual religious activity, creating a facade so complete that they actually had to attempt transmutation?

Two flaws in current thought prevent the real facts from being understood. The first is that people tend to judge the people of the past by themselves. The second is the usual difficulty which faces the external theorist—he has not been inside the doors of a Sufi school. The Sufis have a tradition which has been maintained for many centuries. This can be summarized in the term "undertaking." A Sufic undertaking may not seem scientific by contemporary standards, but it is nevertheless widely applied. The Seeker is given an enterprise to complete. It may be an alchemical problem, or it may be the effort to reach the conclusion of an enterprise just as unlikely of attainment. For the purposes of his self-development he has to carry that undertaking out with complete faith. In the process of planning and carrying through this effort, he attains his spiritual development. The alchemical or other undertaking may be impossible, but it is the framework within which his constancy and his application, his mental and moral development, is carried out. To this extent it is secondary. Insofar as it is permanent for him and for his lifetime, perhaps, it is not secondary at all, because it becomes his permanent anchor and frame of reference. It is in something slightly like this spirit that all competitive undertakings are carried out in sport, or mountaineering, or even in physical culture, in other societies. The mountain or the muscular development are the fixed points, but they are not the element which is actually being transformed by the effort. They are the means, not the end. The whole concept may seem strange, but it is ultimately based upon its own logic. It is not the framework which is altered by the effort, but the human being himself. And it is the development of the human being which counts, nothing else.

When the Sufic concept of the deliberate evolution of humanity is grasped, the other elements fall into place. In a similar spirit, perhaps, Latin is taught in some schools to develop a part of the mind. An externalist or literal observer might say that the study of Latin is one of the least useful of occupations. All depends upon his use of the word "useful." I recently heard a man refer to a cigarette smoker as "a mechanism for the consumption of tobacco." So he is, but only from one point of view—just as an automobile might be looked upon as a means of burning gasoline. Its other functions have been overlooked in this statement, which nevertheless may be said to remain true within a narrow context.

There is a Sufi allegory about alchemy, which is interesting because of its connection with Western thought. A father has several idle sons. On his deathbed he tells them that they will find his treasure hidden in his field. They dig up the field and find nothing. So they plant wheat, which provides an abundant crop. For several years they do this. They find no gold, but indirectly they become both enriched and accustomed to constructive labor. Ultimately they become honest farmers, and forget the digging for gold.

The search for gold through chemical methods, then, produces gains which are other than those apparently sought. This story was certainly known in the West, because it is actually quoted both by Bacon and by Boerhaave, the seventeenth-century chemist, who stresses the importance of the work rather than the supposed objective. In his De Augumentis Scientiarum, Bacon says: "Alchemy is like the man who told his sons that he had buried gold for them in his vineyards. They dug and found no gold, but this turned the mold for the vine roots and caused an abundant harvest."

The thirteenth-century *Speculum Alchemiae*, attributed to Bacon, gives a hint of the evolutionary theory of alchemy: "I must tell you that Nature always intends and strives to the perfection of Gold: but many accidents, coming between, change the metals."

Numerous Sufi commentators of Rumi's evolutionary poems ("Man first of all appeared in the mineral domain") say, "The human metal must be refined and expanded."

The function of the Philosopher's Stone as a universal medicine and a source of longevity shows another aspect of spiritual alchemy which dovetails exactly with the Sufi procedures. The interesting fact here is that in Sufi tradition the stone or elixir is a state of mind, concentrated by the doctor within himself and transmitted to the patient by means of his mind. If some of the Western accounts of reviving sick patients with the stone are read in this assumption, we can see what the stone was. After the mind is concentrated and transformed in a certain way (salt, mercury and sulphur combined), the result is the stone—certain power. This stone is now projected upon the patient, who recovers.

The secret (because concealed within the mind) stone (force) is the source and essence of life itself.

Recent historical research has unearthed the fact that alchemy, using similar ideas and symbolism, was practiced in China as early as the fifth century B.C. Chinese and Japanese and Western scholars claim that the development of alchemy in China was originally spiritual, and that it was only later that the metallurgical aspect arose. It is possible that the metalworkers adopted the theme from the Taoist divines, and not the other way about, as immediate assumption would tend to believe. Many, if not all, of the ideas of alchemy as a spiritual process are present in the teachings of the Chinese sage Lao Tzu, the founder of Taoism, who was probably born in 604 B.C.

We also find the elixir theory, of a preparation or method which confers immortality, in the philosophers of China connected with alchemy, and in the Hindu *Atharva Veda,* whose date is earlier than 1000 B.C. Chinese philosophers specifically state that there are three alchemies, as Professor Read notes. The first is to produce longevity through liquid gold; the second is to produce a red sulphurous ingredient in goldmaking; the third was to transmute other metals into gold.[4]

Dr. O. S. Johnson, in *A Study of Chinese Alchemy,* which he completed at the University of California, details some remarkable material which he has extracted from Chinese sources on the antiquity of this art and its equation with the search for immortality through human efforts of self-development.

The Chinese alchemist Lu Tsu (quoted by William A. P. Martin, *The Lore of Cathay,* 1901, p. 59) gives what some writers have thought a deliberately baffling "chemical process" for transmutation. In the light of what has already been said it can be read straight through as a reference to the potential development of the essence of man. It is only baffling if one is trying to find laboratory instructions: "I must diligently plant my own field. There is within it a spiritual germ that may live a thousand years. Its flower is like yellow gold. Its bud is not large, but its seeds are round and like unto a spotless gem. Its growth depends upon the soil of the central palace, but its irrigation must proceed from a higher fountain. After nine years of cultivation, root and branch may be transplanted to the heaven of the higher genii."

Translated into Sufi terms this would read: "Man must develop by his own effort, toward growth of an evolutionary nature, stabilizing his consciousness. He has within him an

[4] Dr. John Read, *Prelude to Chemistry,* London, 1936.

essence, initially tiny, shining, precious. Development depends upon man, but must start through a teacher. When the mind is cultivated correctly and suitably, the consciousness is translated to a sublime plane."

For those who are interested in such things as chronology, the foregoing seems to be an indication that, as the Sufis say, their lore is timeless and reaches back to the most remote antiquity. In the hymns of the Aryans assigned to about 2000 B.C. there are indications of a formulation of doctrines which have come to be considered Sufic in the sense of the carrying out of certain practices of sublimation and development. The engendering of metals is also mentioned here.

That the alchemists of the West knew that they were pursuing an internal goal is clear from their admonitions and the innumerable cryptic illustrations in their works. Alchemical allegory is by no means difficult to read if one bears in mind Sufi symbolism. In the seventeenth century, a thousand years after the time of their original inspirer, Geber (born circa 721), the European alchemists were keeping lists of successive masters, reminiscent of the Sufi "spiritual pedigrees." One of the most interesting things about this fact is that these chains of succession refer to people who are linked in the Sufic and Saracen tradition, but otherwise have no common denominator. In the records, we find the name of Mohammed, Geber, Hermes, Dante and Roger Bacon.

Recent research has shown that Sufi materials were sources of Dante's illuminist work, such as the *Divine Comedy*. His Sufic affiliations must, however, have been known to the alchemists all the time. Raymond Lully, the Majorcan mystic, is again and again cited as an alchemical Adept. Yet from his works we learn that his exercises were actually taken from the Sufis, whom he names as such.

The Arab and Jewish illuminist Sufis invoke the succession as Hermes (symbolizing the most ancient wisdom, of celestial origin), Mohammed (and some members of his family and companions), Jabir or one of his associates, and thence to the modern orders. The Latin Western alchemists trace their lore from Hermes to Geber, thence through the illuminists. Bacon was one, Lully another, as well as various other Western practitioners.

The Sufi concept of gaining unity from diversity, integrating the mind and then the inner consciousness, through the appearance of a master who shall provide the key,[5] through the proper application of the homonyms for salt, sulphur and mercury—to reach the "light," according to the illuminists—is found in alchemical doctrine again and again.

Only its concealment in chemical phraseology prevents its being attacked as private-enterprise human progress, outside the Church. Here is a typical example, the caption to an alchemical diagram symbolizing the Work, in the *Viridarium Chymicum*—a great collection published in 1624:

The Whole Work of Philosophy. Those which were formerly enclosed in many forms are now seen in one. The start is the Master ["elder," literally] and he brings the Key. Sulphur with Salt and Mercury will give *wealth*.

That this cryptic utterance was symbolic and should be applied to the secret teaching of self-perfection and human alchemicalization is stressed as far as the author dares in the final sentence, warning in effect against physical alchemy:

If you see nothing here, you will not be able to seek further. You will be blind, even though you are in the midst of light.

What is more than interesting is that alchemy, for the West as for the East, was not a sterile, repetitious tradition,

[5] "Norton [fifteenth century] lays down the principle that the secrets of 'holi Alkimy' can only be imparted verbally to the chosen neophyte by a divinely appointed Master—and 'of a *Million*, hardly *three* were ere ordained for Alchimy.'" (J. Read, *op. cit.*, p. 178.)

relying upon ancient lore alone. It was constantly renewed from the teachings of people who had been in contact with Sufi study. This is evidenced by the constant succession of names which appear, many of whom we can trace as having been in contact with Sufis, Sufi schools, or who use Sufi terminology. Bacon, for instance, did not merely read the works attributed to Geber. He went to Spain and found the source, as we know from his quotations from Sufi teachings formulated by the twelfth-century illuminist Sufis. Lully not only studied Sufism in practice and used certain exercises, but he passed on this knowledge, to become a name constantly invoked by later alchemists. The same trend was carried on by Paracelsus and others.

Paracelsus, who traveled in the East and received his Sufic training in Turkey, introduced several Sufi terms into Western thought. His "Azoth," is identical with the Sufi *el-dhat* (pronounced in Persian and hence in most Sufi poetry as *az-zaut*). *Paragranum* is merely a Latinization of the science of the inner nature of things.

Owing to the Reformation, Paracelsus had to be careful how he expressed himself; since he was projecting a psychological system different from either the Catholic or Protestant ways. In one place he says: "Read with the heart until at some future time the true religion will come." He also used the "wine" analogy of Sufism, in referring to interior knowledge. As a result he was accused of being a drunkard. Only from a Sufi point of view could this passage of his be accepted:

"Let us depart from all ceremonies, conjurations, consecrations, etc., and all similar delusions, and put our heart, will and confidence solely upon the true rock. . . . If we abandon selfishness the door will be opened for us, and that which is mysterious will be revealed." (*Philosophia Occulta*)

He even quotes Sufi dicta:

"Salvation is not attained by fasting, neither wearing

certain clothes, nor by flagellation. These are superstitions and hypocrisy. God made everything pure and holy, man need not consecrate them. . . ." (*Ibid.*)

Many occultists, in spite of this, continue to try to follow the alchemical and Cabalistic ideas attributed to Paracelsus.

Henry Cornelius Agrippa (born 1486) was another example of what the Sufis call "precursors" or "scouts" (*rah-bin*). He is supposed to have been an alchemist and magician, and even today there are people who attempt to reach the truth through the magical system ascribed to him. He wrote on the method of Raymond Lully, lectured on Hermes, and undoubtedly knew of the Sufic interpretation of alchemy.

Those who followed him, and those who consider him a fraud alike, would do well to reexamine his words in the Sufi light. He said of alchemy: "This is that true and occult philosophy of the wonders of nature. The key thereof is the understanding—for the higher we carry our knowledge, the more sublime are our attainments in virtue, and we perform the greatest things with more ease." The stone of the alchemists who followed the "Art" literally was "vain and fictitious," so long as they practiced that art literally, since "it is an internal spirit within us, which can very well perform whatsoever the monstrous mathematicians, the prodigious magicians, the wonderful alchemists and the bewitching necromancers can effect."

Since this is as far as any Sufi could go, especially surrounded by people who wanted to believe in the supernatural in a crude form, and since orthodox religion had a vested interest in maintaining supernaturalism of the implausible sort, it is not surprising that such men as Agrippa have been considered deluded, magicians, or insane.

Mysteries in the West
I. Strange Rites

In an instant, rise from time and space.
Set the world aside and become a world
within yourself.

(Shabistari, *Secret Garden*)

It is the night of Saturday, especially consecrated to a ritual which is awesome to us, faithfully followed by the devotees of a certain cult.

Two groups of twelve, dressed in colorful costumes, carry out complicated movements within an enclosed space. They at times respond to musical stimuli applied through a primitive instrument by a man of seeming authority who, with a few assistants, supervises their activity. Entirely surrounding the area devoted to the ritual, a congregation gives its responses. At times the people sing, sometimes they shout, sometimes they are silent. Some wield an instrument which gives forth a strange sound.

Much care has evidently gone into the planning of the geometrically designed arena. Around it are colorful insignia, flags, banners, decorations probably designed to raise the emotional pitch of the individual and the group. The atmosphere is eerie partly because of the abrupt changes in emotion. Their reaction to the ecstatogenic processes being enacted in their midst is so explosive at times that one wonders why they do not spill over into the sacred enclosure. Both joy and sorrow are manifested among the votaries.

We are observers at a floodlit association football game. What is missing from the observer's account is a knowledge of what is actually happening, and why. If we have this knowledge, we can identify the players, crowd, referee, the use of the chalked lines. If we do not, we continue: Here a man writhes on the ground, another grimaces, sweat pouring from his face. One of the audience strikes himself, another his neighbor. The totem rises into the air, and is hailed by an awesome roar from the assembly. . . . Then we see that blood has been shed.

Other forms of ritual are subject to a similar approach by those who have not been through the experiences which precede their staging. Even more important, very many rituals of one kind or another have undergone alteration throughout the ages, the original intention or force being lost. When this happens, there is a mechanical or associative substitution of other factors. The ritual is distorted, even though there may be apparent reasons for its every aspect. This development is what we can call the dereliction of cult behavior.

Here, now, is an externalist account of a dervish ritual, in which events are described from the point of view of the observer alone. The author is the Reverend John Subhan, of the Methodist Episcopal Church, who was present at this event in India:

Tonight is Thursday night, the night which is specially sacred to the Sufi. Come, let us visit some shrines and see for ourselves what strange religious rites are practiced almost at our very doors.

We enter a dimly lighted room where a number of men are gathered. As we do so a signal is given by a man who appears to be the leader of the assembly, and the doors are shut. There is a hush as twelve men form into two parallel lines in the center of the room.

The glimmer of a solitary hurricane lamp falls on dark faces in which only the eyes seem to live. The rest of us fall back to the sides of the room. The Dhikr is about to begin.

With a startling clap of the hands the leader starts swaying from right to left. Very slowly he begins, and the men fall into the rhythm of his swaying. Every time they sway to the left they call "Hu!" in chorus, "Hu . . . Hu . . . Hu."[1]

The dervish ritual is not of the same nature of the football game—far from it. Since, however, it is not symbolic but concerned with an interior activity, the advantages of describing such an event in this out-of-context manner are few.

The atmosphere engendered by Sufic activity produces for the Sufi himself a perception, leaves a trace which he is able to recognize. It is, however, useless to say that one can recognize in the very being of a certain cult divorced from its origins a "sensation" that it was once a Sufic one. Material has to be made available in the form in which it can be shared by the reader, at least to some extent.

For this reason it is necessary to start with the inner perception that certain Western phenomena are of this origin, then to see what relatively acceptable formal material exists through which one can illustrate the fact. There are two main methods available for this. The first is to refer to the parallel phenomenon, if there is one, in the East. The other is to seek tracer elements, like technical terms and concealed meanings. In our case we use both, to shed light here upon at least one aspect of what has come to be called the witch cult of Western Europe.

"Witch," as we are widely informed, simply means "wise." This word could occur anywhere, and need not be a translation from Arabic or anything else. "Wise" is a name used

[1] John A. Subhan, *Sufism, Its Saints and Shrines*, Lucknow, 1938, p. 1.

by dervish cults, and also by the followers of other more or less undiluted traditions.

In Spanish, the word for witch is *bruja*. And it is in Spain that we find early and relatively complete accounts of the rituals and beliefs of the people of Western Europe who celebrated similar festivities and were considered by the Church to be votaries of the Black One.

We can follow up the clue which is contained in the fact that the *maskhara* dervishes, although they are found nowadays mostly in pockets of Central Asia and occasionally in India, use the Arabic word whose radical is BRSH.

The *maskhara*, "revelers," are also called *mabrush*, "marked on the skin," or possibly "intoxicated by the thorn apple." In Spanish, *maja* is the Latin-based word, while *bruja* (pronounced *brusha*) is the word which appeared in Saracen Spain to describe these people. If we assume, for the moment, that *brusha* might be a descriptive term adopted by a Reveler group, we can try to decode allied descriptive uses by means of Arabic poetic method. What, in fact, does *brusha* mean, both in its root form and in its derivations? According to our poetic code-method, a number of words of the same consonantal group are taken to add up to a description of a cult—as we have seen in the case of "Sufi."

Dictionary words give us a selection of—a hallucinogenic substance, a symbol, and a ritual mark, all under this general consonantal grouping:

BRSH = *Datura stramonium* (thorn apple), pronounced BaRSH. Alternatively, by similarity of sound:

YBRUH = root of the mandrake (Syriac loanword), pronounced YaBRUUHH. Both of these contain alkaloids. Both were reputed to have been used by witches, to induce visions, sensations of flying, and in rituals.

What is a symbol associated with witches? A broom:

M-BRSHa = a brush, broom, scraper (Syrian[2] dialect), pronounced MiBRSHA.

[2] Under the Saracens, there were huge numbers of Syrians in Spain. The Norman-Syrian contact could have been as early as 844 A.D. when Seville was pillaged.

Translating from the group of words, we can therefore
describe a community of people associating themselves with
this letter arrangement as: "Associated with the mandrake
(or thorn apple); using the symbol of the broom, identified
by a mark on the skin, wearing a particolored or motley
garb." Such people would be most accurately described in
Arabic, and in medieval Spain, as *brujo* (masculine) or
bruja (feminine), pronounced at the time *brusho, brusha.*
If we accept the connection with the Revelers, we can associate further. Their use of the mandrake would provide a
further homonym—the colloquialism *mabrush, mabrusha,*
"frenzied," a reference to their dancing. The traditional
witches' dance has been identified with, or at least compared to, two forms of dance known in Europe—that of the
Saracens, the waltz (which is supposed to have come from
Asia through the Balkans), and the *dibka,* the Middle
Eastern ring dance, known from the Mediterranean to the
Persian Gulf.

But there are still numerous other witch facts which can
be added to this. Arabic sources quoted by Arkon Daraul
speak of the "dance of the two-horned," and give us the clue
to the meanings of the "barbarous" words used by witches,
which members of the fraternity even today cannot understand. Here are some of them, with their Arabic equivalent:

The ritual knife, cryptically called "Athame." From
adhdhame, a bloodletter. "Athame" is a very fair attempt at the sound represented by *adh-dhame.* The
Sab(b)at(h), confused by confluence with the Hebrew word, turns up in our Arabic text about the
Spanish two-horned people as in fact originating in
Az-ZABAT, "the forceful (occasion)." A fanciful
later etymology is through French *s'ebattre,* "to frolic."
The same association of sound converted into *Robin,
Robinet,* the perfectly apposite Semitic *Rabba,* "lord,"
the elusive and mysterious lord or functionary of the

Sabat. Rabbana! (O our lord!) is part of the Moslem prayer, emphatically stressed aloud five times a day.

The very word "coven" eventually found an apparent identification with the idea of convening or gathering together. Yet in the recital of the ritual by a former member of the ancient Hispano-Semitic cult, *kafan* refers to the shroud which is placed over the heads of the Revelers while they are dancing, reported in witch material from as far away as Scandinavia. By later association it may have come to mean the meeting or the members, but *Kafan* was certainly used in the earlier form, and means winding-sheet.

We can now go on to a further stage—the witches' ointment and what it might have been composed of. Why was the ointment originally used? In Arabic, "ointment" is RHM, the word which also stands for blood kindred. Ointment was given to the witch, male or female, after initiation, and after being marked. *Marham*, ointment, is rubbed on to the skin with a view to establishing a symbolic form of blood kinship. Thus, by an "anointing," if we can talk in Semitic roots, the ointment (RHM) is applied to help create the condition of blood kinship (RHM). It was to be used in the future, to take the witch to his or her kindred, RHM. So the RHM formed the mental, pharmacological link with the RHM.

But was there no alkaloid or other active principle in the witch ointment? There most certainly was. It will be remembered that the witches made a brew from the bodies or severed members of unbaptized babies. The mandrake root, it will be remembered, is "human" in shape. It is traditionally thought of as a tiny simulacrum of a human being. A tiny human being is a child. As a plant, we could hardly expect it to be duly baptized. And ingredients of the ointment seem to be this form of an "unbaptized one."

Too many analogies have been sought for witch practices in Christianity or pagan cults of a pre-Christian kind. If you read works on witchcraft in Europe, you will find that as far as most of their authors are concerned, there was no such thing as centuries of Saracen rule in Spain, or generations of absorption of Eastern culture on every level. Even the name (the Wise Ones) could be a direct translation of *arifin*, the title assumed by people in the East who believed in the possibility of direct communication with the supernatural.

Modern witches seem uncertain about the significance of the size of their circle (nine feet in diameter) and know little about their old numerology. But this material is available elsewhere, even to the measurements. Their own tradition is, incidentally, that they come from the "Summer Land," which is taken by their present-day members to mean the East. Their black man (Moor) and horned fetish (the devil, confused with the moon) belong to the realm of recent operation ("working") for recently there has been an attempted rationalization of their cult, tracing it to seasonal and other festivals, and an amalgamation with ecstatic cults, using the Arab code system to formulate their rituals.

Who brought the witches to the West? In the medieval form, from which most of our information derives, undoubtedly the Aniza tribe. We have to go back to the deserts of Arabia.

The mighty Aniza Bedouin clan, most numerous in fighting men and richest in pedigree camels, is marked in Arab literature for its bitterness in desert war. Bedouin wars provided material for the development of the chivalric code, and for love and battle epics. Not to mention the *dibka* dance and the bloodletting knife. The patterns of poetry developed by tribal bards was to influence the literature of a score of nations after the expansion of Islam to the north, east and west.

The genesis of the Bedouin life lay in pre-Islamic times, in the *Days of the Arabs,* each *Day* being an epic of some battle whose origin may be forgotten, but whose cultural by-products, in verse, nobility of conduct or military tactics, remained a part of the tribe's heritage.

This is the Bedouin of the storybooks—the untamed warrior whose gentleness with women and children is proverbial and balanced by his determination to fight to the death for a trickle of possibly muddy water or a palm tree; but who would give absolutely everything away in one magnificent gesture.

One of the earliest and most bloody of the *Days* was that which lasted forty years at the end of the fifth century, fought between two sections of the Aniza. Starting with the theft of an ailing she-camel belonging to an old woman, it ended—as the *Days* often did—by an act of mediation. Its end product, characteristic of Saracenic romance, and which influenced all Western literature, was the most famous heroic romance tale of Arabia, the *Story of el-Zir*.

History brought these people to Europe, and with them much of their culture. One of them was a dervish teacher, deeply involved with the musical, romantic and tribal traditions of his tribe.

The parent tribe of the Aniza are held by all Bedouin bards to be the Fakir ("humble in spirit") clan. This appellation was adopted by dervishes, and in one of its deteriorations is applied to itinerant Hindu imitation yogis who autoanesthetize themselves and lie on sharp barbs, to no clearly ascertainable purpose; unless it be that a moity of onlookers may hope to be able to emulate them.

The Fakir tribe still lives in northwest Arabia, near their ancestral settlement of Khaibar, the ancient town which was a stronghold in Mohammed's time. The Aniza have many legends, one of them associated with their necessary outward proliferation. According to this story, Wail, the Fakir and ancestor of the whole Aniza, on one "Night of Power" (probably the twenty-seventh of the month of Ramadan) made a supplication. He laid one hand on himself and one on his magnificent she-camel, and prayed that the seed of both should multiply. The result, we are told, is that the Aniza are now fertile in both fields, with a current strength of some thirty-seven thousand men and about

a million head of camels. They have fertility-increasing
powers as well. Their tradition has passed, too, into the beliefs of those cults which are dependent upon Aniza membership.

Today they are plentiful in the Syrian desert, having
fought their way into occupation there over a period of
nearly two centuries, ending about the year 1600 A.D. The
cult of the Revelers which is connected with their name,
however, goes back at least to Abu el-Atahiyya (748–c. 828).
A potter and contemplative, he yearned for a greater balance
between the glories of Baghdad at the time of Haroun el-
Rashid the great Caliph, and the development of innate
human faculties. He said so to the Caliph, who settled upon
him an annuity of fifty thousand silver pieces.

He became a writer, and left a collection of mystical verse
which "entitle him to the position of father of Arabic sacred
poetry."

His circle of disciples, the Wise Ones, commemorated him
in a number of ways after his death. To signify his tribe,
they adopted the goat, cognate with the tribal name (*Anz,
Aniza*). A torch between goat horns ("the devil" in Spain,
as it later became) symbolized for them the light of illumination from the intellect (head) of the "goat," the Aniza
teacher. His *wasm* (tribal brand) was very much like a
broad arrow, also called an eagle's foot. An alternative name
for the Aniza is a kind of bird. This sign, known to witches
as the goosefoot, became the mark for their places of meeting.
Some of his followers, especially the young females, were
marked with a small tattoo or other mark, in conformity
with Bedouin custom. After Atahiyya's death before the
middle of the ninth century, tradition has it that a group of
his school migrated to Spain, which had been under Arab
rule for over a century at that time.

The symbols and customs associated with the tribal affiliation continued to be used. This is in conformity with
dervish practice. Each teacher gives a special flavoring to his
school, which changes when the school is taken over by

another teacher. The object here is to retain group feeling.[8]

All this is not to say that there was no earlier cult in Europe of much the same type. But it does seem to show the elision of the two into what eventually frightened the Church of the middle ages, and has remained a piquant mystery to all kinds of people ever since. Even the female lore of the witches is in parts so close to the Sufi love poetry of the middle ages, especially that of the Spaniard Ibn El-Arabi, that little more need be said on this point.

The Quresh are the noblest tribe of Arabia, and the supreme clan is the Hashimite. They can be considered something apart, for they are the prophetic and royal blood. Next to them, however, come the mighty Aniza. Three rulers today are from this clan—the Saudi-Arabian king, the Sheikh of Kuwait, and the Ruler of Bahrain.

This material gives us three main possibilities, or ways of assessing and describing, the meetings of the witches of the West. The first we could call the survival of the old (pre-Christian) religion; the second, the importation of the Saracenic cult; the third, an antichristian development. Any or all of these, of course, can contain outside elements.

The supporters of the "old religion" theory have pressed everything they can find into service. Horns can for them only stand for the survival of a hunting or fertility rite; the dance for this, the animal guise for that. The clerical observers have stressed the feast as a blasphemous sacrament, the marking as a travesty of baptism, and so on.

Like our different versions of a football game, the interpretation depends upon knowing what was actually going on, not upon our assumptions that because something was found in a certain place at a certain time it must accord with our theory or assumption as to what it was. "Devil, horns, boiled babies" is the one version. "God and goddess, fertility dance, secrecy to maintain the old religion" is the

[8] Among the witches, primitive tribal ritual derived from the Aniza overwhelmed the Sufi element. Successive inductions of Bedouins into the cult was almost certainly responsible for its reversion to tribalism.

other. The third is—"symbol of the Aniza tribe, its teacher, the hallucinogen."

The term "old religion," which witches and others accept as an indication of the prehistoric origins of the cult, is a standard Sufi phrase, often used, as "antique faith," "old one," "ancient tradition." It was stressed by Ibn El-Arabi the Spanish Sufi, in his love poems.

If the ancient tradition did indeed exist in Europe before the eighth century, when the Saracens occupied its main centers, it undoubtedly underwent a complete penetration of the poetic code-system, Sufi terminology and Arab tribal symbolism for which there can hardly be a parallel analogue of equal depth of influence.

What more can we find out from the phrase "the antique faith," or "the ancient tradition?" Translate "antique," "ancient" into the basic Arabic triliteral root of QDM[4] and we get the poetic meaning:

$$QDM = \text{concept of precedence.}$$

Here are some of the main derivations from this root, to be found in any Arab dictionary:

Qidam (QiDM) = precedence, preexistence
Qidman (QiDM^{an}) = old, olden times
Qadam (QaDaM) = high rank, bravery
Qadam (QaDaM) = human foot, step, stage of movement
Qadum (QaDUM) = an axe
Qadim (QADiM) = future
El-Qadim (EL-QaDiM) = the Ancient One (God)
Qaddam (QaDDAM) = chief, leader

This strange word stands for eternity in the sense that it shows that time is eternal. An equivalent in English might be "precedence," which carries the meaning of preceding (hence being past) and going forward (meaning ahead). The axe carried by dervish wanderers is called qadum.

---

4 Cf. Asrarel Qadim wa'l Qadam (the Sufi Secrets of the Past and Future).

There are two Ancient Ones—the Ancient (Sheikh, Pir) of the Sufis, and the Ancient One (the deity). This possibility of two sorts of preeminent and ancient ones, one human (the leader of the group) and the other the higher (divine) one, is intended to convey a very subtle concept. The Sufis have often been accused of believing that their leaders are divine. Through the special, or poetic, use of this word they actually show that there are two versions which this Ancient may take.[5] The one is the teacher who has certain qualities of a supreme character, as near to deity as may be perceived in a man. Both the Sufis and the witches use a ceremonial limp or staggered step to convey the sense of the Arabic word *qadam*, a step. There is one important difference in the Eastern and Western versions. In the East the word *qadam* (step, stage) is mimed for purposes of cryptographic transmission. The Sufi takes a step sideways, or stamps, in order to commemorate the actual root word. When he makes a definite step, either as a recognition signal or during a ceremony, he is doing this to affirm the continued transmission of the three-letter word QDM. By working this word into the proceedings, the framers of the ritual or password system have made sure of his survival—at least among people who can understand Arabic words to any extent.

In my own experience, when instructed in the method of making a certain step-signal, I was sent away to study all the elements of the word for "step." From this study, in turn, emerges the realization that the system is the "antique faith," that it is divided into stages or steps, that it proceeds step by step, that it is ahead as well as of the greatest antiquity.

It is more than obvious that in the transmission of outer forms in non-Arabic speaking countries, a similar adaptation

[5] "There is another peculiarity of this language, the suggestive and meaningful nature of its words. Arabic words to a Sufi strike them as eloquent. They do convey what, in other languages, need pages to explain. They therefore are most suitable to convey occult conceptions." (Sheikh el Mushaikh, *Tasawwufal Islami*, London, 1933 [*Islamic Sufism*, by I. A. Shah] p. 39.)

of words has not taken place. Ideally, if the idea of an antique faith with a progressive destiny were translated into English by witches or whatever they might be called, they should have chosen such a word as "succeed." Succession means to "come after," but it also connotes something which is to be in the future, something which can be attained. Speaking from the point of view of the process which is being described, then, the ancient knowledge would have to become known in its Western transition as "succeed."[6]

The change from one language to another where the old allusions remain is against the evolutionary idea of the Sufis. And it is this very metamorphosis which makes the Sufic development very difficult to study in an academic way. Generally speaking, only the moribund versions, which have lost their movement, will be available.

[6] The Swedish witches of Mohra adapted the concept correctly when they hailed their leader as "Antecessor."

Mysteries in the West
II. The Chivalric Circle

When you are still fragmentated,
lacking certainty—what difference
does it make what your decisions are?
(Hakim Sanai, *The Walled Garden of Truth*)

A group of Sufis is formulating an association which shall enable them to carry on their work of human development toward self-fulfillment. The work, as with all Sufic activities, has three parts. The individual himself must live up to certain personal standards, and they choose the medieval ideal of chivalry as their format. This, in turn, gives them an opportunity of forming a visible elite. The existence and appearance of this elite fulfills the second function—the impact upon humanity in general. The third element, reverence for the teacher, is invested in the Sufic "king" figure, who leads the community.

They choose, as an external form, the hooded woolen robe of blue which is standard wear among Sufis. For color symbolism they adopt gold and blue, to signify the essence within the body or mind—the sun in the sky or the "speck of gold within the sea," as the Sufi sage Attar puts it. The basic unit of the Sufi is the Circle, the *halka*. In their commemorative rituals they carry out the exercises or movements collectively known as the "dance." As their slogan they take an Arabic motto, about a cupbearer. This is translated in the Persian branches in a rhyming sentence, with almost the same sounds as the motto of the Garter Order.

Their patron saint is Khidr, the Green One.

The *halkas* are composed of thirteen people. There are two reasons for this number being used. In the first place, these Sufis wish to emphasize their inner teaching as being the same as that of all religions. It is the secret, concealed message of all faiths—the need for organized development. In this case, the other religion with which these Moslem Sufis are most concerned is Christianity. The acceptance of the identity of Christianity and Islam is conveyed by simple numerology.

"Unity," the Sufis of the Khidr Order explain by their symbolism, is the same as "three" for practical purposes. They demonstrate this by pointing out that the Arabic word "unity" (*ahad*)—the adjective used for Allah the One—is composed of three letters in Arabic—AHD. Therefore three is one, because the difference between monotheism and Christianity is one of terminology.

But where does the thirteen come into the picture? Quite simply. In Arabic notation, A equals one, H has the numerical value of eight, and D is equal to the number four. Add these together and the result is thirteen. Thirteen therefore becomes a number important to this Sufi group.

Halkas of this persuasion are thus always grouped into thirteen. Thirteen men form one unit.

The reputed date of the formation of this organization is about the year 1200 of the Christian era.

About a century and a half later (nobody is quite sure of the date) a mysterious organization came into being in England. It was inspired by the King himself. The members were divided into two sections of thirteen each—one under King Edward III, the other under the Black Prince. Its colors were blue and gold, its robes woolen and hooded, its aims overtly chivalric. Its patron saint was St. George, who is equated in Syria, where his cult originates, with the mysterious Khidr-figure of the Sufis. It was, in fact, called the Order of St. George, which would translate direct into Sufi phraseology as *Tarika-i-Hadrat-i-Khidr* (the Order of St. Khidr). It became known as the Order of the Garter. The word "garter" in Arabic is the same as the word for the Sufi mystical tie or bond, and also "religious or monkish asceticism." The word for the basic Sufi unit (*halka*) is interchangeable in Sufi parlance with the very same radical from which "garter" is derived.

The early records of the Order of the Garter are lost. Speculation as to the derivations and origins of the Order have replaced them. The pretty story that the Order was instituted as a result of someone sneering at a real garter, while discounted by some serious historians, may in fact have a very interesting basis in fact. It may be recalled that this incident is said to have taken place at a dance. If we look at the facts from the Sufi historical point of view, we can ask something which may not have occurred to others. What kind of dance was it? The whole incident looks like an attempt to explain away a dance ritual which was in some way interrupted and had to be justified. A garbled version is likely to have come down to us. Why, for instance, was a garter being displayed at a dance, if this is what was happening? Either because the garter was chosen to represent in visual form the "tie" of the Order; or because "some lady's garter had fallen off."

What is the slogan of the Order of the Garter, and does it have any connection with the Khidr Order? Superficially there is no connection between "Dishonored be he who thinks evil of it," and the secret "cupbearer" phrase. If we approach the matter from conventional method, we will never see the connection. But if we go by sound rather than meaning, for the time being, a strange fact emerges. The French version of the slogan and the Arabic and Persian ones sound almost like the same words.

Those who have read even translations of Persian Sufi

poets, with their cupbearers as the medium of the enlightenment of the Sufi, will see the connection.

The process by means of which a foreign word or phrase
becomes adopted into another language is well established
in literature and custom. There are numerous examples,
and the system has even been named, being catalogued in
dictionaries as Hobson-Jobson. The interminable religious
chant in India, *Ya Hasan Ya Hussein* (O Hasan! O Hussein!) is accepted in English under the sound Hobson-
Jobson, an attempt by British soldiers to reproduce the
chant. The standard Indian dictionary of Anglo-Indian
terms, containing many examples of the process, is actually
called Hobson-Jobson. In West Africa the Arabic word
el-ghaita (a bagpipe) has been anglicized into "alligator."
Nearer home, all Londoners are familiar with the name of
a certain tavern, the "Elephant and Castle," originally
named the *Infanta de Castile*.

Quite recently, a Middle Eastern friend of mine presented an astonished barrow-pushing scrap collector with a
shilling in a London street. The man had been repeating,
with fervor, in that plaintive tone of the hawker, "Any old
iron?" The way in which he drew out the sounds was for
my friend indistinguishable from the mendicant dervish cry
of *O Imam Reza!* which shouting dervishes repeat hundreds
of times a day as a pious invocation, heard by all in some
areas.

Shakespeare's name is sometimes rendered in perfectly
correct and acceptable Persian as *Sheikh-Peer*, "the ancient
sage."

A society with secret phrases, or which had to suffer an
interruption during a ritual, would have need to explain
what a barbarous phrase meant, and what exactly was the
basis for elevating a garter. There is a great deal of other
material which links these two movements, much of it initiatory in character and which cannot be reproduced here.
It may be said, however, that an alternative name for a
branch of the Khidr Order is *el-mudawwira* (the round

building), associated with the great palace of Baghdad which belonged to Haroun el-Rashid. The entire city of Baghdad was constructed in 762 A.D., in certain geometrical proportions based on the wheel. Traditional Sufi groups, like the Freemasons of the West, associate their dedication with this round building. It may only be a coincidence that the Garter Order was concerned with the Round Table revival, and that King Philip of Valois was also anxious to start a new Round Table group.

Until the time of Edward VI (died 1553) the Order was called that of St. George, patron saint of England; although the traditional connection with a garter reaches back to the origins of the Order. It is just possible that two hundred years after its first institution the meaning of the word "garter" was sufficiently well understood for this to become the actual name of the Order. Successive alterations to the ritual and numbers of the knights have virtually changed the originally Sufic coincidence.

Today the Order of the Garter is still the most important and proudest institution of England. The idea that it may be of foreign derivation is unwelcome to some people. These, however, are only those who fail to realize that, whatever its origins, it is in England that the Order has attained its greatest distinction, worthily maintaining an honorable roll of elite.

Those who have sought in the Garter a connection with the strange tradition of the witches may not be as wide of the mark as others might think. At least one branch of this fragmentary cult in Britain is heavily influenced by Spanish-Saracen transmission of a deteriorated Sufi type, where a vague "magical power" idea has replaced the theme of *baraka*.

There is a very coherent reason for the Sufi group combining the elements of blue, gold, kingship, Khidr (St. George) and the protection of women into their formulation. It is all based upon a single word root and its manipulation, though a similar consistency cannot be found in the

Order of the Garter. This might lead one to suppose that
the Garter is a translation of the essential qualities of the
Khidr group, all of which can be found assembled in the
triliteral root KHDR.

The elements used in the format and rituals of the group
are all found here:

KHaDiR = to be green (Islam, the matrix of the
group)

KHuDDiR la fi hi = he was blessed in it (the bene-
diction of the group)

KHiDaR, KHiDiR = St. George, Elias, the Patron
of the Sufis, Khidr

ElKHuDRat = the sea (the ocean of life, in which
the Sufi finds truth; the sea, of which the Sufi is a
wave, much used in poetry; the blue in which is
the gold)

AKHDaR = suspicious; fine woman (chivalry, referring to the first Islamic order of chivalry, when
Mohammed early in the seventh century founded
a body of men to protect women and caravans)

KHaDRa = chief of a tribe

ElKHaDRa = the sky, firmament (from which the
sun breaks through, another allusion to the gold in
the blue)

ElaKHaDiR = gold, meat and wine. (The gold element of the sky or sea—the meat and wine which
are common denominators with Christian ritual.
The Christian ritual itself is regarded as symbolical of the totality of the whole community and
individual development, so that the sacraments of
the Church are to the Sufi merely a fragment of
the whole undertaking as given above.)

The emblem of the group is the palm tree, which is derived from the root *khadar*, to cut a palm tree. The tree itself, as noted elsewhere in this book, signifies *baraka* and
other basic elements of Sufism, emblazoned upon the cryptic

Hohenstaufen coronation robe of the kings of Sicily and the Holy Roman Emperor, who were known to have Sufi contacts.

The time of Edward III in England certainly did see an extension of Saracenic elements into Europe. English national dancing, the Morris, must be of these origins. Cecil Sharp—the authority on English folk dance—has linked European "Moorish" dancing and the probable date of its entry into England:

> The Morris, then—once also the Moresc—of England; *Le Morisque* and Morisco of France; the *Moresca* of Corsica . . . is in all reasonable probability Moorish in origin: never mind if in our own country it is become as English as fisticuffs. . . . Holland, as is told by Engel, was infected too; industrious research, in fact, will probably show that the Morris in some shape or other was known throughout Europe, and beyond. As for the date of its introduction into England that is impossible to state with certainty; but most authorities point to the time of Edward III. Maybe when John of Gaunt returned from Spain is probably the earliest when Morris-men were seen in England.[1]

These dances may have been imported direct from Moorish Spain in those times, but they are traceable to Sufi fraternities much further back in time. The riding of a hobbyhorse (Basque *zamalzain*, from Arabic *zamil el-zain*, "gala limping horse"[2]) is only a part of Sufic ritual. These entertainers are not only "certainly reminiscent of Arab minstrels;" they are representative of the humorous poets in gaudy dress, long hair and painted faces who act out certain metaphysical teachings to this day among the Sufis. Sometimes they rode hobbyhorses, sometimes canes, feigning idiocy as "fools of God." One such dervish stick rider

[1] C. J. Sharp & H. C. Macilwaine, *The Morris Book*, London, 1907, p. 15.
[2] *Legacy of Islam*, ed. Arnold and Guillaume, Oxford, p. 372.

character is interviewed by Rumi in his *Mathnawi*. This is a connection with the BRSH (*bruja* = witch) riders of Spain.

The first Sufi record of a teaching journey to England[3] —such is contained in the travels of Najmuddin (Star of Faith) Gwath-ed-Dahar Qalandar. He was born about 1232, or perhaps earlier. His son, or another successor (Najmuddin Baba), "followed his father's footsteps" from India to England and China in 1338.

The first Najmuddin was a disciple of the illustrious Nizamuddin Awlia of Delhi, who sent him to Rum (Turkey) to study under Khidr Rumi. Khidr Rumi's full name was Sayed Khidr Rumi Khapradari—the Cupbearer—of Turkestan. It will be remembered that the Khidr Order (equated with the Garter) has as its slogan a salutation to the cupbearer. This cup had miraculous qualities.

Legend has it that this dervish carried with him the interpretation of the Sufi sign *hoo* (which in stylized calligraphy looks like the number four)—the Mason's mark found on Gothic buildings in the West. In addition to its forming a framework for the Sufi "magic square," it is also used by the Qalandars as a diagram of the three devotional positions (upright, kneeling and lying down), which may be equivalent to the "instruments" of the Masons.

Najmuddin's teacher, Sayed Khidr, was an associate of the Sufi teacher Suhrawardi (of the Path of the Rose, sometimes equated with the Rosicrucians); of Abdul Qadir, Rose of Baghdad; and the father of Jalaluddin Rumi (some of whose stories are found in Chaucer, and who was writing at the time of the alleged journey to England); as well as other very important Sufi teachers like Fariduddin Shakarganj and Shah Madar. Shah Madar taught the essential unity of all religions, especially the esoteric way of Islam and Christianity. He followed the teachings of Tayfuri and

---

[3] John A. Subhan; *Sufism, Its Saints and Shrines*, Lucknow, 1938, pp. 311 et seq., probably quoting *Kitab-i-Qalandaria*, in which this journey is detailed.

the formulation of the King or Lord of the Fish, Dhu'l-Nun the Egyptian, or the "Black."

Fariduddin Shakarganj (Father Farid of the Sweet Treasure) was of the Chis(h)ti School of Sufis, and was originally a nobleman of Afghanistan. He died in India in 1265, where his tomb is revered by people of all faiths. His functions were healing and music. The Chis(h)ti musicians, who wandered through Asia with fife and drum, assembling the populace and telling stories of Sufi meaning, may be connected with the Spanish *chistu* or jester, whose costume was strikingly similar.

The Sufi wanderers called Qalandars and Chis(h)tis must have brought to the West other dances, as well as rhythmic ritualistic procedures, and those which are in part represented by the Morris man.

Hugo of Reutlingen, as an instance, in his *Weltchronik* of 1349, quoted by Dr. Nettl, speaks of the song in F major used by dancing bands which "reminds us of the Arabian dance of the dervishes."[4]

[4] Paul Nettl, *The Story of Dance Music*, New York, 1947, p. 49.

Mysteries in the West
III. The Head of Wisdom

This day and that alike you do within your
    garden spend. . . .
Neglectful of the nightingale, the crow your
    chosen friend.

Yet such companionship must leave its trace
    upon your soul:
Do you think fire shall cease to burn, or oil
    and water blend?
(*Divan of Bedil*, Johnson Pasha's translation)

When they were suppressed, the Knights Templar were accused of worshiping a head, sometimes called the Baphomet or Bafomet. This was considered to be an idol, and probably connected with Mohammed (Mahomet). The head was described, but no head which could positively be identified as one of these Bafomets could be located.

Probably relying upon contemporary Eastern sources, Western scholars have recently supposed that "Bafomet" has no connection with Mohammed, but could well be a corruption of the Arabic *abufihamat* (pronounced in Moorish Spanish something like *bufihimat*). The word means "father of understanding." In Arabic, "father" is taken to mean "source, chief seat of," and so on. In Sufi terminology, *ras el-fahmat* (head of knowledge) means the mentation of man after undergoing refinement—the transmuted consciousness.

It will be noted that the word "knowledge, understanding" used here is derived from the Arabic FHM root. FHM, in turn, is used to stand both for FHM and derivatives, meaning "knowledge;" and FHM and derivatives, standing for "black, Coalman" and so on.

The Baphomet is none other than the symbol of the completed man. The black head, negro head, or Turk's head which appears in heraldry and in English country-inn signs is a crusader substitute word (cant word) for this kind of knowledge.

It may be noted that the shield of Hugues de Payen, the founder (with Bisol de St. Omer) of the Templars in 1118 A.D., carried three black human heads—the heads of knowledge.

The use of this term, especially the "wondrous head" theme, recurs throughout medieval history. Pope Gerbert (Silvester II) who studied in Moorish Spain, is stated to have made a brazen head, among many other marvelous "magical" things.[1] Albertus Magnus spent thirty years making his marvelous brass head. Thomas Aquinas, pupil at the time to Albertus, smashed the head, which "talked too much."

The head appears again and again.

It should be remembered that the Templars and graduates of the Spanish magical schools had one thing in common, apart from being suspected of heresy and magical powers and belonging to secret organizations. They all spoke and used Arabic. By means of this initiatory language, they could communicate with one another, pass punning messages, put up signs (like the "bat" of Majorca) to illustrate some message.

This artificial head is not made of brass. Artificial it is, in that it is the product of "work" in the Sufic sense. Ultimately, of course, it is the head of the individual himself. At least one chronicler gets close to the mark when he says that the "head was flesh and blood, like unto an ordinary man's." The emphasis which is put on the statement, however, leads the ordinary reader to the conventional idea

[1] He is said to have introduced Arabic numerals into northern Europe in 991, from Saracen Spain.

of artificiality, and like a good conjuring trick, diverts attention from the method of making the head, which might be suspected if it were thought that "head" was a code word for the result of a (heretical) formative process.

In Arabic, "brass" is spelled SuFR, connected with the concept of "yellowness." The "head of brass" is a rhyming homonym for "head of gold," which is spelled in exactly the same way. The Golden Head (*sar-i-tilai*) is a Sufi phrase used to refer to a person whose inner consciousness has been "transmuted into gold" by means of Sufic study and activity, the nature of which it is not permissible to convey here.

The three heads of black wisdom on the shield of the founder of the Templars are shown on a background of gold—"On gold, three Moors' heads black."

The phrase, "I am making a head," used by dervishes to indicate their Sufic dedication in certain exercises, could very well have been used by Albertus Magnus or Pope Silvester, and transmitted in the literal sense, believed to refer to some sort of artifact.

Albertus Magnus (born 1193) was well versed in the Saracenic and Sufi literature and philosophy. As Professor Browne notes, he exceeded the usual customs of Western Orientalists, for, "dressed as an Arab [he] expounded at Paris the teachings of Aristotle from the works of al-Farabi, Ibn Sina (Avicenna) and Ghazali."

Mysteries in the West
IV. Francis of Assisi

Even though you tie a hundred knots
—the string remains one.

(Rumi)

Most people know that St. Francis of Assisi was a light-hearted troubador of Italy who experienced a religious conversion and became a saint with an uncanny influence over animals and birds. It is on record that the troubadors were a relic of Saracenic musicians and poets. It is often agreed that the rise and development of the monkish Orders in the middle ages was greatly influenced by the penetration of Moslem dervish organization in the West. Studying St. Francis from this point of view, certain interesting discoveries become possible.

Francis was born in 1182, the son of Pietro Bernardone, a merchant of fine stuffs, and his wife, Madonna Pica. He was originally named Giovanni, but his father was so attached to France (where he spent much of his commercial life) that "for love of the land he had just quitted" he renamed the child Francesco.

Although considered an Italian, Francis spoke Provençal, the language used by the troubadors. There is little doubt that he felt in the spirit of the troubadors a glimpse of something deeper than appeared on the surface. His own poetry so strongly resembles in places that of the love poet Rumi that one is tempted to look for any report which might connect Francis with the Sufi order of the Whirling Dervishes. At this point we come across the first of a number of tales considered inexplicable by Western biographers.

The Whirling Dervishes can attain intuitive knowledge partly by a peculiar form of spinning, presided over by an instructor. Rumi's school of Whirling Dervishes was in full operation in Asia Minor, and its founder was still alive, during the lifetime of St. Francis.

Here is the puzzling "spinning" tale:

Francis was walking through Tuscany with a disciple, Brother Masseo. They arrived at a fork in the road. One path led to Florence, another to Arezzo, a third to Siena.

Masseo asked which branch they should take.

"The road which God wills."

"And which is that?"

"We will know by a sign. I command you, by your path of obedience, turn round and round as children do, until I tell you to stop."

So poor Masseo twirled and twirled, till he fell down from giddiness. Then he got up and looked beseechingly at the saint; but the saint said nothing, and Masseo, remembering his vow of obedience, began again to twirl his best. He continued to twirl and to fall for some time, till he seemed to have spent all his life in twirling, when, at last, he heard the welcome words: "Stop, and tell me whither your face is turned."

"To Siena," gasped Masseo, who felt the earth rock round him.

"Then to Siena we must go," said Francis, and to Siena they went.

That Francis felt the source of his troubador inspiration to lie in the East, and that he was connected with the Sufis, seems clear from much evidence. When he went to the Pope, trying to have his Order accepted, he used a parable which shows that he must have been thinking in terms of the orphaning of a tradition and the need to reestablish its reality. The phrases which he uses in the parable are of Arabia, and the terminology, of a King and his court, of a woman and her sons in the desert, is not Christian but Saracen.

"Francis," says Bonaventura, recording an audience with Pope Innocent, "came armed with a parable. 'There was,' he said, 'a rich and mighty king who took to wife a poor but very beautiful woman, who lived in a desert, in whom he greatly delighted and by whom he had children who bore his image. When her sons were grown their mother said to them, 'My sons, be not ashamed; ye are the children of a King.' And she sent them to the court, having supplied them with all necessaries. When they came to the King, he admired their beauty; and seeing in them some resemblance to himself, he asked them, 'Whose sons are ye?' When they replied that they were the sons of a poor woman dwelling in the desert, the King, filled with much joy, said, 'Fear not, ye are my sons, and if I nourish strangers at my table, how much more you, who are my legitimate children.'"

The tradition that the Sufis are the esoteric Christians out of the desert, and that they are the children of a poor woman (Hagar, wife of Abraham, because of their Arab descent) fits completely with the probability that Francis had tried to explain to the Pope that the Sufi stream represented Christianity in a continuing form.

At his first meeting with the Pope, we are told, Francis did not make much impression, and he was sent away. Immediately afterward, however, the Pope had a strange dream. He saw "a palm tree gradually grow up at his feet until it grew a goodly stature, and as he gazed upon it wondering what the vision might mean, a divine illumination impressed on the mind of the Vicar of Christ that this palm tree signified the poor man whom he had that day driven from his presence."

The palm tree is the symbol used by the Sufis, and this

dream is probably the consequence of Francis using it as an
analogy during his audience.[1]

In the early part of the thirteenth century, Pope Innocent III, convinced of the validity of the saint's mission,
granted permission for the foundation of the Minor
Brothers, or Franciscans. The "Lesser Brethren," considered
to be a title assumed from pious humility, might lead one
to ask whether there was any Order known as the "Greater
Brethren." If so, what might the connection be?

The only people known in this way who were contemporary with St. Francis were the Greater Brothers, an appellation of the Sufi Order founded by Najmuddin Kubra,
"the Greater." The connection is interesting. One of the
major characteristics about this great Sufi teacher was that
he had an uncanny influence over animals. Pictures of him
show him surrounded by birds. He tamed a fierce dog merely
by looking at it—just as St. Francis is said to have cowed
the wolf in a well-known tale. Najmuddin's miracles were
well known throughout the East sixty years before St.
Francis was born.

When St. Francis was praised by anyone, it is reported,
he replied with this phrase: "What every one is in the eyes
of God, that he is no more."

It is related that the dictum of Najmuddin the Greater
was: *El Haqq Fahim ahsan el-Haqiqa*—"The Truth it is
which knows what is True."

In or about 1224, the most important and characteristic of
all of St. Francis' songs was composed: the *Cantico del Sole*
—Song of the Sun. Jalaluddin Rumi, the Whirling Dervish
chief and greatest poet of Persia, wrote numerous poems
dedicated to the Sun, the Sun of Tabriz. He even called a
collection of his poems the *Collection of the Sun of Tabriz*.
In this poetry the word "sun" is used again and again.

If it were true that St. Francis was trying to establish
contact with the sources of his troubador poetry, we would

[1] *Tariqat* (palm tree) is a code word for "Sufism." See annotation
"Tarika."

expect him to visit, or try to visit, the East. We would also expect him to be well received by the Saracens if he reached them. Further, he would be expected to produce Sufic poetry as a result of his Eastern travels. Now we can see whether these facts accord with history, and whether they were understood by his contemporaries.

When he was thirty, Francis decided to try to reach the East, and specifically Syria, which abutted upon the area of Asia Minor where the Whirling Dervishes were established. Prevented by financial troubles, he returned to Italy. Then he started out again, this time toward Morocco. He set off with a companion and traversed the whole kingdom of Aragon in Spain, though nobody can say why he did this, and some biographers are actually puzzled. Spain was very much penetrated with Sufi ideas and schools.

He did not actually reach Morocco, being driven back by illness. In the spring of 1214 he returned home.

Now he set out for the Crusades, where the siege of Damietta was in progress. Sultan Malik el-Kamil was encamped across the Nile—and Francis went to see him. He was well received, and the theory is that he went there to try to convert the Sultan to Christianity. "The Sultan," says a chronicler, "not only dismissed Francis in peace, with wonder and admiration for the man's unusual qualities, but received him fully into his favor, gave him a safe-conduct by which he might go and come, with full permission to preach to his subjects, and an entreaty that he would frequently return to visit him."

This visit to the Saracens is assumed by biographers to be prompted by a desire to convert the Sultan. And yet it is said of him that "These two aimless journeys break in somewhat strangely upon the current of his life." They would be strange if they were not those of a troubador looking for his roots. His desire to get to Morocco is dismissed in terms such as these: "It is impossible to tell what incident in his unrelated story may have suggested this new idea to the mind of Francis."

The Saracenic armies and the courts of their princes were at that time foci of Sufi activity. There can be hardly any doubt that it was here that Francis found what he was looking for. Far from having converted anyone in the Moslem camp, his first action upon recrossing the Nile was to try to dissuade the Christians from attacking the enemy. By the usual process of hindsight this is explained by historians as being due to the saint's having had a vision of the forthcoming calamity to Christian arms. "His warning was received with contempt, as he had forseen; but in the month of November following was fully verified when the Crusaders were driven back with great loss from the walls of Damietta. The sympathies of Francis under such circumstances must have been divided, for it is impossible that he could have been without some personal feeling toward the tolerant and friendly prince who had received him with such kindness."

The "Song of the Sun," hailed as the first-ever Italian poem, was composed after the saint's journey to the East, although because of his troubador background it is impossible for his usual biographers to believe that he was not composing similar poetry before this:

> It is impossible to suppose that during all these years [before 1224, when he wrote the "Song"] Francis, who was the leader of the young troubadors of Assisi in his early days, and who went through the woods and fields, after his conversion, singing to himself, still in French, songs which could not surely be the same songs he had sung through the streets among his joyous companions—the lays of war and love—it is impossible, we say, to suppose that it was for the first time at this late date that he had woven together canticles to the glory of God; but we are assured that these quaint and unskilled rhymes were the first beginning of vernacular poetry in Italy.

The atmosphere and setting of the Franciscan Order is

closer to a dervish organization than anything else. Apart from the tales about St. Francis which are held in common with Sufi teachers, all kinds of points coincide. The special methodology of what Francis calls "holy prayer" indicates an affinity with the dervish "remembering," quite apart from the whirling. The dress of the Order, with its hooded cloak and wide sleeves, is that of the dervishes of Morocco and Spain. Like the Sufi teacher Attar, Francis exchanged his garb with a mendicant. He saw a seraph with six wings, an allegory used by Sufis to convey the formula of the *bismillah*. He threw away spiked crosses which were worn for purposes of self-mortification by many of his monks. This action may or may not have been exactly as it is reported. It may resemble the dervish practice of ceremonially rejecting a cross with the words, "You may have the Cross, but we have the meaning of the Cross," which is still in use. This, incidentally, could be the origin of the Templar habit, alleged by witnesses, that the Knights "trod on the Cross."

Francis refused to become a priest. Like the Sufis, he enrolled into his teaching laymen, and again like the Sufis but unlike the Church, he sought to spread the movement among all the people, in some form of affiliation. This was "the first reappearance in the Church, since its full hierarchical establishment, of the democratic element—the Christian people, as distinguished from the simple sheep to be fed, and souls to be ruled."

The striking thing about the rules laid down by Francis was that, like the Sufis and unlike the ordinary Christians, his followers were not to think first of their own salvation. This principle is stressed again and again among the Sufis, who consider regard for personal salvation to be an expression of vanity.

He "began his preaching everywhere with the salutation which God, he said, had revealed to him—'The peace of God be with you!'" This is, of course, an Arab salutation.

In addition to Sufi ideas, legends and practices, St. Francis retained many Christian aspects in the Order.

The consequence of this amalgam was to produce an organization which did not fully mature. A nineteenth-century commentator sums up the inevitable development:

> We who, with all the enlightenment of six additional centuries, can look back and see the Inquisition grimly shadowing from under the robes of the Spanish priest, and see hordes of mendicant friars, privileged and impudent beggars, appearing behind the genial countenance of Francis, may perceive how much of evil mixed with the good, and how the enemy of all truth had cunningly mixed the seed of the tares with that of the wheat.

Mysteries in the West
V. The Secret Doctrine

I asked a child, walking with a candle,
"From where comes that light?"
Instantly he blew it out. "Tell me where
it is gone—then I will tell you where it
came from."

(Hasan of Basra)

Whether nominally of the East or West, we are all heirs in one way or another to the strengths and weaknesses of the medieval Arab philosophy. One of the drawbacks of this method was the attempt to apply its working outside its most successful field. This field was, of course, the collection, comparison, authentication and explanation of the traditions of the Prophet.

The adoption of this technique and its traditions, itself an expansion of scholarly methods derived by the Saracens from the Christian Greek theologians, was rapid. It could easily be learned, because it meant collecting facts and piling them one upon the other, with a view to form something complete.

There was another factor which existed side by side with this system in the Saracen lands. It was the formulation of schools of study and practice of a special kind in which the teacher, the teaching and the taught formed, in at least one sense, a unity. This part of the method was not transmitted unaltered, because it did not lend itself to institutionalization, the format which was developing most rapidly in the West. Even before the Moors were expelled from Spain, it was mainly their books which were translated, and this "single-line" knowledge was accepted, together with material which had already filtered through from earlier eastern Mediterranean sources. "The can of pineapples was imported, and recipes concocted based on canned pineapple. The growing and packing of the pineapple was something else, which in most quarters received little attention," says a modern Sufi on this theme.

Because the personal element of a teacher with special attainments militated against the needs of a continuing organization, this concept was dropped. It lingered, uneasily, among the independent people who were termed occultists and preached a doctrine dangerous to institutionalism—the unacceptable one of the need for a completely qualified teacher, one who knew things which were not in books.

After the fall of Constantinople, Greek original material —again in the form of books—provided more "single-line" material, more cases of pineapples. The institution of discipleship, tied to the concept of maintaining the monastic or academic institution, regarded advanced products in the form of personalities of greatness with wonder and admiration. The object of the institution was not to produce such people. They occurred in spite of, not because of, it. They were labeled saints. This was the function of religious organization.

The intellectual movement, on the other hand, specialized in producing more intellectuals and more enlightenment through the use of the human brain, employed more or less as we would today use a machine, but regarded as almost a form of sanctified performance, mainly because of its comparative novelty.

The Saracens themselves were not guiltless of transmitting the purely intellectual approach, though this was with them generally considered to be a phase rather than a dedication.

Strong traces of the various kinds of thinking and reaction are still strongly with us. There is the devout scholastic; the pious ecclesiastic; the pure pedant. Then there is the man who dislikes organization so much that he overreacts against it, harking back to the unlettered seer of antiquity in the belief that the whole of human greatness is the result of inspiration. The psychological and other new sciences follow close behind, pointing out the inadequacies of all the rest. In many cases this has already become a monotony referable to arguing from a new fixed idea and partaking of the nature of religious dogmatism and all the rest.

Even in formalized Arab (which often meant Greek) philosophy, there were often saving graces—strains of inner teaching or emphasis which were ignored in their adoption by the Western scholastics of the university type. In the East the tradition of a master and his disciples continued, in spite of the overlay of sheer scholasticism.

It is acknowledged that the "intellectual movement initiated by Ibn-Rushd [in the twelfth century] continued to be a living factor in European thought until the birth of modern experimental science."[1] From the eighth century, the Arabs had been studying and adapting Greek thought to their own ideas. Like the later Westerners, most of them worked from books alone, on the assumption that a book can contain the sum total of a teaching.

Ibn Rushd asserted the thinker's right to submit everything, except supernaturalism, to the force of reason. He was a doctor, a commentator on Aristotle, and an astronomer. He also studied music, a monograph upon which was published in his famous Aristotelian commentary, and which was taught at Paris, after being expurgated by the Church. This Córdoban was known to the West as Averroës, and he exercised a tremendous effect upon Jewish thinkers. Like his master, Ibn Tufail, he is said to have passed down a Sufic system alongside the permitted phil-

[1] Professor Philip Hitti, *History of the Arabs*, p. 584.

osophical one. Ibn Tufail (known to the West as Abubacer, after his first name, Abu Bakr) was also a physician, philosopher and ultimately Vizier at the Court of Granada. He wrote the extraordinary romance called the *Story of Hayy ibn-Yaqzan*. This, in the opinion of Western students, is the prototype of *Robinson Crusoe*; Alexander Selkirk merely serving as the news peg to provide topicality. It is based upon a story by Avicenna the Bokharan (980–1037), whose teaching was almost entirely philosophical. He, too, was a physician, philosopher and scientist. Avicenna followed yet another giant philosopher, Alfarabi (Alfarabius), whose Sufic ideas have been labeled Neoplatonic. He died over a thousand years ago.

All these names form a vital part of the modern heritage of thought. The reaction against medieval attempts to form a coherent idea of life and creation has, in the opinion of many, not served us very much better than credulity. The questing mind of the scientist, full of the desire for discovery, has been recognized in more recent times as overreaching itself. The scientist who has to keep his mind and concentration fixed upon an ever-narrowing field of study is in danger, and nowadays he admits it. He can become too concentrated or too diffused. His intellectual development is sometimes won at a sacrifice of emotional adjustment. This danger has long been apparent to those Sufis who were interested in scientific work. One of them, Anwar Faris, says:

> The twin exercises of identification and detachment are valuable in the training of the self. Too much identification produces an atrophy of the faculty of detachment. Fanaticism is the frequent result. A man becomes attached to something and cannot escape. When the Sage ibn-Sina (Avicenna) was writing his work on minerals, he used to study the mineral world, in general and in particular. He concentrated upon individual examples, then detached from this and ab-

sorbed himself in the whole. Thus did he strike a balance, together with concentration and detachment in other fields of thought and essence.

The superficial remedy to this is expressed in the "complete man" which the Moors considered to be a reflection of the inner complete man. Joseph McCabe (*The Splendour of Moorish Spain*, London, 1935) refers to the outer appearance of the cultivated man in his Spanish setting:

. . . all but a few literary cranks now see that the main line of human progress is in the extension of the scientific spirit to the whole of life. But it must be kept carefully in mind that this is only half of the Arab ideal of life. To most of their thinkers it would have seemed meaningless to ask if science were not in some danger of making men hard, calculating, overintellectual, cold, insensitive to beauty and art. Their students of science were quite commonly poets and musicians. That there was any antagonism between the intellectual and the emotional life, that both could not be cultivated by the same person, would have seemed to them a paradox.

This way of life, still less the Sufic one, was not widely adopted by the newly emergent West. In the Renaissance the cultural ideal was attempted, but not the one within that, the thesis of internal change, balance, extension of perception. The arts, studies and theories were adopted piecemeal and studied or reproduced, even developed. The inner sense was lost, lingering in places to be derided by the victorious sheer scholasticism and pure art-worship. The materials were studied and handed on in fragments as philosophy, astronomy, medicine. Many developing schools of learning in northern Europe, under severe ecclesiastical pressure or control, found it necessary to expurgate from this material non-Christian sentiments. This further limited the vitality of the material.

From Sicily, through the German "Baptized Sultans" of the Hohenstaufen strain, northern Europe received a form of this knowledge, but it was undoubtedly processed in a similar way. And this notwithstanding the adoption of Sufi architecture for the great Hohenstaufen castle, nor the Sufi symbolism of the coronation mantle of King Roger I.

It is almost not too much to say that those who persisted in thinking Sufistically were soon branded occultists. Their followers accepted the label. The result was a distorted, rather pathetic belief, in mastership, illumination and the personal triumph through occultism. Roger Bacon cites the *Secrets of Illuministic Wisdom*, a Sufi book by Ibn Sabin, who was in correspondence with Frederick II von Hohenstaufen. (Hitti, *op. cit.*, pp. 587, 610.) Bacon's fate was to be considered as an occultist, not because of his preaching as officially accepted, but because of his having impressed the "living transmission" theory upon those who disliked dogmatism and were therefore themselves cast into the scholastic wilderness. Nowadays their spiritual heirs accept the occultist label, and wander still—like the Indian untouchables who actually refer to themselves as outcasts.

The West (which mostly meant the Church) had taken what it thought it needed, and slammed the door with what seemed finality. Books were burned, Spain reclaimed for the true faith. At the other side of the threshold were left a strange assortment of people, things and ideas. Among them was material for future puzzlement, not strange to a Sufi—the troubadors, the game of cards, the harlequin, certain initiatory societies.

There were cracks in the door, which let something, but very little, in and out.

At the end of the eighteenth century, Napoleon invaded Egypt. A general with his forces founded the Order of the Seekers of Wisdom, otherwise known as the *Sufiyin*—the Sufis.

In a book perhaps correctly entitled the *Mélange*, he explained how he located among the Eastern Adepts the sources of the "orphan" secret wisdom of the West. "This was the Fount. We had been for centuries following the wide but muddied river."

Why and by what process the river had repeatedly become muddied in the West seems to have been eventually understood by the *Sufiyin,* who in microcosm repeated the fate of their predecessors—though through no fault of their own. They had assumed that all they needed to import into the West was the doctrine and the methodology, without the teacher.

Only six years after the reputed date of starting the Order, the "Affirmation of the Sophiens of France" admitted failure: "We must dissolve rather than continue repetitiously to practice rituals and operations which in the absence of the active teaching master cannot produce the essential man. The process is of a complexity which only superior perceptions of needs will meet. The secret which the master has, this he uses to cause and make grow the change in others, who shall take his place. Without him, the community cannot really progress, though it may retain its outward form."

But Sufi masters cannot be recruited or imported. The notice of dissolution continues piteously: "Who can force to himself the presence of the living illuminate? He knows the needs, and he fulfills them. For us there is only yearning."

At least the *Sophiens* had learned something. Fragments seem to have lingered on, because many years later an offshoot was reported to be persisting in India.

Was the door slammed for good? It seemed so. Not only did the West have enough science, art and other materials to digest, but it had the weapon of propaganda. The geopolitical struggle so well delineated by Professor Toynbee,[2]

[2] A. J. Toynbee, *A Study of History,* Vol. VIII: Heroic Ages—Contacts between Civilizations in Space, Oxford, 1956, pp. 216 et seq., "The Encirclement of the Islamic World by the West, Persia and Tibet."

coupled with the Crusades mentality, proceeded to stigma-
tize everything Saracen, "paynim" or Arab as not only
heretical, infidel and unpleasant, but diabolical and dangerous. The West inherits this tradition, steadily reinforced by
events. First it was the Spanish Arabs who had to be beaten
back from the borders of France. Then the infidel who was
holding the Holy Land. Then the Turks were preparing
to storm the gates of Vienna. Mohammedanism lumped together in the Western mind, constituted a threat and an
evil which must be contained and counterattacked. The last
phase was ably sustained by the missionary interests which
intended to overcome Islam for the greater glory of the
Church. The existence of the Turkish Empire only proved
that the infidel foe was still a threat. Little was to be learned,
in any case, from people who were in many cases now members of dependent communities, whether the sun set on
them or not.

Only cranks interested themselves in Eastern philosophy.
Cranks were to be found in every community. Was one to
turn Turk or go native? Unhygienic people who did not
even accept the Gospel and whom one ruled were hardly
likely to be able to teach anything. Let them, in any case,
put their own house in order first.

And yet there were people who looked beyond this temporary view of human development, even though they
would never have believed that the circumstances in which
they found themselves were as temporary as we now know
them to be. And the process started early, earlier than one
would believe. The Sufic current was at work.

We must go back several hundred years, to Majorca, to
find a trace of the double life which was being led by
mystics at that time—Christian anchorites doubling as Sufi
teachers.

Brother Anselm of Turmeda was a Majorcan mystic of
the dark ages—and saint to the Christians. But this was very
far from being all. Among the Moslem Spaniards he was the
sanctified Sufi Abdullah el Tarjuman. What did he teach?

His book, *Dispute of the Ass with Brother Anselmo*, is a sometimes literal translation of a part of the *Encyclopaedia* of the Arab Brethren of Purity. Since his Arabic name literally means "Servant of God," "the Translator," there is no reason why he should not have tried, by translation, to pass on Sufi teachings. A modern Spanish scholar (Angel Gonzalez Palencia, in *Hispania*, XVIII, 3, October, 1935) draws attention to him and calls him *el estupendo plagiario* —but in the middle ages learning was not always considered to be the property of individuals; especially the knowledge published by a secret society, a band of anonymous sages like the Brethren. Copyright was unknown.

This living link between Arab teaching and Christianity is carried on by another strange character, a renegade priest. In 1782, Father Juan Andres, an expelled Jesuit, published a remarkable book *Origen, progresos y estado actual de toda la literatura*. He tried to show the debt of Europe to Spanish-Arabian learning. He pointed to the diffusion of science, even recognized the debt of St. Thomas to this source. Spanish poetry, he noted, sprang from the Arabic development in Spain, including the Provençal and troubador romances and Italian lyric verse, as well as the development of the novel, fables and the music of the Arabic-speaking Alfonso the Sage.

How did the renegade Jesuit know all these things? There was no documentation at the time available to him. And yet, in some so far unexplained manner, he discovered facts about the Arab—and particularly Sufic—heritage of the West which was later to be pieced together, almost point by point, largely through a study of the documents of Arab Spain. Even the probable origins of the Jesuit system in the Fatimite schools of Egypt[3] can hardly account for the perception which ex-Father Andres showed, because this was not a Sufi School. Was there a current of hidden teaching, a vein of ancient lore, which the expelled Jesuit had tapped?

[3] The correspondences are listed in Ameer Ali's authoritative *Short History of the Saracens*.

There was, indeed. The Eastern impact in the dark ages was absorbed on several levels. Of these the most important are the theological and the occultist. Lully, Assisi, Scot and dozens of others passed on the theological version. But we only have to glance at the list of the famous names of occult illuminati of Europe to see what was the nature of the secret doctrine which they were passing down, in however garbled a form.

Raymond Lully, according to the occultists, was an alchemist and illuminate. According to the devout, he was a Christian missionary. According to his own writings, he was an adapter of Sufi books and exercises. Roger Bacon, another hierophant of occultism, wrote on Sufi illuminism. Paracelsus, who tried to reform Western medicine, presents Sufi ideas. He, too, is one of the heroes of the "magicians" and alchemists. Geber the alchemist was one of the best-known Sufis of Iraq. He is known as a master of occultism. Also in the occult tradition is Albertus Magnus, both scholastic and magician, who studied in Arab schools and inspired St. Thomas Aquinas. Numerous Popes supposed to be magicians or transmitters of a secret doctrine, the hidden teaching, were graduates of Arab schools—such as Gerbert, Pope Silvester II. Laurence, Archbishop of Malfi, is charged with having learned his secret lore from Silvester. And so the process continues.

In organizations it is the same story. If the Franciscan Order bears the stamp of Sufi origins, so do the Rosicrucians and the Masons. The terminology of contemporary witches in England contains (as "unknown words") ordinary untranslated Arabic phrases. The salutation "Blessed Be!" is the least significant, but provides an instance of a direct rendering of the Sufi salutation *Mabaruk bashad*—the calling down of the *baraka* upon an individual or assembly.

The secret teaching, in most of its expressions accessible to us, therefore, boils down to very little other than simplicity for whoever has the patience or the general knowledge of what was on which side of the door when it was banged, all those centuries ago.

There are times in the lives of all scholars when, with all the drama and excitement of discovery, the thrill of realization bursts upon them. It may be the result of a tiny thought, working in the mind, patiently collecting unaccounted scraps of information, bursting forth into blinding light. Inventors, scientists, historians, all have known this experience. Miguel Asín y Palacios, the renowned Spanish Arabist, devout Christian though he was, knew this thrill when he came across the work of the illuminist school of Sufi philosophers, and realized what they had given to the world—even the highest reaches of the Catholic world.

It was in the ninth century that Ibn Masarrah of Córdoba taught to a select group of disciples what he knew of the heights to which the human consciousness could attain. From these beginnings the illuminists were to provide the substance of the allegories of Dante; the teachings of the school known as the Augustinian scholastics of the middle ages; the wisdom of some of the founders of modern Western philosophy—Duns Scotus and Roger Bacon from Britain, Raymond Lully of Majorca, St. John of the Cross among the canonized. Solomon ibn Gabirol, a Jewish thinker of Málaga, based his *Fount of Life* on Masarrah's work. This, in turn, inspired the Franciscan School. (Hitti, *History of the Arabs*, pp. 580 et seq.)

As he delved more and more deeply into the rare manuscripts which had lain almost untouched in Spain since the expulsion of the Moors, Professor Asín's excitement mounted. There, in the sometimes crabbed, strange Maghribi script of the Sufi Spaniards of a millennium ago, was not only the idea of the illuministic philosophy—but in many cases he found literal quotations cited in the works of mystics and philosophers whose names were household words to the devout of Europe. Asín was not alone in this discovery, however, for Professor Ribera had noted such facts as the statement by the great Majorcan mystic Lully that he had written his masterwork *Book of the Lover and the Beloved* on the pattern of the Sufis.

All this is all the more remarkable because the Sufi illuminists are among the most famous and yet the most secretive of all Sufi schools. Such intellectual giants as Suhrawardi, Ibn El-Arabi of Murcia and El-Ghazali rigidly adhered in their public writings to noncommunication of the vital data which was to bring about the actual transformation of the human mind and complete the "alchemy of happiness," as Ghazali called it. The strange seeming contradiction that gnosticism and agnosticism actually meet somewhere along the Sufi path baffled the externalists who sought to penetrate the experiences of the schools. It still baffles some people.

And yet there is evidence that at the deepest levels of Sufic secrecy there is a mutual communication with the mystics of the Christian West. And the influence of the illuminist philosophy profoundly affected the East as well —the Persian, Turk, Afghan mystics all followed the illuminists. Arkon Daraul (A History of Secret Societies, New York, 1962) has shown that the process of illuminism as the host to a secret within a secret extends until the present day. The illuminati of England, France and Germany, organized as a secret society, the *Alumbrados* of Spain and numerous other initiatory circles, continue to transmit the teachings of these Spanish scholars.

Before turning to a consideration as to what illuminism is, it will be as well to note what its followers had to say about its origins. Here again we come across the secret-doctrine theory in its full development. The secret book *Wisdom of Illumination* states that the philosophy is identical with the inner teachings of all the ancients—the Greeks, the Persians, the Egyptians—and is the science of Light and the deepest truth, through whose exercise man can attain to a status about which he can normally only dream.

Roger Bacon repeated this assertion, and from him the

idea was taken up all over Europe, giving rise to numerous secret schools, some of them genuine, others entirely bogus. This knowledge, said Bacon, was known to Noah and Abraham, to the Chaldean and Egyptian masters, to Zoroaster and Hermes and Greeks such as Pythagoras, Anaxagoras and Socrates—and to the Sufis. Suhrawardi, who wrote his secret book a century before Bacon (and was judicially murdered for it) is quoted by Bacon himself—or rather his book is, as Baron Carra de Vaux has shown (*Journal Asiatique*, XIX, p. 63).

Among the strange byways of history we may note Bacon named as a Rosicrucian, a follower of the path of the Rose Cross—a late mistranslation of the Sufi phrase "Path of the Rose."

It was inevitable that religious zealots and others should counterattack the Western scholars who unearthed the Sufi teachings as being the basis of work which had been for centuries admired and applauded by the most orthodox Christians. Hence we find Asín replying (*Obras Escogidas*, I, Madrid, 1946) with all the emphasis at his disposal:

"Recently publishing a doctoral thesis—*Character and Origins of the Ideas of the Blessed Raymond Lulle*, (Toulouse, 1912)—its author, Mr. Probost, with completely infantile audacity, calls Menedez y Pelayo, Ribera and me liars and romantics for maintaining the Arab affiliation of the Lullian system. This inexpert youth does not know my study *Psychology According to Mohiedin Abenarabi*, published in the *Actes du XIVme Congrès des Orientalistes* seven years ago, in which I had demonstrated *documentarily* the copying of the allegory of the Lights." Even in those days, before his studies of the illuminism of the Sufis were complete, Asín was ready and willing to produce documents to prove his point.

In the work of men like Asín, the pendulum is swinging back, and the Sufi influence is being recognized. But the discovery that Christian contemplatives used Sufi books, Sufi methods, Sufi terminology has stimulated the inevitable

results, expressed in the explanations which are now pouring out from the cells of the modern scholastics. Sufism, it
is now declared, is able to produce true mystical experience
because the Sufis revere Jesus. Further, Sufism was profoundly influenced in its early days by Christianity. The
implication is that Sufic ideas are not to be rejected. If St.
John of the Cross and Lully could use them, there must be
some good in them. The scholastics have retraced a part of
their path, and are rewriting their history to allow for uncomfortable facts. The only danger in this activity is that,
as new material comes to light, new reshaping of the official
attitude becomes necessary. Mental gymnastics. Those who
do not adhere so strongly to the theological line are busy
tracing Sufism back to "coincidences" in ancient doctrines.

Contact with Sufis, who were discovered not to be ogres
after all, provoked another interesting development in
Western thought, a process which is still continuing. This
development can best be termed recognition. A realization
of the affinity of Sufic thought with Western intuition and
ideas has brought many people to the point where they are
taking a close look at the system. By Sufic thinking this
comes about for two reasons—firstly because the bases of
Sufi ways are inherent in the human mind ("there is only
one Right Way") and again because in modern Western
training of all kinds are the scattered seeds of the ideas of
the Sufi transmitters from Spain, Sicily and elsewhere. The
Sufic sentiments of Khayyam and others, which have almost
become naturalized into the West, is another source of the
diffusion of this current. We have various aspects of this
diffusion in this book, chosen in order to illustrate it, not as
any complete enunciation.

The teachings of a continued vein of secret teaching, of
which the books of philosophers were merely a part without
the key, the arguments without the action, was transmitted
to the West from the illuminist Sufis of Spain, and possibly
the Near East as well. One channel is known to us—from
Andalusia the dissemination of this idea has been traced

by Asín and his associates to Roger Bacon and Raymond Lully. Others have followed the trail in the work of Alexander Hales and Duns Scotus, and have noted the determining influence upon the so-called Augustinian scholastics of the West.

The traditional account of how the teachings are transmitted and from where is partially contained in the *Wisdom of Illumination*, written by the martyr Suhrawardi. He lived from 1154 to 1191, an Easterner domiciled in Aleppo, and was killed by the order of the orthodox, whose pressure Saladin's nephew, the local ruler, was unable to resist. Thus he is known as "Suhrawardi the Murdered." He is one of the greatest Sufi teachers; and his school, as Asín has demonstrated, provided Dante with his ideas. The "Murdered Sheikh" did not originate the illuministic theory of Sufism, nor the tradition of a chain of masters from the remotest antiquity. But in the preface to his book we have a sketch of his teachings on this point. Most copies were committed to the flames, but some have survived, especially in the East.

As with most Sufi books, this was written in response to repeated requests, as he observes—written for his friends and companions. Philosophy has always existed, and there has always been a true philosopher in the world. The differences between the ancients and moderns is one of proof and demonstration. Aristotle was a great teacher, but dependent upon his forerunners. Among these were Hermes, Aesculapius and others, in very long succession. They may be divided into classes, some more elevated than others, according to the balance between intellection, speculation, belief and so on. The importance of the philosopher is so great that if a fully balanced one is found, he is the representative of God on earth. But the inner philosopher is always superior to the scholastic. There is never an age in which a great theosopher is not in existence. The speculative philosopher has no right or claim to rulership. This rulership may not be political power; but if wisdom and power of a material sort are combined, the age is illuminated. Yet the philosopher may, because of his endowments, remain unknown and yet have the mastery of the world.

It is best for the philosopher to combine insight with experience, rather than one or the other. Nobody can benefit from a study of Sufism unless he has freed himself from the mental habits of formal philosophy. Such an undeveloped person should only frequent ordinary philosophers. In Sufism certain perceptions have to be developed and further development depends upon these. This is the equivalent of the scholastic method in which the experiences are formed and ideas built of ideas. Unless this method of the Sufis is followed, the practitioner cannot be considered a real philosopher.

The ancient doctrines of Egypt and Greece are in direct line with Sufism, and with them, of course, exposition had to take its place and relationship to experience, which means the development of the Sufi perceptions. The terminology of the illuminists indicates that the theory embraces the ancient wisdom of the Semites as well as that of the Persians, hence showing the theme of the essential unity of "complete" philosophy at the theory and practice level.

In formal scholasticism, of course, the division between intellect and inspiration is so great that it is difficult at first for the uninformed reader to grasp that these two things are considered by this school to be inseparable if the truth is to be reached. Hence the Sufi insistence that this step of cognition must be made.

The Higher Law

There are three indications of real
generosity: to remain steadfast without
resisting, to praise without the emotion of
generosity, and to give before being asked.
(Maaruf Karkhi)

One of the most interesting productions of Western Sufic
literature is the long poem *The Kasidah,* written a century
ago by the explorer Sir Richard Burton, himself a Sufi, and
composed on his return journey from Mecca. This "Lay of
the Higher Law," which appeared in small editions, aroused
a great deal of interest. Even Lady Burton, who was not
oversympathetic to her husband's heterodox beliefs, con-
fessed that she had read it many times, and "never without
bitter tears, and when I read it now it affects me still more;
he used to take it away from me because it impressed me
so." There is no doubt that the poem is a powerful composition, steeped in Sufi lore.

Burton, in his foreword to *The Kasidah,* called himself
"the translator," and attributed the work to one Haji Abdu
al-Yazdi. He summarizes it thus:

The principles which justify the name, Higher Law,
are as follows:

"The Author asserts that Happiness and Misery are
equally divided and distributed in the world.

"He makes Self-cultivation, with due regard to others, the sole and sufficient object of human life.

"He suggests that the affections, the sympathies and the 'divine gift of Pity' are man's highest enjoyments.

"He advocates suspension of judgment, with a proper suspicion of 'Facts, the idlest of superstitions.'

"Finally, although destructive to appearance, he is essentially reconstructive."

"Only an admirer of Omar Khayyam could have written *The Kasidah*," says Justin Huntly McCarthy. And yet, according to Lady Burton, the poem was written eight years before FitzGerald introduced Burton, Swinburne and Rosetti to Omar. What the two poets have in common, of course, is that they are both Sufis.

Although only a few hundred copies appeared, *The Kasidah* ("The Tinkling of the Camel Bell") was included in Lady Burton's biography of "the greatest Oriental scholar England ever had and neglected." As a result, the work became very widely known, and its hidden influence upon those who studied it must have been great. Summing it up, Isabel Burton shows how the outlines of Sufic thinking can influence even one who is devoutly Christian and unsympathetic to the author's commitment: "It is a poem of extraordinary power, on the Nature and Destiny of Man, anti-Christian and Pantheistic. So much wealth of Oriental learning has rarely been compressed into so small a compass."

What Burton has done has been to comment in verse upon Western methods of thought, modern theories and philosophies, from the Sufi point of view. More, he has (like Khayyam) taken it upon himself to ask questions to which he does not supply fixed answers. This is the technique of the teaching Sufi who poses questions and waits to see whether his hearers will seek the explanation or not. The Sufi message had something for Western thinkers, and was even recognized as the essence of Burton's life. Burton's

Life was described thus by one enthusiast: "to me its great *raison d'être* / is that *Tinkling of the Camel Bell.* It is hard to judge of a thing in the first heat of admiration, but it seems to me worthy to stand level with the greatest poems of the Earth, and in front of most."

It is a long poem, in twenty pages of type, and an author's commentary upon the supposed Haji upon whom he fathered it is even longer. Burton follows in his notes the method of Sufi teachers, and this is the part of the work which most clearly shows that he has been through a course of Sufic study under a master. There seems little doubt that Burton was trying to project Sufi teaching in the West. To this extent he must be considered a part of the process which has been continuous—the interchange between the East and West which is studied in this book.

In Sufism he finds a system of application to misguided human faiths "which will prove them all right, and all wrong; which will reconcile their differences; will unite past creeds; will account for the present, and will anticipate the future with a continuous and uninterrupted development." This is to be by a process "not negative and distinctive, but, on the contrary, intensely positive and constructive." Like all Sufis, he often uses the method of approaching his subject from a number of different angles —and then breaking away, leaving the reader to complete the process. The reason for this is that a Sufi is only made by passing through both discipleship and self-work (*amalinafs*).

Above all, Burton, writing in a time when science and reason were in the full flow of their ecstatic self-discovery, insists that "there are things which human Reason or Instinct matured, in its undeveloped state, cannot master; but Reason is a law to itself. Therefore we are not bound to believe, or to attempt belief in, anything which is contrary or contradictory to Reason."

The Kasidah opens with the desert, the dark, the pilgrims
on their way to Mecca:

> The hour is nigh; the waning Queen walks forth to rule
>   the later night;
> Crown'd with the sparkle of a Star, and throned on orb
>   of ashen light:

The night passes, while the travelers experience various
emotions, and Burton takes leave of the pilgrim caravan,
the undeveloped human continuity. He is following another
road, a Sufi way:

> Friends of my youth, at last adieu! haply some day we
>   meet again;
> Yet ne'er the self-same men shall meet; the years shall
>   make us other men;.......
> Go, vanish from my Life as dies the tinkling of the
>   Camel's bell.

Now the poem speaks of the endless questions which
mankind asks, the dreadful fears which beset him. He
quotes the Sufis Hafiz (the "Bard of Love and Wine") and
Khayyam, who "would divorce old barren Reason from his
bed, / And wed the Vine-maid in her stead." Taking his
questioning a stage further in typical Sufi style, he shows
that there is something still deeper beyond their imagery:
". . . fools who believe a word he said!" He quotes the Sufi
who says that anyone who knows that he has a soul is entitled to ask questions about it; and he shows that the seeming pessimism of the Sufi at times hides something else—
exposing the absurdity of selfishness:

> And this is all, for this we're born to weep a little and
>   to die!
> So sings the shallow bard whose life still labors at the
>   letter "I."

The Sufi insistence carries Burton on to Jesus. He be-
wailed our sorrows and our sin; why was a little glimpse of
paradise not offered to man? Why could ears never hear and

eyes never see bliss in the heavenly kingdom? Mansur, the Sufi martyr who was publicly disembodied by the forces of tyranny, is now put into juxtaposition with Jesus, and quoted: "I am the truth! I am the truth. . . . The microcosm abides in ME." Mansur was wise, "but wiser they who smote him with the hurled stones."

To eat, drink and make merry is something which may sound all very well, but it does not show any distinction between man and swine. The ascetic, fanatic that he is, answers Burton, as he stalks the earth, that he is completely confident in a life to come, adjusted to his vale of tears. Wiser is he than Moses (who ignored future rewards and punishments), who shows the future state—the future when he does not know the past, and to whom the present is a mere dream. Our Sufi does not like him at all:

> What know'st thou, man, of Life? and yet, for ever
> twixt the womb, the grave,
> Thou pratest of the Coming Life, of Heav'n and Hell
> thou fain must rave.

The feeling of one's own importance, while according to the Sufi it may be necessary in some ways, has to be moved into correct perspective, otherwise the human being becomes useless—though he may not seem so to other useless people.

> The world is old and thou art young; the world is large
> and thou art small;
> Cease, atom of a moment's span, to hold thyself an All-
> in-All!

The section which follows this admonition studies the contradictions of human speculation about life, and especially the theme of sorrow which runs through it. Illustrations are taken from Hinduism, Buddhism, the ancient Egyptians; the creator is seen as an enlarged human being, a potter, weaver, playing with what is only human sentiment. The way in which diety works or seems to "plan" is not explicable in human terms:

> Cease, Man, to mourn, to weep, to wail; enjoy the
> shining hour of sun;
> We dance along Death's icy brink, but is the dance less
> full of fun?

Selecting sayings from ancient teachers, the English Sufi shows that the mere experience of life teaches nothing. Buddha and Confucius are quoted, and the manmade God is again attacked. Now the lowly ascetic, the religionist who merely affirms that he chooses to call the "Maker" God is assailed by the Sufi Drawer of the Wine. A changeful, finite creature cannot fathom the infinite depths of Power with "a foot of twine." The Sufic echo is treading close to the agnosticism of which the Sufis have sometimes been accused. It is only here, in this narrow strip between faith and disbelief, that the truth is to be found.

The childish fears of lost humanity seek a sure God, make him in their own image, then "pray the Law its laws to break." In one form or another we find the gloomy Brahman in India, the Chaldean star-oracle, the Zoroastrian dualist, the Jewish Jehovah—"Adon or Elohim, the God that smites, the Man of War." He sweeps past the gods of Greece, fair and frail humanities, to the Odin of the North. Looking at religion as a developing human movement, Burton watches the death of Great Pan; the Nazarene comes and seizes his seat beneath the sun: "the votary of the riddle-god, whose one is three and three is one."[1] And, of course, the miserable creed of inherited sin.

After Christianity, Islam. The lank Arab, a lizardeater, overwhelms the lands of the grail of Jamshid, the Persians' idyllic traditions of old are gone. These are the ways of organized religions: "they rose, they reigned, they fought,

---

[1] The "riddle" refers to the Sufi use of three-letter roots. The "three is one" stands for the three letters AHD, together spelling the word "unity."

and fell, / as swells and swoons across the world the tinkling
of the Camel's bell."

There is no good, no bad, as it is measured by ordinary
standards. This Burton affirms, without the usual Sufic rider
that just what this means is experienced only in the Sufi's
inner consciousness. As soon as it is expressed in the limited
frame of words, it sounds destructive. But he is writing in
the grip of Sufic exhilaration and he is now addressing himself to Sufis alone. Good, he points out, is to man what he
likes; evil what does him harm. These ideas change with
location, with race and time. Every vice has been a virtue,
every good has been called a sin or crime.

Good and evil intertwine. Only Khizr (the completed
Sufi) can see where one begins and the other ends.

The literalist, who claims that man's early state was the
ideal one, is now brought under heavy fire; Burton takes
his ammunition from the modern knowledge of evolution.
Before man walked the earth, torture and suffering were the
continuous tone. Primitive animals tore each other apart.
Before that, the fair earth was alternately burning hot and
frozen solid; the sun an orb of whirling fire; the moon a
mere corpse of what had been a world. Early man was anything but refined:

His choicest garb a shaggy fell, his choicest tool a flake
of stone;
His best of ornaments tattoo'd skin and holes to hang
his bits of bone;
Who fought for female as for food when May awoke a
warm desire;
And such the Lust that grew to Love when Fancy lent
a purer fire.

This primitive man learned from beavers and ants how to
build; and it was when he mastered fire that the lord of
beasts became a lord of men. "Conscience was born when
man had shed his fur, his tail, his pointed ears."

The heritage of animality is still in man, and it is to be

seen in the behavior of one toward another. In defiance
of his known history, mankind cannot accept an explanation of himself based upon literal belief in tales and fables.

Then, if tradition is not true, what is truth? What we
think is truth is not such at all. This kind of truth is tem-
peramental, changing. Burton explains this in his commentary upon "Haji's" poem: "The perceptions, when they
perceive truly, convey objective truth, which is universal;
whereas the reflectives and the sentiments, the working of
the moral region, or the middle lobe of the phrenologists,
supply only subjective truth, personal and individual."

Objective truth is the goal of the Sufi, and it is obviously
toward the need for finding this that Burton is directing
his audience.

All mere theories, repetitious observances, are nothing.
Burton now shouts at the priest to baptize the dead, as the
Marcionites did, following a quotation from Paul (1 Cor.
XV, 29): "Else what shall they do which are baptized for
the dead, if the dead do not rise at all? Why are they then
baptized for the dead?"

Truth cannot be found by the means which are generally
used to seek it:

Yes, Truth may be, but 'tis not Here; mankind must
seek and find it There.
But Where not I nor you can tell, nor aught earth-
mother ever bare.

The struggle to find truth comes partly, in its real form,
through not struggling at all. This is the Sufi paradox which
is contained in the next lines:

Enough to think that Truth can be; come sit we where
the roses glow;
Indeed he knows not how to know who knows not also
how to unknow.

Even the meaning of faith itself has to be approached
by the Sufi in what seems to the ordinary person an el-

liptical manner. Like the masters before him, Burton approaches this by seeming paradox. All faith, he says, is both false and true. "Truth is the shattered mirror strown in myraid bits; / while each believes his little bit the whole to own." The kind of faith which unregenerate man takes for real faith is so often unmoved and fixed because it is merely what today would be called a conditioning. This false faith stands, "and why? Because man's silly fancies still remain, / And will remain till wiser man the daydreams of his youth disdain." This is precisely the thought of Rumi, when he asks when the hearer will stop coveting the sweets of childhood.

Now into the discussion. After Burton dismisses the conventional teaching on the soul, the zealot strikes back with a harsh condemnation of materialism, which is what he thinks the Sufi is advocating:

> "Tush!" quoth the Zahid [devotee], "well we ken the
>   teaching of the school abhorr'd
> That maketh man automaton, mind a secretion, soul
>   a word."

Burton spares him little time. Faith is due to an accident of birth; the faith that men normally know is a product of their environment. The author again pits one religionist against another; the Hindu despising the Frank; the Moslem crying about polytheism; the Buddhist calling the Confucian a dog; the Tartar claiming that attention to a future state is betraying the efficiency and duties of man in the world. And the Sufi chimes in:

> "You all are right, you all are wrong," we hear the
>   careless Sufi say,
> "For each believes his glimm'ring lamp to be the gorgeous light of day."

Man's ignorance of his own ignorance is the real enemy. He must seek truth in the right way, must gladden the heart, ". . . abjure the Why and seek the How."

Looking to the future, because he finds no response in the people of his own time, Burton tells himself that, having delivered his message, in days to come when wisdom dwells with men, "These echoes of a voice long stilled haply shall wake responsive strain."

Wend now thy way with brow serene, fear not thy
  humble tale to tell:
The whispers of the Desert-wind; the tinkling of the
  Camel's bell.

Burton's burst of Sufi activity in *The Kasidah,* published sixty years ago, was paralleled by Wilberforce Clarke's translation and adaptation of the *Gifts.* This cleared a great deal of ground in showing that the dervish philosophy was different from normal Western assessment of it at the time. This supplied at least a basis for the further examination of Sufic ideas, if not practices. Burton, by relating Sufi thought to modern Western feelings, provided a bridge whereby the thinking Westerner could accept essential Sufi concepts. It remained for Cartwright to leave an equally important book, one which in the guise of pseudo-Oriental romance presented some of the actual experiences of being a Sufi.

Since the complete work-and-thought system of Sufism has not been much used in the West, and because of prejudice or a difference of thought, until recently seemed unlikely to "naturalize" itself where it was needed most, it is to be expected that few original literary works of a Sufi nature would be found in Western European languages. The textbooks in the East are generally couched in poetic or devotional terms, and the active part of the teaching is supplied by a master whose major function is actually to be a master, to exist among his students. Cartwright did the next best thing: he wrote an account of his experiences in such a school.

The *Mystic Rose from the Garden of the King* first appeared in 1899. Superficially the book looks like a fantasy.

Its author was Sir Fairfax L. Cartwright, a member of the
diplomatic service. The book was reprinted in 1925, and
it contains two important sources of Sufi experience for
those who can understand it. The portion devoted to stories
is designed to lift momentarily the veil between ordinary
thought and the inner questioning of the mind. The other
portion gives a series of inner experiences, which are numbered and which represent one person's varied realization
of the extra element possible to man's attainment before he
comes to the point where he can make use of this perception.

Like Burton, Sir Fairfax found it necessary to attribute in
the first edition the authorship to an Oriental—"Sheikh Haji
Ibrahim of Kerbela." He uses the Eastern imagery and setting because it does lend itself to the projection of Sufi
thought through the objectivization of the content. Like
the fable with which this book begins, it enables the
reader to detach himself from associations, and to participate to some extent in the reality which the author is trying
to convey. The reader does not really think of himself as a
dervish or Oriental king. To this extent he can safely enter-
tain ideas in theory and even more that he would reject if
they were presented within his own culture pattern.

This book is no substitute for Sufi experience, but it contains material well suited to the Western mind trying to
grasp a mode of thought which in its culture lacks many
agreed bases. The idea that ecstatic experience is Sufism or
really mysticism of any kind is one of the numerous points
scotched by Cartwright:

"The man who is despondent seeks consolation in intoxication, but intoxication may be produced by good wine or
by bad wine; the good wine will raise him into a state of
material ecstasy and make him forget his despondency; the
bad wine will make his state worse than it was before. So
it is with the spiritual wine; if it be pure it will lift the
disciple who drinks thereof into the realm of the perfect
contemplation of the truth, but if it be adulterated and

impure it will throw his soul back even further than the point which it has already attained."

The allegory of alchemy, a traditional Sufi tale in which the great work of transmutation is accomplished, is given a fresh form in the book. The book is full of allegories, and one of the best is a Western adaptation of the "Tale of the Sands," which loses nothing in the form which he gives it:

A bubbling stream reached a desert, and found that it could not cross it. The water was disappearing into the fine sand, faster and faster. The Stream said aloud, "My destiny is to cross this desert, but I can see no way."

This is the situation of the disciple who needs a master, but who cannot trust one, the pathetic human situation.

The voice of the Desert answered, in the hidden tongue of nature, saying, "The Wind crosses the desert, and so can you."

"But, whenever I try, I am absorbed into the sand; and even if I dash myself at the desert, I can only go a little distance."

"The Wind does not dash itself against the desert sand."

"But the Wind can fly, and I cannot."

"You are thinking in the wrong way; trying to fly by yourself is absurd. Allow the Wind to carry you over the sand."

"But how can that happen?"

"Allow yourself to be absorbed in the Wind."

The Stream protested that it did not want to lose its individuality in that way. If it did, it might not exist again.

This, said the Sand, was a form of logic, but it did not refer to reality at all. When the Wind absorbed moisture, it carried it over the desert, and then let it fall again like rain. The rain again became a river.

But how, asked the Stream, could it know that this was true?

"It is so, and you must believe it, or you will simply be sucked down by the sands to form, after several million years, a quagmire."

"But if that is so, will I be the same river that I am today?"

"You cannot in any case remain the same stream that you are today. The choice is not open to you; it only seems to be open. The Wind will carry your essence, the finer part of you. When you become a river again at the mountains beyond the sands, men may call you by a different name; but you yourself, essentially, will know that you are the same. Today you call yourself such and such a river only because you do not know which part of it is even now your essence."

So the Stream crossed the desert by raising itself into the arms of the welcoming Wind, which gathered it slowly and carefully upward, and then let it down with gentle firmness, atop the mountains of a far-off land. "Now," said the Stream, "I have learned my true identity."

But it had a question, which it bubbled up as it sped along: "Why could I not reason this out on my own; why did the Sands have to tell me? What would have happened if I had not listened to the Sands?"

Suddenly a small voice spoke to the Stream. It came from a grain of sand. "Only the Sands know, for they have seen it happen; moreover, they extend from the river to the mountain. They form the link, and they have their function to perform, as has everything. The way in which the stream of life is to carry itself on its journey is written in the Sands."

The Book of the Dervishes

If you know not these states, pass
on, nor join the infidel in ignorant
counterfeit . . . but all learn not the secrets
of the Way.
(Shabistari, *Secret Garden*, Johnson Pasha's
version)

If there is any standard dervish textbook it is the "Gifts of
(Deep) Knowledge"—the *Awarif el-Maarif*—written in the
thirteenth century and studied by members of all Orders.
Its author, Sheikh Shahabudin Suhrawardi (1145–c. 1235)
presided over the coalescing of theory, ritual and practice
which took place in his time, established teaching schools
close to the courts of Persia and India, and was Chief of the
Chiefs of Sufis in Baghdad.

The book is of interest to us both because it shows the
outward and early stages of attraction into the dervish
corpus, because it contains the basic contents of thought
and action of these mystics, and because of Lieutenant
Colonel Wilberforce Clarke. Colonel Clarke was himself a
dervish, probably of the Suhrawardi Order. He translated
more than half of the *Gifts,* for the first time, into English,
and published it in 1891. Also the first English translator of
Hafiz' *Orchard*, Nizami's *Story of Alexander*, and Hafiz'
Works, he was a worthy follower of the tradition of distinguished Sufic adapters such as Raymond Lully.

Taken as a whole, Clarke's work can be seen as an attempt to present dervish thinking to an English audience which was thinking of the dervish as an insane, bloodstained fanatic. Dervishes there were, in the Sudan. They were taken to be some kind of savage. Others were known in Turkey—but Turkey was rather beyond the pale, of course. Clarke brought the original text more up to date with quotations from Sir William Jones, Malcolm, the *Secret Garden* of Shabistari, Brown's *Darvishes* and other available material. He pointed out that the great Hafiz had been "mistranslated and misunderstood" by the poet Emerson and others. He did not shrink from printing parallel extracts showing mistranslation, to the advantage of the dervish, not for his own academic reputation.

Clarke attains a great deal of lucidity by rearranging the materials with which he is working in such a way as to reflect, with added information to make the picture intelligible to the English reader, the working of Sufism as a semiorganized activity within the religious context of Islam. It is difficult to see how this could have been better done, given the prevailing need in Britain for religious matters to be presented in a way analogous to the current brand of Protestant practice. This book is now nearly impossible to obtain.

Islam, he noted, forbids monasticism. The people who were later known as dervishes took, in the year 623, an oath of fraternity and fidelity in Arabia. They chose the name of Sufi, which stands for wool (*suf*), pious (*sufiy*) and other meanings. These were the nucleus of the Moslem Sufis, the original forty-five contracting individuals of Mecca, together with an equal number from Medina.

The practice of these people was given expression in various ways. The First Caliph and the Fourth (Abu Bakr and Ali) formed special assemblies at which exercises were held. These schools were paralleled by Uways, the founder of the first austere Order, in 657. Buildings were first dedicated to the movement's use in Syria in the eighth

Christian century. Thus far the overt expressions of Islamic Sufism.

The parallel Sufic lore which sees Sufism as a continuum, Clarke records, uses the "wine" allegory to show the gradual development of the teaching until it became a more or less public manifestation, before retreating again within itself in the seventeenth century. This is expressed thus:

> The seed of Sufism
> was sown in the time of Adam
> germed in the time of Noah
> budded in the time of Abraham
> began to develop in the time of Moses
> reached maturity in the time of Jesus
> produced pure wine in the time of Mohammed.

Quoting attacks made on Sufis for "voluptuous libertinism" and for being derived from external systems, the Colonel affirms its essential unity and individuality. It is not, he says, introduced from Greece or India. He explains the meaning of the dervish claim, "Neither fear we hell, nor desire we heaven," which sounds so strange from the mouth of one whom every external assessment identifies as a religious man.

He is well aware of the Sufi experience that at every stage of development a new mystery or change in perception and understanding is involved. "Traces of Sufi doctrine," he says, very bravely for his time, "exist in every country—in the theories of ancient Greece; in the modern philosophies of Europe; in the dream of the ignorant and of the learned; in the shade of ease and the hardship of the desert."

But enlightenment can come only through the rarest of all men, no matter how frequent a patchy illusion of truth may break through the Seeker's confusion. This teacher is the Perfect and Excellent Guide: "When he exists, to discover him is impossible." The teacher discovers the disciple, not the other way about. "False teachers and deceived Seekers vainly pursue the desert vapor—and wearied return, the dupe of their own imagination."

The problem of the would-be Sufi is in recognizing his teacher, because he is not yet sufficiently refined to know who he may be. "Perfection who shall discover save he who is perfect? The jewel's price who shall tell, save the jeweler?" Hence the disarray into which some repetitious dervish systems have fallen, as have other bodies of doctrine. Clarke quotes Mohammed: "By pious fools my back hath been broken."

The desire of the teacher is that the real desire of the disciple be fulfilled; that his base qualities be transmuted into laudable ones; that understanding come to him.

Because it is necessary to use certain methods of overcoming undesirable mental states, the dervish described by Clarke must never shun temptation in the sense of fleeing from evil just to avoid it. He uses the externals of religion, and seeks to soak himself in its lore, as an insurance against losing his way. At the same time he knows that "Paradise, hell, all the dogmas of religion are allegories—the spirit whereof he alone knows." This he terms the creed of the "men of heart, the inward people." Evil, for them, exists only as not-being. Being itself, if attained completely, removes the possibility of the negation, so-called evil.

By divine illumination, man sees the world to be illusion (in the sense that there is a greater reality of which the world is a gross distortion), and hence he calls the world evil. He tries to shake off not-being, in the Sufi phrase used by Clarke.

It is not possible to understand Sufi poetry unless one is steeped in the imagery and almost unbelievable depth of feeling which is cloaked in allegory. Clarke's book now gives some of the technical terms which have been explained in the *Secret Garden* for the guidance of the would-be Seeker. Cleverly selecting points which would be most difficult for Western readers, Clarke explains the use of the wine allegory. Ecstasy and rapture, for instance, are not the states

necessarily referred to when drunkenness is mentioned by
Sufis. Because the intellect is dulled by alcohol, the Sufi
state, hostile to superficial logic, is seen as a development
consequent upon the paralysis of what most people regard
as thought. To the Sufi the automatic thought-processes
(the associative functions) are useful only in the fields in
which they work—scholasticism, mechanical thinking.

The self-righteousness which was such a marked feature
of much Victorian thinking is a target for Clarke, and he
selects Sufic matter whose emphases would be meaningful
in his time. This concentration upon self, or what one assumes to be oneself, is the Veil of Light. The Veil of Darkness is the state of mind of the evil man who knows he is
evil. Freed from this kind of self is the "tavern haunter,"
the dervish. He is neither a believer nor an infidel, in any of
the meanings of the word perceptible to the intellect or
familiar emotion.

This admirable recension of essential parts of the *Gifts*
begins in substance with the character of the Sheikh—the
Guide of the dervish. As far as the disciple is concerned, his
first real step in his new life is the finding of such a person.
The function of this director is to remove the rust, in the
Sufi phrase, from the mind, so that eternal (objective) fact
may be accessible to him. In a manner which adequately
anticipates modern psychology, the *Gifts* early stresses the
need for the Guide to be free from subjective reasons for
seeking leadership. He must not seek precedence, being a
Guide, or have a desire to be followed. The true leader will
delay accepting applicants as disciples until he is sure that
he has no such subjectivity.

The Guide must be able to determine the capacity of the
disciple. He will have to deal with this disciple in accordance with his potentiality. If there is little promise, he will
have to use severe methods, such as admonishment. He
orders him to follow certain attitudes of mind in order to
change his unbalanced concentration upon certain things.

Unless he has this perception, the Sheikh cannot be a Guide at all.

The Guide must have no desire for, nor part in, any of the property of the disciple. He can only accept material things from a disciple when he is impelled to use them for the common good. When a disciple wants to bestow his property on the Sheikh, the dervish teacher may take it, because he is able to exchange it for the tranquillity which the disciple needs. But if the disciple is still attached to property, he will be allowed to spend some.

The encouragement of the sincerity of the disciple is one of the major concerns of the Sheikh; as also the severing of undesirable attachments of mind. An important part of this activity is charity and distribution of material substance. The disciple should choose poverty rather than riches, though to the Sufi, poverty and riches are as one.

The Sheikh has to extend kindness and compassion. He abridges the austerities of the disciple as far as is possible within the needs of the work. Too strong privations may prevent the disciple from integrating himself with the dervish effort at first.

The effect upon the disciple of what the Sheikh says is a most important one. It is likened to a seed, and only from good seed can a good crop be raised. Pollution in the mind of the learner can stem from the Sheikh having a desire to influence the hearer, or any pride in himself. The Sheikh does not talk to a disciple without an objective reason. "Objective speech is when it means the same to the speaker as to the hearer."

Advice is given to disciples in a disguised or allegorical form, especially when it is a criticism.

The inner development of the disciple is something which the Guide keeps secret. Expectation of developments on the part of the former is undesirable, and the Sheikh will explain that anticipation of certain states of mind will close the road to them.

The disciple must honor the Sheikh deeply. Therein lies his hope. But, conversely, the Sheikh must not expect to be honored by the disciple. The rights of the disciple are always respected by the Sheikh.

The teaching Sheikh does not spend much of his time in association with the community. He allots times for retirements and movements (*khilwat* and *jilwat*). The teacher has his own special exercises. These are personal, for himself and others, and for devotion to the activity. He has to practice detachment from people as such.

He also engages in special acts of devotion and benevolence, in various forms, including religious ones.

Clarke now places the section dealing with the duties of the disciple or learner (the Directed One) after the functions of the Sheikh, in variation from the original version. The first important point stressed is the necessity of the teacher to the disciple. The teacher's acceptance is the nearest thing to divine acceptance, and represents it as far as it can. The disciple's right to Sheikhly guidance is in part gained by a correct attitude toward his teacher. The Sheikh has this right of being honored. The disciple observes fifteen Rules of Conduct:

He must repose complete faith in his Guide in instructing, directing and purifying disciples.
He must attend the teacher carefully and closely.
He is obedient to the Sheikh.
He abandons opposition, outwardly and inwardly.
He accords his will with the will of the Director.
He observes the thoughts of the Sheikh.
He refers his dreams to the Sheikh for diagnosis of his thoughts.
He is expectant of the words of the teacher.
He lowers his voice before the Sheikh.
He does not allow his selfishness to extend at large. He addresses his teacher as O *Sayed* (prince) or O *Maula* (master).

He addresses his teacher with observance of the convenience of the time.

He must not speak of stages of mind and experience which are not his own; neither must he speak much to the teacher of his own stage.

He must conceal the miracles of the teacher of which he may learn.

He must reveal to the Sheikh his own experiences.

He speaks to the Sheikh in a manner which the Sheikh will understand.

Having arrived at the stage when the conventions of a dervish community may be studied, Colonel Clarke now summarizes Suhrawardi's fifth item in his own third section.

When the dervish arrives at the convent, he tries to make it before the afternoon. He salutes the spot in prayer, and then shakes hands with those present. An offering, probably of food, is made to the dwellers. Dervishes are divided into two sections—dwellers and travelers. Dervishhood itself is often considered to be a certain condition or phase of being a Sufi, not invariably a vocation or permanent state. In this sense it cannot be compared with the monastic organization of, say, Christianity or Buddhism.

The dervish may stay three days at a convent as a guest. After this, he can stay if he can find some employment within the precincts which will occupy him correctly. Those who are engaged in a phase of continuous devotion do not perform physical service about the convent.

There are three stages or conditions of dervishes to be found in the community considered dwellers. The first group, at the earliest stage, are the People of Service (Ahl-i-Khidmat). They serve the regular dwellers, and are at the earliest stage. They are at a stage before they can be given inner exercises, and can only carry out external ones, coupled with inner "intentions" which are not really developmental processes, though the servers may take them as such.

Only by service do they become actually worthy of the degree of real service.

The People of Society (*Ahl-i-Suhbat*) are often the younger ones, who spend time in sitting in house assemblies and carrying out mutual activities designed to provide the bond (knowledge) which reveals their reality and capabilities for the "work."

The People of Retirement (*Ahl-i-Khilwat*) are generally the senior people, who spend much time in solitude, conforming to the exercises which are proper to their stage.

It is often the case that such an assembly of dervishes has no teacher among them. If this is the case, they are handicapped. They are able only to prepare themselves for the association of a master. They cultivate trust and patience and contemplation. They must eat together, so that they be associated outwardly as well as inwardly. They have to strive at all times to be not only in agreement with each other, but also in a state of complete equality, one with the other. No hierarchical organization or leadership is possible to them.

Travel, both physically and metaphorically, can be an important part of dervish activity. The dervish travels in his own land (internally) and also through the countryside and from land to land (externally). Some Sheikhs spend no more than forty days in one place. "On dead skins, by tanning, the effects of purity, of softness, and of delicacy of texture appear; even so, by the tanning of travel, and by the departure of natural corruption and innate roughness, appears the purifying softness of devotion and change from obstinacy to faith." Yet dervishes may not travel at all. Those who have no teacher sometimes travel almost permanently.

There are detailed programs for travel and the way in which its experience is utilized by the dervish. These are generally known as the Twelve Rules of Travel.

The "dance" of the dervishes, the subject of so much misinterpretation, is divided into audition and movement. The real dervish is not a musician, in the sense that he does not actually play instruments. Outside musicians or servers may do so. The Islamic authorities, "outward sages," deny the permissibility of these activities, but they are permitted and encouraged in special circumstances and in accordance with needs by dervish saints and spiritual directors. There are grave disadvantages, amounting to complete negation of the "work," inherent in the use of music and movement without an inner perception of what these are. Especially deleterious is any movement made during the audition of music, contrary to the custom when hearing music in a more lay situation, when movement is expected.

The mantle (khirqa) has a great deal of symbolical importance to the dervish. He sews his own cloak, generally made up of patchwork pieces. The bestowing of the mantle is a mark of passing impalpable blessing or power (baraka) from one person to another. The succession of teacherhood is referred to as the inheritance of the mantle. The dervishes, in addition to much other lore, refer to the investiture by Mohammed of the Mother of Khalid with a mantle that nobody else wanted. It was a small black cloak, with yellow and red stripes, of the Bedouin sort. The Sufi mantle is dark blue or white.

The selection of a deputy is marked thus:

"When the Sheikh seeth in the disciple the effects of holiness and the marks of acquisition to the degree of excellence and instruction; and wisheth to appoint him his own successor—he clotheth him with the Robe of Holiness, and with the honor of his own favor, whereby may be effected the perpetuating of his Order and the obeying of the people."

Amid much else, the tradition about robes divides dervishes into three classes. The first take the mantle which the Sheikh allots for their use; the second have no special garb because they are in a "working" condition; the last choose their own garb because their choice has become an absolute, necessary, complete (objective) choice.

The remainder of the material presented by Clarke is

best considered theoretical mixed with initiatory doctrine. The complexity is increased by the fact that many of the stages and experiences are conditional upon several factors. Sufism not being a static or simple proceeding, trying to freeze any stage can cause serious generalization and consequent distortion. For this reason the material is to be seen as primarily illustrative, yet not without internal motion.

Knowledge is represented in the dervish codex, as in current and ancient usage, as knowledge in general. The divisions of knowledge, and its gradation, are the subject of important Sufi "work," because each stage in the journey is characterized by its appropriate knowledge. The general assumption that knowledge can be divided into two sorts—information and experience—is not accepted by Sufis.

There are two forms, for instance, of *aql*, intelligence—the intelligence of the ordinary man, and that of the religious one. The first is fit for this world and its affairs, the latter for the next world. This is characterized by guidance, sometimes referred to as illumination.

Then there is ordinary knowledge, contrasted with inner, or deep knowledge. The first may be characterized by piety, the latter by perception of the workings of a divine activity. There is another form of knowledge, that of the theologist, which deals in such things as commands and prohibitions.

These knowledges are pursued by three kinds of sages. The first is the sage of God, who has the three knowledges. The second kind of sage is he who contains the wisdom of the next world. The third path is that of the sage of this world. He knows only the outward forms of devotion.

The real knowledge is a kind of nutrition, like food.

Deep knowledge (*maarifat*) is characterized by three subordinate forms of knowledge. The first is the wisdom of how each word or agent acts. The second is the recognition of each agent in the "work." The third is the recognition of the agent through thought. The man who recognizes instantaneously the meanings of happenings and actions, without ordinary reflection, is the *arif*, the Wise, the "arrived" Sufi, or the Mature One.

There are forms of understanding and reunderstanding knowledge. These are described as:

The Science of Inner Wisdom;

The Wisdom of Science;

The Science of the Wisdom of Wisdom.

These are the simplest terms in which the succession of refinements of knowledge and wisdom can be rendered.

The so-called mystical state (*hal*), and its relationship with the stage of the traveler, is the subject of the next section dealt with by Clarke.

The mystical experience, which in other systems is considered to be the be-all and end-all of the quest, is for the dervish nothing more than a prelude to the attainment of true association with objective reality. The way in which it is received and in which an interaction between it and the receptor takes place will determine whether it is producing a valid progress.

This is a most important consideration, because it sharply divides Sufism from all other so-called mysticisms, whether induced by drugs, or any other ecstatogenic cause.

"Stage" (*makam*) is the degree of permanent knowledge of truth (objectivity) which has been attained. Ecstasy, therefore, is or can be the instrument for the establishment of *makam*.

"The *hal* is a gift; the *makam* is an acquisition."

And the mystical state, according to the Sheikhs of Khorasan, "is the heritage of deeds. Like lightning it appeareth, and effaced becometh." Its manifestation is followed by concealment. It is transmuted, or transmutes the consciousness, providing contentment (*riza*). It is necessary to beware of the idea of progression or chronological development in these states, and Junaid has warned against this. He says: "From one *hal* one may advance to a higher one. From there he gains information wherewith he can amend his first state."

There is a ratification of each state, which makes possible advance to another, and also makes possible the permanency of progress, of stage. Without a certain methodology, state (*hal*) is sporadic and repetitious, useless.

The dervish conception of the nature of God is now given, although it appears in the original almost at the beginning of the textbook.

The Sufi does not worship anything but God, the Unique, One.

At the same time, the nature of God as understood by the Sufi is not susceptible to enunciation in the crude words which serve for other purposes. God's abode, for instance, is not where God is. The answer to the question is "He." He is in the time of "He." He made things resemble and suffice by means of "He."

There is no possibility of arguing the existence or place of God, because God is not susceptible to the criteria which are available.

This knowledge is the product of what is called certitude (*yakina*), which has a modus operandi of its own, not an intellectual one. Therefore Sufism has its own science whereby it approaches the question. This science relies upon practice, not speculation.

Dealing with matters which are generally termed "of the next world," the book stresses the dangers of assumption that this form of being will be something which we can conceive within the coarse perceptions which we habitually employ for crude measurement.

Attempts to reason out the relationship between the familiar and the concept of the next world will end in loss. When reason passes beyond its own limits, error results.

Similarly, there is a limit to the efficient working of imagination and fancy. The imaginary picture evoked by the name of a person not so far seen may or may not approximate to the reality.

Two main forces are used by those who have no insight, to combat those who have. The first force is that of the Men

of Power, who kill, punish and harm. The second is that of
the People of Learning, who use deceit, hypocrisy and
heresy.

"Steadiness" is a technical term which is associated with
remaining steadfast, conscious of the presence of God, considering that God is watching. This causes awareness of
oneself and what one is and what doing.

In this condition the worshiper maintains an outward
and inward adornment of rules. The inward knowledge on
the basis of which this is done is called contemplation,
watching (*muraqiba*).

Those who are in this stage say, "Yesterday is dead;
tomorrow is not born; today is in the agonies of death."

Those concentrating upon exercises connected with the
past or the future are in a state of destruction. "The safety
and the salvation of the people is in their being engaged in
the ordinance of the time."

One of the specialist Sufic sciences is called the Science
of State (*ilm-i-hal*). The usage of this science varies in accordance with the capacities of the practitioners. There is
no Sufi science greater than this, because it is the methodology whereby the gradations of *hal* are observed and applied.

The science involves the interaction of states of mind
and their relation to the physical happenings in the surroundings.

The Science of Certainty is the revelation of truth (objective reality) through special states by experience, not
by cerebration as we understand it in the conventional
world.

There are three phases of the Science (practice and perception) of Certainty, allegorized by calling the Sun objectivity: The first, seeking guidance from the splendor and
understanding of the heat of the Sun. The second, by
actually seeing the body of the Sun. The third, the dispers-
ing of the eyes' light in the light of the Sun itself.

There are three stages of "certainty," then, which Suhrawardi summarizes as:

The Knowledge of Certitude, in which it is known, verified and evident;

The Essence of Certainty, manifest and witnessed;

The Truth (Reality) of Certainty, a double way in which there is a conjoining of the witnesser and witnessed.

Beyond this point words do not suffice, and the dervish is accused of pantheism and more. An attempt at explaining produces the word sequence, "The seer becometh the eye, the eye, the seer." A distortion of meaning, originating from the attempt to enunciate the process in formal terms, is perpetuated by the reader, who cannot penetrate by the unaided intellect the real significance of the phrase.

The doctrine of essence, and its connection with the personality and the self, is a most important part of dervish study. There are, for illustrative purposes, two kinds of essence:

The first is the essence of a thing, which is the inner essence (*dhat*) and the truth (*hakikat*) of that thing. Truth here means objective reality, the inner meaning. People normally see or perceive only the outward use of a thing, are ignorant of any ultimate function of that thing. A lamp, for example, gives light. It may be used for heating, or for decoration. But other functions of its true reality are imperceptible to the ordinary man. If, by a stretch of imagination, it were found through delicate scientific measurement that the lamp was giving off certain communication rays, this activity might be the expression of the true reality or essence of that lamp.

Then there is the human essence, called the rational essence (the human spirit) which is known as the "luminosity." This is the sum total of the grace (*baraka*, impalpable qualities) of the individual.

The perceiving of the operation and being of these elements is an extremely sensitive one. True, inner knowledge of the essence is hinted at in the religious life. Hence: "Hints as to the knowledge of essence are found in the links and conditions of the knowledge of God."

This assertion shows how all dervish teaching is based not on the concept of God, but on the concept of essence. There is a slogan which summarizes this, and which clearly establishes that the religious context of dervish thinking is merely the vehicle for the self-realization which is aimed at: "He who knows his essential self, knows his God." Knowledge of the essential self is the first step, before which there is no real knowledge of religion. Sufis are accused of paganism because they first apply themselves to this problem, retaining the religious context as a practical working shape, rather than as any indication of final and objective truth.

The means of appreciating the various stages and conditions of the essence and its progressive refinement are themselves an essential part of dervish activity. It is here that the dervish parts company with the mere theoretician. The latter says: "I will think this out;" the dervish: "I will prepare myself to perceive this, without using limited, obstructive thought, a childish process."

The "veiling" or interruption of the correct use of the human spirit (essence) is caused by an unbalanced indulgence in certain coarse sentiments which together constitute a pattern of imprisonment (conditioning) characteristic of most people. These "veils" or "blameable qualities" are listed as ten:

1. *Desire.* Desires based on ignorance of what should be, and on assumptions as to what is good for the individual. Austerity, correctly used, is the antidote to irrational desire. This is the stage of "I want a lollipop."

2. *Separation.* This is a type of hypocrisy, when the person uses rationalization to justify thoughts and actions which are centered upon himself, not upon an ultimate reality. The antidote is the practice of sincerity.

3. *Hypocrisy.* Characterized by self-pride, glorying in possessions, pseudoindependence, violence. This is overcome only by the practice of qualities which are reprehensible in the eyes of the people, but laudable in God's sight. They include submission of the right kind, humility and the

poverty of the Fakir. These qualities are recognized only by correct assessment of the true worth of their opposites.

4. *Desire for Praise and Love.* Narcissism, which precludes objective assessment of oneself; lack of a balancing factor which amounts almost to self-contempt.

5. *Illusions* of almost divine importance. Countered only by the glory of the qualities of God.

6. *Avarice and Parsimony.* Give rise to envy, the worst of all characteristics. This can be dissolved only when the power of certainty (*yakina*) comes.

7. *Greed* and the desire for more. This is dangerous because it causes the person to be like the moth, insensately dashing itself against the candle flame. It is countered only by austerity and piety.

8. *Irresponsibility.* This is manifested by the desire to attain something which has been conceived in the mind. It is always in motion, like a globe continually turning. It can be made to depart only by patience.

9. *Haste to Fatigue.* This is lack of constancy of purpose, in its usual manifestation. This is what prevents people from realizing that there is a succession of objectives which will replace present, crude ones. "From this calamity it is impossible to escape save by the establishing of the ordered thanks." Exercises are employed to overcome this tendency.

10. *Negligence.* Slothfulness of a deep kind is shown by lack of awareness of the needs of a situation or an individual. Alertness is cultivated through remedies applied by the "Physicians of the Essence"—the dervishes.

It will be noted that ordinary, contemporary psychotherapy attempts the treatment of some of these conditions, but only in order to guide the mind into a pattern which the psychological doctrine assumes is normal. According to the dervish, the conditions which have to be treated are due to an unharmonious state of the mind, groping for balance and evolution. It is impossible, from this point of view, to attempt to restore a mere equilibrium without a dynamic forward movement. The psychologist tries to make a warped wheel turn smoothly. The dervish is trying to make the wheel turn in order that it may propel a carriage.

"The Deep Knowledge of the Spirit"—Section III of the dervish book and placed eleventh in Colonel Clarke's version—involves a form of exposition where many theories meet. This chapter, when read in the light of Sufi technical terminology, shows how the progress of the human mind to realization accords with the symbols of religion. Words like "angels," "Adam and Eve," "grace," are here used in such a manner as to show how the Sufi thinkers interpreted the religious lore to give an insight in exactly what processes were symbolized by what have been widely accepted as historical or legendary tales, or supernatural phenomena.

Whatever the literal truth of the making of Eve from Adam's rib may be, the dervish Suhrawardi teaches the Sufi understanding of the event as a continuously repeated process of a mystical kind.

"In every person of mankind, another exemplar becometh —by the union of spirit and essence (in part)—transcribed from the exemplar of Adam and Eve." What is called "heart" is the combination of Adam and Eve, the soul and the essence. The male element comes from the universal soul. The female element comes from the universal essence. It is this essence which man (Adam) contacts within himself and brings forth in the form of Eve. Eve being brought forth from Adam therefore represents the special, inner, cognition of the true (objective) essence, produced by mankind from its interior resources.

For explanations of this psychological kind, the result of actual experiences of a successive nature, the dervishes were considered by orthodox theologians to be apostates, discounting the literal interpretation of the Scriptures. But the historical reality or the folklore version of Scriptural stories are of no interest to the dervish. He has transcended the vehicle. "To Adam, all names became known."

All created things are the outcome of an interchange between the two principles which are called essence and soul:

"By reason of active deed, of passive deed and power, of weakness, the attribute of male and female appeareth; in the soul of increase and universal essence, the custom of love-making became confirmed by the link of temperament; by means of marriage, the races of worlds became existing and by the hand of the midwife of Fate appeared in the apparent world."

There are successive rarefications of true reality, each one appearing as absolute in its own field of perceptivity. "Breath is the result of spirit, spirit of order."

The angels, as other dervish teachers have stressed, are the higher developments of the mind. Some are spoken of here as being of the nature of *jamal* (beauty), others of the nature of *jalal* (grandeur).

The doctrine of "collection and dispersion" (*jam'* and *tafrika*) as expounded in this section deals with the relationship between life in the world and life in other dimensions. The Knower, the Complete Sufi, is in the world, yet not of it. He is in a state of correct harmony with the continuum of which apparent existence is only a minor portion. He is aligned with the body and the non-body, as they must be represented in ordinary exposition. He understands the modalities which give rise to the belief in the existence of creation and the absolute which underlies it.

"Shining and concealment" are the twin terms which deal with the manifestation and lack of perception of God in humanity. "Shining" means the breaking through of the sun of the reality of God from the clouds of humanity. The clouds are the aspect of hiddenness of this objectivity.

The famous romance of Majnun ("the madman") and Layla is used to allegorize the power of the "shining" and the inability of the traveler (madman) to sustain the brilliance of that shining without having passed through a necessary preparation.

The tribe of the madman interceded with some of the people of Layla, asking that Majnun be allowed to be illuminated with the "sight of Layla's beauty."

Layla's tribe replied that there was no harm in this: "But Majnun hath not the power of beholding Layla's beauty."

They brought the madman, and for him lifted a corner of Layla's tent. "Immediately his glance fell on the fold of Layla's skirt—senseless he fell."

Illumination cannot be sustained by someone who is not ready for it. At the best it will throw him into an ecstatic state in which he is paralyzed, as it were, and unable to consummate the contact. This is why, although dervish poets speak of being "mad for love," they emphasize that this madness is the result of preview, not of genuine experience. It is recognized that genuine experience must take an active, mutual, meaningful form, not a form of useless intoxication.

Inebriation mystics are those who stop short at this stage, and try to reproduce the experience repetitiously, or approximate them on paper or in emotional art. This is the stage at which much experimentation in mysticism becomes bogged down.

"Rapture" (*wajd*) and "existence" (*wujud*) refer to two states of which the first is the prelude to the second (*Junaid*). In rapture, the individual is immersed in a sensation which is opposite to the one which he formerly felt. He also becomes attuned to a form of cognition other than that to which he is accustomed. A person experiences this state when he is still at the stage when he is primitively linked with sensual qualities and has little understanding of any deeper perspective to them.

Existence is the name given to the state of "acquisition," when real existence, as opposed to simple physical existence, is perceived by the devotee.

"Period" and "moment" are two concepts which are associated with a moment of perception on contact, a momentary cognition, the instrument of fashioning further states of being. Several other concepts and exercises are associated with these two. One such is the exercise of the freezing of movement, temporarily stopping ordinary associative processes. Another is the use of the Pause of Time, and the

Pause of Space, which enable the operation of constructive "time" to take place.

A Complete Sufi may be called a Master of Time, meaning master of starting and stopping, of modifying cognition. The individual who can operate in this sphere is called (by the sage Shibli) one who has escaped from being under the sway of *hal*, the mystical state of rapturous but generalized joy.

Moment is the term given also to "breath." It stands for the physical exercises connected with breathing, and also for the illustration of the fact that Sufi development is a succession, like the pulsation of breath, not a static condition or irregular motion.

Thus: "Moment is a state in a place of 'stopping.' Breath is a state free from 'stopping.' 'Time' is for the beginner. Breath is for the finisher, completer."

"Presence" and "absence" (*shuhud* and *ghaybat*) are terms which connote states of Sufihood which may be quite imperceptible to the ordinary man or woman. The dervish may be present as far as the invisible world is concerned, yet absent as far as the familiar one is concerned.

Sir Sayed Ahmad Khan defines absence of this kind as whatever is outside our sight, like the force of gravitation.

Shibli went to visit another great sage, Junaid. The wife of the latter was about to conceal herself modestly behind a screen. Junaid said, "Stay where you are—Shibli is absent." At that moment, Shibli began to weep. Junaid said, "You must now be absent, for Shibli has returned." Being absent or hidden means that the dervish is working in another dimension, and appears to be absent.

This is not the same as absentmindedness, which is not itself a constructive or positive state. Junaid's wife could not see Shibli's absentness; Junaid had to perceive it. Similarly, the ordinary man denies even the possibility of such a state, because he cannot perceive it. For him, it is not only absent, but hidden, concealed, like the concealment of Shibli.

Presence, of course, is another variety of absence, depending upon the point of view: "Present with God is absent to men." Some dervishes alternate between this polarity, perhaps slowly, perhaps instantaneously. When the complete alchemicalization has taken place, there is no duality. They are constantly in the state of presence, and they are not hidden from either world.

The methodology of the dervishes includes the use of exercises designed to produce *tajrid* (outward detachment) and *tafrid* (interior solitude). The correct balance of integration of the special faculties can be attained by "outwardly abandoning the desires of this world, and inwardly rejecting the compensation of the next world and of this world." This is *tajrid.*

Tafrid is not essential to *tajrid.* But it is associated with it, or may be so. It involves the "rejecting of the increase of deeds of himself, and the concealing of their appearance by regarding on himself God's favor and bounty."

This method illuminates the developmental shortcomings in ordinary religion, which focuses the attention upon the next world. This, for the dervish, is a primary stage, which has to be shed when the time of actual *amal* (labor) starts.

The obliteration and confirming of the slave's existence is the interpretation of the twin words *mahw* (obliteration) and *isbat* (confirmation). This schematic representation of an aspect of dervish being is widely misunderstood by laymen. Every obliteration is a confirmation—obliteration of undesirable or negative qualities produces the activation of equal and opposite positive qualities. Superficial conjecture has labeled this theory and its processes as a negation of the intellect or mind of the dervish. By default, because dervishes are working and not theorizing or concerned with exegesis, this label has adhered to the words.

"Change" (*talwin*) and "rest" (*tamkin*) refer to attitudes of mind and body, as well as inner conditions. Rest is the term used for the permanency of manifestation of Truth. In this condition the dervish experiences a permanent tran-

quillity of heart which enables him to perceive true reality,
or objective fact, generally called Truth.

Change is the exercise and also the condition of tranquillity of the heart, by the pursuance of exercises of presence
and absence, as already noted, and other procedures.

The prayer exercises, in which the special interpretations
and uses of the formulas of Islam are concentrated upon,
form a great part of the rest of Colonel Clarke's version of
the *Gifts*. Then come the allegorical meanings of austerity,
of poverty and humility, of celibacy and marriage, trustful-
ness, contentment and love.

Love is the great theme which runs through the ocean of
Sufi poetry and the personal teachings of the masters alike.
Love is essentially the creator of states of experience, which
are themselves referred to as "gifts." There are two general
forms of love—Ordinary Love and Special Love. Those who
have not followed the developments possible in this field of
the Sufis constantly confuse the one with the other, in a
blurring alternation which deceives their perception. Such
people make, for instance, serious errors in assessment of
individuals, groups and situations. Aware of this, they generally are at pains to try to retrieve their mistakes subsequently
(rationalization), and in consequence may appear absurd
to those who observe them, whether initiates or otherwise.
Self-deception is a symptom of this form of love, whose sincerity is not questioned. Its quality is, however, subject
to fluctuations imperceptible to the individual.

The comparisons between Ordinary and Special Love
are listed. A perception of *baraka* (impalpable beauty, grace)
in the form or apparent being of a thing is a quality of
Ordinary Love. When this becomes profound (Special) love,
it is transmuted into the self's inclination to viewing the
beauty of the essence (*dhat*)—not the form. The effect of
love is shown by contrasting love which beautifies existence
(Ordinary Love) with love which refines existence (Special
Love).

Real love, of the essential type, is not general but specific.

It may observe beauty in all forms, but its attention is actually directed upon the essence which is the only love in a final sense. A person does not love in this sense if his love is capable of distraction. This is illustrated by a tale:

A man once met a beautiful woman. He revealed his love to her. She said, "Beside me is one who is more beautiful than I, and more perfect in beauty. She is my sister." He looked to see this woman. Then the first one said: "Boaster! When I saw you from afar, I thought that you were a wise man. When you came near, I thought that you were a lover. Now I know that you are neither."

The wisdom of the dervishes portrays a characteristic of love which is so rare as to be almost unconceived by the rest of humanity. The lover thinks greatly of even slight regard from his beloved. But of his own regard for her, he thinks little. Seen in this light, the feelings of Ordinary Love reflect egocentricity.

Clarke retains in his version a number of definitions of Sufi individuals and states which are not susceptible to simple exposition. In the seventy-odd years since his book appeared, it must be admitted that the Sufi sense of varying definition in accordance with many factors has not been established in, say, English. But this is probably inevitable while dictionaries retain the assumption that brevity is possible in all definitions.

A Fakir, for instance, is one who is poor. He is not necessarily a *zahid*, which is an austere man who may or may not be poor. But a Fakir may be a person who is at one time austere and at another time not. Similarly an austere person may not be a Fakir in the sense of deliberate intellectual poverty or humility. The Fakir has abandoned belief in the exaggerated significance of familiar chattels. To this extent he is good, or suitable for the Path. He may even abandon all idea of stages of development, of states or even deeds. But he can do this only when he has arrived at the condition when this is possible to him; when this becomes his function, not his choice. The Sufi is superior to the Fakir, because the

Fakir initially desires Fakirhood, and the Sufi desires
nothing. So a Fakir may become a Sufi, in which case his
Fakirhood is negated, nullified.

No stabilization of Sufic terms is ultimately possible,
though looking at the whole of the Sufi lore and some uses
of the names given to Sufis can give an impression as to how
the system works.

What is a dervish?

The Rev. Joseph Wolff made a perilous journey through
Asia in the nineteenth century, seeking Stoddard and
Conolly, two British officers held by the Emir of Bokhara.
A former Jew and priest of the Church of England, he had
the blessing of influential people in Britain. He was able
to travel freely in Central Asia only because he called himself "the Christian Dervish," capitalizing on the prestige of
the noun.

A dervish is a Sufi. In North Africa, "dervish" is a term
of respect, denoting something less than an *arif* (Knower,
Wise One), while a Sufi is looked at askance as someone
engaged in mysterious processes. In England, a Sufi is
thought to be "a Mohammedan mystic of the pantheistic
type," while a dervish is something weird—what a North
African might call a "Sufi."

Although even kings may sign themselves "Fakir," the
label can be embarrassing in some places. A distinguished
Indian academician said: " 'Fakir' is confused with Hindu
jugglers—and worse. I regard you not as a Fakir, but as a
Man of the Path."

Putting the word into a phrase helps to establish the
usage. "He is a dervish," means, "a good, simple person,
devoted to truth." "He is a Fakir," means, "one who struggles
to improve himself, with humility." "He is a Sufi," means,
"one who follows the Sufi Way," also, "one who has attained
progress in the Way."

The confusion arises because of several factors. Not least
of these is the fact that the Sufis themselves do not use
labels to denote fixed states or stages, since there is no such

thing in Sufism. You can label a pound of butter "butter," but a Sufi is never entirely a dervish or a Knower. His status changes in relation to the infinite gradations of truth and objectivity.

In Sufi literature, the words "Sufi," "dervish" and "Fakir" are used more rarely than "Knower," "lover," "follower," "traveler." The other words tend to be externalist labels.

In Sufism, the shortcomings of dictionary definitions are exposed perhaps more strikingly than in other fields. Thus *Chambers' Dictionary* (1955 edition):

DERVISH: "A member of one of numerous Mohammedan
                fraternities. . . ."
SUFI: "A pantheistic Mohammedan mystic. . . ."
FAKIR: "A religious (esp. Mohammedan) mendicant,
                ascetic. . . ."

The meanings of the word "Mohammed"—or even "Mohammedan"—"fraternity," "pantheism," "mystic," "religion," "mendicant" and "ascetic" are different in Eastern usage, and especially in Sufi application, than in English.

A Persian dictionary, perhaps more poetically, if with less seeming precision, says: "What is a Sufi? A Sufi is a Sufi" —and succeeds in rhyming the entry: *Sufi chist?—Sufi Sufi'st*. This is actually a Sufi quotation. The compiler does not believe in trying to define the indefinable. An Urdu one says: "Sufi refers to any one of numerous special, but successively necessary, stages of being, open to humanity under certain circumstances, understood correctly only by those who are in this state of 'work' (*amal*); considered mysterious, inaccessible or invisible to those who have not the means of perceiving it."

Clarke quotes Sufi literature of most of the classical authors over a period of seven hundred years (from 911 to 1670)—Persians, Afghans, Turkestanis, Arabs, Indians. His Western sources range from 1787 to 1881, nearly a hundred years. His translation of the *Gifts* was published by the Government of India's press at Calcutta.

This particular work is suited to exposition outside its nominal cultural pattern partly because it is itself the product of a school which interlaces, crossing and recrossing the traditional Sufic stream over the centuries during which the dervish format has been familiarly overt.

This interplay is important, because it shows how the Sufic stream meets, blends and recombines in a manner which superficial observation of the dervish orders would not expect.

The author of this book was Sheikh Shahabudin Mohammed the Suhrawardi, a disciple of the founder of the Suhrawardi Order of dervishes. The Order was founded on the teaching school by Ziyauddin Najib Suhrawardi, who died in 1167. He wrote the *Observances of the Disciples*. His life, like that of many initiating teachers, is not well documented. This is a part of deliberate policy, when the founder of a school intends to focus attention upon the school and not upon personalities.

Our author, his disciple, was the chief Sufi teacher of Baghdad, a source of the concentration and transmission of the Sufic lore for his time.

His disciples traveled far and wide, carrying the methodology of the Order. Sayed Nurudin of Afghanistan (Ghazna) brought the system to India, where King Altamash made him the highest ecclesiastical dignitary of the State. Another disciple was Najmuddin Kubra, who founded his own Order—the Kubravi—and who was master of all manner of miracles. He exercised, for instance, an uncanny influence even on animals, merely by means of thought projection. So many of his disciples became masters through his *baraka* that his title is "Fashioner of Saints." Few Sufis have excelled these in their power or popularity. The Suhrawardi Order is found throughout the Moslem world, from the Atlantic to the Pacific.

In one place, a Bokhara Suhrawardi dervish master (Shamsuddin Hussein) made four hundred thousand disciples. He married the daughter of the Turkish Sultan Bayazid I, Nilufer Khanum.

The great poet Saadi of Shiraz was a disciple of our author, who was himself the nephew and successor to the founder of the Order.

The *baraka* of the Order is traced to the same classical Sufi masters who provided the inspiration for the other Orders and schools. Therefore the essential character of the teaching is to be seen as colored only slightly by its representation in the organization known as the Suhrawardi Way, the last word normally translated by Westerners as "Order."

Stemming from the same origins were the Sufi masters who considered that the *Suhrawardiyya,* as it is called in Arabic, represented the correct alignment of Sufi teaching of the time. Hence there is a sort of interchangeability in membership of Orders which can appear confusing. Some of the famous masters were Sayeds, descendants of Mohammed; others were direct descendants of other Orders, like Bahauddin Zakaria, grandson of the founder of the Qadiri Order. The Grand Sheikh Jalaluddin of Tabriz was nurtured by the *Suhrawardiyya,* then joined the Chishti Order after seven years with Shahabudin at Baghdad. Sufism here is to be seen as a means of concentrating a certain teaching and passing it on, through a human vehicle, through climates prepared for its reception. Before and after Clarke, this has been attempted in Europe, with varying success. In most cases the effect has been to draw the individual back to the roots of the teaching in the East, where it is still concentrated. There have been many Sufis living and working in the West, but it is only recently that the correct conditions have existed for the naturalization or reintroduction of a genuine transmission school in the Western world. The impatience of many would-be students is only faintly useful in the evolution of such a work.

Among the cornerstones for this kind of development, Colonel Clarke's version of the *Gifts* is undoubtedly to be mentioned.

The Dervish Orders

Because of superficial thought
What appears to be hypocrisy in
The enlightened ones
Is in fact better than
What is felt to be sincerity in the beginner.
(Hadrat Bayazid el-Bistami)

Almost all Sufis, at one time or another, are members of one of the Ways which are called by Western scholars "Orders," in allusion to their supposed similarity to the Christian religious orders of the middle ages. There are several very important differences between the two kinds of organizations.

The Order, for the Sufi, is not a self-perpetuating entity with a fixed hierarchy and premises, forming a training system for the devotee. The nature of Sufism being evolutionary, it is by definition impossible for a Sufi body to take any permanent form as rigid as this. In certain places, and under individual masters, schools appear and carry out an activity designed to further the human need for completion of the individual. These schools (like that of Rumi and Data Ganj Bakhsh, for example) attract very large numbers of people who are not Moslems, although Sufi schools have always, since the rise of Islam, been presided over by people who originate in the Moslem tradition.

Again, while Sufi Orders have specific rules and set forms

of dress and ritual, these are not invariable, and the extent to which the Sufi adheres to these forms is determined by his need for them, as prescribed by his master.

Some of the great Ways have detailed histories, but the tendency to divide into departments of specialization means that schools at times share each others' nominal characteristics. This is because the Way is being developed by means of an inner necessity, not piloted by the externals of its apparent organizational framework.

So secret are many of the schools that when one of the greatest of all Sufis, Hujwiri (died 1063) wrote a book[1] dealing with Sufism and the Orders in the eleventh century, giving inside information about them, it was actually assumed by some that he had invented or concocted part of the material.

Even this development itself, contrary to what people assumed, was a part of inevitable dervish policy. Data ("dervish" in Hindi) Ganj Bakhsh (Munificent One) is the name by which Ali el-Hujwiri is known in India.

Born in Ghazna (Afghanistan), he is referred to by the Sufis as "the Selected," the man chosen to make known certain facts about Sufism and Sufi organization, for the purpose of its projection in the Indian field. Although by no means the first Sufi to settle in India (he is buried in Lahore, Pakistan, and his beautiful tomb is venerated by people of all creeds), his task was to establish there by his life and works a claim that Sufism was thoroughly consistent with the principles of Islam. His importance can hardly be overemphasized. As the Christian writer John Subhan says:

Ali el-Hujwiri's tomb may still be seen in Lahore near the Bhati gate. It has been an object of veneration and a place of pilgrimage for the best part of nine hundred years. All sorts and conditions of men, kings and beggars, have resorted to it through the centuries, seeking

[1] *Kashf el-Mahjub* (The Revelation of the Veiled).

spiritual and temporal blessings. Most of the Moslem invaders and wandering dervishes, on entering the land, made a point of paying their homage at his shrine.[2]

Hujwiri's place among Sufis is next only to his importance as an interpreter of Sufism to the Moslems themselves. For the Sufi, *The Revelation of the Veiled* contains material which only he can understand, concealed within the form of a book designed to be read by pious Moslems to introduce them to the Sufi way of thought through the familiar terminology of their formal tradition.

The book is carefully studied by members of most of the Orders. Hujwiri himself studied under Abu el-Qasim Gurgani, a great teacher of the Naqshbandi Order, and his main work is the *Revelation*, which is the first book in Persian on Sufism and the Orders.

The book contains lives of notable Sufis, of ancient and contemporary times, references to doctrines, alms, prayer, faith and mysticism. It is addressed to those who wish to approach Sufism through the prevailing context of Islam. Beyond this obvious presentation, the *Revelation* conceals, in a manner discernible only to Sufis, information about the use and meaning of the secret language which the Sufis use in order to communicate and carry on their special training.

All that can be revealed about this for the moment is contained in the chapter on the patched robe. The wearing of patched cloaks is a Sufi custom, the mark of the practicing Sufi on the Path. It might be called the uniform of the wandering dervish, and it has been seen in almost every part of Asia and Europe for nearly fourteen hundred years. The Prophet Mohammed and some of his companions showed their adherence to the Sufi Way by their adoption of this garb. Many Sufi teachers are on record about the

[2] John A. Subhan, *Sufism, Its Saints and Shrines*, Lucknow, 1938, p. 130.

method of sewing on the patches, whether they should be large or small, who should wear the robe, who can confer it, and so on. The whole phenomenon is a part of the mystery of the Sufis.

Hujwiri's chapter on patched robes, read for its superficial value, might satisfy a devout theologian. Dwelling upon the connection between patches and poverty, upon the industry needed to sew a patch correctly, upon the outward affirmation of asceticism which the patches conveyed, the chapter could read as a rather pious, very unsatisfactory collection of ideas and facts, assembled for sentimental purposes. The fact is very different.

When reading the text, the student has to know, first of all, that he cannot translate the word as "patch" and leave it at that. He must look for the concepts which are contained in the Arabic word, and keep them all in mind, applying them to the text in a certain manner. Then he will see whether the writer means "patch," or "walking," or "divine fool," and so on.

The effect of the book upon the Sufi is now very different from the rendering which he would get from a superficial reading. Here is an example of semiliteral translation, taken from Professor Nicholson's translation of the chapter:

"To take pains in sewing patched robes is considered allowable by the Sufis because they have gained a high reputation among the people; and since many imitate them and wear patched robes, and are guilty of improper acts, and since the Sufis dislike the society of others than themselves—for these reasons they have invented a garb which none but themselves can sew, and have made it a mark of mutual acquaintance and a badge. So much so that when a certain dervish came to one of the Shaykhs wearing a garment on which the patch had been sewn with wide stitches, the Shaykh banished him from his presence."

The Arabic root from which the word "patch" is derived also embraces an important group of meanings. Among these we may note:

1. Nonsensical (*raqua'*). How the Sufi appears when he is talking or behaving in terms of an extra cognition, imperceptible to the ordinary man. The motley of the jester is a fair translation of this quality. "Fool," in the Sufi sense, is also from the same root, spelled *arqd'a*.

2. To be addicted to wine (*raqaa'*). Sufis use the analogy of intoxication to refer to a certain mystical experience.

3. Heedless (*artaqa'*). The Sufi appears to be heedless of things which seem most important to the ordinary man, but which, objectively, may have another significance.

4. Seventh Heaven (*raqa'*). An allusion to the celestial or divine quality of Sufism.

5. Chessboard (*ruqd'at*). The black and white alternation of light and dark, part of the checker pattern of the floor of certain dervish meeting places.

6. Patched garment (*muraqqa'*). The only word of this group other than the last one which can be used as a symbol or implement, an allegorical object summarizing the root as a whole and all its Sufi meanings.

7. To patch a garment; to walk quickly; to epigrammatize; to hit a target with an arrow are all derivations of the same root through the word *raqd'a*.

8. To repair (a well). Symbolizing the rectification of the existing "well" of human knowledge in humanity by the Sufis shares the same root.

One of Hujwiri's tasks was to pass on in written form, concealed in Sufic cipher, essential elements which were to be used by dervish schools.

Hujwiri's coming to India was in accordance with the travel technique practiced widely in the Orders. He was told by his teacher to go and settle in Lahore. This was the last thing that he wanted to do, but since he was under the complete discipline existing between student and master, he set out for India. The moment he arrived at Lahore he saw that the body of Sheikh Hasan Zanjani was being taken to his grave. Hujwiri was his successor, and realized now that he had been sent for this reason. Such examples of replacement of Sufi teachers who are about to die by one sent from a great distance are not rare in dervish annals.

Hujwiri founded no Order, but remains a teacher shared in general. His name stands in the list of teachers whose *baraka* extends throughout the whole of the dervish community, irrespective of the time in which he lived. After he died, it is believed, his authority continued on earth, because his perfection had reached such a degree that ordinary death did not dissolve it.

Sufi Orders may be organized in a monastic form. On the other hand, the Sufi monastery or school may consist of a linking of people and activities spread over an immense area and invisible to the outsider. Hence there are Orders —and especially branches of Orders—with some members in India, others in Africa, some in Indonesia. Collectively they constitute the organism of the school. Since the Sufis believe in the possibility of communication without physical presence, such a concept of a diffused Order is easier for the Sufi to accept than it would be for people familiar with more conventional views about human society and purpose.

Branches of Orders exist in guilds, in student bodies, in military formations. In more modern times the kind of unit represented by the conventional monastery has become the exception. The Sufi monastery, outwardly similar in many ways to that of the Christian, Hindu or Buddhist, is in reality the product of economic and political conditions, not of any esoteric necessity. According to the Sufis, "the monastery is in the hearts of men." This, again, is in line with the dervish idea that Sufism is a developing entity, and cannot remain a system for reproducing forms, however attractive they may be.

In places where a feudal type of life still continues, Sufi monasteries, tied to the produce of the land, continue to flourish. In urban life, Sufi centers are more yoked to the tempo of town living, and derive their income from shops donated to the community, or from a levy upon the earnings of the members of the Order.

The Sufi Order, then, stands for the body of people who are specializing in the acceptance, using and transmission of Sufism. It has no traditional shape, and its outward appearance will depend upon local conditions and the necessities of the "work."

One Arabic publishing company is a Sufi organization. In some areas all the industrial and agricultural workers are Sufis. Certain professions in some countries are dominated by Sufis. These specialist groupings of Sufis may consider themselves to be Orders or monasteries, engaged in a specific task of acceptance, preservation and transmission. The central factor in the Orders is, of course, the production of the human exemplar of the teaching, as distinct from the propagation of the Order or any mechanical promotion in terms of identifiable rank. Sufis have no bishops.

This is not to say that the hierarchy of Sufis is not well defined. But a Sufi is known by another, insofar as rank is concerned, by methods other than the displaying of insignia. A certain degree of development of the individual, in spite of its having to be confirmed by a master, is held by Sufis to be perceptible to others of similar attainments.

It is within the school of the Order that the initial acceptance and development of the candidate takes place. Unlike other systems of instruction, there is nothing of the nature of conditioning. The aspirant must be attached to the principles of the Order and to the person of the teacher, but before this can take place he has to be tested. The testing is carried out with the intention of shedding those individuals who are unsuitable. Rejected are those who feel the desire to attach themselves to an organization or individual because of their own weaknesses. People who have been attracted by the repute of Sufis and the desire to attain miraculous powers are weeded out. The initial tasks given to a probationary member have two main functions—the first is to determine his suitability, the second to show him that he must desire Sufihood for its own sake.

Very often the teacher in whose charge the candidate is

placed will do all he can to deter him—not by persuasion, but by playing a part which may seem to reflect discredit upon himself. The Sufis believe that only by these methods can they communicate to the essence awaiting to be awakened the fact that the Sufi impulse is available. The nominal communication with the outward personality of the candidate is relatively unimportant. When the mind is not yet capable of grasping Sufism coherently, the Sufi will not attempt to persuade it. He has to communicate at greater depth. People of this sort, who could be convinced by conventional means of the importance of Sufism, would not be genuine converts.

Many of the reports of absurd and unacceptable behavior of Sufis stem from the working out of such plans.

Many of the main Orders have been nicknamed. The Rifa'i are called the Howling Dervishes; the Qalandari "Shaven"; the Chis(h)ti "Musicians"; the Mevlevi "Dancing"; the Naqshbandi "Silent."

These Orders are generally named after the founder of the specialization which they represent. Rumi, for instance, organized his "dances" in accordance with what he considered to be the best way of developing in his disciples the Sufic experiences. This was done, as ancient records show, in accordance with the mentality and temperament of the people of Konia. Imitators have attempted to export the system outside of this cultural area, with the result that they are left with what amounts to a pantomime, and the original effect of the movements has disappeared.

The rhythmic (and arhythmic) movements called dance are used in many Orders, always in response to the needs of the individuals and the group. Sufi movements can thus never be stereotyped, and do not constitute what is elsewhere called dance, calisthenics or the like. The using of movements follows a pattern based upon certain discoveries and knowledge which can only be applied by a teaching master of a dervish Order.

It seems likely that the religious dances which are known

in Christianity, Judaism and even primitive tribes are a degeneration of this knowledge, ultimately pressed into the service of spectacle, magic or superficial mime.

"If the scissors are not used daily on the beard," says the celebrated Sufi poet Jami, "it will not be long before the beard is by its luxuriant growth pretending to be the head." (*Baharistan*—Abode of Spring)

The dervish Order may be looked upon as an organization with the minimum amount of regulation. Like any other body of people associating for a purpose, the rules of the Order cease to be operative when this objective has been attained.

The schematic diagrams used by the Orders help to convey this idea. The chain circle of the Orders shows how the groupings stem from the schools which surrounded certain classical teachers. These schools took their inspiration from the private assemblies of Mohammed and his close companions. Hence, in one such geometrical chart, the center shows the companions Abu Bakr, Ali and Abdul-Aziz the Meccan in a circle. Arranged around this are seven smaller circles, each one containing the name of a great master. The seven main Ways of Sufism, the specializations of teaching, emanate from these individuals.

The dervish Orders all claim the spiritual transmission (*baraka*) from one or more of these masters. It must be remembered that since Sufism is not static, the total *baraka* of the founders of Orders is held to interpenetrate all the Orders.

The circular format and interlinking of circles indicates this interdependence and movement. In poetry, such authors as Rumi have emphasized this by saying: "When you see two Sufis together, you see both two and twenty thousand."

The objective of the temporary organism called an Order, agreed by all masters, is to provide circumstances in which the member can attain the stabilization of his inner being comparable or identical with those of the early transmitters.

The motive for creating an Order around a group of words, chosen to illustrate certain activities or characteristics of the Order, is obvious. All members know that the format is not mystical, but arbitrary. They are, in consequence, unable to attach their emotional side to the emblems of the Order. The concentration is thus held upon the chain of transmission (the individuals whose substance is being contacted). Again, since it is believed that the Complete Man (*insan-i-Kamil*) is both a real individuality and also a total part of the essential unity, it is not possible for the Sufi to attach himself to a personality alone. He knows from the start that his interior powers are being guided from one objective to the next. Hence, in the austerely pious dervish Orders, there is a fixed succession of progress through one individual. The disciple has first to attach himself to the teacher. When he has reached the maximum development possible, the teacher transfers him to the reality of the founder of the Order. From here he transfers his consciousness to the substance (the "foot") of Mohammed, the originator of the doctrine in contemporary form. From here he is transferred to the reality of God. There are other methods, whose application depends upon the character of the school and especially the qualities of the personality dealt with. In some exercises the disciple has to immerse himself in the consciousness of various other teachers, including Jesus and others considered by the Sufis to be of their number.

One of the objects of pilgrimages to the burial places or former residences of teachers is to make a contact with this reality or substance. In neutral phraseology it could be said that the Sufis believe that Sufic activity in producing a Complete Man accumulates a force (substance) which itself is capable of alchemicalizing a lesser individual. This is not to be confused with the idea of magical power, because the power exercised upon the Seeker will operate only insofar as his motives are pure and he is purged of selfishness. Further, it will act in its own way, and not in a manner which can be anticipated by the Seeker. Only his teacher, who has traveled the way before, will be able to judge as to what effect such an exposure will have.

Within the Orders, when the disciple has been accepted for a training course under a master, he has to be prepared for the experiences which his unaltered mind is incapable of perceiving.[3] This process, which follows the dissipating of conditioning, or automatic thinking, is termed the "activation of the subtleties."

There is no word in English which can be used as a true equivalent of the technical term "subtlety." The original word is *latifa* (plural *lataif*). It has been rendered "purity spot," "place of illumination," "center of reality." In order to activate this element it is assigned a theoretical physical situation in the body—generally considered to be the center where its force or *baraka* is most strongly evidenced. The *latifa* is theoretically considered to be "an incipient organ of spiritual perception."

The root in Arabic is from the triliteral grouping LTF. From this the terms used in Arabic include the concepts of subtlety, gentleness, kindness, gift or favor, delicacy. Hence, in the phrase "the gentle sex," the word rendered as "gentle" is in Arabic derived from this root.

The disciple has to awaken five *lataif*, receive illumination through five of the seven subtle centers of communication. The method, presided over by the instructor (Sheikh), is to concentrate the consciousness upon certain areas of the body and head, each area being linked with the *latifa* faculties.

As each *latifa* is activated through exercises, the consciousness of the disciple changes to accommodate the greater potentialities of his mind. He is breaking through

[3] Nearly a century ago, John P. Brown published his *The Dervishes or Oriental Spiritualism* (1867), which has since been one of the very few sources for elements of dervish activity available in the West.

the blindness which makes the ordinary man captive to life and being as it ordinarily seems to be.

In more than one sense, therefore, the activation of the centers is producing a new man. Lest the reader unconsciously link this system with others which may resemble it, we must note that the activation of the *lataif* is only a part of a very comprehensive development, and cannot be carried out as an individual study.

The five centers are named Heart, Spirit, Secret, Mysterious and Deeply Hidden. Another one, strictly speaking not a *latifa* at all, is Self, composed of a complex of "selves." This is the totality of what the ordinary (raw) man or woman considers his personality. It is characterized by a shifting series of moods and personalities whose rapidity of movement gives the individual the impression that his consciousness is constant or a unity. It is not in fact so.

The seventh subtlety is accessible only to those who have developed the others, and belongs to the real sage, the repository and transmitter of the teaching.

The illumination or activation of one or more of the centers may take place partially or accidentally. When this happens, the individual may gain for a time a deepening in intuitive knowledge corresponding with the *latifa* involved. But if this is not a part of comprehensive development, the mind will try, vainly, to equilibrate itself around this hypertrophy, an impossible task. The consequences can be very dangerous, and include, like all one-sided mental phenomena, exaggerated ideas of self-importance, the surfacing of undesirable qualities, or a deterioration of consciousness following an access of ability.

The same is true of breathing exercises or dance movements carried out of correct succession.

The nonbalanced development produces people who may have the illusion that they are seers or sages. Due to the inherent power of the *latifa*, such an individual may appear to the world at large to be worthy of following. In Sufi diagnosis, this type of personality accounts for a great number of false metaphysical teachers. They may, of course, themselves be convinced that they are genuine. This is because the habit of self-deception or of deceiving others has not been transmuted. Rather has it been supported and magnified by the awakening but still undirected new organ, the *latifa*.

The areas which are involved in the activation of the *lataif* are: Self, under the navel; Heart, at the place of the physical heart; Spirit, on the side of the body opposite the heart position. The Secret *latifa* is exactly between the Heart and Spirit positions. Mysterious is in the forehead; Deeply Hidden is in the brain.

The actual meanings of these locations is something which comes as a special realization to the Sufi when the *latifa* in question is being activated. It is only at the outset of the study that they are given these locations.

In the dervish schools there is the special interchange between the teacher and the learner—something which cannot take place unless there is a real teacher present in the community, and until other conditions are ready for the interchange. In this, of course, Sufism differs from a philosophy or a practice which can be learned at second hand.

The special interchange includes the technique called *tajalli*—irradiation. *Tajalli* influences and affects everyone, though it is perceptible only to a few. A person, for instance, may find that he is "in luck" or "does just the right thing," or that he "cannot put a foot wrong." This may be a consequence of accidental *tajalli*. Not realizing the source of the phenomenon, the individual will attribute the cause to something else, say to luck. He feels well because someone has said something complimentary to him; or because he has had a raise in pay. These are the reasons, the rationalizations. This, too, is the wasteful form of *tajalli*; because its operation has a content which far exceeds in importance and even usefulness the secondary advantages which warm the heart of the unconscious recipient.

Being unconscious of the mechanism, however, he cannot proceed further in acquiring the advantages of *tajalli*.

The ecstatic condition, when the human being feels himself at one with creation, or a Creator, rapture, something like intoxication; when he feels that he has entered paradise; when all senses interchange or become one sense—these can be the inability to accept and participate in *tajalli*. What is considered by the individual to be a blessing is in fact a flooding-out of potentiality. It is as if a flood of light has been shone into the eyes of someone who was until recently blind. It has a glory and a fascination. But it is of no use, because it dazzles.

There is a further stage, when the blindness has been removed, and when the personality is wakeful and versatile enough to accept *tajalli*. Then there is the illusion of *tajalli*, sometimes a foretaste, sometimes a reflection, which is useful for artistic creativity or self-indulgence, but is—for the Sufi—a fictitious state. This can be easily discerned because it is not accompanied by an access of knowledge. It counterfeits the true state by giving merely a *sensation* of knowledge or fulfillment. In this respect it resembles a dream in which a wish is fulfilled, thus enabling the disturbed dreamer to continue with his sleep. If he had not provided out of his own mind a happy outcome to his problem he would have woken up and delayed the rest function.

The false *tajalli* experienced by those who do not carry their development along in a balanced way may give rise to a conviction that it is a true mystical state, especially when it is found that supranormal faculties seem to be activated in this condition. Sufis discriminate between this experience and the true one in two ways. Firstly, the teacher will at once identify the counterfeit state. Secondly, as a matter of self-investigation, it can always be discerned that the gains of perception are of no exact value. There may be, for instance, an access of intuition. One may know something about someone—thought reading is an example. But the actual function, the value of the ability to read thought, is nil. The person suffering from false *tajalli* will be able to report some fact or series of facts about someone else, indicating a breakthrough of the limitations of time and space. The test of the *tajalli* for anyone who cannot instantly recognize that it is genuine is whether the "supernatural" perception is accompanied by a permanent increase in intuitive knowledge—the seeing of things as a whole, for instance; or the knowing of the course which one's self-development will take; or the course of that of another; or performing "wonders." Abdul-Qadir Jilani explains that miracles, which are so often reported of Sufis, are not due to any sort of power as generally understood: "When you acquire divine knowledge, you are merged with the intention of God. . . . Your internal essence admits no other thing. . . . People attribute miracles to you. They seem to originate with you, but the origin and intention is God's." (Muqala VI of the *Futuh el Ghayb*)

As with other branches of Sufi action, many different things have been said and written about the *tajalli* of the subtleties. These only serve as guides, and may be completely wrong when applied without regard to prevailing conditions. For the Sufi, every situation is unique, and there are no textbooks as generally understood.

In spite of this shortcoming, which would deter many people from what they consider to be an investigation of Sufi illumination, the practice of activating the *lataif* is essential if real progress is to be made. The real teacher is he who can nurse his disciples in such a way that the awakening of the subtleties takes place concurrently and in accordance with what the individual can bear. Give a child one sweet, the saying runs, and he will be happy. Give him a large box of sweets and he will be sick.

In the stage of activating the *lataif* the student must first recognize the effects of the Self in its myriad facets upon his personality. This is something which his teacher introduces to him. Then, almost parallel but a little behind this development, he finds the activation of his *lataif* encouraged by the efforts of the teacher. This is something which he cannot start by himself if it is to be successful.

His first Sufic experience will be associated with the illumination of a *latifa*. Before that stage has been reached, he will find that he has to work on himself in the area of Selfhood. If he concentrates too much and too long on the problem of Selfhood, the master will have greater difficulty in encouraging the *latifa* illumination. In communities where this factor is not properly understood, the struggle with the Self becomes almost the be-all and end-all of the effort. The attachment to the teacher remains, and the liberation of the personality cannot be effected.

It is in this field more than any other that occultists and fragmented schools, as well as lone experimenters, go astray and in the end peter out or merely become self-propagating systems for the self-struggle, without the benefit of the experience, the *tajalli*, which tells them that they are capable of the development which they seek. In accepting a disciple, the master is always careful to assure himself that the former has the capacity to progress from self-concentration to *latifa*-release.

Generally speaking, Sufi doctrines are both studied and practiced concurrently in the schools of the dervish Orders. This means that there must be a balance between the intellectual presentation and understanding of a doctrine, and its application. Further, there must be a balance between one set of ideas and another. Concentration as a method of doing an exercise is one thing; but it must be balanced by the use of nonstruggle absorption of impacts. How this is done is a part of the intimate and very effective methodology of the dervish Orders.

Some Orders specialize in certain varieties of technique. When a disciple has been taken as far as possible in the school of one Order, he may be sent to another one in order to give him the elements which are the specialization of that school. This, again, has to be done with extreme care, because there can be no question of a one-sided development. If certain faculties are to be developed, this must be done in such a way as to leave room for correct and parallel development at a later date in another school.

Among the specializations of the schools are the *qiff* or *ist* exercise, when a teacher calls out "Halt!" and all physical movement is frozen until he allows the students to relax. The exercise is carried out by teaching masters of the Naqshbandi Order, and it is the Ninth Secret Rule of the Order, being a method which has been found to be effective in breaking through the web of associative thinking and making possible the transmission of *baraka*.

Something of the atmosphere in a dervish Order's school can be felt by this statement, which is a verbatim extract from a preliminary discourse by Sheikh el-Mushaikh (Sheikhly Sheikh), addressing a number of candidates for admission to the Azamia (Greater) Order recently:

"The object of the Sufis is to refine themselves to such an extent that they attain the irradiation [*anwar*] of what we call the several attributes of God, or Beautiful Names. No Sufi can become a part of the 'texture of God' by such an ultimate refinement. Yet only by getting rid of his material slough can he enliven his true essence, which can be called the soul [*ruh*].

"Your attention is invited to the anecdote reported by the Sage Sanai, in his *Walled Garden of Truth*. In it he shows that the superficial perception of religion is inaccurate, so that when I speak of God and Soul and so on, you will have to remember that these are things, as Ibn El-Arabi stresses, which have no correct parallel to you, and which have to be perceived, not merely named and associated with emotionalism.

"The Sage Sanai says:

" 'A man of discernment asked an unreflective one, seeing that he was prone to accepting facile assumptions, "Have you seen saffron, or only heard of it?" '

" 'He answered, "I have seen it, I have eaten it a hundred times (in tinted rice) and more." '

" 'Said the Sage, "Bravo, unfortunate one! Do you know that it grows from a bulb? Can you continue to talk like this? Does he who is ignorant of himself know the soul of another? He who knows hand and foot, how can he know divinity? . . . When you experience, then you will know the meaning of belief. . . . The scholarly are entirely misdirected." '

"To continue. Inasmuch as the accretions weigh down the inner spark [ruh] of the Seeker and thus prevent his progress toward completeness, for the scaling off of these accretions certain exercises have to be performed. They have to be in accordance with the needs of the Seeker. Exactly how this is done is dependent upon the action and knowledge of a Special Guide [murshid or pir, Guided One or Ancient, Wise One]. Some have the impression that this enlightenment can be attained by a Seeker (salik) by reading books on Sufism, and by practices of his own. This is neither theoretically sound nor borne out by experience, quite apart from our inner cognition of its falsity. A Guide is absolutely essential.

"Certain terms have to be noted. Nafs in Sufic terminology is both ego and 'breath.' How the word is used is important and comes through attention to its use in actual fact, not by a study of dictionaries. It is often said that the nafs-i-ammara (Commanding Self) has to be subdued. This may mean that certain cravings and physical and mental attitudes have to be seen for what they are and treated accordingly. In this usage, the word is seen to mean self or ego. In another usage, it simply means breath. For example, in the exercise known as habs-i-dam it means 'imprisoning the breath,' under the strict supervision of a Guide, who uses this exercise for a specific and limited purpose.

"The word bayat means taking the pledge, pact engagement or undertaking, and it signifies the occasion when the Seeker places his hands between those of the Spiritual Guide for the dual pledge. One, on his part, binds himself to seek the Way indicated by the Guide. The other, on his own part, undertakes to guide the Seeker on the Path. This is a special, solemn, meaningful moment. There is a dual, mutual interaction in the pledge; a contractual relationship is formalized by it. It is at this juncture that the Seeker may be allowed to call himself *murid* (disciple), Directed One.

"The term *muraqiba* covers forms of concentration. In it the disciple strives to remove certain thoughts from his mind and concentrate upon things which will make possible his illumination and lay a basis for his permanency. The term also corresponds with sitting with the head down, chin on knee, the correct Sufi posture.

"The word *zikr* (*dhikr* in Arabic) literally means repetition or recital. It conveys the action of the disciple repeating as many times as directed that which he has been given to repeat. It is also, in another sense, called *wird*.

"The technical term *tajalli*, luminizing, and the word *nur* (light—plural: *anwar*) are both associated with the process of activating which is carried out on the way toward independent reality through the force contained in the power of Love. In this we work with the Beautiful Names. Generally considered to be ninety-nine in number, corresponding to the number of beads on a Sufi rosary, they are in another sense limitless. In active 'work' they are limited at first to the names or concepts which are needed to help activate the special organs of perception and communication.

"There is no point at all in activating special new organs of perception and communication unless the individual at the same time is able to keep up with the realization of what is being communicated, to whom, and why. The improvement of communication in itself is best limited to spheres where it belongs—among intellectuals who assume that they have something to communicate. For the rest of us, present methods are adequate to ordinary purposes.

"The word *qalb* (heart) may be considered an anatomical localization of the organ which has to be awakened.

Its position is where the pulsation of the physical heart is normally to be determined on the left breast. In Sufi belief and action, this organ is considered to be the seat of the main, initial inner perceptiveness involved in the 'search' or 'work.'

"The total illumination of this and certain other organs precedes the *walayat-i-Kubra* (major saintship), which is the goal of the Sufi and which corresponds, in other systems, with illumination. At this stage there are certain powers available, powers which seemingly control natural phenomena. It must be remembered that miraculous powers relate to a sphere in which they are coherent and meaningful, and cannot be examined from the viewpoint of the sensationmonger.

"The unification which the Sufi attains is termed *fana* (annihilation). Self-mortification is not permitted, and the proper physical upkeep of the body is essential.

"Before the exercises can take place, either the Greater Balance or the Lesser Balance must have been achieved by the candidate. This balance is connected with the fact that ordinary humanity is not able, except for very short periods, to concentrate at all. Rumi, in *Fihi Ma Fihi*, stresses this, a matter of first importance in any teaching situation:

Innumerable changes of mood are yours, and they are uncontrolled by you. If you knew their origin, you would be able to dominate them. If you cannot localize your own changes, how can you localize that which formed you?

"A great deal of Sufi poetry, in addition to its formal content, refers to degrees of wholeness or ability to concentrate the mind and as a result find a way to the place where truth is not fragmented. When Shabistari in the *Secret Garden* speaks of a spark being whirled and giving a mere illusion that it is constituting a circle of light, he is speaking of a Sufi experience, known to all dervishes, of a certain stage of 'collection.'"

The dervish belief, as affirmed in the practices of the working Orders (as distinct from repetitiously devout ones which specialize in saint worship), is that there is a special state which has to be activated. This is not emotional, certainly not intellectual as ordinarily experienced. The frequent references to refining, purifying and discriminating are connected with this. The dervish refines his consciousness so that he can become aware of states of mind and conditions of reality which are only crudely grasped by the ordinary mind. It might be said that people are normally aware of intellect only in terms of quantity; of emotion as a quantity. The quality, a subtler side which is nonetheless essential to completeness, is difficult to train or elicit, hence abandoned by most people, who make do with very rough approximations of their total capacities.

And, of course, perception of these infinite subtleties is not possible to the ordinary individual. Just as a child has to learn to distinguish between objects in terms of coarse and fine, so has the unregenerate human perception to be trained in this respect.

The full dynamic of the Organ of Evolution becomes operative only when something akin to detachment has been attained. This happens only when certain educational preparations have been made. Before the stage of conscious development, various indisputable experiences mark certain stages of advance. These give the individual both proof of his progress and strength to continue to the next stage. Unless he receives these illuminations in correct succession, he will stay at a stage of partial awareness or occasional concentration power. One of the least desirable results of such out-of-sequence development is when the candidate is not weaned from dependence upon his instructor.

When what we have called the Organ of Evolution is developed and working, the functions of instinct, emotion and intellect are transmuted and work in a new key. A fresh and ever-widening series of experiences is open to the dervish.

Infinite possibilities and intricate mechanisms are now seen in things which formerly seemed inert or of limited use. A dervish example is found in the teaching reference to the permissibility of listening to music. The great Shibli says: "Hearing music deliberately seems outwardly to be a disruptive thing; internally it is a warning. When the Sign is known, such a person may listen, for he hears the warning. Unless he has the Sign (awakening of the Organ of Evolution), he is submitting himself to the possibility of danger." The sensual nature of music is here referred to, as well as the mere emotional and limited intellectual value of music. These are dangers, both because they may lead to sensuality and because, through producing a taste for the secondary indulgence (music because one enjoys music), it veils the real usefulness of music, which is to develop the consciousness.

This is a sense of music which is not only unknown in the West, but energetically denied by many people in the East. Because of the peculiarities of music, some dervish Orders, especially the powerful and highly adaptable Naqshbandi Order, refuse to employ it.

Also a specialization of dervish schools is the real value of poetry, employed as a mystical exercise. All poetry has several functions. In accordance with its "reality," so will it be meaningful for the Sufi. All Orders allow on theological grounds the hearing of poetry, because Mohammed the Prophet approved of it. He said, "Some poetry is wisdom;" and "Wisdom is like the lost she-camel of the devout. Wherever he finds her, he still has the best right to her." He actually used an Arab rhyme to assert what is the Sufi theme of a complete reality which is God: "The most true Arab statement is in the rhyme by Labid that 'Everything but God is unnecessary, for events change.'"

When he was asked to comment on poetry, the Prophet replied, "What is good of it is good, and what is bad, is bad." This is the dictum followed by Sufi masters regarding the permissibility of hearing, reading or writing poetry.

But, according to the great teacher Hujwiri, poetry must in its essence be real and true. If there is unreality or untruth in it, it will contaminate the hearer, reader and writer with its faults.

The manner in which poetry is heard, and the ability of the hearer to benefit from it, is important to Sufism. The dervish teachers will not allow that the real essence of poetry can be appreciated by those who are not correctly prepared for its full understanding, however much an individual may believe that he is extracting the whole from hearing a poem.

Hujwiri passes on the dictum from dervish schools that those who are stirred by the hearing of sensual music are those who are hearing in a sense which is not real. Real hearing, of poetry as of music, is of development value, giving a range of experiences far more varied and valuable than fleshly or ecstatic ones. This, however, can only be enunciated in the present context as an assertion. It is not susceptible to verification outside a Sufi circle.

For the Sufi there are four Journeys. The first of these is the attainment of the condition known as *fana*, sometimes translated as "annihilation." This is the stage of unification of the consciousness, in which the Sufi is harmonized with objective reality. It is the production of this condition which is the objective of the dervish Orders. There are three stages after this. Niffari, a great teacher of the tenth century, describes the Four Journeys in his *Muwaqif*, written in Egypt nearly a thousand years ago.

After he has reached the stage of *fana*, the Sufi passes into the Second Journey, in which he truly becomes the Perfect Man by the stabilization of his objective knowledge. This is the stage of *baqa*, permanency. He is now not a "God-intoxicated man," but a teacher in his own right. He has the title of *qutub*, magnetic center, "point toward which all turn."

In the Third Journey, the teacher becomes a spiritual director to each kind of person in accordance with that person's individuality. The previous kind of teacher (of the Second Journey) is able to teach only within his own immediate culture or local religion. The third kind of teacher may appear to be many different things to different men. He is operating on many levels. He is not "all things to all men" as part of a deliberate policy. He can, on the other hand, benefit everyone in accordance with that person's potentiality. The teacher of the Second Journey, in contrast, is able to work only with selected individuals.

In the Fourth, and last, Journey, the Perfect Man guides others in their transition from what is generally considered to be physical death, to a further stage of development which is invisible to the ordinary person. For the dervish, therefore, the apparent break which takes place at conventional physical death does not exist. A continuous communication and interchange exists between him and the next form of life.

In a dervish community, as in ordinary life, the spiritual attainments of an individual Sufi may not be apparent except to those who are in a position to perceive the emanations of a higher order which truly characterize the dervish.

It is to these stages which Ghazali refers in his standard work, the *Ihya*. He approaches his description of them from the viewpoint of their relevancy to one another and their function for the external world. There are, he says, four stages, which may be likened to a walnut. The choice of this nut is made, incidentally, because in Persian the walnut is called the "four-kerneled" which can also be translated as "four essences" or "four brains."

The nut has a hard shell, an inside skin, a kernel and oil. The shell, bitter in taste, serves as a covering for a period of time. It is thrown away when the kernel is taken out. The skin is of more value than the shell, but is still not to be compared to the kernel itself. The kernel is the object if one is attempting to extract oil. Yet even this inner meat contains matter which is rejected in the pressing out of the oil.

Although Niffari's book is well known and much studied by scholars, the practical application of his method, and the real use of the technical term *waqfat* which he uses, is not to be gleaned from reading alone. Although *waqfat* is associated with the Divine Pause and the Halt exercise which enables a man to break through time and space, it is a highly complex factor which is only roughly indicated by the word used. For example, it also has the quality of a luminosity which removes the darkness caused by multiplicity. Multiplicity is caused by accepting secondary phenomena as primary ones, or differentiation as difference. In the earliest stages of dervish training it is made clear by examples and exercises that when one is, for instance, working with the concept of "fruit," one must not concern oneself with the immense variety of fruit, but with the essential concept.

The dervish schools, whether they exist in a monastery or in a café of Western Europe, are essentials to Sufism because it is in the school situation that such materials as those of Niffari are studied and experienced, in accordance with the peculiarities of the student and the needs of the social clime in which he operates.

This is why the Sufi development has to take root in a certain way in various societies. It cannot be imported. Neither can the methods of working suited to tenth-century Egypt or Yogic India operate effectively in the West. They can naturalize themselves, but in their own way. The lure of mystery and of the colorful East has for centuries obscured for the Western mind the fact that it is the human development which is aimed at, not the trappings.

Seeker After Knowledge

I fear that you will not reach Mecca,
O Nomad!—For the road which you are
following leads to Turkestan.
> (Sheikh Saadi, *Rose Garden,*
> "On the Manners of Dervishes")

I was sitting one day in the circle of a Sufi teacher in northern India, when a young foreigner was brought in. He kissed the hand of the Sheikh and started to talk. For three and a half years, he said, he had studied religions, mysticism and occultism from books, in Germany, France and Britain. He had moved from one society to another, looking for something which would lead him to the right path. Formal religion did not appeal to him. Collecting all the money he could lay his hands on, he journeyed to the East, and he had wandered from Alexandria to Cairo, from Damascus to Teheran, through Afghanistan, India and Pakistan. He had been in Burma and Ceylon, as well as in Malaya. In all of these places he had talked to, and taken copious notes from, spiritual and religious teachers.

There was no doubt that he had covered an immense amount of ground, physically and otherwise. He wanted to join this Sheikh because he wanted to do something practical, to concentrate upon ideas, to improve himself. And he

showed every sign of being more than ready to submit himself to the discipline of a dervish Order.

The Sheikh asked him why he rejected all the other
teachings. There were various reasons, he said; different in
almost every case. "Tell me some," said the teacher.

The great religions, he said, did not seem to go deep
enough. They concentrated upon dogmas. Dogmas had to
be accepted before anything else. Zen, as he had met it in
the West, was out of touch with reality. Yoga required a
fierce discipline if it were not to be "just a fad." The cults
which centered around the personality of one man were
based upon concentration upon that man. He could not
accept the principle that ceremony, symbolism and what
he called mimicry of spiritual truths had any true reality.

Among such Sufis as he had been able to contact, a
similar pattern seemed to him to obtain. Some had whole-
hearted discipleship; some used rhythmic movements which
seemed like mimicry of something to him. Others taught
through recitals indistinguishable from sermons. Some Sufis
were wedded to concentration upon theological themes.

Would the Sheikh help him?

"More than you know," said the Sheikh. "Man is developing, whether he knows it or not. Life is one, though in
some forms it appears inert. While you live, you are learning.
Those who learn through deliberate effort to learn are
cutting down on the learning which is being projected
upon them in the normal state. Uncultivated men often
have wisdom to some degree because they allow the access
of the impacts of life itself. When you walk down the street
and look at things or people, these impressions are teaching
you. If you *try* actively to learn from them, you learn certain things, but they are predetermined things. You look at
a man's face. As you look at it questions arise in your mind,
and they are answered by your own mind. Is he dark, is he
fair? What sort of a man is he? There is also a constant
interchange between the other person and yourself.

"This interchange is dominated by your subjectivity. By

that I mean that you are seeing what you want to see. This has become an automatic action; you are like a machine, but also a man, only superficially trained. You look at a house. The general and particular characteristics of that house are split up into smaller elements and assessed in your brain. But not objectively—only in accordance with your past experiences. These experiences in modern man include what he has been told. Thus the house will be big or small, nice or not so nice; like your own or not like it. In greater detail, it will have a roof like another, it will have windows which are unusual. The machine is going around in circles, because it is merely adding to its formal knowledge."

The newcomer looked dazed.

"What I am trying to convey," said the Sheikh, relentlessly, "is that you assess things in accordance with preconceived ideas. This is almost inevitable for the intellectual man. You do not like symbolism in religion, you have decided. Very well, you will seek a religion without symbolism." He paused. "Is that what you mean?"

"I think I mean that the use of symbolism by various bodies does not satisfy me as being genuine or necessary," said the youth.

"Does that mean that you would know if you found a form of using symbols which was correct?" queried the teacher.

"Symbolism and ritual, to me, are not fundamental," replied the would-be disciple, "and it is fundamentals that I seek."

"Would you recognize a fundamental if you saw one?"

"I think so."

"Then the things which we say and do would seem to you to be mere matters of opinion, or tradition, or superficiality; because we *do* use symbols. Others use chants, and movements, and thinking and silence, concentration and contemplation—a dozen other things." The Sheikh paused.

The visitor spoke.

"Do you think the exclusivity of Judaism, the rituals of

Christianity, the fasting in Islam, the Buddhist shaven head, to be fundamentals?" Our guest was now warming up to a characteristic intellectual theme.

"The Sufi dictum is that the 'apparent is the bridge to the Real,'" said the Sheikh. "This means, in the case which we are considering, that all these things have a meaning. The meaning may be lost, the performance a mere mockery, a sentimental or misunderstood acting of a part. But, properly used, they are connected in a continuous sense with the true reality."

"So originally all ritual is meaningful and has a necessary effect?"

"Essentially all ritual, symbolism and so on is a reflection of a truth. It may have been concocted, adapted, diverted to other ends; but it represents a truth—the inner truth of what we call the Sufi Way."

"But the practitioners do not know what it means?"

"They may know in one sense, on one level; a level sufficiently deep to propagate the system. But as far as reaching reality and self-development, the use of these techniques is nil."

"Then," said the student, "how do we know who is using the outward signs in the right way, the way of development, and who is not? I can accept that these superficial indications are of potential value, inasmuch as they *could* lead to something else, and we have to start somewhere. But I, for one, could not tell you which system I should follow."

"A moment ago you were applying for admission to our circle," said the Sheikh, "and now I have succeeded in confusing you to such an extent that you admit you cannot judge. Well, that is the essence of it. You *cannot* judge. You cannot use the instruments of carpentry for watchmaking. You have set yourself a task: to find spiritual truth. You have sought this truth in the wrong directions, and interpreted its manifestations in the wrong way. Is it surprising that you will remain in this state? There is one other alternative for you, as you are at present. The excessive concentration upon the theme, the anxiety and emotion which is engendered in you, will ultimately pile up to such an extent that you will seek a relief from it. Then what will happen? Emotion will swamp intellect; and you will either hate religion or—more likely—become converted to some cult which takes the responsibility. You will settle down with the notion that you have found what you sought."

"Is there no other alternative, even assuming that I accept your belief that my emotion can swamp my intellect?" The intellectual training does not take kindly to any suggestion that it is not comprehensive; nor that it can be swamped by emotion. The slight asperity in tone showed that the thinker was asserting itself. This was not lost on the Sheikh.

"The alternative, which you will not take, is detachment. You see, when we detach, we do not do so in the way in which you do. Intellect teaches you to detach your mind from something and view it intellectually. What we have to do is to detach from both intellect and emotion. How can you become accessible to anything if you are using intellect to judge it? Your problem is that what you call intellect is really a series of ideas which alternately take possession of your consciousness. We do not regard intellect as sufficient. Intellect, for us, is a complex of more or less compatible attitudes which you have been trained to regard as one single thing. According to Sufi thinking, there is a level below this, which is a single, small, but vital one. It is the true intellect. This true intellect is the organ of comprehension, existing in every human being. From time to time in ordinary human life it breaks through, producing strange phenomena which cannot be accounted for by the usual methods. Sometimes these are called occult phenomena, sometimes they are thought to be a transcending of the time or space relationship. This is the element in the human being which is responsible for his evolution to a higher form."

"And I have to take this on trust?"

"No, you cannot take it on trust, even if you wanted to do so. If you took it on trust, you would soon abandon it. Even if you were intellectually convinced that it was necessary as a hypothesis, you might very well lose it. No, you have to experience it. This means, of course, that you have to feel it in a way which you feel nothing else. It comes into your consciousness as a truth different in quality from other things which you have been accustomed to regarding as truths. By its very difference you recognize that it belongs to the area which we call 'the other.'"

Our visitor found this difficult to digest, and returned to his established way of thinking. "Are you trying to produce in me a conviction that there is something deeper, and that I feel it? Because if not, I do not see the point of spending so much time on this discussion."

"You will think it very rude of me, I am sure," said the Sheikh amiably, "but I have to say that things are not as you see them. You see, you come here and talk. I talk to you. As a consequence of our talk and thought many things happen. As far as you are concerned, all that has happened is that we have talked. You may feel that you are convinced, or you are not. To us the meaning of the whole event is far greater. Something is happening as a result of this talk. It is happening, as you can well imagine, in the minds of all the people here. But something else is also happening—to you, to me, and elsewhere. Something which you understand when you understand it. Take it on the very simple level of cause and effect as normally understood. A man goes into a shop and buys a piece of soap. As a result of this purchase, many things can happen—the shopkeeper has that much more money, more soap may be ordered, and so on. Words spoken in the course of the transaction have an effect, depending upon the condition of mind of the two parties. When the man leaves the shop, there is an additional factor in his life that was not there before—the soap. Many things can happen as a result of this. But to the two main characters, all that has *really* happened is that a piece of

soap has been bought and paid for. They have no awareness
of the ramifications of this, and little interest in it. It is only
when something noteworthy—from their point of view—happens that they think about it again. Then, they will say,
'Fancy that, the man who bought my soap was a murderer;'
or perhaps he was a king. Or perhaps he left a counterfeit
coin. Every action, like every word, has an effect and a place.
This is the basis of the Sufi system-without-a-system. And,
as you will have read in innumerable stories, the Sufi moves
among the incredible complex of actions and happenings
in a state of inner awareness of their meaning."

"I can see what you mean," said the visitor, "but I cannot
experience it. If it is true, of course it accounts for quite a
number of things. Some occult happenings; prophetic experiences; the failure of all but a very few people to solve
riddles of life by merely thinking about them. And it could
also mean that a person who is aware of the complex developments all around him can harmonize himself with them
to a degree impossible to others. But the price of trying this
is the price of throwing away one's previous knowledge. I
could not do that."

The Sheikh did not want a verbal victory, and did not
close in for a *coup de grâce*. "My friend, a man once hurt
his leg. He had to walk with a crutch. This crutch was
very useful to him, both for walking and for many other
purposes. He taught all his family to use crutches, and they
became a part of normal life. It was a part of everyone's
ambition to have a crutch. Some were made of ivory, others
adorned with gold. Schools were opened to train people in
their use, university chairs endowed to deal with the higher
aspects of this science. A few, a very few people started to
walk without crutches. This was considered scandalous,
absurd. Besides, there were so many uses for crutches.
Some of them replied, and were punished. They tried to
show that a crutch could be used sometimes, when needed.
Or that many of the uses to which a crutch was put could
be supplied in other ways. Few listened. In order to over-

come the prejudices, some of the people who could walk without support began to behave in a way totally different from established society. Still they remained a few.

"When it was found that, having used crutches for so many generations, few people could in fact walk without crutches, the majority 'proved' that they were necessary. 'Here,' they said, 'here is a man. Try to make him walk without a crutch. See? He cannot.' 'But we are walking without crutches,' the ordinary walkers reminded them. 'This is not true; merely a fancy of your own,' said the cripples—because by that time they were becoming blind as well; blind because they would not see."

"The analogy does not fit completely," said the young man.

"Does any analogy fit completely?" asked the Sheikh. "Don't you see that if I could explain everything easily and completely, by means of a single story, there would be no need for this talk? Only partial truths are expressed exactly by analogy. For instance, I can give you a perfect pattern for a circular disc, and you can cut out thousands from it. Each one may be a duplicate of each other one. But, as we all know, a circle is only relatively circular. Increase its dimensions proportionately by several hundred times, and you will find that it is not a true circle any more."

"This is a fact of physical science; I know that all scientific laws are only relatively true. This is all that science itself claims."

"And yet you seek complete truth through relative methods?"

"Yes, and so do you, because you said that symbols and so on are 'bridges to the real,' though they are incomplete."

"The difference is that you have chosen one single method of approaching truth. This is not enough. We use many different methods, and we recognize that there is a truth which is perceived by an inner organ. You are trying to boil water, and you do not know how. We boil water by bringing together certain elements—the fire, the container, the water."

"But what about my intellect?"

"That must fall into its right perspective, find its own level, when the present lack of balance of the personality is restored."

When the visitor had left, someone asked the sage, "Will you comment upon this interview?"

"If I comment upon it," he said, "it would lose its perfection."

We had all learned, each in accordance with his status.

The Sufi doctrine of equipoise between extremes has several meanings. Where it applies to discipleship, the capacity to learn from another, it means that the individual must be free from incorrect thinking before he can start to learn. Our Western would-be disciple has to learn that he cannot bring his assumptions about his own capacity to learn into a field where he does not in fact know what it is that he is trying to learn. All he really knows is that he is in some way dissatisfied. All the rest is his own collection of ideas as to what the reason for the dissatisfaction might be, and an attempt to find a cure for the illness which he has diagnosed without first asking himself about his diagnostic abilities.

We have chosen an actual incident involving a Westerner; but this form of thinking is not confined to the West. Similarly, the opposite extreme—the man who wants to submit himself completely to the will of a master—which is said to be characteristic of the Eastern mind, is next to useless. The Seeker must first attain some measure of balance between these two extremes before he can be said to have the capacity to learn.

Both types learn about their capacity to learn mainly from the observation of the Sufi teacher and his way of behaving. As the human exemplar, his doings and sayings are the bridge between the relative incapacity of the student and the position of being a Sufi. Less than one person in a hundred will normally have any conception of either of these two requirements. If the student, by careful study of Sufi literature, does glimpse the principle upon which discipleship works, he will be more than fortunate.

He can find it in Sufic material, providing that he is prepared to read and reread it, to school himself to avoid the automatic associations which pigeonhole or label Sufi (and all other) thought for him. Generally speaking, he is more likely to be temporarily attracted to some more plausible school, which lays down inflexible principles which he can lean upon.

The Creed of Love

One went to the door of the Beloved and knocked.
A voice asked, "Who is there?"
He answered, "It is I."
The voice said, "There is no room for Me and Thee."
The door was shut.
After a year of solitude and deprivation he returned and
    knocked.
A voice from within asked, "Who is there?"
The man said, "It is Thee."
The door was opened for him.

                                                    (Jalaluddin Rumi)

Sufism has often been called the creed of love. All Sufis, irrespective of the external appearance of their schools, have
made this theme a matter of essential concern. The analogy
of human love as a reflection of real truth, so often expressed
in Sufi poetry, has often been literally interpreted by others
than Sufis. When Rumi says: "Wherever you are, whatever
your condition is, always try to be a lover," he is not speaking
of love as an end in itself; nor of human love as the ultimate
possibility in the potential of the human being.

The deterioration of the Sufic love-ideal in the West is
seen to develop fairly after the loss of a linguistic grasp of
the word groupings adopted by Sufi teachers to convey the
fact that their idea of love was much more than idyllic
fantasy. Spreading from Spain and southern France into
western Europe, undergoing a change of language which
robbed it of its effective content, the creed of love lost many
of its essential characteristics. In order to recapture, for a
Western audience, the comprehensive nature of this Sufic

specialization, we have to look at the development of the troubadors.

One aspect of love poetry arising in Saracen Spain, that of the elevation of womankind, was rapidly diverted by the Church, as has been noted by historians, into the idealization of the Virgin Mary. This development is seen in the collection of poetry made by Alfonso the Sage from Saracen sources. An authority on this subject freezes this moment for us in referring to these *Cantigas de Santa Maria:* "The subject—the praise of the Virgin Mary—is a logical development of the troubador's idealization of the lady of the manor; while the poems of the troubadors . . . are, in matter, form and style closely connected with Arabic idealism and Arabic poetry written in Spain."[1]

Professor Hitti and others are fully persuaded of the Arab origins of the troubadors: "The troubadors . . . resembled Arab singers not only in sentiment and character but also in the very forms of their minstrelsy. Certain titles which these Provençal singers gave to their songs are but translations from Arabic titles."[2]

The derivation of the word "troubador" from the romance word for "finding" is a secondary one. They were "finders" in the sense that this was the nearest applicable naturalization of the original term, which is an Arabic word, itself a play between two words. The first is RBB (viol), used by Sufi minstrels, and applied by both Khayyam and Rumi to themselves, as Professor Nicholson has pointed out.[3] The second is the root TRB. There is a third, associated sound, RB—which literally means, when transformed into RaBBat, "lady, mistress, female idol."

As shown again and again in this book, Sufi names for specialist groups were invariably chosen with the greatest possible care and regard for the poetic niceties of the situa-

[1] J. B. Trend, *The Legacy of Islam,* Oxford, 1931, p. 31.
[2] P. Hitti, *History of the Arabs,* New York, 1951, p. 600.
[3] R. A. Nicholson, *Selections from the Diwan-i-Shams-i-Tabriz,* pp. xxxvi et seq.

tion. We should remember that the "-ador" part of the word is merely the Spanish agental suffix, and is no part of the original concept.

Following up the dictionary derivations of the RB and TRB roots, if used to describe the activities of a group of people, we find ten main derivative words:

1. TaraBaB = to perfume, rear a child.
2. RaBBa = to collect, rule people, have authority over.
3. TaRaBBaB = to claim mastership.
4. RaBB = the Lord, God, Master.
5. RaBBat = lady, mistress, female idol.
6. RiBAB = covenant, friends, tithes.
7. MaRaB = gatherer, abode, meeting place.
8. MaRaBBaB = preserve, confection.
9. MuTriB = musician, Sufi exponent, teacher, guide.[4]
10. RaBAB = viol, adjective for Sufi singer used by Rumi, Khayyam, etc.

Seen in the light of Sufic usage, therefore, we are not dealing with a phenomenon of Arab minstrelsy, but with the efforts of a group of Sufi teachers, in which the love theme was a part of a whole. The idealization of woman or the playing of the viol are insignificant but nonetheless partial aspects of the whole.

The teachings of Sufi schools contain all the elements collected in the special name of troubador. Sufis gather together at a meeting place. Some live in convents (RaBAT), still commemorated in such Spanish place names as the *Arrabida, Rabida, Rapita, Rabeda* of today. They call themselves, and are called, "lovers," and also "masters." Although masters, they are also, as they frequently emphasize, "slaves of love." They play the viol, and use a certain password containing the two alliterative words for "confec-

4 Prof. Edward Palmer, *Oriental Mysticism*, p. 80.

tion" and "beloved" to emphasize or commemorate that the name of the group has several distinct yet allied meanings. The phrase could roughly be translated as "be a darling (RB) and pass the jam (RB)." They speak of divinity as female, idol, mistress. Ibn El-Arabi (the "greatest master" of the Sufis), the Spaniard, used this imagery to such a degree that he was accused of blasphemy.

The troubadors are a derivation from a Sufic movement originally grouped around their name, which stuck to them after its many facets were forgotten. The Arabs ruled Spain from the early part of the eighth century, and flourishing Sufi schools are noted during the ninth century. The first Provençal poets wrote at the end of the eleventh century. The correspondence between troubador feeling, however diluted a form of the Sufi stream it became, and original Sufi material was noted even by people who had no specialist knowledge of the interior contact. Emerson equates the great Sufi love poet Hafiz and the troubadors, and claims for them the true essence of poetry: "Read Hafiz and the *trouvères*: fact books which all geniuses prize as raw material and as an antidote to verbiage and false poetry."

That there was something deeper than the superficial appearance about the troubadors was noted by Robert Graves in *The White Goddess*. Writing at a time when he had not investigated Sufism to any extent, he realized that there had been a process at work in the poetry which had altered its original sense and direction:

"Fancy played a negligible part in the development of the Greek, Latin and Palestinian myths, or of the Celtic myths until the Norman-French *trouvères* worked them up into irresponsible romances of chivalry. They are all grave records of ancient religious customs or events, and reliable enough as history once their language is understood and allowance has been made for errors in transcription, misunderstandings or obsolete ritual, and deliberate changes introduced for moral or political reasons."[5]

In order to orientate ourselves, to taste the atmosphere of those days when Sufi thinking through poetry and music was providing a leaven to Western thought which is still with us, we can turn to Michelet, the French medievalist.[6]

"The darkness of scholastic Christianity is being replaced by the light and warmth of Saracen life, in spite of the eclipse of its military power," he says. The picture which he draws for us shows very clearly the effect of Sufi, not "Arab" thinking. This passage might almost have been designed for the purpose. Its very existence underlines Michelet's intuitive sense of an underlying process, just as much as Emerson and Graves, the poets, feel the Sufi impulse in Hafiz and the troubadors.

He tells us, for instance, that Dante and St. Thomas Aquinas look upon Satan in one of two ways—the Christian way, "grotesque and coarse-minded . . . such as he was in his earliest days, when Jesus could still drive him to enter into the herd of swine." And the other (the Sufi way) as "a subtle reasoner, a scholastic theologian, a phrasemongering jurist." This latter view is again and again insisted upon by the Sufis: "Seek the real Satan in the scholastic sophist, or the hairsplitting doctor—for he is the opposite of Truth."

The second trend emphasized by Michelet as a legacy of Islam to the West—a new realization of love, maternity, art, color, verve—is strongly marked in the ideas and activities of the Sufis, not the austere scholastics of Moslem Spain who in 1106–43 burned publicly the books of Ghazali, one of the greatest Sufis:

"From Asia, that men thought they had abolished, rises a new dawn of incomparable splendor, whose rays strike far, very far, until they pierce the heavy mists of the West. Here is a world of nature and art that brute ignorance had called

[5] Faber and Faber edition, London, 1961, p. 13.
[6] Jules Michelet, *Satanism and Witchcraft* (tr. A. R. Allinson), London, 1960, pp. 71–73.

accursed, but which now starts forth to conquer its conquerors in a peaceful war of love and maternal charm. All men yield to its spell; all are fascinated, and will have nothing that is not from Asia. The Orient showers her wealth upon us; the webs and the shawls, and carpets of exquisite softness and cunningly blended colors of her looms, the keen, flashing steel of her damascened blades, convince us of our own barbarism. . . . Is there one being of sanity strong enough, where sanity is so rare, to receive all this without giddiness, without intoxication. . . . Is there a brain that not being petrified, crystallized in the barren dogmas of Aquinas, is still free to receive life, and the vigorous sap of life? Three Wizards essay the task (Albertus Magnus, Roger Bacon, Arnold of Vallaneuve) by innate vigor of mind they force their way to Nature's source; but bold and intrepid as their genius is, it has not, it cannot have, the adaptability, the power, of the popular spirit."

The Sufi stream was partially dammed. The West accepted the bases of much luxury, love poetry and the enjoyment of living. Certain elements, necessary to the whole and impossible without a human exemplar of the Sufi Way, remained almost unknown. The Sufi Guide, in his distorted form of a mysterious near-occultist figure, lingered on in strange places. He was for the most part someone heard about, not met.

Centuries later, reaching back toward the sources of the love cult which had shaped his own Western heritage, no less a personage than Professor Nicholson, the great scholar, himself composed a Sufic verse:

> Love, Love alone can kill what seemed dead,
> The frozen snake of passion. Love alone
> By tearful prayers and fiery longing fed,
> Reveals a knowledge schools have never known.[7]

Such was the vitality of the inner Sufic theme of this poetry that it laid the foundation of a great deal of sub-

[7] R. A. Nicholson, *Rumi, Poet and Mystic*, London, 1956.

sequent Western literature. As one writer puts it: "Without the Provençal and troubador singers there would be precious little in our contemporary music worth the name. True, we could have had dirges and folk songs, but the strange insistent call to something else, something which awaits us, something which as human beings we have to accomplish, would probably be missing from poetry and music alike."[8]

Sufi transmission, in however attenuated a form, must be considered to be a basic ingredient of modern life. This is not to say that its goals are understood today, because the tradition as known in the West is necessarily incomplete. The greatest authority upon the Arabs, Professor Philip Hitti, regards this Provençal and troubador transmission as marking a new civilization for the West:

"In southern France the first Provençal poets appear full-fledged toward the end of the eleventh century with palpitating love expressed in a wealth of fantastic imagery. The troubadors (TaRaB: music, song) who flourished in the twelfth century imitated their southern contemporaries, the *zajal* singers. Following the Arabic precedent the cult of the dame suddenly arises in southwest Europe. The *Chanson de Roland*, the noblest monument of early European literature, whose appearance prior to 1080 marks the beginning of a new civilization—that of Western Europe—just as the Homeric poems mark the beginning of historic Greece, owes its existence to a military contact with Moslem Spain."[9]

European music as we know it today was transformed by this development from Sufi sources.[10]

[8] G. Butler, *The Leadership of the Strange Cult of Love*, Bristol, 1910, p. 17.

[9] P. K. Hitti, *History of the Arabs*, 1951 ed., p. 562.

[10] *Ibid.*, "Adelard of Bath, who studied music at Paris, was probably the translator of al-Khwarizini's mathematical treatise *Liber Ysagogarum Alchorism.* He was, therefore, one of the first to introduce Arab music into the Latin world. . . . It is significant that in this same period a new principle appears in Christian European music, the principle that notes have an exact time value or ratio among themselves. . . . The term Ochetus (rhythmic mode) is probably a transformation of Arabic *iqa'at* (plural of *iqa*). Mensual music was

The association between love and poetry, between the poet and the musician, and between these and the magician in the widest sense, runs through Sufism, as through the Western tradition which it undoubtedly contacted and reinforced. It is as if the twin streams of the ancient teaching mingle on this dimension, far removed from the coldly rationalizing intellect. The object of the poet-lover-magician is not, however, in Sufism, merely to be absorbed in the effulgence of the truth which he learns. He is transformed by it, and as a consequence has a social function—to inject back into the stream of life the direction which humanity needs in order to fulfill itself. This is the role of the "secret garden" experience beyond which comes the understanding of the poet's mission. Florence Lederer grasps this sense strongly when commenting upon Shabistari's wonderful poem *The Secret Garden:* "But the man must not rest in this divine union. He must return to this world of unreality, and in the downward journey must keep the ordinary laws and creeds of man."[11]

Anwari, like the Western magician-poets of old, emphasizes that the poet and lover shade into one another:

If to be a lover is to be a poet, I am a poet;
If to be a poet is to be a magician, I am a magician;
If to be a magician is to be thought evil, I can be
     thought evil;
If to be thought evil is to be disliked by worldlings, I
     am content to be such.
Disliked by worldlings is to be a lover of the true real-
     ity, more often than not.
I affirm that I am a Lover!

A Sufi poet of the seventeenth century says, in the *Key of the Afghans:*

---

probably the greatest, but certainly not the only contribution the Arabs made in this branch of knowledge."
[11] F. Lederer, *The Secret Garden*, London, 1920.

The arrow needs an archer, and poetry a magician. He must ever hold in his mind the scales of meter, rejecting the long and the short. Truth is his mistress, astride a black steed, veiled in allegory. From beneath her lashes shoot a hundred unerring glances. The poet will decorate her fingers with multihued jewels, adorn her with the perfume and scent of saffron metaphor. Alliteration will ring like footbells; on her bosom will be the mystery of concealed rhyme. Together with the secrets of inner meaning, the concealing eyes, these make her body a perfection of mystery.[12]

What exactly was lost in the transition of the love theme from East to West? First of all, the knowledge, which can be imparted only by human association, of the wider significance of love, and where it connects with other elements in life. The individual who merely equates love with divinity is a barbarian from the point of view of the person who has found the connection with the reason of life. Secondly, the intricacies, the depth within depth, contained in the works of art which were produced by the Sufi Adepts. The barbarian takes what nutrition he can from what he sees or handles. The color-blind man may see all colors in shades of white, gray and black. This may be adequate to his desires, but according to the Sufi, it is not adequate to his needs. The intricacy of much Eastern and other art is not merely a display of versatility or skill. It is an analogy of the infinite successions of meanings which can be transmitted by one and the same thing. Further, those who have glimpsed the Sufi experiences realize that the multiple meanings contained in such a work of art are there, so far as the human being is concerned, in order to lead him to a true perception of what the inner reality is. It is the perception of this inner reality which enables him to take himself forward to the greater evolution which is the destiny of man.

Most people will see in a series of Chinese boxes, one

[12] Translated by T. C. Plowden.

inside the other, only an excellent artistic or craftsmanlike achievement. The Sufi, having found the key to "eternal succession" will realize that this produce is an analogy, not something to puzzle or delight the barbarian. So it is with the entire love theme for the Sufi. With the analogy of love, and the literary use he makes of it, he can help to bridge the gap in understanding for others who are at an earlier stage of the Path.

Love is a common denominator for mankind. The Sufi, having penetrated its secrets to the tasting of the true reality which lies behind, returns to the world in order to convey something of the steps of the Path. Those who remain intoxicated by the wayside are not his concern. Those who wish to go further must study him and his works.

Miracles and Magic

The ritual of him who has seen the Shah (Truth) is above anger and kindness, infidelity and religion. . . .

(*Mathnawi*, IV)

A writer named Abdul-Hadi recorded six centuries ago that his father told him one day, "You were born as a result of a prayer by the great Bahaudin Naqshband of Bokhara, whose miracles are innumerable." He conceived as a result of this statement such a desire to see this Sufi master that as soon as he was able to detach himself from his affairs he traveled from Syria to Central Asia. He found Bahaudin (died 1389), the head of the Naqshbandi Order, sitting surrounded by disciples, and told him that he had had to come to him, because he was curious about his miracles.

Bahaudin said, "There is a food other than ordinary food. This is the food of impressions [*naqsh-ha*], which are penetrating into man ceaselessly from many directions of his environment. Only the elect know what these impressions are, and can direct them. Do you understand?"

Abdul-Hadi did not see the connection, and remained silent.

"The meaning of this is one of the secrets of the Sufis. The master makes the food which is a 'different' nutriment available to the aspirant, and this aids his development. This is outside the laws of happening which can be understood.

Now, as to what you call miracles. Everyone present here has seen miracles. What is important is the function of miracles. Miracles may be destined to supply a part of the food which is an extra food, and may act upon the mind and even the body in a certain way. When this happens, the experience of the miracle will perform its due and proper function on the mind. If the miracle acts only on the imagination, as with the crude mind, it will stimulate uncritical credulity or emotional excitement, or a thirst for more miracles, or a desire to understand miracles, or a one-sided attachment to, even fear of, the person who is apparently responsible for the miracle."

This, he continued, made the miracle something which could not be explained satisfactorily, because of the many different trains of thought which it prompted, different in every mind, and the many chains of effect it caused, different in everybody.

There was nobody, except for the mature Sufi, who could recognize the true interpretation of a miracle. This applied with an inexplicable miracle. How much more did it apply to a miracle which happened, but which was not palpable. There were miracles in continuous operation which humanity did not perceive through the senses, because they were undramatic. An example was a process whereby, against all probability, a man might gain or lose moral or material things in a frequent succession. Sometimes these are called coincidences. All miracles were in fact coincidences—a series of things happening in a certain relationship to one another.

"Miracles," said Naqshband, "have a function, and that function operates whether they are understood or not. They have a true [objective] function. Hence, miracles will in some people produce confusion, in others scepticism, in others fear, in others excitement, and so on. It is the function of the miracle to provoke reactions and supply nutriment; nutriment in this case which varies with the personality acted upon. In all cases the miracle is an instrument of both influence and assessment of the people acted upon."

All miracles, according to the Sufis, have thus such a multifarious action on humanity that they cannot be (a) performed except when needed, and generally develop as incidental happenings; (b) diagnosed or defined because of the complexity of their nature. The nature of a miracle cannot be detached from its effect, because it would not be of any importance if a human being were not involved.

A typical statement of a miracle attributed to what might be called a short-term requirement is contained in a vast collection of materials referring to Abdul-Qadir of Jilan, the founder of the Qadiri Order of Sufis.

Sheikh Umru Osman Sairifini and Sheikh Abdul-Haq Harini deposed as follows:

"On the third day of the month of Safar, in the year 555 of the Flight, we were in the presence of our Master [Sayed Abdul-Qadir] in his school. He rose and put on wooden sandals, and performed an ablution. Then he performed two prayers and gave a loud shout, throwing one sandal into the air, when it seemed to disappear. With a further cry the Master threw the second sandal into the air and this also vanished from our sight. None of those who were present dared to question him about the event.

"Thirty days after this incident a caravan arrived in Baghdad from the East. Its members said that they had some gifts for the Master. We consulted him, and he allowed us to accept the presents. The members of the caravan gave us some silken and some other cloth and a pair of sandals which were the same ones which the Master had hurled from him. Their account was as follows:

" 'On the third day of the month of Safar, that day being a Sunday, we were on the road with our caravan when there was a sudden Arab attack, under two chiefs. The robbers killed some of our number and plundered the caravan. They immediately entered a nearby forest for the purpose of distributing the loot. We survivors reassembled at the edge of the forest. It occurred to us that we could invoke the aid of the Sayed in our calamity, for we had no recourse and no means wherewith to continue our journey. We resolved to offer him presents in token of thanksgiving, should we at least arrive safely in Baghdad—an improbability as the situation then seemed to be.

" 'As soon as we had made this decision, we were alarmed by one, and then another, cry which echoed through the glades. We concluded that the first band of Arabs had been attacked by a second one, and that a fight between them would now follow. Soon afterward a party from the bandits came to us and said that there had been a disaster. They begged us to accept our property back. We proceeded to the place at which our merchandise had been collected by the Arabs, and found that their two captains were lying dead—each with a wooden sandal near his head.'

"It appears to us indubitable that the Master, having perceived the calamity of the caravaneers, moved by a desire to aid them, had been able to project his sandals in such a way that the leaders of the band, the ultimately guilty parties, were killed.

"Preserved by us as a matter of record and committed to writing in the presence of Almighty God, the Distinguisher and Requiter of truth and falsehood."

The Naqshbandi tradition referring to such events as these has it that "when a Friend perceives that a wrong is to be righted, he will seek guidance as to the method and permission as to the propriety in a state of contemplation; when the necessary effect will follow instantly and continuously or subsequently and appropriately."

"Miracles," says Afghani, "may make you feel conviction about a thing. Be sure that whatever they make you feel, this is not their actual effect, nor the end of their effect."

This functional attitude toward miracles underlines, even for the outside observer, deeper possibilities of inexplicable happenings. If we start from the lowest level of miracles, we can see that an action or happening which is familiar and explicable to us might be puzzling or conclusive "magical" evidence to a more ignorant person. Hence, a savage seeing fire made by chemical means might consider the happening miraculous. At his stage of development, this event might produce in him the degree of religious awe necessary to make him venerate the performer or obey his injunctions. In any case there would be a mental and physical effect upon him. At the other end of the scale, happenings which cannot be explained by current physical science will influence even the most sophisticated modern. In the case of the invisible miracles referred to by Naqshband, a similar mechanism would be operative. A long succession of coincidental and favorable (or unfavorable) happenings involving a human being will be certain to exert over him a mental and physical effect, even if the latter is only that he will eat more than usual because he can afford to do so through his run of luck.

This theory goes much further than ordinary thinking about miracles, and differs from the usual reactions only insofar as it insists that nothing is truly accidental or isolated.

This is underlined by the Sufi teaching that "effect is far more important than cause, because effect is varied, while cause is ultimately only one." Even the most hardened materialist would agree with this, if it were put into his own phraseology, something like this: "All action is ultimately physical action; and the differences in its effect is determined by what is being acted upon." No Sufi would quarrel with this, apart from saying that the pure materialist is capable of only a limited view of origins and causation, seeing them in a one- or two-dimensional way, because of the rigidity of his outlook.

Miracles are connected with causation problems, and causation, according to the Sufi, with the problems of space and time. Many miracles are considered such because they seem to defy the conventions of space or time or both. A breakthrough into an extra dimension would rob them of

their inexplicable quality. But, say the Sufis, since miracles
have physical effects, it is the effect of the miracle which
may generally be a part of the food which is not a food,
which can be significant. It is only on a crude level that an
investigation into miracles can be attempted.

A miracle is therefore accepted calmly in Sufi perspective
as the working of a mechanism which will influence a
man or woman to the extent to which he is attuned with it.
A crazed savage who wants to immerse himself in the over-
whelming emoting of apparent miraculousness is not a
candidate for spiritual development; though he may make
a very much improved and law-abiding member of a conventionally religious society as a result of his experience.

My own teacher once commented on a question about
miracles by saying, "Contemplate the phrase 'Why is the
sound of an onion?'" to show that some questions cannot
be put by those who have not the capacity to pose them nor,
consequently, the potentiality of understanding the real
answer.

The evidential miracle as interpreted in conventional
religion may be of multiple value, according to the Sufis.
That is to say, it may convey one impression to a man at one
stage of development; and a form of food to someone more
advanced.

We can be even more specific. Professor Seligman was
surprised to find that incisions made by certain dervishes in
the flesh stopped bleeding with inexplicable rapidity. Other
observers have noted that Rifai dervishes could cause
wounds which seemed to heal without any scar, and with
absurd rapidity. Until Dr. Hunt in 1931 showed a film of
Indian Rifais performing these practices, the ordinary reaction had been to discount the whole thing, or else to attribute it to hypnotism. The Qadiri dervishes are seen walking upon water; the Azimia are reputed to appear, like many
of the ancient Sheikhs, at different places at one and the
same time. Why do these things happen, or seem to happen?

The dervish has a completely different attitude toward

them than the ordinary man, whether he be a credulous simpleton or a twentieth-century scientist. It must be remembered that the Sufi claims that things are not what they seem. In demonstrating his ability to do things that others cannot do, which appear contrary to accepted physical laws familiar to everyone, he states his case. This is as valid a method of expressing oneself as any literary form, and more effective than most. The fact that this form of statement has been abused, misunderstood and counterfeited does not invalidate the basis of it.

The outside observer, especially if he is what is generally considered to be objective or educated, is heavily hampered when approaching this problem. His pressing need is to explain the phenomena in terms understood by him. He has no sense of a duty to extend his own perceptions into the phenomena which he is investigating. Yet, from the dervish point of view, this man is getting only such nutrition as he allows himself to get out of the miracle. When a child is afraid of a bogey, he must find an explanation, or have a plausible one found for him. When an insensitive man looks at inexplicable happenings, and knows that "there must be a logical explanation," this explanation will be supplied to him—I do not say how or by whom.

In Sufism, the secret protects itself. Hallucinations, as they are called, work both ways, according to Sufi experience. A man may think that he sees something which is not in fact there. He may also see something other than what is really there. How he sees it and what he sees will depend upon his own capacity of understanding. I am not now talking about deliberate deceit and conjuring tricks. To assume, just because a thing can be explained in rational terms, that this is the only explanation for it is not an absurdity in ordinary experience. But it is incorrect if one is living on a level where several different explanations are actually seen to be possible, in accordance with the quality of the percipient to profit by them. Modern science has not yet acquired this special refinement of differentiation—its dimensions are not sufficient for the purpose.

A traditional Sufi method of referring to this situation is to use an analogy. Sufis, also traditionally, use analogies familiar to the people whom they are addressing. Western readers of this book will all know the story of Hans Christian Andersen, generally called the tale of the Ugly Duckling. The duckling thought that it was ugly; and so it was, seen from the point of view of the ducks. All ended well, because it was discovered that he was a swan. The germ of this story is to be found in Jalaluddin Rumi's *Mathnawi*, where a point is stressed which has been lost in the Danish version, aimed at a different audience. Rumi tells his hearers that they are "ducks, being brought up by hens." They have to realize that their destiny is to swim, not to try to be chickens.

While the subject of magic and miracles is looked at from a chicken standpoint by a duckling, his opinions, to say the least, are likely to be inaccurate.

The Scandinavian fabulist gave the story an encouraging flavor. The duckling became a swan by the inevitable process of growing up. Rumi, always an evolutionist, points out that the chick must realize that it is destined to become a duck.

Miracles are now seen as a part of the development pattern of human life. This attitude removes them from the preoccupation of the theologian, who seeks to justify them on the lower level; and from the sceptic, who seeks to explain them in terms of scientific theory. They have a significant function of their own. In communities where the "age of miracles is past," the miracle phenomenon therefore continues to operate. One might say that, although the volcano is no longer a dragon belching fire, it is still in existence as a volcano.

Retaining our metaphor, we can now descry a sense of process in physical phenomena, though the symbolism may change. The Turkish secret society in Cyprus, dedicated to unifying and projecting the dynamic of a community in its evolution, was known as *Volkan* (volcano), thus neatly translating the feeling of inner or underground force from the physical, transplanted from seemingly independent nature-force to the human community.

This approach to miracles means that, however attractive a recital of wonders performed by anyone may be, such a rehearsal will not have the same function as the actual event which is being reported. This is the explanation of the Sufi teaching, "Let the miracle act," reflected in part by the Spanish proverb *Haga el miraglo, si hagalo Mahoma*—Let the miracle be done, even though Mohammed do it.

A degeneration of this sense is the doctrine "The end justifies the means."

The Sufis, however, do not lose sight of the attendant belief that, if the seeming miracle is of importance in the development of a group (in this case the Sufis), it is more likely to occur in a progressing group, in order to make the progress of the group faster or more solid. "The miracle," says Kamaluddin, "is a foretaste of the power of the group, which is developing organs capable of attaining miracles. Two things are developing simultaneously—the right attitude toward miracles and the harmonious yoking of the Seeker with the miracle factor." Again looking at the question in an evolutionary light, it might be said that the man who is lost in crude wonder at the marvels of a motorcar, a miracle of a thing, will be slow to step into his proper function, which is to use that car, or to be transported by it.

This limiting effect of the sense of wonderment is the reason why Sufi teachers have spoken against indulgence in the ecstatic experience, which is only a stage in the development of the Sufi. Lost in awe and wonderment, the Sufi Seeker is halted when he should be going forward to the realization beyond. The seeking of temporary (or even permanent) mystical experience is therefore spoken of as a "veil."

True reality is held to be beyond ecstasy, as Kalabadhi of Bokhara says in his *Kitabel-Taaruf*. Junaid (of Baghdad, died 910—one of the first classical authors) says that in

ecstasy man is delighted; but when truth comes, it takes
ecstasy's place. He mentions passing through the standard
Sufi experience of ecstasy followed by unawareness of
ecstasy.

A man pestered the teacher Nourettin for information
about magical powers, healing gifts, and inner satisfaction
through the Sufi Way.

Nourettin said, "You are prowling around our campfire,
brother. Shed wolfish acquisitiveness and sup with us, not
upon us. You are in the wrong order of thinking. One thing
must come before another."

The visitor said, "Then give me some impressions of you
and your friends, that I may decide whether to make common cause with you." The teacher said, "If you measure us
against your present ideas, you will be looking through a
cloudy glass at the sun. This will make you represent us
in relation to your present ideas and those of your friends
or enemies. If you collect odd facts about us, your collecting will be determined by a method of selection different
from the method used in making a posy like ours. Unfortunately for the final aim, the posy may look good, but it will
not provide the scent which you need."

While there is no need to consider honest scholars as
wolves prowling around the Sufi campfire, the bafflement
inseparable from trying to study something which is interior
change through external methods remains, and is often expressed: "Who were the Adepts to whom he [Ghazali] *did*
communicate these thrilling secrets? . . . Was there really
anything to communicate? If so, what?"[1]

"[Lane] mentions the regret which a converted Muslim
felt at having to abandon these religious exercises. It is interesting to note that this particular man said that as a dervish
he had developed unusual telepathic power, so that he knew
what was going on at a distance and could even hear words
that were spoken there. Claims to such powers are common-

---

[1] Gairdner, Introduction to the *Niche for Lights,* p. 6.

place in Sufi literature. Certainly stories one has heard from people of unimpeachable veracity confirm the existence of very remarkable powers, whatever the explanation may be."[2]

Speaking of Najmuddin Kubra (died 1221), precursor of Francis of Assisi, the Rev. John Subhan provides a sample of the unusual endowments of Sufi Sheikhs: "The influence of this founder of the Great Brethren (*Ikhwan-i-Kubrawiyya*) was not limited to human beings, but extended to birds and animals. Phenomena of a very similar kind to this are exhibited even today. . . . Standing at the door of his *khanaqah*, his glance fell on a passing dog. Instantly the condition of the dog was changed and it showed such behavior as to correspond to that of a man who had lost himself (i.e., in the mystic sense). Wherever it went dogs gathered round it who would put their paws in his (in token of allegiance) and then withdraw themselves and stand at a respectful distance surrounding it."[3]

In the seesaw of magical belief and literature from ancient times to the middle ages, and then again until today, certain features of magical practice are important Sufistically. Magic surrounds Eastern symbolism in a way which has not yet been understood outside; and the way in which it is understood within Sufi groups is not generally available beyond their walls.

Alchemy is known to be of allegorical as well as literal usage. Magical literature veils a good deal of Sufic material. Exactly how it is used, and what the allegories are, cannot be conveyed satisfactorily. But *sihr*, and *sihr al halal* (permitted magic), according to Islamic legal definition, covers Sufi material part of which is inaccessible elsewhere in written form. Fragments are found in *Jawahir-i-Khamsa* (*Five Jewels*) and is religio-magical. Magic is, then, in this usage, the vehicle for the transmission of allegorical teaching. Sufism has used the permitted terminology of magic

[2] The theologian Professor A. Guillaume, *Islam*, London, 1954, p. 152.

[3] *Sufism, Its Seeds and Shrines*, Lucknow, 1938, p. 182–83.

(as of alchemy, philosophy, science) to convey Sufic material. This technique of using the terms of one discipline to represent another was brought to the West fairly early. As Professor Guillaume notes, the illuminist Sufi Ibn Masarra of Córdoba, for instance, "was the first to introduce into the West an intentionally ambiguous and obscure use of common words, and his example has been followed by most subsequent esoteric writers."[4]

Five Jewels itself is derived in part from the magical books of El-Buni, the Western magician of the Arabs; and the whole high magical tradition of medieval Europe is strongly influenced by literal adaptations of the Spanish Arab schools whose work includes magical documents. One of the reasons for adopting the magical cover was the well-established survival value of magical texts, one of whose characteristics is that no word shall be altered. It may therefore be accepted, as personal investigation has showed, that much of the Sufic lore which would not pass muster in a theological guise was transmitted in a magical one.

Magic is a training system as much as it is anything else. It may be based upon experience, upon tradition of celestial or other ascription, upon religion. Magic not only assumes that it is possible to cause certain effects by means of certain techniques; it also schools the individual in those techniques. Magic, as we know it today, may be subject to every form of rationalization. It embodies, taken as a whole corpus of collected material, minor processes such as small hypnotic techniques, and beliefs which attempt to duplicate natural happenings. While Sufism cannot be taken apart to see what its constituents are, the magical tradition, because it is a truly composite one, can in fact be so dissected. We are only concerned with that part—a very large part—of magic which is involved in the effort to produce new perceptions and to develop new organs of human development.

Looked at in this light, a great part of the human

---

[4] *Op. cit.*, p. 266.

heritage of magical practice (which often includes religious practices) is seen to have been concerned with this quest. Magic is not so much based upon assumptions that things can be done which transcend the normal man's capabilities, as upon the intuitive feeling that, if you like, "faith can move mountains." Those magical activities which are designed to exercise the projection of thought or ideas at a distance, or to see the future, or to attain a contact with a source of superior knowledge, all carry their echo of a dim human consciousness that there is a possibility of man's taking part consciously in the work of evolution; and the feeling of a stirring, evolving organ of perception beyond those senses which are formally recognized by physical science as it stands today.

Magic, then, to the Sufi, is judged according to Sufic criteria. Is it involved in the development of man? If it is, where does it stand in relation to the main Sufi stream? Magic is seen, Sufistically, as generally a deterioration of a Sufic system. The methodology and repute of the system continues, but the essential contact with the continuing destiny of the system is lost. The magician who seeks to develop powers in order to profit by certain extraphysical forces is following a fragment of a system. Because of this, the warnings against the terrible dangers in magical dabbling or obsession are frequent, almost invariable. It is too often assumed that the practitioners imposed a ban on casual magic because they wanted to preserve a monopoly. From the long-term viewpoint it is far more evident that the practitioners themselves have an imperfect knowledge of the whole of the phenomenon, some of whose parts they use. The "terrible dangers" of electricity are not dangers at all to the man who works continuously with electricity, and has a good technical knowledge.

Magic is worked through the heightening of emotion. No magical phenomena take place in the cool atmosphere of the laboratory. When the emotion is heightened to a certain extent, a spark (as it were) jumps the gap, and what appears to be supernormal happenings are experienced. Familiar as an example to most people are poltergeist phenomena. They occur only where there are adolescents or others in a state of relatively continuous nervous (emotional) tension. They hurl stones, seem to cancel the force of gravity, move tremendously heavy objects. When the magician is trying, shall we say, to move a person or an object, or influence a mind in a certain direction, he has to go through a procedure (more or less complicated, more or less lengthy) to arouse and concentrate emotional force. Because certain emotions are more easily roused than others, magic tends to center around personal power, love and hatred. It is these sensations, in the undeveloped individual, which provide the easiest fuel, emotion, "electricity" for the spark to jump the gap which will leap to join a more continuous current. When the present-day followers of the witchcraft tradition in Europe speak of their perambulation of a circle, seeking to raise a "cone of power," they are following this part of the magical tradition.

But the seer, who places himself into a certain state in order to penetrate beyond the time barrier, and the magician, who undergoes a course of training in order to attain a specific object, differ from the Sufi. The Sufi's task is to so organize himself as to make it possible for the meaningful operation of an organ of perception and action which will have a continuing effect. The seer and the magician, like many of the Christian mystics, are not wholly regenerated or reconstituted by the process. The Yogi is altered but not made any more meaningful. The Buddhist contemplative may have attained what he was striving for; but this has no connotation of usefulness or dynamism in the sense of activity, particularly for the community.

Everyone should read Miss Underhill's book, *Mysticism*; and almost anyone who is interested in mysticism will generally be found to have done so. She points out a similarity of thinking between the religious and the magical, between the mystic and the magus. To the Sufi, this similarity is in the end contained in the concept of "forward-reaching." This is the origin of the human movement toward, among other things, civilization, toward progress, toward more knowledge. Miss Underhill considers that the mystic wants to "be" and the magically minded wants to "know." The Sufi attitude is undoubtedly that of "being;" but, unlike the familiar type of mystic, he will use "knowing" as well. He distinguishes between the ordinary knowing of facts and the inner knowing of reality. His activity connects and balances all these factors—understanding, being, knowing.

Sufi methodology, too, organizes the emotional force, which the magician tries to explode, into a correctly running fuel for operating the mechanism of being and knowing.

Both high magic and ordinary mysticism, viewed in this light, become for the Sufi merely the struggling on of a partial methodology which will simply reproduce its own pattern. Unless it evolves far enough to enable it to reproduce more than it inherited, unless, in fact, there is a genetic amplification of scope and sufficient power of reproduction of that scope, the whole thing is a creaking anachronism. At the best it is an escape from the destiny of the individual and the community.

Are magical-type rituals a part of the genuine tradition of the Sufis? They are not. For the Sufi, certain symbols will have certain associative and certain dynamic functions. These he will use, or be influenced by, instinctively. The ritual is not used by the developed Sufi for the developed Sufis, but it may occur, for the concentrating of the thinking involves an exercise of emotional "attachment," and can take place without an equivalent exercise of detachment. Pageantry and ritual as used in non-Sufi life (including processions, regalia, symbolic actions) are viewed by the Sufis as undesirable because they increase the attachment of the attention to something without developing the balancing factor which most people who enjoy traditional pageantry have never even heard of, and obviously often cannot quite grasp if they are simply told about it.

Sufi psychology points to an inner mechanism which attempts automatically to balance emotion-causing impacts. This is in operation when people react against something that they have been told, or which the community or any group is trying to implant in their minds. In the modern West it has given rise to a literary method sometimes known as "debunking." The debunker cannot help doing it, for it represents his own need for fulfillment by balance. His public accept it gratefully because it feeds a hunger caused by emotionality without proper channeling. Intellect does not balance emotion at all, because emotion in this sense is more clearly portrayed as a ballast which has to be correctly distributed, or a burden which has to be well placed, or a force which is being properly used. It is not something which can be suppressed or bypassed by intellect, or which can be inhibited in its expression by thinking; or even which can be properly redirected by exploding it and starting again. When Western psychologists use, say, catharsis to explode emotion or release it, they may apparently fail. If they seem to succeed, they cannot be said to have done more than make the patient more socially acceptable. As far as anyone can tell, he is less troublesome than he was before. This may suit the present phase of society well enough. It is not enough for the Sufi, who considers the human being as something which is "going somewhere," not something which is being kept at, or restored to, some sort of a norm assessed by purely logical or mainly expedient criteria.

All this does not mean that the Sufis are not psychologists. On the contrary, their psychosomatic treatment is of such intense importance to the ordinary world that in many places "Sufi" means "physician," and they are of course considered magicians in consequence; or mystics. But primarily the Sufi is aiming for something, not working with the halt and the lame as a vocation. Indeed, his psychological and healing (making whole) abilities come from his primary objective's operation. His knowledge of the imperfections of supposedly sound humanity is the source of his ability to help obviously unsound humanity. Even in "public," ordinary, traditional mysticism, saints did not become saints because they were healers; they became healers because they were saints—even the greatest of them. This leads back to the question of developed intuition: "When the lion is sick, he eats of a certain shrub and cures himself. He does this because the illness has an affinity for a certain plant, or for the essence of it. The cure is always known to the disease. Release this knowledge and you will know more than the doctor who can only recall facts and memories which seem to apply. There is a difference between hopeful assumptions and positive knowledge. And every case of sickness is slightly different." [*Tibb-al-Arif* (Medicine of the Gnostic), by Abdul-Wali, Salik.]

The *Ikhwan El Safa* (Faithful Friends, generally called in English the Brethren of Sincerity) comprised a secret group which became known through their fifty-two treatises, published from Basra in about 980 A.D. An objective of this school was to make available the whole body of knowledge of tho time. Their field covered philosophy, religion, science and every other branch of learning. They have been accused of being magicians. Like the European Rosicrucians, who may have been influenced by them, they are supposed to have reserved an inner knowledge. The first step toward the realization of this, however, as they saw it, was the establishing of a medium for the dissemination of more ordinary learning. Their individual identity was never established as authors, but their connection with the Sufis is undoubted. Their name—*Safa*—is assonant with one interpretation of the word "Sufi," and the concept of faithfulness in loving friendship is a Sufic one. Their name seems to have been adopted from a group of animals in the collection of allegorical stories called the *Kalilah,* who by their steadfastness preserved themselves from a hunter.

The great master Ghazali shows his debt to them in his *Ihya* (Revival); and among other Sufic teachers, El-Maari, the predecessor of Omar Khayyam, is known to have attended their meetings. El Majriti, the astronomer of Madrid, or his disciple El Karmani of Córdoba, and Averroës took these teachings to the West, including the musical theories which influenced music so profoundly and the moral philosophy which was linked with illumination by the Sufis.

The great Rumi advises harmony with the Brethren of Purity (Sincerity), showing the Sufi character of the mysterious encyclopaedists:

> Think well of the Brothers of Purity
> Even though they show harshness toward you;
> For when evil suspicion takes hold of you
> It severs you from a hundred friends.
> If a tender friend treats you roughly to try you,
> 'Tis contrary to reason to distrust him.[5]

The reference alludes to the Sufi teaching method in which the master may have to test the fortitude of the disciple, or use what seem harsh measures in order to develop bases for Sufic experience.

At some time before 1066, El Majriti (The Madridian) of Córdoba or his disciple El Karmani brought the *Encyclopaedia* of the Brethren to Spain from the Near East. Majriti's scientific work was translated by the Englishman Adelard of Bath, Britain's first Arabist and the greatest English scientist before Roger Bacon.[6] Adelard's importance in Western studies is very great indeed, for he provided an early channel for the transmission of Sufic ideas during the classical phase. Studying in both Spain and Syria, he must have come into contact with the Sufi centers in both areas which were working for the dissemination of book learning plus inner teaching.

Because of his outlook, Adelard has been considered a Platonist, though from the Sufi point of view Platonism is considered a variety of the current later named Sufism. A

---

[5] Whinfield's version, *Mathnawi*, Bk. V, Story X, London, 1887.
[6] Professor P. K. Hitti, *History of the Arabs*, London, 1960, pp. 573 et seq.

contemporary medievalist[7] shows how Sufic views were propounded by him, as a part of his great contribution to the
"center of humane studies and Platonism" of the School
of Chartres: "Adelard's view amounts to making the individual the same as the universal; it is the senses which
impede our minds with the individual. . . . He was the
first thinker of this period to trace the immediate connection between divine ideas and actual being. This was largely
the result of his knowledge of Greek and Arabian science."

But the impact of the Brethren was even more startling
on other forms of mysticism and transcendental thinking in
the West.

Since the eleventh century some of the great minds of
the East and West have been fascinated by the system
known as the Cabala—the Jewish mystical concept of microcosm and macrocosm, with its theoretical and practical
branches. By means of the Cabala, man could understand
himself, wield incalculable power, perform wonders, do and
be almost anything. Eagerly studied and practiced by Jews
and Christians alike, the teaching of the Cabala was
thought to be anchored in the very essence of ancient He-
braic doctrine; the true and ancient teaching which was, in
fact, the inner, secret doctrine. There is no occult school,
no magician, no mystic of the West who is not to some extent influenced by it. The very word is redolent of mystery,
of power. What are the origins of the Cabala?

It is a characteristic of Jewish scholarship that honesty and
detachment are wedded to a search for truth. And hence we
may not be surprised to find that the *Jewish Encyclopaedia* stresses the determining role of the Brethren of Sincerity
on the production of the mighty Cabala system: "The Faithful Brothers of Basra originated the eight elements which
form God," it says, "changed by a Jewish philosopher in
the middle of the eleventh century into ten."[8]

---

[7] Gordon Leff, *Medieval Thought*, London, 1958, pp. 116 et seq.
[8] This alteration of basic Cabalism deprived the Western development of the system of a great deal of its meaning and usefulness.
And Hebrew and Christian Cabala literature later than the twelfth

The Cabala came from the region of the Faithful Brothers
to two places—Italy and Spain. Its system of word manipulation may be derived from parallel and ancient Jewish
teaching, but it is founded upon Arabic grammar. There is
a most intriguing link between the Sufistic stream and the
Jews here, which has caused Sufi teachers to stress the underlying identity of the two. These are some of the facts which
link the Sufis and the Judeo-Christian mystics:

Ibn Masarrah of Spain was a precursor of Solomon Ibn
Gabirol (Avicebron or Avencebrol), who propagated his
ideas. These Sufi tenets "influenced the development of the
Cabala more than any other philosophical system," says the
Jewish Encyclopaedia. And, of course, Ibn Gabirol, the
Jewish follower of the Arab Sufi, exercised an immense and
widely recognized influence upon Western thought. God
is called by the Jewish teacher Azriel in his system of the
Cabala EN SOF, the absolutely infinite, and it was he who
undertook to explain the Cabala to philosophers after its appearance in Europe. There is no doubt that the Arab study
of grammar and the meanings of words is at the base of the
usage of words in the Cabala for mystical purposes. Arabic
grammar was the model for Hebrew grammar. The first
Hebrew grammar was written by the Jew Saadi (died 942)
and was, like all the early ones, in Arabic, and entitled
Kitab al-Lugha, "in Arabic and under the influence of
Arabic philology." (*Jewish Encyclopaedia,* Vol. 6, p. 69) It
was not until the mid-twelfth century that Hebrew grammar started to be studied by Jews in Hebrew.

The Sufis and the Brethren had produced what they considered to be the most ancient teaching, the secret lore of
fulfillment and power, and handed it to the Arabized Jews.
The Jewish Cabalists adapted this teaching to contemporary Jewish thinking, and the Cabala of the Arabs became
the Cabala of the Jews, and later of the Christians. But the
mystical schools of Sufism, which never regarded organized

---

century is therefore only of partial meaning. This includes all aspects
of the Cabala of ten elements, as distinct from the "Eight Cabala."

book knowledge as a sufficient source, continued to ally practice of the Sufic rites with the essentials of the old Cabala teaching, and it was in this form that mysticism among the Jews was influenced, not primarily through the Jewish Cabala.

This Sufi tradition is underlined by the *Jewish Encyclopaedia*, which says: "To the spread of Sufism in the eighth century was probably due the revival of Jewish mysticism in Mohammedan countries at that period. Under the direct influence of the Sufis arose the Jewish sect called Yudghanites." (Vol. xi, p. 579) The effect of the Sufi system upon the mystical Jewish Markabah-riders was so profound that some of the phenomena (the transition of colors and then to colorlessness, for example) produced in the mystic are identical with those of the Sufi. Hasidism, the mystical piety in practice which arose in Poland in the eighteenth century, is not only "the real continuation of the Cabala; but it must be based on Sufism or a part of the Cabala, which is identical with it." The same source notes the "striking analogy" between the practice of the two systems and the "many points in common with Sufism" of the Hasidist activity, including the relationship of the disciples to the master. The very first book of the ethical writings of the Judeo-Arabian period is on a Sufi model. Hence "Sufism has a special claim upon the attention of Jewish scholars, because of its influence on the ethical and mystical writings of the Judeo-Arabian period."

It need hardly be added that the words "Arabian" and "Jewish" have little meaning to the Sufis; and this is one reason why there was such an entente between the Spaniards who followed the Sufi way and transmitted so much of it to the Christian West.

The Cabala was, of course, a formulation, a frame for the attainment of certain objectives. Like most other systems—the framework of Sufi Orders is another—of this kind, it lingered on as a husk after the time for its dissolution and readaptation had passed.

Magic and miracles, for the Sufi, have a similar, active function. They apply for the time and place and other conditions. Since they are both the product of the time and the means of a development, they have to be considered as limited in one respect and continuing in another. While people persist in trying to examine them by other criteria, they will continue to convey a bizarre and useless aspect.

The Teacher, the Teaching, the Taught

> By yourself you can do nothing: seek a Friend.
> If you could taste the slightest bit of your
> insipidity, you would recoil from it.
>
> (Nizami, *Treasury of Mysteries*)

It is often said that the mentality of the Oriental is such that he will readily place himself under the instruction of a teacher, and will follow directions with an obedience which is rare in the West. To anyone who has any real experience of the East, this belief is as erroneous as another Western generalization—that all Eastern countries are more or less the same. The most that can be said about Eastern attitudes toward spiritual teachers is that there are more teachers available, and also more evidence that they are doing some good.

Almost all human beings are reared with some measure of self-reliance, which becomes a habit of thought. Through a quite natural lack of true reasoning, the idea of accepting guidance becomes confused with a loss of freedom. Most people—in East and West alike—do not realize that putting oneself in the hands of an expert implies no loss of personal importance. Inconsistently, they will allow a surgeon to remove their appendixes, but will dispute the superior knowledge or experience of a teacher in a field in which they are as ignorant as in surgery.

Since the Sufis do not preach or try to attract followers, material relating to the approach to a teacher is only found in the statements of developed Sufis, and generally not from those who are themselves teachers. "You go to the priest," says one, "from habit or belief, and because he affirms certain things. You visit the doctor because you have been recommended to him, or because you have a sense of urgency or desperation. You frequent the company of magicians because of an inner weakness; the swordsmith because of an outer strength; the shoemaker because you have seen his wares and want to possess yourself of some. Do not visit the Sufi unless you want to benefit, for he will drive you forth if you start to dispute."

The Sufi belief is that the attraction of a Sufi teacher is essentially because of intuitive recognition; the reasons which the would-be Sufi gives are secondary, rationalization. One Sufi says, "I knew the master was a great and good man before I met him. But only when he brought enlightenment to me did I realize his greatness and goodness to be of a far greater order, far beyond my initial capacity to understand."

The sense of freedom and the reverse tends to be a subjective one in the ordinary man. A Sufi records: "My teacher liberated me from the captivity in which I was; the captivity in which I thought I was free, when in fact I was actually revolving within a pattern."

The uncritical carry-over of the sense of self-reliance into fields where it does not in fact operate is illustrated in this autobiographical fragment from a Sufi: "I resolved that I should tread the mystic Path alone, and struggled to do so, until an inner voice said to me, 'You go to a pathfinder to show you a road through a wilderness—or will you prefer to seek your own way and destroy yourself in the process?' "[1]

[1] See annotation "Nonrational Concern."

While some Sufic faculties may develop spontaneously, the Sufi personality cannot mature in solitude, because the Seeker does not know exactly which way he is heading, in which order his experiences will come. He is at the beginning subject to his own weaknesses, which influence him, and from which a teacher "shields" him. For this reason Sheikh Abu al-Hasan Saliba said: "Better place a disciple under the control of a cat than under his own control." Just as a cat's impulses are varying and uncontrollable, so are those of the would-be Sufi at an early stage.

This parallel of unregenerate man as largely animal, endowed with faculties which he cannot yet properly use, is frequent in Sufi teaching: "The more animal the man, the less he understands of teachership. To him the Guide may seem like the hunter, requiring him to enter a cage. I was like this," states Aali-Pir. "The untrained hawk thinks that if he is captured, as he calls it, he will be enslaved. He does not realize that the hawkmaster will give him a fuller life, perched freely on the wrist of the King, without the perpetual preoccupations of food and fear. The only difference between human and animal here is that the animal fears everyone. The human claims that he is assessing the reliability of the teacher. What he is really doing is smothering his intuition, his inclination to place himself in the hands of one who knows the Way."

There is, again, an interaction between the teacher and the taught, which can hardly exist if there is no teacher. The Sufi pattern of words, action and cooperation requires three things: the teacher, the learner and the community or school. Rumi refers to this complex of activity when he says:

> Ilm-amozi tariqish qawli ast
> Harfa-amozi tariqish fa'li ast
> Faqr-amozi az sohbat qaim ast.

"Science is learned by words; art by practice; detachment by companionship."

And, since the very manner of learning must itself be learned, Rumi says in another place: "That which is a stone to the ordinary man is a pearl to him who knows."

The function of the teacher is to open the mind of the Seeker, so that he may become accessible to a recognition of his destiny. In order to do this, man must realize how much of his ordinary thinking is cramped by assumptions. Until this point is reached, true understanding is impossible, and the candidate is only fit for one or another of the more usual human organizations which train him to think along certain lines: "Open the door of your mind to the waif of understanding; for you are poor and it is rich." (Rumi)

Sufism may be viewed in one sense as struggling against the use of words to establish patterns of thinking whereby mankind is kept at a certain stage of ineptitude; or made to serve organisms which are ultimately not of evolutionary value.

A Sufi was once asked why the Sufis use words in a special sense, possibly removed from their accustomed significance. His answer was: "Rather ponder upon why the ordinary man suffers from the tyranny of words, immobilized by custom until they only serve as tools."

The relationship between the teacher and the person taught cannot be understood in Sufism apart from the teaching. A part of the teaching stands outside time and space. This corresponds to the element in the teacher and the learner which has a similar status. A part of the teaching is within all of the many aspects into which the ordinary human consciousness splits up experience, life and the world of forms. An interaction of a special kind is producing a transformation. This relationship, therefore, far transcends in ultimate meaning the usual scope of teaching and learning. The Sufi teacher is more than one who is passing on formal knowledge; more than one who is in a state of harmony with the learner; more than a machine which imparts a portion of a stock of information that is available in stored form. And he is teaching more than a method of thinking, or an attitude to life; more even than a potentiality to self-development.

The Czech Professor Erich Heller, in his preface to a book which rapidly became a classic of teaching in the mid-twentieth century, touches on the problem of studying literature, and especially of teaching it. He says that the teacher "is involved in a task which would appear impossible by the standards of the scientific laboratory—to teach what, strictly speaking, cannot be taught, but only 'caught,' like a passion, a vice, or a virtue." (*The Disinherited Mind*, London, 1952)

The function of the Sufi teacher is even more complex than this. Unlike the teacher of literature, however, he has no task in the usual sense of the word. His task is in being, being himself; and it is through the proper functioning of that being that his meaning is projected. Thus it is that there is no division in the public and private personality of the Sufi teacher. He who has one face in the classroom and another at home, who has a professional attitude or a bed-side manner, is not a Sufi. This consistency, however, is within himself. His external behavior may very well appear to change, but his inner personality is unified.

The actor, who gets "into the skin of the part," cannot be a Sufi teacher. The man or woman whose official face runs away with him, so that he is carried away by a temporary personality, cannot be a Sufi teacher. One does not have to be as advanced a case as Walter Mitty, the creation of James Thurber, to experience "involvement," a state which is possible only to those at a low level of Sufi awareness. Teachership cannot come through anyone prone to temporary possession by a character.

Yet, so firmly established in the ordinary man is the habit of alternating personality that it is socially accepted to "act a part." In a very large proportion of instances of this standard social procedure, there is a carry-over of the synthetic or alternate personality. This is not in itself considered to be an evil; it is undoubtedly an indication of immaturity in the Sufic sense.

This inner unification of personality, expressed through a diversity of ways, means that the Sufi teacher does not resemble the outer, idealized personality of the literalist. The calm, never-changing personality, the aloof master, or the personality which inspires awe alone, the "man who never varies" cannot be a Sufi master. The ascetic who has attained detachment from things of the world and is thus himself an externalized incarnation of what seems to the externalist to be detached is not a Sufi master. The reason is not far to seek. That which is static becomes useless in the organic sense. A person who is always, as far as can be ascertained, calm and collected, has been trained to have this function, the function of detachment. He "never shows agitation;" and, by depriving himself of one of the functions of organic as well as mental life, he has reduced his range of activity. The overtrained becomes muscle-bound.

Detachment, for the Sufi, is a part, only a portion, of dynamic interchange. Sufism works by alternation. Detachment of intellect is useful only if it enables the practitioner to *do* something as a result. It cannot be an end in itself in any system which is dealing with humanity's self-realization.

In partial or derelict metaphysical systems, of course, the means has become an end. The attaining of detachment, or immobility, or benignity (which are all parts of any individual's development) are considered to be so strange, or desirable *in themselves*, and so rarely attainable, that the practitioner "settles for" them.

A further development comes when rationalizations are provided, intended to prove that the attainment of detachment, or asceticism, or any of the other partial developments, has some sort of sublime or infinite meaning. "So-and-so attained complete detachment, and as a result he was supremely enlightened," and much more of this becomes the legend. Of course the one does not follow from the other, but somehow it seems to follow. In Western

Europe you will hear, from otherwise quite sensible people, such non sequiturs as "So-and-so is wonderful; he can control his heartbeat. I always go to him for advice about my personal problems." If the same person were told: "So-and-so is wonderful; he can type ninety words a minute—take your problems to him," the reaction would be instant indignation.

A person can only teach, in the metaphysical area and giving him the benefit of any doubt about sincerity, what he actually believes to be true. If he teaches you that through standing on your head you will reach some sort of mystical goal, he must first arouse in you some degree of belief that it has already been attained by this method. This is what might be called positive affirmation, and may be accepted or rejected. The Sufi teaching method embraces a wider field. By drawing attention to other points of view than conventional ones, and by practicing a complex of activities collectively termed Sufism, the teacher endeavors to make available to the learner the materials which will develop his consciousness. His procedure, as Sir Richard Burton remarks, may even appear to be destructive, but is "essentially reconstructive." Rumi refers to this factor when he talks about pulling down a house in order to find a treasure. A man does not want his house pulled down, even though the treasure is of greater use to him than the building for which (for the purposes of this illustration we may assume this) he has no special affection. The treasure, as Rumi says, "is the reward of the pulling down of the house." It is not a matter of being compelled to break eggs before an omelet can be made; but of the eggs doing their own breaking in order to be able to aspire to omelethood.

The "guide, philosopher and friend" who is the Sufi teacher, then, performs what may be considered to be many functions. As a guide he shows the Way—but the aspirant must himself do the walking. As a philosopher he loves wisdom, in the original meaning of the term. But love, to him, implies action, not merely enjoyment or even the despair of one-sided love. As a friend he is a companion and adviser, provides reassurance and a point of view which is influenced by his perception of the other's needs.

The Sufi teacher is the link between the disciple and the goal. He embodies and symbolizes both the "work" itself, of which he is a product, and also the continuity of the system, the "chain of transmission." Just as the army officer symbolizes, for practical purposes, the State and its objectives for the private soldier, so the Sufi symbolizes the *tarika,* the wholeness of the Sufi entity.

The Sufi teacher cannot be an earthshaking personality who attracts millions of adherents and whose fame reverberates into every corner of the earth. His stage of illumination is visible for the most part only to the enlightened. Like a radio receiving apparatus, the human being can perceive only those physical and metaphysical qualities which are within his range. Therefore the man (or woman) who is bemused and impressed by the personality of a teacher will be the person whose awareness is insufficient to handle the impact and make use of it. The fuse may not blow, but the element becomes destructively or inefficiently incandescent. "A blade of grass cannot pierce a mountain. If the sun that illumines the world were to draw nigher, the world would be consumed." (Rumi, *Mathnawi,* Bk. I, Whinfield's version) The evolving man can only glimpse the qualities of the stage next above him. Obviously, even on the physical analogy, the generality of people cannot even perceive the real qualities of the sage, the man of the fourth stage of Sufic development, when he is at the first or second stage.

The comparison which is used by Sufis is this—a little light is useful to the bat. The brilliance of the sun is useless to him, even though he may become intoxicated by it.

The so-called free or rational mind, when approaching problems of teachership, makes the most amazing assumptions. A person who says, "I will follow someone who satisfies me that he is genuine," is only saying, together with the savage, "If a person appears to me to have strange powers or otherwise defeats my mechanism of assessment, I shall be prepared to obey him." Such a person is useful to the jungle witch doctor who has just imported "miraculous" magnesium flares from Germany; but he is of little use to himself. Still less use is he to the Sufi cause; because he is not ready for truth, however ready he may be for bewilderment. He must have intuitive capacity for recognizing truth.

A man came to Libnani, a Sufi teacher, while I was sitting with him, and this interchange took place:

Man: "I wish to learn, will you teach me?"

Libnani: "I do not feel that you know how to learn."

Man: "Can you teach me how to learn?"

Libnani: "Can you learn how to let me teach?"

The variety of teachers is enormous in Sufism, partly because they consider themselves to be a part of an organic process. This means that their impact upon humanity may be taking place without any consciousness on the part of humanity of the relationship. As one example, the Sufi of the middle ages might move from place to place dressed in a patchwork garment, and teach by signs, perhaps not speaking, perhaps saying cryptic words. He established no formal school himself, but made sure that the message of Sufihood was communicated to people in the countries through which he passed. This strange figure is known to have operated in Spain and elsewhere in Europe. The name given the silent teacher who performed strange movements, incidentally, was *aghlaq* (plural *aghlaqin,* pronounced with gutteral "r" and European "q" as *arlakeen, arlequin*). This is an Arabic play upon the words for "great door" and "confused speech." There can be little doubt that his appearance to the uninitiated is perpetuated in the Harlequin.

A Sufi Adept may dress in a patchwork coat or in ordinary clothes. He may be young or old. Hujwiri mentions an encounter with a youthful teacher of this kind. A man who wanted to learn about Sufism saw the youth dressed as an Adept, but with an ink bottle at his side. He thought that this was unusual, for Sufis are not scribes. He approached the "imposter" whom he took to be a scribe profiting by the repute of the patchwork robe, and asked him what Sufism was. "Sufism," was the answer, "is not to think that because a man carries a pot of ink he is not a Sufi."

While a Sufi may attain illumination within a long or a short time, he cannot actually teach until he has received the Robe of Permission (to enroll students) from his own mentor; and by no means are all Sufis material for teachership. The esoteric interpretation of a certain joke sums this up:

> Nim-hakim khatrai jan
> Nim-mulla khatrai iman.

> The half-physician is a danger to life;
> The half-priest is a threat to faith.

The half-Sufi, in this sense, may be a man who is liberated from the need for being himself a disciple, but who has to continue along the Way himself to the final attainment. Being preoccupied with his own development, he cannot teach.

The teacher is referred to as the Sage (arif), guide (murshid), Elder (pir) or Sheikh (leader, chief). A great many other words are used, in different shades of meaning denoting the precise nature of the relationship between members of a group and their teacher.

There are three routes which can be indicated by the teacher for the postulant. In most Sufi systems, the beginner goes through a novitiate of a thousand and one days, in which his ability to receive instruction is assessed and increased. If he does not fulfill this period (which may be figurative, and consist of another period of days), he will have to leave the precincts of the school (madrasa). The second route is when the teacher accepts an applicant directly, without having him attend the general assemblies of the group or circle (halka or daira), and gives him special exercises to perform in concert with himself and independently. The third route is when, after assessing the capacities of the student, the teacher accepts him formally but sends him to another teacher who specializes in the exercises which will more directly benefit him. Only the teachers of certain schools apply all the exercises which might be indicated—generally the schools of Central Asia, and especially the Naqshbandi element called the Azimiyya, who incorporate numerous teaching methods in a form of overlap procedure.

Such teachers have a combined method which is centered within their inner circle, technically termed the *markaz*, "centrifuge, center of a circle, headquarters." A session of Sufis performing such exercises is referred to as a *markaz*; though when not actually engaged in exercises they might be termed a *majlis* (a session).

All Sufi teachings being disposed toward multiple meaning, depending upon how much or on what level the individual can grasp them, there are many illusions in literature to the role of the teacher which are sometimes translated literally. Rumi, as an instance, says: "The worker is concealed in the workshop." This is generally taken to refer to the immanence of God. In the theological sense this is completely true, and like all Sufi teachings it is considered to convey objective truth. This means that it is true in every possible interpretation. Insofar as it is applied to teachership, however, it means that the Sufi Guide is a part of the "work" as well as the teacher of the Sufis—the whole process, teacher, teaching and taught, is a single phenomenon.

The implicit consequence that teachership cannot be studied in isolation where the Sufis are concerned is considered a central fact of high initiatory importance. The would-be student of the Sufis may not be able or inclined to grasp it; but unless the Sufi grasps it, he cannot be a Sufi at all.

For this reason the function and character of the Sufi

teacher is always allowed to grow in the perception, by means of such material as has been assembled above, together with the actual practice of Sufism.

Professor A. J. Arberry of Cambridge, who has approached Sufism from a consistently sympathetic, academic viewpoint, shows the difficulties which have to be faced by the externalist or intellectual worker, the "obscurity of a doctrine based largely on experiences in their very nature well nigh incommunicable."[2]

I was present one day when a Sufi Sheikh in the Near East was being closely questioned by a foreign student of the occult who was desperate to know how he could recognize a Sufi teacher, and whether the Sufis had any Messianic legends foreshadowing the possibility of a Guide who would bring people back to metaphysical awareness. "You yourself are destined to be a leader of this sort," said the Sheikh, "and Eastern mystics will be prominent in your life. Keep faith." Later he turned to his disciples and said, "That was what he came here for. Do you refuse a child a sweetmeat, or tell a lunatic that he is insane? It is not our function to rehabilitate the ineducable. When a man says, 'How do you like my new coat?' you must not say, 'It is horrible,' unless you can manage to give him a better one, or teach him better taste in dress. Some people cannot be taught.

"Rumi said: 'You cannot teach by disagreement.'"

[2] Arberry, *Tales from the Masnavi*, London, 1961, p. 19.

The Far East

Fishes, asking what water was, went to a
wise fish. He told them that it was all
around them, yet they still thought that
they were thirsty.

(Nasafi)

The influence of Sufism upon Indian mystical life has been
so great that several schools which had been considered to
be the product of ancient Hinduism are revealed by scholars
to have originated in Sufi teachings. This historical fact is
of less importance to the Sufi than the fact that the mystical
stream, its source, is essentially one. The different outward
aspects of mysticism in the Far East have generally caused
it to be assumed that the cults are independent products of
the culture in which they are rooted. But such a view of life
is impossible to those who believe that there is only one
truth, and that those who know it must communicate and
cannot remain in compartments.

Over a thousand years ago the seed which was to bloom
into a variety of meditative schools of apparently Hindu
origin was planted in India. The love mysticism of the
bhakti type is one example, here noted by Dr. Tara Chand,
in the *Cultural History of India*:

Certain other characteristics of South Indian thought

from the ninth century onward, however, strongly
point to Islamic influence. They are the increasing
emphasis on monotheism, emotional worship, self-
surrender (*parpatti*) and adoration of the teacher
(*guru bhakti*), and, in addition to them, laxity in the
rigors of the caste system and indifference to mere
ritual . . . absorption in God, through devotion to a
teacher. . . . The Sufi conception of the deified teacher
was incorporated into medieval Hinduism.

Dr. Chand, great scholar though he is, fails to note here
that the significant points which he lists are, in their grouping and emphasis, Sufic rather than directly Islamic in the
usual sense—in the sense in which they are understood
by the Moslem clergy. In most Indian cults the role of the
deified teacher has been perverted from its originally Sufi
nature, and has undergone a transformation which has
given later Hindu schools a non-Sufi emphasis. All too often
these are the cults which fascinate Western students, anxious to find spirituality in action in the East, who tend to
be reduced to attachment to mere derivatives of Sufi schools,
which use the trappings of Hinduism.

Although they undoubtedly had something to build upon,
it was the Sufi teachers who were responsible in great measure for the establishing of what became known as great
Hindu schools of mysticism. Auguste Barth notes in his
Religions of India the correspondence between the geographical and chronological settlement of Sufis in India and
the rise of what were later to be thought Indian mystical
schools of great antiquity:

It is precisely in these parts that, from the ninth to
the twelfth century, those great religious movements
took their rise which are connected with the names of
Sankara,[1] Ramanuja, Ananda Tirtha and Basava, out

[1] Vedanta is a revival, based upon the ancient Hindu scriptures
interpreted over a thousand years after their composition by Sankara
(788–820). This system (Vedanta means "completion of the Vedas")

of which the majority of the historical sects came and to which Hinduism presents nothing analogous until a much later period.

One factor has prevented students from being able to check the claims to great antiquity made for the mystical movements among the Hindus. This was, strange though it may seem to most readers, the fact that the early Hindu religious literature was written down only in the late eighteenth and early nineteenth centuries, at the instance of such British scholars as Sir William Jones.[2] "Ancient documents scarcely exist. The oldest Indian manuscript is thought to be a Buddhist fragment on birch bark of the late fifth century A.D., from Taxila. The Bakhshali manuscript, of the same material, seems the next claimant for high antiquity, though this is only of the twelfth century."[3] The Bhakti and reformist movements in Hinduism, which produced such great names as Madhva, Ramananda and Kabir, are based to a great extent upon Sufi thought and practice, introduced into India after the Islamic conquest. Kabir "spent considerable time with Moslem Sufis;" Dadu "manifests perhaps even greater knowledge of Sufism than his predecessors . . . perhaps because the Sufis of Western India wielded greater influence upon the minds of the seekers after God, Hindu or Moslem, than those of the East," says Tara Chand, who is not himself a Sufi.

The Sikh religion, it is a matter of historical fact, was founded by the Sufized Hindu Guru Nanak, who freely admitted his debt to Sufism. Of him the *Cultural History* says:

covers the ground introduced by Ghazali, Ibn El-Arabi and Rumi, following the Sufi ancients. The resemblance of Kant's work to Vedanta is attributable to the Sufi philosophical stream. See: *The Absolution of Sankacarya as Compared with Mawlana Jalal Uddin Rumi's School of Thought* by the Turkish scholar Rasih Guven, in *Prajna*, Pt. I, 1958, pp. 93–100.

[2] Professor S. Piggott, *Prehistoric India*, London, 1961, p. 235.
[3] *Ibid.*, p. 252.

Manifestly he was steeped in Sufi lore, and the fact of the matter is that it is far harder to find how exactly he drew from the Hindu scriptures. His rare references to them lead one to imagine that Nanak was only superficially acquainted with the Vedic and Puranic literature.

The name "Sikh" means Seeker, the style used for the Sufi traveler.

Maharshi Devendranath Tagore (1815–1905)—the father of Rabindranath Tagore—spent two years in the Himalayas. During this time he was not studying the scriptures of his Hindu patrimony, but a poem from the Sufi master Hafiz, as a consequence of which he was rewarded with a beatific vision, according to another Hindu savant, Professor Hanumantha Rao.

The later Sufi teachers in India, many of whom followed the Turkish, Afghan and Persian conquerors, had an effect upon the country which is second to none. One of the consequences of their arrival was that the Hindus actually adopted the Arabic word for a dedicated Sufi—Fakir—and applied it to themselves.

Whole books have been filled with the amazing deeds and miracles attributed to these men, and even today millions of people of every persuasion gather to worship or invoke their aid as saints.

Muinuddin Chishti, the founder of the Chishti Order in India, was sent to Ajmer in the middle of the twelfth century, to bring his teaching to the Hindus. The Raja Prithvi Raj, who resented his arrival, is reputed to have assembled soldiers and magicians to stop him entering the city. The soldiers were struck blind when the saint, following a precedent of the Prophet, threw a handful of pebbles toward them. One glance from the eyes of Muinuddin, we are told, and three hundred Yogis and Pandits were unable to open their mouths, and became his disciples. But by far the most impressive tale is that of the supernatural combat between the famous Hindu magician Jaypal Yogi and the Sufi Fakir.

Jaypal brought with him some thousands of his Yogi disciples, according to the Chishti legend, and cut off the water supply to Lake Anasagar. One of the Chishti's new converts, under Muinuddin's orders, took one bucketful of water out of the lake—whereupon every stream and well in the area became dry.

Jaypal sent hundreds of apparitions, including lions and tigers, to attack the saint and his following. They were all destroyed as soon as they touched the magic circle which Muinuddin had drawn for protection. After a number of similar feats, Jaypal surrendered and became one of the Chishti's most famous disciples, known as Abdullah of the Wilderness, because he is supposed to wander eternally in the vicinity of the great shrine at Ajmer.

There are, quite perceptibly, three levels of contact between the Sufis and the Hindu or Sikh mystics. A misunderstanding of this has been responsible for much confusion. In the historical and cultural context, as well as in the truly metaphysical one, all parties share a sense of unity of aims in the role of mysticism to develop man. They are also at one in their essential harmony. It is in the field of rigid and repetitious ritual, fossil dogma and personality veneration that there are very considerable rifts.

The narrow, morbidly formalist Moslem who is following a superficial Sufic way will clash almost invariably with his opposite number, the professional Hindu ascetic wedded to a deteriorated tradition.

Since it is these last who make the most noise and show, it is they who are taken, all too often, by outsiders as genuine representatives of the mystical stream of India. Their studied asceticism and worldly endowments are almost always far more striking and attention compelling than the schools of the real mystics. They also tend to burst into print, to provide material for documentary photographers, to recruit disciples from abroad, to try to spread their teaching as widely as possible. Many of the Eastern-based cults of the Western world are in fact nothing more than derivations of these menageries, which have assumed the traditions and superficial color of the authentic tradition.

They tend not to accord with the advice of the great teacher, Sheikh Abdullah Ansari, felicitously translated by a distinguished Sikh, the Sardar Sir Jogendra Singh:

"Fasting is only the saving of bread. Formal prayer is for old men and women. Pilgrimage is a worldly pleasure. Conquer the heart—its mastery is conquest indeed. The Sufi Law of Life requires:

> Kindness to the young
> Generosity to the poor
> Good counsel to friends
> Forbearance with enemies
> Indifference to fools
> Respect to the learned."

There is an interesting interaction between Hindu thought and Sufi teaching, an example of which is contained in the commentary on the *Slokas*. A great deal of Hindu popular wisdom is contained in a series of sayings called *Slokas*, passed on from a teacher to his disciple. Sufi commentary, such as that of Ajami, holds that the *Slokas* as generally circulated are one half of a double system of instruction. Like the fables of Aesop or the tales of Saadi, they may be read either as merely good advice upon which one could rear one's children, or for their inner meaning.

Here are some of the *Slokas* (s), together with Ajami's comment (c) which is used as an exercise by Indian Sufis. These *Slokas* have been numbered in accordance with Abbe Dubois' great work, *Hindu Manners, Customs and Ceremonies* (Oxford, 1906, pp. 474 et seq.):

(s) V. In the afflictions, misfortunes and tribulations of life, only he who actively helps us is our friend.

(c) Study whether you know what help is. Enlightenment is necessary before the wild one knows it.

(s) XI. The venom of a scorpion is found in its tail, that of a fly in its head, that of a serpent in its fangs. But the venom of a wicked man is to be found in all parts of his body.

(c) Meditate upon the good of a good man, equally well distributed.

(s) XVIII. The virtuous man may be compared to a large leafy tree which, while it is itself exposed to the heat of the sun, gives coolness to others by covering them with its shade.

(c) The virtue of a good man will assist the sincere, but will weaken the indolent. Shelter is only a respite from work.

(s) XLI. A shameless man fears the maladies engendered by luxury, a man of honor fears contempt, a rich person fears the rapacity of kings, gentleness fears violence, beauty fears old age, the penitent fears the influence of the senses, the body fears Yama, the god of death; but the miser and the envious fear nothing.

(c) Be a wise man, for he understands the nature of fear. It is therefore his slave.

There had been a thousand years' interchange between the Sufis and Hindu mystics before any Western scholar interested himself in Indian mysticism. In the seventeenth century Prince Dara Shikoh of the Mogul line carried out a thorough assessment of Vedic literature and a comparison between Islamic and Hindu modes of thought. Like the Sufi teachers before him, he came to the conclusion that Hindu scriptures were the remnant of an esoteric tradition identical with that of Islam, and in its most inner sense precisely the same as the Sufi one.

His researches included also the sacred books of the Jews and Christians, studied from the point of view that they might represent the exteriorization of an inevitable development of human consciousness concentrated from time to time in certain population groups. It is upon the basis of his work, which itself follows the attitude of the scholars of Haroun el-Rashid of Baghdad, that a great deal of subsequent, even quite modern, mystical comparison rests.

The work of Dara Shikoh, striking because carried on by a Moslem prince of a family ruling a land of unbelievers, is only one expression of the contact carried on by Sufis throughout India for centuries. In this respect the process can be seen as closely approaching that which took place in medieval Europe, when the existence of a strong and authoritarian Church did not prevent the development of groups such as those Sufi-organized ones which we have unearthed in previous chapters.

The role of Sufism, however, should not be considered to be one of projecting the results of comparative religious study and stressing the theosophical theory of the essential unity of religious manifestations. There has never been a time when the Sufis did not regard themselves as being involved in a task—the task of transcending outward forms and making common cause with the religious *fact*, the acquisition of knowledge about religion by means of itself. While it might be difficult to explain in the cruder terms of accepted formal religion that there was a unity in experience, that unity was nevertheless there all the time. The nearest that one can get in familiar terminology to this fact is to say that for the Sufi and other mystics of the Sufic stream, this was a psychological study, not an academic one. The object of the study, again using the limited phraseology available to us here, was to make oneself available to the inner motivation which was trying to produce a further development in human consciousness. Mysticism and religion, therefore, are looked upon as the yoking of the individual and the group with the destiny of mankind as expressed in a mental urge.

A resemblance between Sufi thought and practice and the strange, allegedly typical Buddhistic cult of Zen as practiced in Japan is of great interest. Zen claims to be a secret transmission outside of the canonical Buddhist field, passed on by individual example and teaching. Historically it is of no great age, and it is not connected even by its practitioners with any special event in the life of Buddha.

Its earliest records date from the eleventh century, while the earliest school to be founded in Japan was brought from China in 1191.

The period during which Zen was imported into Japan corresponds with the modern growth of Indian schools under Sufi impetus. Its place of origin—South China—is the location where there were settlements of Arabs and other Moslems for centuries. Buddhism itself in Japan only dates from the year 625, and mainly came into the islands between the second half of the seventh century and the beginning of the ninth century. Moslem and Sufi penetration and conquest of the traditional Buddhist shrines of Central Asia was well under way by then; it was from the great Buddhist strongholds of Afghanistan that the Buddha cult entered Tibet, after the Moslem conquest.

There are legends connecting Chinese Zen with India, and Sufi tradition asserts that the early classical Sufis made spiritual contact with the followers of *bodd*, just as they had found a common denominator with the mystics of the Hindus.

The similarities between Zen and Sufism, both in terminology, stories and activities of masters, are considerable. From the Sufi viewpoint, the practice of Zen as given in popular literature resembles irresistibly the working of a part of the techinque of the "impact" (*zarb*) of Sufism.

Dr. Suzuki, the foremost literary Zen exponent, would seem to be right in considering Zen adapted to the Far Eastern mind, but ideas, allegories and examples contained in Sufi teaching were well established centuries before the Zen teacher Yengo (c. 1566–1642) wrote the letter quoted in answer to "What is Zen?" Those who have read the foregoing chapters of this book will be well familiar with such phraseology as this, if allowance is made for a Far Eastern staccato turn of speech:

> It is presented right to your face, and at this moment the whole thing is handed over to you. For an intelligent fellow, one word should suffice to convince him of the truth of it, but even then error has crept in. Much more so when it is committed to paper and ink, or given up to wordy demonstration or to logical quibble, then it slips further away from you. The great truth of Zen is possessed by everybody. Look into your own being and seek it not through others. Your own mind is above all forms; it is free and quiet and sufficient paternally stamps itself on your six senses and four elements. In it light is absorbed. Hush the dualism of subject and object. Forget both, transcend the intellect, sever yourself from understanding, and directly penetrate deep into the identity of the Buddha-mind; outside of this there are no realities.[4]

It would be easy to attempt to build upon these striking facts a case for the transmission of Sufism and the ultimate derivation of what is now called Zen from that source. But, according to Sufi belief, the basis must always have been there, working in the human mind. Any Sufic contact would merely have helped to rekindle the inner consciousness of the only true reality.

A Chinese Sufi, Mr. H. L. Ma, speaking at a meeting of the Hong Kong Metaphysical Association a decade ago, shows how the way of putting ideas can seem to vary with the cultural environment:

> With respect to all the Seekers of Truth, I must say that Su-fi is hard to impart. Why? Because new hearers expect the unfolding of a system to follow their accepted pattern of thought. They do not know that this pattern is what is wrong with them. Su-fi is in you al-

4 Suzuki, *An Introduction to Zen Buddhism*, London, 1959, p. 46.

ready. You feel it but you do not know what it is. When you feel certain feelings of kindness, love, truth, wanting to do something with all of you—that is Su-fi. You think of yourself first—that is not Su-fi. You have a strong sympathy for a worthy sage—that is Su-fi. . . . A master, asked what Su-fi is, hits the questioner. He means by this, "Show me the pain and I will show you Su-fi." You say to master, "Where did the Light come from?" He blows it out. He means: "You tell me where it is gone, and I will tell you where it came from." You cannot tell in words what you ask in words. . . .

This may sound extremely Oriental to the Western reader, but the illustrations used (the pain and the candle) are not Far Eastern analogies at all. They come directly from the teachings of the "Western master," Rumi. The method of presentation of the ideas, rapid and parabolic, however, seem very Chinese. Yet they retain the spirit of the Sufi.

It is Colonel Clarke's way of putting his impressions of the Sufis, however, which gives the more Western mind a chance to grasp what the orientation of the schools is, and produces an atmosphere which is necessary to the Western mind:

"The sublime love poetry of the Sufi saints, the wholly practical nature of their teachings, the fervor allied with a deeply underlying sense of mission, of attainment of needs, both spiritual and physical, the confidence of the message and the future of the human race: these are some of the outstanding contributions of this wonderful body, admission to whose numbers conveys the undoubted and abiding sensation of membership of an ancient elect."[5]

[5] Col. A. Clarke, *Letters to England*, Calcutta, 1911, p. 149.

APPENDIX I
Esoteric Interpretation of the Koran

For the Sufis of the classical period, the Koran is the encoded document which contains Sufi teachings. Theologians tend to assume that it is capable of interpretation only in a conventionally religious way; historians are inclined to look for earlier literary or religious sources; others for evidence of contemporary events reflected in its pages. For the Sufi, the Koran is a document with numerous levels of transmission, each one of which has a meaning in accordance with the capacity for understanding of the reader. It is this attitude toward the book which made possible the understanding between people who were of nominally Christian, pagan or Jewish backgrounds—a feeling which the orthodox could not understand. The Koran in one sense is therefore a document of psychological importance.

Chapter 112 of the Koran is an excellent example of this synthesizing capacity of the book. This is one of the shortest chapters, and it may be translated thus:

> Say, O messenger, to the people:
> "He, Allah, is Unity! Allah the Eternal.
> Fathering nobody, and not himself engendered—
> And absolutely nothing is like him!"

For the devout and conventional Moslem this is the basic declaration of faith. Allah is God; He has no equal, is the Eternal.

Christian commentators, from the earliest times, have considered this passage to be a direct attack upon the doctrine of the divinity of Christ, and they wax very fierce about it.

It is one of the most quoted passages of the Koran, and millions of Moslems use it in their prayers every day.

Viewed on this basis, the "chapter of the Unity" seems to draw a distinct line between the believers and the rest. The devout Moslem can use it against the Christian, whom he considers to be a heretic of the monotheistic tradition. The Christian reacts by considering it an insult to his central beliefs. Such a situation obtains, however, only where there is a certain psychological climate—a clash between two power groups which struggled during the middle ages for power in a medieval manner.

If we accept these assumptions, we place ourselves within the conflict which, for the Sufi, never existed except for those who chose a conflict within this psychological state.

Such an interpretation of the meaning of Chapter 112 was never accepted by the Sufis. Setting aside the Sufi claim to be able to perceive the real meaning of this chapter, we can find a bridge between ordinary thinking and a possible intention of this passage by referring to the opinion of the great Ghazali about it.

Like all the chapters of the Koran, he says, this one cannot be reduced to similarity with other books by assuming that it has a single, simple meaning of the sort familiar to the ordinary thinker. The Unity has no simple, single aim, no mere superficial meaning. Its impact depends upon understanding and experience, just as much as upon its poetic rhythm.

He refers to the context in which the chapter was revealed. It was in answer, not to a Christian nor to a religious man, but to a party of Bedouin Arabs who approached the Prophet Mohammed with this question: "To what may we compare Allah?"

The answer is that Allah may not be compared to anything. There is no analogy possible between this being (Allah—that which is to be worshipped) and anything familiar to humanity. Allah is the word used to denote the final objectivity, uniqueness, something which has no relationship with numbering, anything in time, anything which propagates in a sense familiar to man.

It is on this level, not even an initiatory or mystical one, that the common ground between Moslems and Christians was laid. By understanding this we can much more easily understand how Sufism bridged the gap between the official interpretations of Christianity and Islam and the needs of the thinking man.

This sense of the meaning of "Allah," coupled with the original rhythm of the poetry, may be conveyed more readily by this sort of reconstruction:

> O Messenger—
> Say: "He, Allah, is but One!
> Of days neither ended nor begun,
> Fathering not, a son of none—
> And none is like to him, not one!"

It is this spirit and this claim to the essential unity of divine transmission which is what has been referred to as the "secret doctrine."

Unless this feeling about the Koran is conveyed correctly, the inevitable conclusions about the limited clash between church Christianity and formal Islam becomes the only frame of reference for the scholar. It may give rise to such translations as the following, bereft of the Sufic connotation:

"ALLAH is the One God; Unbegetting, Unbegotten, Unequaled."

APPENDIX II
The Rapidness

There is no aspect of Sufism more attractive to the impatient than this. Considerable interest and excitement has been aroused since the "rapid technique" of Sufi development was brought to India by Sheikh Shattar.

"The Rapidness" (the Shattari Method) traditionally emanates from the Naqshbandi Order of Sufis, most widely distributed in Afghanistan, Turkestan, other parts of Central Asia, and Ottoman Turkey. Bahaudin Naqshband gave his name to this phase of Sufi teaching. He died in 1389. His chain of transmission reaches back to Mohammed, his companion Abu Bakr, Salman the Persian, the Sayed family and the Imams, and others, including Bayazid of Bistam (died 875), another of the greatest masters.

Sheikh Abdullah Shattar visited India in the fifteenth century, wandering from one monastery to another, and made known the method. His procedure was to approach the chief of a Sufi group and say, "Teach me your method, share it with me. If you will not, I invite you to share mine."

Shattar died in the first quarter of the fifteenth century in India, and his successors powerfully influenced various Mogul emperors. One Shattari leader, Shah Gwath, was persecuted by the official religious authorities, but eventually enrolled their spokesman as a disciple. The Shattari Order ceased to be of any public account in the early nineteenth century of the present era, having—in Sufi parlance—become a mere self-perpetuating organization centered in Gujerat. The Shattari Methods, which have been strenuously sought by Indian and other Seekers ever since, remain in the custody of the Shattari-trained element of the Naqshbandi, the parent school.

Annotations

ARAB DIFFUSION IN EUROPE

The Western tradition of learning is as much a Saracen tradition as anything else; if by Saracen we mean the concentration point, in Spain, Sicily and elsewhere, of the many stimuli which make up a great part of what is considered to be an outgrowth of Greek and Latin culture.

"The period during which the literary scepter was held by France coincided with the growth and high development of the Arabist school of Montpellier, which came under the influence of the Arabized Jews of Spain. Montpellier, owing to its geographical relation to Andalusia on the one hand, and Sicily and the Italian peninsula on the other . . . drew numbers of students from the Latin West, who after having imbibed at the Arabized sources available at that time, once more scattered themselves in Europe, thus permeating the whole fabric of medieval culture with the gloss of Arabian erudition. The subsequent teaching of the alumni of Montpellier, who exercised a dominating influence over medical literature on the Continent and in England, is one of the outstanding historical facts of the middle ages. The newly developing varieties of romance, combined with the steady inpour of Arabic works from southern Spain, which were in the main rendered into indifferent Latin, rendered both the liquid languages and sciences (including medicine) particularly susceptible to Arabian influences." (Dr. D. Campbell, *Arabian Medicine*, I, London, 1926, pp. 196–97)

ASCENT

There are four major "conditions" of man. All mankind is in one of these. In accordance with these conditions, the individual has to have his progress planned. He will behave in a different way, may appear a different person, will take decisions, according to the condition and the degree of that condition which he has attained. Not everyone reaches every stage of every condition, according to Sufi doctrine. The difference in Sufi formulation will depend upon the existence of conditions of this kind, their completeness, and their relationship with all humanity. Shah Mohammed Gwath, in *Secrets of the Naqshbandi Path,* expresses the conditions in religious terms:

1. Humanity (*nasut*), the ordinary condition.
2. On the Path (*tarika*), equated with "angels" in the cosmic sense.
3. Force, equated with what is called "power" (*jabarut*), or real capacity.
4. Absorption (*lahut*), referring to the condition of "divinity" in another sphere.

The individual Sufi is concerned with passing from one stage of conditions to another. The teacher is responsible for making this possible through the training which he offers. The Guide is responsible for relating the individual progress to that of the total needs of humanity. Innumerable techniques and activities of the Sufis ultimately relate to the application of this concept.

BARAKA
ROOT AND DERIVATION (*Arabic*)
BaRK b- = to stand firm, dwell in.
BaRK 'ala = to sit down.
BaRRaK l- = congratulate. (Syrian dialect)
BaRRaK 'ala = to bless.
TaBARaK = to be exalted.

TaBaRRaK b- = to bode well of.
BaRaK-at = blessing, abundance.
BiRK-at = pool, tank, puddle.
BaRIK = happy, fresh dates with cream.

BaRRAK = miller.

MuBARaK = blessed.

BaRRaK = make kneel down, bend the knees.

The Italian *Carbonari*, originally a mystical fraternity, made use of the coincidence between the Arabic *baraka* and the Italian *baracca*. The latter means "a covering without walls, a barrack, storehouse, undertaking, enterprise." They used it as the term for the Lodge. In July 1957, Mr. John Hamilton published in the *Hibbert Journal* a paper in which he proposed that the word *baraka* be used in English to denote certain qualities in people or objects, such as "the virtue emanated by Jesus and other great healers." Professor Robert Graves independently advocated the same course in an important lecture in America. The word is familiar to many who have lived in the East, but has a meaning wider than its usual employment. President De Gaulle of France, in saying, "I have *baraka*," used it in the sense of personal invulnerability made necessary because of a sense of the need to complete a mission or function.

BEDIL

Mirza Abdul-Qadir Bedil, who lived at the time of the Indian emperor Aurangzeb, is greatly admired as a Sufi teacher in India and Central Asia. A collection of thirty-one thousand of his extraordinarily originally constructed poems was published by a committee of savants in Afghanistan in 1962.

BLACK AND WISE

The idiomatic usage of the word "black" in Europe to denote something unpleasant has obscured its special, technical usage during the middle ages. Reference may be made to the use of the idea of "dark," occult, for something hidden may form a bridge toward reestablishing the sense of this concept in its connection with hidden wisdom—and also, by extension, with leadership. The Kaaba (cubic temple, the Holy of Holies) in Mecca is draped in black, esoterically interpreted as a play upon words of the FHM sound in Arabic, alternatively meaning "black" or "wise," "*understanding*." The word *sayed* (prince) is connected with another root for black, the SWD root. The original banner of the Prophet Mohammed was black, collectively standing for wisdom, lordship. The association of the ideas is not, of course, preserved in the translation of the Sufi phrase: "In the darkness, the Path." (*Dar tariki, tariqat.*) The black-and-white checker effect (light—understanding—comes from darkness) said to have been handed down to the Sufis from the very greatest antiquity, symbolizes this duality. In many ways, Sufi meetings ritualistically perpetuate the alternation of light and darkness, of black and white. One such method is to lay cloth of alternate black and white on the floor of the meeting place. Another is to alternately kindle and extinguish a lamp.

CLASSICAL TEACHERS

There are three "generations" or "waves" of teachership during the classical period. All Sufis believe themselves to be recipients of the *baraka* accumulated by these teachers, who are thus their spiritual ancestors.

In the first generation: Abu Bakr, Umar, Ali, Bilal, Ibn Riyah, Abu Abdullah, Salman the Persian—the Seven Great Ones.

In the second generation: Uways el Qarni, Hiran ibn Haya, Hasan el-Basri; the Four Guides ("Crowns").

In the third generation: Habib Ajami, Malik Ibn Dinar, Imam Abu Hanifa, Daud of Tai, Dhu'l-Nun the Egyptian, Ibraham Ibn Adam, Abu Yazid, Sari el-Saqti, Abu Hafa, Maaruf Karkhi, Junaid—the Eleven Sheikhly Transmitters.

These are the masters who concentrated the teachings and passed them on in such a manner as to make possible the school developments which later appeared as dervish Orders.

CONFLUENCE

Just as students of comparative religion have noted similar-

ities in the externals and doctrines of many faiths, in
mysticism Sufism has continuously stressed the essential
identity of the stream of transmission of inner knowledge.
In the East the Mogul prince Dara Shikoh wrote the *Confluence of the Two Seas,* stressing the meeting between
Sufism and early Hindu mysticism. The Rosicrucians in
the West adopted almost literally the teaching of the Spanish illuminist Sufis in claiming an unbroken succession of
inner teaching, in which they included "Hermes." The
Western illuminati included Mohammed in their chain of
transmitters. Count Michael Maier in 1617 wrote *Symbola
Aurea Mensae Duodecim Nationum* (Contributions of
Twelve Nations to the Golden Table), in which he showed
that the Sufi tradition of a succession of teachers was still
being maintained. Among the alchemical teachers were
several whom the Sufis also recognize, including Westerners
who had studied Saracen lore. They are: Hermes of Egypt,
Mary the Hebrew, Democritus of Greece, Morienus of
Rome, Avicenna (Ibn Sina) of Arabia, Albertus Magnus of
Germany, Arnold of Villaneuve of France, Thomas Aquinas
of Italy, Raymond Lully of Spain, Roger Bacon of England,
Melchior Cibiensis of Hungary, and Anonymus Sarmata
(Michael Sendivogius) of Poland. All Western alchemy, of
course, is attributed by tradition to Geber (Jabir Ibn el-
Hayyan) the Sufi.

CONSCIOUSNESS

The communication between minds which is established by
Sufism has several aspects. By means of the *tasarruf* exercises, which "clear" the individuality, there is an interaction
of minds. This is used by Sufis for purposes of healing, and
it is through this technique that most of their inexplicable
cures are effected, aside from the application of simpler
techniques. (See J. Hallaji, "Hypnotherapeutic Techniques
in a Central Asian Community," International Journal of
Clinical and Experimental Hypnosis, October, 1962) Jung's
theory of the collective unconscious is expounded by the

Spaniard Ibn Rushd (1126–1198). It was also often referred to by Rumi, and its meaning and force are subjects of Sufi specialization. Rumi notes that this phenomenon is one of a higher consciousness: "Animality has division in the spirit; the human spirit has one soul." This is generally referred to as the "great soul."

DEATH AND REBIRTH

The theme that man must "die before he dies" (Mohammed) or that he must be "born again" in his present life is to be found in very many forms of initiatory observance. In almost all cases, however, the message is taken symbolically, or is commemorated by a mere mime or ritual. The Sufis, believing that they preserve the original sense of this teaching, mark the three main grades of initiation with a "death" process. In this, the candidate has to pass through certain specific experiences (technically termed "deaths"). The actual initiation ceremony merely commemorates this happening, and does not simply dramatize it as a symbol. The three "deaths" are:

1. The White Death
2. The Green Death
3. The Black Death

Leading up to the spiritual experiences referred to as "deaths" are a series of psychological and other exercises which include three outstanding factors:

1. Abstinence and control of physical functions.
2. "Poverty," including independence from material things.
3. Emotional liberation through such exercises as overcoming avoidable obstacles, and "playing a part" in order to observe the reactions of others.

Discipleship under a master follows a special pattern in which the Seeker is given opportunities for exercising his consciousness of these three stages. Since Sufism uses the normal organization of "the world" as a training ground, the three "deaths" always involve specific enterprises carried out in human society, leading to the spiritual experiences marked by the three "deaths" and successive "rebirth" or transformation which results from them.

Dots

Among the Sufis, NQT—"dot," "point," sometimes "abbreviation"—has an important value in conveying teachings. In one aspect this is connected with the mathematical part of Sufism. The Arabic word for "geometrician" or "architect" is *muhandis*. It is composed of the letters M, H, N, D, S, which are equivalent to the numbers 40, 5, 50, 4, 60. These total 159. These numbers, resplit conventionally into tens, hundreds and units, yield

$$100 = Q$$
$$50 = N$$
$$9 = T.$$

These three consonants, combined in the order 2, 1, 3, provide the root NQT. This root means "dot," "point." In certain ceremonial usages, therefore, the word "point" is used to convey the concealed word which is its parent—the word *muhandis*, the Prime Builder. There are many other ingredients in this grouping of numbers. An example is this: The first two letters (Q,N) mean in Arabic "deep meditation," a word for Sufism. The remaining letter, the T, stands in the Arab "occult" list for "inner knowledge." Hence, in certain situations special dialogues are used. An example is when an individual at an early stage of membership is being tested for his formal knowledge of how the word code works. A certain dialogue may take place:

QUESTIONER: "What does the Geometrician mean?"
APPLICANT: "I is represented by the dot (NQT)."
Q: "How is it spelled?"
A: "Like a dot."
Q: "What comes after meditation (QN)?"
A: "The inner knowledge (the letter T)."

Q: "Will you tell it to me?"
A: "I have only two thirds—N and Q."
Q: "I have the third third—T, standing for 'hidden.'"

ELEMENTS OF SUFISM

The Ten Elements of the Sufis refer to the framework of individual effort within which the Seeker gains the potential to become awake, or alive, in the greater dimensions which lie outside familiar experience. El-Farisi has listed them thus:

1. Separation of unification.
2. Perception of audition.
3. Companionship and association.
4. Correct preference.
5. Surrender of choice.
6. The rapid acquisition of a certain "state."
7. Penetration of thought, self-examination.
8. Traveling and movement.
9. Surrender of earnings.
10. Lack of acquisition or covetousness.

Sufi exercises and training are based on these Ten Elements. In accordance with the need of the disciple, the teacher will choose for him programs of study and action which give him the opportunity of exercising functions summarized by these Elements. These factors are therefore the basis of preparing the individual for the development which he could not otherwise sustain or perceive, let alone attain.

HAFIZ

Khaja Shamsuddin Hafiz (literally Master Sun of Faith, the Protector, he who knows the Koran by heart) died in 1389. One of the greatest of all Persian poets, his works are known as the *Interpreter of the Secrets* and the *Speech of the Invisible*. His collection, the *Diwan*, conceals, in seemingly sensual verse, many Sufi experiences. It is used as a textbook, and also (by the vulgar) for omens, by opening it at random. Originating in Isfahan, the family migrated to

Shiraz. The date of his death is concealed in a poem which appears on his tomb, which itself gives the clue to the fact that it is concealed in the numerical cipher used by the Sufis: "If thou would'st know when he sought a place in the dust of Musalla, seek the date in the dust of Musalla." "Dust of Musalla" (*khak-i-Musalla*) decodes to the numbers 791, the equivalent in the Moslem calendar for the year 1389. Hafiz was the teacher of kings and at the same time beloved of the people. His influence is still second to none in Persian literature.

HALLAJ

Hussein Ibn Mansur el-Hallaj is the great martyr of the Sufis. Like many Adepts, he took as his surname a vocational name—Hallaj, the wool carder or cotton dresser—which has caused most commentators to assume that this was his trade or that of his family. The cloaking of Sufi groups and their assemblies within the cover of guild organization is one of the reasons for the choice. Ghazali the Spinner and Attar the Chemist are other examples. But Sufis always chose vocational names which could be (by double meaning) associated with their Sufic commitment. Hallaj is chosen because of the association of wool (*suf*) with the vocation; and also because an alternative meaning for the HLJ root in Arabic is either "to walk slowly" or "to let forth lightning."

Although known popularly as Mansur, this was actually the name of his father, a former Magian. He was executed in 922 for saying such things as "I am the Truth" (*Ana el-Haqq*), and refusing to recant, thus uttering the ultimate blasphemy. He was alleged to be an alchemist, like many Sufis, and extant hostile literature paints him as a wily pretender. For the Sufis, some of the greatest of whom were his friends and contemporaries, he is one of their greatest masters.

He held secret meetings at his house, and became very powerful through his teaching and by performing miracles.

He was, in short, a political threat. He taught that Sufism was the internal truth of all true religion, and because he emphasized the importance of Jesus as a Sufi teacher, he was accused by fanatics of being a secret Christian. One of the counts against him was that he had a number of books, wonderfully embellished and decorated. His assertion that the Mecca pilgrimage could be performed anywhere, by making suitable dedications and preparations, was considered to be impossibly heretical. Hujwiri (*Revelation of the Veiled*) authoritatively defends Hallaj on the grounds that things done or said by Sufis are not to be interpreted by lower criteria. The attempt to express Reality, he says, in ordinary terms, is an impossibility. Similarly, the attempt will not create the meaning.

On Tuesday, March 26, 922, Hallaj walked to the place of his execution, condemned by the Inquisition of the Caliph el-Muqtadir. He was tortured and dismembered, but showed no fear. This was his last public prayer, while he could still speak:

> "O Lord, make me grateful for the *baraka* which I have been given in being allowed to know what others do not know. Divine mysteries which are unlawful to others have become thus lawful to me. Forgive and have mercy upon these Thy servants assembled here for the purpose of killing me; for, had Thou revealed to them what Thou hast revealed to me, they would not act thus."

HANIFS

The loss of the Sufic thread in many metaphysical schools, with the resultant failure of these schools to provide a real fulfillment for the followers, is considered by the Sufis to be one cause of the quest, the search for a teacher, which preoccupied so many people in ancient times. Certain companions of Mohammed themselves described this quest as applied to themselves. One of them was Salman the Persian.

He related how he tired of the mere rituals of the Zoroastrians, and set off southward seeking the faith and practice of the Hanifs. He attached himself first to a Christian teacher, then to another. When the latter died, he told Salman to journey southward in search of an exponent of the Hanifite lore. After being captured and sold into slavery he found the immediate circle of Mohammed's disciples at Medina. What was this practice of the Hanifs, which the Sufis equate with Sufism?

The choice of this word, as with many others which are only attempts to convey a varied meaning with one root, is believed by the Sufis to explain itself. The triliteral root HNF is basically associated with the concept of "leaning on one side"—a reference to the rhythmic movements of the Sufis. A derivative of HNF is the form TaHaNNaF, which means "to act like a Hanifite;" and *tahannafi* means "to do a thing accurately." Here we have a word picture of exercises performed according to a set plan; but also potentially "on one side"—which Sufis teach means in an eccentric as well as rhythmic manner. The word *hanif*, also from the same root, is the noun. It also stands for straightforwardness. Such a variety of meanings would seem baffling if it were not realized that such ideas as "to do a thing accurately" and "to lean on one side" can be equated within a certain system—that of the Sufis. This is not to say, of course, that the root form was invented by the Sufis; or even that the words are not in everyday use in straightforward meanings. The important thing to note is that for the Sufis certain words are chosen to describe a complex of ideas which accord with a number of Sufi ideas and practices, and build up, on close examination, a word picture.

It is as if we were to take a word in English, one with a number of meanings, and use it because within the meanings were found several which, taken together, carried a message or composite presentation of certain essentials. This procedure is rather more elaborate than punning or simple rhyme. It extends the dimensions of meaning, as it were, through the word and its derivatives.

HIDDEN SUFIS

There are several forms of invisible saints ("friends") corresponding with the general human need for a certain representation of psychic or psychological activity in the whole community, according to Sufi teaching. Hujwiri (*Revelation of the Veiled*, Nicholson's version, p. 213) says: "Among them there are four thousand who are concealed and do not know one another and are not aware of the excellence of their state, but in all circumstances are hidden from themselves and from mankind. Traditions have come down to this effect, and the sayings of the saints proclaim the truth thereof, and I myself—God be praised!—have had ocular experience of this matter."

E. H. Whinfield (*Mathnawi*, London, 1887, p. xxvii et seq.) related this concept more closely with current ideas as to who or what such people might be:

"A very remarkable doctrine is that of unrecognized saints. There are always on earth four thousand persons who are, so to speak, saints without knowing it. These are they who are born with a natural goodness, which lifts them without effort to a point that most labor to reach in vain—loyal, gentle, unselfish souls, endowed with a natural intuition of good and a natural inclination to pursue it, the stay and comfort of those who enjoy the blessing of their society, and, when they have passed away, perhaps canonized in the hearts of one or two who loved them. Spontaneous goodness of this sort is not to be submitted to rules or forms; the inward inclination, not the outward ordinances, is the source of their goodness. 'Against such there is no law.' They have a standard of thought and character of their own, quite independent of the praise or blame of 'men of externals.'"

Sufi teaching accords such people a place in the total evolutionary pattern of mankind.

JAMI

Mulla Nurudin Abdarahman Jami (literally Master Light of Faith, Servant of the Merciful, of Jam) was born in Khurasan in 1414 and died in Herat in 1492. Jami was spiritualized by the glance of the great Master Mohammed Parsa, who passed through his birthplace when the poet was a small boy, according to his own belief. He was a teacher of the Naqshbandi Order. His Sufi teachings are sometimes displayed, sometimes concealed, in his extraordinary poetical and other works. Among these are the romances of Salman and Absal and the epic of Joseph and Zuleikha, allegorical tales which are among the greatest pieces of Persian literature ever written. His *Abode of Spring* contains the most important initiatory material. Jami was a great traveler, theologian, hagiographer, grammarian and prosodist, as well as a musical theorist. His intellectual powers were such that after studying under the Master Ali of Samarkand he was soon recognized by the great doctor Rum as superior to him. Addressing a great assembly, he said, "Since the building of this city none equal in mind and the use of it to this youth Jami has ever crossed the Oxus to Samarkand." Jami chose his place-name as a pseudonym because it decodes to the numbers 54, reencodable to the letters ND. This combination of letters in Arabic stands for a group of ideas—idol, opponent, running, compounded perfume—all Sufi poetic concepts connected with the "state" or "movement" of the Sufi.

LANGUAGES

Many of the Adepts of Sufism, though well versed in Arabic, have refused to use it except when they desire to use it for a specific purpose. They traditionally adhere to this practice even in circles where a knowledge of Arabic is considered to be essential to a cultivated man. As a consequence, some even of the very greatest masters have from time to time been considered insufficiently educated by literary observers. There are many stories about this subject. The reasons for not using Arabic are: (1) If the Sufi is following at the time the "path of blame," he finds it necessary to incur certain feelings of opposition in his hearers. This is best done, in the case of a highly language-conscious people like the Arabs, by not speaking their language—from their point of view a serious shortcoming. (2) Because of the fixed idea of Arabic supremacy, the Sufi has to detach the individual from the assumption that all great men must speak Arabic. (3) The Sufi cannot be forced into the scholastic culture pattern devised by others, without compromising his own teachings. (4) There are distinct circumstances when communication on a verbal basis, by familiar methods, is not indicated. The Sufi's "state" tells him what this is. In the case of the ordinary man, such a refinement of perception is not possible, and he therefore strives unthinkingly to communicate information and ideas on the basic assumption that when people meet, their identity of linguistic ability is a good and necessary thing.

The great Sufi and great Sheikh of Khurasan Abu-Hafs el-Haddadi knew no Arabic, it was reported.[1] He spoke through interpreters. When he went to Baghdad to visit such giants as Junaid, he spoke so eloquently in Arabic that he had no equal. This is a typical story. The Sufi, for whom Sufism is more important than anything else, will embody in his own self-development a technique of this kind, and combine it with the impact which he is making upon others. It is never his aim to further his own reputation in academic circles. Those who have viewed Sufism as a Persian cult whose practitioners harbored animosity toward the Arabs and sought to reduce the importance of Arabic as one of their techniques completely misunderstand the role of language in Sufism. Similar techniques are reported in the use of languages other than Arabic.

[1] Hujwiri, *Revelation of the Veiled.*

LATAIF

The activation of the special Organs of Perception (*lataif*) is a part of Sufi methodology analogous to, and often confused with, the *chakra* system of the Yogis. There are important differences. In Yoga, the *chakras* or *padmas* are conceived as physically located centers in the body, linked by invisible nerves or channels. Yogis generally do not know that these centers are merely concentration points, convenient formulations whose activation is part of a theoretical working hypothesis. Both Sufism and Christianity of an esoteric sort preserve a similar theory, combining it with certain exercises. The succession of colors seen by the alchemist in the Western literature can be seen as referring to concentration upon certain physical localizations if we compare it with the Sufi literature on exercises. This is surprisingly easily demonstrated, though it seems that nobody in the West has noticed the connection. In Sufism, the *lataif* are located thus: Mind (*qalb*), color yellow, location left side of the body. Spirit (*ruh*), color red, location right side of the body. Consciousness (*sirr*), color white, location solar plexus. Intuition (*khafi*), color black, location forehead. Deep perception of consciousness (*ikhfa*), color green, location center of chest. In Western alchemy, the "succession of colors manifested" is of very great importance. Among the Christian alchemists the succession black-white-yellow-red is very common. It will at once be noted that this succession, transposed into physical equivalents, forms the sign of the Cross. The alchemical exercises therefore aim at activating colors (locations = *lataif*) in the form of crossing oneself. This is an adaptation of the Sufi method which is thus, in order of activation: yellow-red-white-black-green. In alchemy, again, the succession is sometimes given as black (subsidiary gray = partial development of the black faculty, the forehead)—white (solar plexus, the second point of the sign of the Cross)—green (a Sufi alternative for the right side of the chest)—citrine (left side of the chest, "heart")—red (right side of the chest). Sometimes, as the second stage, the "peacock" (variegated colors) appears in the consciousness. This sign, considered important to the alchemists, is known by the Sufis as a special condition, not invariable, which occurs in the mind when the consciousness is flooded by changing colors or photisms. It is a stage before stabilization of the consciousness, and can in some ways be compared to color illusions produced by hallucinogens. The Sufis wear clothing (often turbans) of the color corresponding to their development in this special system. Literary students of alchemy are left fumbling with a mystery which is thus not complicated if understood in its real meaning.

LIGHT VERSE

The Verse of Light from the Koran (Sura 24, verse 35) itself states that it is an allegory and that its inner meaning must be understood metaphorically.

The idea of illuminism, and especially the analogy of the Lamp in Sufism and its derivatives, comes from this verse. It is the transmitting of the meaning of the Lamp allegory which forms a part of Sufi esoteric development, because the Lamp has to be experienced, as soon as the individual consciousness is capable of perceiving it.

This is the Verse of Light:

ALLAH is the Light of the heavens and earth. His Light is resembled by a lamp within a niche. The lamp is within a crystal, like a shining Star. It is lit from a blessed olive tree, not of the East or the West; of it the oil itself nearly shines, without the effect of any fire. Light upon Light!

This mystical passage gives the essence of Sufism, and conceals the nature of the cognition of the extra dimensions of the human consciousness which comes beyond the intellect.

It is the subject of the great Ghazali's *Niche for Lights,* a Sufi classic.

MIRAMOLIN

The medieval rendering of the Arab title Emir el-Mominin (Commander of the Faithful, Caliph) of Spain and Africa was Miramolin, an attempt to reproduce the sound of the original words. Vulgarly, looked at from the point of view of Spanish, the word sounds as if it was composed of the words "to look" (*mirar*) and "a mill" (*molino*). Transposing this idea of "mill" into Arabic, as it was explained to me by the Moorish descendant of Spanish Arabs expelled in the 1490s, we find the word *rahi.* What else does *rahi* mean in Arabic?

RAHI: Mill; the thick of a fight; chief of a tribe; troop of camels.

MIRAt means "stores, wheat."

The mill which Quixote attacked was, by linguistic analogy and coincidence, a mill, but it also stood for "the thick of a fight; chief of a tribe," etc.

It is impossible to transpose the associations into English, because the humor depends upon the coincidence of sounds. Since Arabic is not now widely known in Spain, this part of the Spanish-Arabic literary interchange cannot take place any longer, and remains only with a few people in Morocco.

The Miramolin of Africa, representing the fanatical element of Islam, was unpopular (to say the least) among the Spanish Arabs and the Sufis.

MYSTERIOUS FESTIVALS

The mysterious "witch" festivals were held on the second of February, first of May, first of August and first of November. They do not accord with the seasons nor the solstices as far as most commentators can make out. It has therefore been concluded that they must be based upon some ancien calendar of animal breeding. These are, in fact, the dates which are celebrated by the Aniza (and other Arabs) heralding the changes of season observed in the Persian Gulf area and still observed there. They correspond exactly with:

Spring, *Rabi'*
Summer, *Saif*
Autumn, *Kharif*
Winter, *Shita*

The "witch" habit of counterclockwise circumambulation, generally considered to be an evil reversal of normal religious clockwise movement, is similar to the Islamic habit of walking around the Kaaba. The Sufis and other Moslems are the only religious group which conducts their worship by means of a widdershins rotation.

NAQSHBANDI

One of the most widespread of the Sufi Orders. The name is literally Painters, on the analogy of the corporations or guilds of the early classical Sufis, such as the Builders. The Order has an inner and an overt branch. Many Persian poets use the word *naqsh* (diagram, painting, map, etc.) to denote a relationship between these Sufis and the whole "plan" of human development which Sufism is believed to be aiding. Rumi uses the word NQSH long before the supposed founder of the Order (Bahaudin Naqshband) taught in Bokhara. He says, "I am a form-making engraver (NaQQASH), each instant I shape an idol." (*Diwan*) Khayyam, even earlier, uses the same imagery: "This circle of the world is like a ring; assuredly we are the seal (NQSH) on its bezel." The Naqshbandi trace their spiritual pedigree to Mohammed through most of the early classical teachers. The Order considers itself a Sufi influence, only partly expressed in its outward form as a dervish school of austere appearance, helping to maintain the cultural identity of the environment. It was powerful in Turkey until the republican revolution, and dominated both the Ottoman and

Mogul courts from time to time. The temporary character of Sufi schools, which causes their reshaping and difference in appearance in various fields, is referred to by Rumi when he says, "I am not of water or fire, nor of the headkilling wind. I am not of the impressed (MUNaQQiSH) clay: I have laughed at all of them." (*Diwan*)

NONRATIONAL CONCERN

The individual reared in a Western cultural setting is often at a disadvantage when faced with the problem of learning, because of his preoccupation with the question of "dominate or be dominated," to which he gives intense and un-discriminating emphasis. He is often aware of the "problem" in only the crude form ("dominate or be dominated"), and his literary and philosophical roots give him little ability to realize that the problem is centered around the assumption that there is no more rarefied possibility than "struggle or be struggled against." Some Western observers have noticed this essential crisis. Under the heading of "Nonrational Concern," the editors of a recent symposium[1] refer to this inherent characteristic:

". . . the inability to make others fulfill one's wishes; and the reverse, the fear of being controlled by others, with the consequent loss of the autonomy that is believed to be fundamental to the conception of the self. These opposites are incongruously exaggerated in paranoid thinking, one of the most prevalent mental symptoms of Western man."

NSHR

    NaSHaR = to expand, spread, display
    NaSHaR = to saw wood; scatter; propagate
    NaSHaR = to become green after rain; to spread
            (foliage)
    NaSHaR = to recall to life, revivify (the dead)
    NaSHiR = to disperse by night in a pasture

[1] A. E. Biderman and H. Zimmer (editors) *The Manipulation of Human Behavior*, New York, 1961, p. 4.

NaSHr = life; sweet smell; reviving herbage after rain
YaUM El-NNuSHUR = day of resurrection
NuSHARa = sawdust
MiNSHAR = saw

Ibn El-Arabi's poetic name derived from the same root as the noun "saw" and was chosen in accordance with Sufi usage. His Sufic mission combined, as we see from the above list of dictionary derivations of the original NSHR root, the dissemination of Sufism, the revival of knowledge, the refreshing influence of rain (*baraka*) upon herbage. "Sawing wood" is also taken to refer to the effort which is put into the life of the Sufi, as well as the production of something new (sawdust) from the material worked upon (wood); a variation of the transmutation or "formation" analogy used by the Sufis. In alchemy there was chemical transmutation; in the QLB root (q.v.) there was the sense of "shaping, forming"; in the NSHR root there is the sense of production, sawdust. The allegory is, of course, of human change, and while the Sufis have kept the concept flexible, in other societies a single aspect (such as alchemy and transmutation) has become fixated and devoted entirely to the limited concept of alchemicalization.

OBJECTIVES OF SUFISM

Dazzled by the outward mystery of Eastern life, or involved in the intricacies of literature soaked in theological and historical allegory, most Western students of the Sufis, particularly the academicians, seem to pause at an earlier stage of experience of Sufi intention than would profit them. A recent (1962) traveler in North Africa, who spent some time with Sufis, brings back from Tunisia a sense of objective which may sound strange to the traditional scholar:

The disciples had to carry out memorizing and meditative exercises, developing powers of concentration and reflection. The others, it seemed, were keeping up a sort of training of which thought and work, as well as exercises like the *dhikr*, all formed a part.

After a few days, the air of mystery and strangeness which I had felt was replaced by a sensation that, however unfamiliar these practices might seem to the outsider, their practitioners did not regard them as supernatural, as we might use the term. As Sheikh Arif once said: "We are doing something which is natural, which is the result of research and practice into the future development of mankind; we are producing a *new* man. And we do it for no material gain." This, then, is their attitude. (O. M. Burke, "Tunisian Caravan," Blackwood's Magazine, No. 1756, Vol. 291 (February, 1962), p. 135)

OUTLOOK

Since Sufism is based upon the realization of truth by the Sufis, its outlook cannot change, though its superficial projection may appear to change. Teaching methods differ in accordance with cultural conditions. In other systems, it is the outlook of the philosophical school which undergoes variation. This "has a great significance in attesting to the ancient roots of the Sufi Way. It indicates that whereas in the progress of history the outlook of other philosophical doctrines has changed according to environments, the Sufi ideals have remained patent to the original form in adhering to the conception of a comprehensiveness without a frontier." (The Sirdar Ikbal Ali Shah, *Islamic Sufism*, London, 1933, p. 10)

Accustomed to looking at philosophy as a makeshift, a groping toward truth, changing in accordance with the acquisition of mere information, there are few people nowadays who can even grasp the assertion that there is an ultimate truth against which everything can be measured, and which is accessible to man.

PEACOCK ANGEL CULT

The Yezidis, reputed devil worshipers, of Iraq, are a secret cult whose symbolism, the peacock and the black snake, have baffled students for centuries. There is, however, no need for this difficulty, given the knowledge that the group was founded by a famous Sufi, and given that we know how Sufic poetic analogy works. Like the Sufi Builders, travelers or Coalmen, the Yezidis were originally a community of Sufis, and their rituals are centered around the use of standard and familiar Sufi symbolism.

Malak tauus, which stands for Peacock Angel, merely means: MaLaK, homonym of MaLiK ("King," the traditional word for a Sufi); and TAUUS (Peacock), which stands here for its homophone TAUUS (Verdant Land). When it is noted that MaLaK (Angel) is used in Ghazali's sense of "angels are the higher faculties in man," it can be seen that the supposed idol of the Yezidis is merely an allegory of two Sufi watchwords—the expansion of the "land," the mind, through the higher faculties. Both of these words are in Sufic usage outside of the Yezidi cult. The Yezidis are divided into grades which use Sufi initiatory titles such as *pir* (elder); Fakir (poor one); *Baba* (chief).

Lady Drower, who studied the Peacock people of Iraq at close range, says of the founder of the group, Sheikh Adi Ibn Musafir (Son of the Traveler, a Sufi cognomen): "Nothing that is known about him speaks of anything but orthodoxy, but he was a Sufi, and the secret doctrines of Sufism have always been suspected of pantheism, and the Sufi sects of cherishing ancient faiths." (*Peacock Angel*, London, 1941, p. 152)

In addition to the peacock emblem, the Yezidis use the figure of a snake, which they blacken with soot. This blackening is symbolic of the word FEHM (charcoal, carbon). The snake itself, far from being a symbol of evil or ancient skin-sloughing-regeneration lore, as some would believe, is chosen for the same reasons as the peacock. In Arabic, snake is HaYYat. This is a near rhyme for another word, HaYYAt, life, which uses the same Arabic letters. The meaning of the black snake is therefore: "Wisdom of Life."

As in the case of other Sufic organizations, the Yezidi system has traveled far beyond its cultural context, and become in places a mere mime. A thriving branch of the cult, which does in fact appear to revere an "angelic peacock," is reported as existing in London in 1962. (A. Daraul, *Secret Societies*, London, 1962)

It is this deterioration of symbolology which is reflected in many strange associations in the West. The real developmental intention has become subservient to the form, which, in turn, is used to produce communal emotion, replacing inner experience.

QALB

The Arabic word QLB is not confined in meaning to the form QaLB (heart), which is one of its most familiar forms. In the Sufi sense, QLB is considered to have the following meanings, all straightforward dictionary derivations of this triliteral root:

QaLaB = to turn a thing upside-down. A reference to the Sufi dictum: "The world is upside down."

QaLaB = to extract the marrow of a palm tree. The palm tree, as noted elsewhere, is the Sufi term for *baraka* and the magic square of fifteen, which contains Sufi diagrammatic and mathematical material. The "marrow" is used in the sense of the essence, vital portion.

QaLaB = to become red. Applied to dates, the product of the palm. An allegory of a Sufi process, later associated with the alchemical idea of the "red elixir."

AQLaB = to be baked on one side. Used for bread, and in a special Sufi sense, denoting a part of a developmental process of transformation, analogized with turning one thing (dough) into what seems to be another (bread).

TaqaLLaB = to be restless. Used of a sleeper, turning in his sleep. Used as a Sufi technical term to describe the uncertainty felt by the ordinary man who is, according to the convention used by the Sufis, "asleep."

QaLB = reverse; invert; wrong side. This is also associated with "molding" and a matrix (QALiB), the formative apparatus.

QaLB = heart, mind, soul; intimate thought; marrow, pith; best part. Also used in the compound phrase *qalb el-muqaddas*, literally "the Sacred Heart," meaning the part of mankind which partakes of the essence of divinity.

The letters Q + L + B add up to 132, equal to the name Mohammed (M + H + M + M + D), the Logos or essence of Mohammed. Thirty-two plus one hundred (Q) make up one third of the total of divinity, the "ninety-nine names of beauty."

QUTUB

This is the reputed invisible head of all the Sufis. The word literally means the Magnetic Pole, Pivot, Polestar, Chief. Transposed into figures, it totals 111—the thrice-repeated unity, the threefold unity, the threefold affirmation of truth, which is a unity. If this is split up into 100, 10, 1, and substituted, we get the letters Q, Y and A. The word QYAA, spelled from these letters, means "to be vacant, voided." It is the vacant, voided, purged "house" into which the *baraka* descends (the human consciousness).

RAYMOND LULLY

I am indebted to Mr. Robert Pring-Mill of Oxford for a textual quotation from Lully's *Blanquerna*, in which he states that he has adopted devotional methodology from the "Sufies," called by him religious men among the Saracens. (Communication dated June 26, 1962, quoting the Els Nostres Classics edition of Lully's *L. de Evast e Blanquerna*, Vol. 3, p. 10 et seq.)

REMEMBERING

The word *dhikr* (pronounced in non-Arab countries as

zikr) refers to certain exercises carried out from the beginning of dervishhood. Basically the word means "remembrance," and the sense is of remembering, commemorating, invocation. "Remembering" is now also defined as the basic term for the religious activity of dervishes. The first stage is remembering oneself, after which the function shifts to one of harmony with the greater consciousness. The disciple has to remember or recognize himself in various ways, shedding this exercise in this form very early, or it becomes an "undesirable cause." Some imitators of Sufism, seeing Sufi assemblies, have copied this technique. The great Hakim Sanai warns against too much remembering, pointing out that it is used only at the early stage:

> Zikr juz dar rahi mujahid nist;
> Zikr dar majlisi mushahid nist.

"Remembering exists not except in the way of struggle; Remembering, repetition is not to be found in the assembly of experience." (*The Walled Garden of Truth*)

ROSE; ROSICRUCIAN; ROSARY

The Christians adopted the rosary from the Saracens. In so doing, they translated the word *el-wardia* (literally the reciter) by another word, almost the same in the original sound, a word standing for "roser," or "rosary." The full Arabic term for the rosary is *el-misbat el-wirdiat* (the Praiser of the Reciter or of the Drawing Near). This term (WRD) is a special technical term for the special exercises of the Sufis or dervishes. The Catholic rendering into Latin is not so much a mistranslation as an adoption of the Sufi poetic (or almost heraldic) method of using a similar word to create a picture. Hence the word *wird* (dervish exercise) was used by the Sufis poetically as WaRD (rose). A similar development took place with the term "Rosicrucian." This is a direct translation of the root WRD plus the word for "cross" in Arabic, SLB. In its original meaning, the phrase means WRD (exercise) plus SLB—"to extract the marrow."

Hence it is only incidentally that SLB (which also means "cross") occurs in the phrase "Rosicrucian." Taking advantage of this coincidence or poetic juxtaposition, the Sufis do, however, say, "We have the marrow of the Cross, while the Christians only have the crucifix," and similar phrases. This loses its meaning in translation. A whole dervish Order (that of Abdul-Qadir el-Jilani) is formed around the idea of Rose in this initiatory sense, and its founder is called the Rose of Baghdad. Ignorance of this background is responsible for much useless speculation about such entities as the Rosicrucians who merely repeated in their claims the possession of the ancient teaching which is contained in the parallel development called alchemy, and which was also announced by Friar Bacon, himself claimed as a Rosicrucian and alchemist and illuminate. The origins of all these societies in Sufism is the answer to the question as to which of them did Bacon belong, and what the secret doctrine really was. Much other Rosicrucian symbolism is Sufic. Martin Luther used the Rose, Cross and Ring (Sufic *halka* group) in his emblem. This must have been supplied to him by an initiate Sufi.

The Sacred Language

Classical Arabic is that version of Arabic which was used by the Koreshite tribe, hereditary guardians of the Temple of Mecca, and to which Mohammed belonged. Long before Arabic became considered a holy tongue because it is the vehicle of the Koran, it was the speech of the sacerdotal class of Mecca, a sanctuary whose religious history legend starts with Adam and Eve. Arabic, most precise and primitive of the Semitic languages, shows signs of being originally a constructed language. It is built up upon mathematical principles—a phenomenon not paralleled by any other language. Sufic analysis of its basic concept groupings shows that especially initiatory or religious, as well as psychological, ideas are collectively associated around a stem in seemingly logical and deliberate fashion which could hardly be fortuitous. Arabic is the nearest that is available to a parent Semitic language, because philologically it is millennia more archaic than, for instance, Hebrew. For this reason, Hebrew grammar is based upon an analysis of Arabic, by a study of which the original meanings of Hebrew words, perverted through long literary usage, were reclaimed by Hebrew scholars.

St. Augustine

It has been the custom among most Christian apologists to represent the religion, and especially their own branch of it, as time-centered, referring back to a certain historical fact—the human transition of Jesus. Other versions of the Christian story are labeled heresies. St. Augustine, who is explained away as being tainted with unchristian (i.e., non-conventional) philosophy, said, "That which is called the Christian religion existed among the ancients and never did not exist from the beginning of the human race." (*Epistolae* Lib. I, xiii, p. 3) The deviation of Christianity from the rest of human religion was, of course, the result of a deliberate choice—the decision to regard the events of the life and death of Christ as unique, not as part of a continuous process. It must clearly be remembered that the versions of Christianity most generally available to the average student are those which have prevailed, being most successful, not necessarily the most accurate, historically or otherwise.

Saki

The Cupbearer, to whom so many Sufi verses are addressed, is generally considered by literary critics to be an imaginary figure. In Sufi practice, however, poems which are addressed to a Saki, or in which a Saki appears, may refer to an individual who plays an illustrative part in the proceedings, because a poem may not stand on its own under all circumstances. When intended to fulfill a certain function, an actual Saki may be present.

Outside of Sufi activity, there are few notices of the presence of a Saki. Sirajudin Ali refers to a Sufi meeting of this kind, when he reports a dialogue between a Saki and a Sufi master (Lai-Khur):

In the Afghan town of Ghazna there was a "madman" called Lai-Khur who used to say the most outrageous things —the Sufi method of attracting attention to something in order to put a point. One day toward the middle of the twelfth century the poet Sanai was walking to the court of Sultan Ibrahim, scourge of the Hindus, to present him with an eulogistic poem on the eve of another expedition into infidel India.

Sanai heard singing from a garden. As he listened, he heard the madman calling the Saki to bring wine—for a toast to the blinding of Sultan Ibrahim. The Saki objected to the toast. Was Ibrahim not a great monarch? "He is blind," said the madman, "to quit this wonderful city to engage upon a useless task—especially when he is needed here."

The next toast was to Sanai, the eavesdropper himself, and to his "blindness." The Saki again said that this must be wrong, for Sanai was an excellent poet, a learned man. "Sanai," said the madman, "has no idea why he was created. When his actions are asked, he will produce only eulogies of kings. This is what he has done during this life of his."

This account of the conversion of Sanai to Sufism is, of course, a report of a dialogue of a Sufic nature, presented in a formalized fashion. Since the Saki's words are never included in the written form of the poems, we have no recorded dialogue form commemorating such encounters; and as far as the ordinary literary man is concerned, they do not exist.

SARACEN-WESTERN CONTACTS

The interchange between Western sovereigns and the infidel Saracens of various brands was extraordinarily close during the whole period of nominal war between the two power groups. Charlemagne, the hero of Christendom, fought as an ally with a Moslem sovereign. Abdurahman II of Spain (821–852) sent an ambassador—Yahya the Gazelle—to a Norman king. Richard the Lionhearted (Arabic *qalb el-nimr*, both Sufi initiatory words) is said to have proposed that his sister should marry the brother of Saladin. She was herself the widow of the King of Sicily, whose rulers were using Sufi phrases in heraldic devices. The Lionhearted's brother, John (excommunicated 1209) sent an embassy from England to the Spanish-Moroccan Commander of the Faithful, offering to embrace Islam. Richard himself married (in 1191) Berengaria of Navarre, whose brother, Sancho the Strong, was a close ally of the Spanish Arabs. John was in 1211 preparing to give military support to the Albigensians, who were undoubtedly saturated with Sufic culture. Isabella of Castile was married to Edmund of Yorke; she was descended from Mohammed II of Seville. The Sufi influence which came from Spain at this time includes Morris dancing. John of Gaunt, who probably brought the dancers, was a patron of Chaucer, who used Sufi materials. Chaucer's wife Philippa was probably Gaunt's third wife, whom Gaunt married in 1396. The lords of Aragon were directly descended from the Moslem kings of Granada. There are said to be 50,000 English descendants of the Beni Omeyya today, from the line of Pedro the Cruel. Thomas à Becket (1119–1170), Chancellor and Archbishop of Canterbury, whose doings and death are linked with speculation as to his spiritual commitment and have given rise to numerous theories, is said to have had a Saracen mother (Hitti, *op. cit.*, p. 652, note 7). Shams el-Doha is the Arabic name of an English or Scottish princess who was married to the Moroccan sovereign Abu el-Hasan (1330–1380), the Mirinid; both have tombs in the ruins of Shilla, near Rabat. The Greek emperor John Cantacuzenus gave his daughter to the Turkish sovereign Orkhan in 1346. Orkhan organized the Janissaries, an elite military organization owing allegiance to the Sufi teacher

Haji Bektash. From the Islamic point of view there is no possibility of Moslem women being offered to unbelievers, and that such marriages took place or were mooted is confirmation of the Eastern tradition that there was an initiatory understanding between the Moslems of the time and the nominal Christians with whose families they were thus closely allied. Both current prudence and subsequent religious propaganda have effaced public acknowledgment of this.

SEVEN MEN

Sufi development requires the Seeker to pass through seven stages of preparation, before the individuality is ready for its full function. These stages, sometimes called "men," are degrees in the transmutation of the consciousness, the technical term for which is *nafs*, breath. Briefly, the stages of development, each making possible a further enrichment of the being under the guidance of a practiced teacher, are:

1. *Nafs i ammara* (the depraved, commanding *nafs*)
2. *Nafs-i-lawwama* (the accusing *nafs*)
3. *Nafs-i-mulhama* (the inspired *nafs*)
4. *Nafs-i-mutmainna* (the serene *nafs*)
5. *Nafs-i-radiyya* (the fulfilled *nafs*)
6. *Nafs-i-mardiyya* (the fulfilling *nafs*)
7. *Nafs-i-safiyya wa kamila* (the purified and complete *nafs*)

The *nafs* is considered to pass through processes which are termed "death and rebirth." The first process, the White Death marks the initiation of the disciple, when he starts to reconstruct the automatic and emotional *nafs*, so that it will in turn provide an instrument for proceeding to the activation of conscience, the second *nafs*. The adjectives "serene, fulfilling," and so on, refer to the effect upon the individual, as well as upon the group and society in general, functions most marked at each stage.

Significant phenomena of the seven stages observed during Sufi exercises include these:

1. The individual out of personal control, believes himself to be a coherent personality, starts to learn that he, like all undeveloped individuals, has a multiple and changing personality.

2. The dawn of self-awareness and "accusation," in which automatic thoughts are seen for what they are.

3. The beginning of real mental integration, when the mind is becoming capable of operating on a higher level than was its previous futile custom.

4. Serene balance, equilibrium of the individuality.

5. Power of fulfillment, new ranges of experience not susceptible to description beyond approximate analogy.

6. A new activity and function, including extra dimensions of the individuality.

7. Completion of the task of reconstitution, possibility of teaching others, capacity for objective understanding.

SIMURGH

The *simurgh* (thirty birds) is the code phrase which means the development of the mind through "China;" "China" standing, in both Persian and Arabic, for the concealed concept of meditation and Sufi methodology. The great Attar clothes this teaching in an allegory:[1]

"Once, from darkness, Simurgh showed himself in China. One of his plumes fell to earth: a picture of it was made and this is still in the Chinese gallery. This is why it has been said, 'Seek knowledge, even unto China.' If this feather of Simurgh had not been seen in China, there would have been no acclaim in the world of hidden things. And this small indication of his reality is a sign of his glory. All souls carry the picture of the outline of that plume. And the matter of his description has neither beginning nor end. Now, People of the Path, choose this way, and start your journey."

[1] *Parliament of the Birds*, ch. II.

This is merely a concealed way of saying: "There is a potentiality in the mind of man. On one occasion it became activated, through a certain form of deep concentration, and was emulated. Without this there is no potentiality for development. Everyone has the faculty, in an embryonic form. It is something connected with eternity. Come, start upon the Way."

SPIRIT AND SUBSTANCE

According to Sufism, what is generally referred to in religious terminology as the Spirit (*el ruh*) is a substance, with physical characteristics, a subtle body (*jism-i-latif*). This substance, as conceived, is not considered to be eternal. It existed before the corporealization of man (Hujwiri, *Revelation of the Veiled*). After physical death, the substantial spirit continues to exist, in one of ten forms, each corresponding to the formation which it has attained during ordinary life. There are ten stages in this sense—the first being that of the "sincere," the tenth being that of the Sufi who has been transformed in nature by his earthly development. The *ruh* is at times visible.

THE SUFI TEACHER

Within mankind is a "treasure," and this can be found only by looking for it. The treasure is, as it were, inside a house (fixed thinking-patterns) which has to be broken down before it can be found. In his "elephant in the dark" house, Rumi teaches that "if there had been a light in the house," multiplicity would be seen to be in fact unity. Man sees only pieces of things because his mind is fixed in a pattern designed to see things piecemeal.

A function of the teacher is to establish this fact to the disciple. Rumi has made this a subject of a poem:[1]

Destroy your house, and with the treasure hidden in it
You will be able to build thousands of houses.

[1] *Mathnawi*, Bk. IV. (Whinfield's translation)

The treasure lies under it; there is no help for it;
Hesitate not to pull it down; do not tarry!

....

That prize is the wages for destroying the house:

....

"Man gets nothing he has not worked for."
Then you will bite your finger, saying, "Alas!
That bright moon was hidden under a cloud.
I did not do what they told me for my good;
Now house and treasure are lost and my hand is empty."

TARIKA, TARIQA

The Sufi wayfarer belongs to a *tariqa* (TaRIQa), the word
meaning more than Path or Way:

Tariqa = course; rule of life; line, streak; chief of a tribe;
means; Order of dervishes. The nearest approximation to the
sense of this word is "way" in English—the way of doing a
thing, the way upon which a person is traveling, the way as
an individual ("I am the Way," in a mystical sense).

As with other Arabic triliteral roots, the TRQ root and
its derivatives contain elements associated with Sufism and
the esoteric tradition:

TaRQ   =   sound of a musical instrument
TaTaRRaQ Li- =   to aim at, to wish, to draw near
                                to
ATRaQ =   to remain silent with downcast eyes
TaRRaQ Li- =   to open the way to
TaRaQ   =   to come to anyone by night
TuRQaT =   way, road; method; habit
TaRIQAt =   lofty palm tree

The use of this word is explained thus in dervish lore:
"The *tariqa* is the Path and also the leadership of the group,

in which resides the transmission. It is a rule of living, a thin line within ordinary life, sometimes maintained through the note of music, expressed visually by the palm tree. The *tariqa* itself opens the Path, and it is connected with meditation, silent thinking, as when a man sits in prayer during the silences of the darkness. It is both the aim and the method." [*Nishan-Nama* (Book of Symbols) of Sufi associations, by Emir Eddin Shadhili, "The Ardent"]

TAROT

The Tarot cards, from which European playing cards are derived, were introduced into the West in 1379. According to Feliciano Busi, a chronicler is quoted as saying: "In the year 1379 was brought into Viterbo the game of cards, which comes from Saracinia and is called by them Naib." *Naib* is an Arabic word meaning "deputy," and the material from which the Tarot cards were copied is still extant. It is "deputy" or substitute material, forming an allegory of the teachings of a Sufi master about certain cosmic influences upon humanity. This is divided into four sections, called the *turuq* (four Ways), the word from which "Tarot" is undoubtedly derived. The Spanish word *naipe* (card) is undoubtedly from the Arabic *naib*. The Tarot now known in the West has been influenced by a Cabalistic and Judaizing process, designed to bring it into line with certain doctrines not implicit in the original. Superficial attempts to link these cards with those in use in Persia or China have not succeeded because the essential cipher element contained in the meanings of the suits and the trumps is still a Sufi property. The pack, as it stands today, is only partially correct, because there have been transpositions of the significances of some of the *atouts*, the trumps or emblematic figures of the pack. This error has been caused by a mistranslation from Arabic of certain words, due to literal conversion into a different culture system. Another factor may be substitution of one picture for another one. This is not a subject upon which I may be much more explicit. Temperance is incorrectly portrayed and interpreted; so is the fifteenth trump; the meaning of the sixteenth trump is a classic case of misunderstanding of a word; the twentieth is wrongly emphasized. Many of the attributions, however, are still in use among the Sufis, though in the West the essential associations with Sufi texts have been lost.

TEMPLARS

That the Templars were thinking in terms of the Sufi, and not the Solomonic, Temple in Jerusalem, and its building, is strongly suggested by one important fact. "Temple" churches which they erected, such as one in London, were modeled upon the Temple as found by the Crusaders, not upon any earlier building. This Temple was none other than the octagonal Dome of the Rock, built in the seventh century on a Sufi mathematical design, and restored in 913. The Sufi legend of the building of the Temple accords with the alleged Masonic version. As an example we may note that the 'Solomon' of the Sufi Builders legend is not King Solomon but the Sufi "King" Maaruf Karkhi (died 815), disciple of David (Daud of Tai, died 781), and hence by extension considered the son of David, and referred to cryptically as Solomon—who was the son of David. The great murder commemorated by the Sufi Builders is not that of the person supposed by Masonic tradition to have been killed. The martyr of the Sufi Builders is Mansur el-Hallaj (858–922), juridically murdered because of the Sufi secret, which he spoke in a manner which could not be understood, and was thus dismembered as a heretic. The pillars of the Temple are not physical ones, but follow the Arabic custom of calling an individual (elder) a pillar. One of the Sufi pillars is Abulfaiz, sometimes called Abuazz. He is the great grandfather (third in teaching succession) of "David" (Maaruf Karkhi), and is none other than Thuban Abulfaiz Dhu'l-Nun the Egyptian, founder of the Mala-mati Order of Sufis, whose similarity to Freemasonry has often been pointed out. He died in 860 A.D., and is also known as the King and possessor of the Egyptian secrets.

TRANSLITERATION

There is no standard European or American transliteration of Arabic or Persian. Various attempts at reproducing the pronunciation by means of Latin letters have failed. When adaptations have been made to the Latin alphabet the result has been that those who already know the Arabic letter are able to write the letter in Arabic upon seeing the Latin modified letter. Those who cannot write Arabic are no better off, because the modified letter does not help them in pronunciation, and there is no value in their knowing anything about differentiation of letters if they cannot write or read them. There is no possibility of applying phonetic rules to Arabic because certain sounds are only learned by ear and made possible of utterance by practice. For the purposes of this book the approximations of spelling used in Latinized words are as useful to the ordinary reader as any artificial system. Arabs, Persians and Hindustani-speakers are able to know which letter to use in writing a word by their knowledge of the language and of its orthography. Orientalists of other origins have for many years attempted to substitute for this knowledge cumbersome transliterations whose main function has, in the event, been to cause them to rely upon the Latinization instead of their memories. This is opposed to the practice of the languages with which they have to deal. Any literate child in a country using the Arabic script knows how the word *abdussamad* is spelled. An equal competence should be expected from a foreign scholastic. Failing this, the approximation in ordinary Latin letters should suffice him. There is no middle way, although one is still being sought.